John Row

WRITTEN FOR CHILD

25TH ANNIVERSARY EDITION

*An Outline of English-Language
Children's Literature*

Fourth Revised Edition

HarperTrophy
A Division of HarperCollins*Publishers*

WRITTEN FOR CHILDREN:
An Outline of English-Language Children's Literature
Copyright © 1965, 1974, 1983, 1987, 1990 by John Rowe Townsend

First published by Garnet Miller, Great Britain, 1965
Revised edition published by Kestrel Books, Great Britain, 1974
Second revised edition, 1983
Third revised edition published by Penguin Books, Great Britain, 1987
Fourth revised edition published by The Bodley Head Children's Books,
an imprint of the Random Century Group Ltd, Great Britain, 1990

LC Number 92-11650
Trophy ISBN 0-06-446125-4
First Harper Trophy edition, 1992.

Contents

Contents (contd.)

List of illustrations

The author and publisher wish to thank the following for permission to reproduce
copyright illustrations:

Title page and page 235, Oxford University Press; pages 65, 184 and 287, Penguin
Books; page 101, Methuen (British Commonwealth), Macmillan (U.S.); pages 125
and 134, Curtis Brown (British Commonwealth), E. P. Dutton (U.S.), McLelland
and Stewart (Canada); page 147, Jonathan Cape (U.S.); page 159, Faber and Faber
(British Commonwealth), Coward McCann (U.S. and Canada); page 161, Elaine
Greene (British Commonwealth), Random House USA (U.S. and Canada); page
177, The Bodley Head (U.S.); page 207, Gollancz; page 214, Hamish Hamilton
(British Commonwealth), HarperCollins Publishers (U.S. and Canada); page 244,
Penguin USA (U.S.); page 247, Collins; page 287, Penguin Australia (U.S.); page
299, Macmillan; page 305, HarperCollins Publishers (U.S.); page 312, Gotham Art
and Literary Agency (U.S.); page 320, William Morrow and Company (U.S.); page
323, Macmillan (U.S.).

ACKNOWLEDGEMENT AND DEDICATION

MANY people have helped me in the preparation of one or other edition of *Written for Children*. I am grateful to them all. But I know they will forgive me for not according them the rather small honour of inclusion in a list of acknowledgements. I wish to associate this book with the name of only one person. That is my wife, Vera, who died when the 1974 edition was a few chapters short of being finished. My debt to her is overwhelming: specifically for help, advice and encouragement during many years of reading and discussion; generally, because I owe to her everything I did during our life together that was worth doing.

I dedicate this book to her memory. J.R.T.

Foreword to the 1990 edition

THIS BOOK is a revised and expanded version of a study first published in 1965. In the original edition I tried to give a brief and readable account of prose fiction for children in Britain from the beginnings to the (then) present day. Later editions extended the scope to cover other works of imagination in book form first published in the English language. Poetry and picture books were added to fiction, and I sought to deal with American, Australian and other writers and artists on the same basis as the British.

Over the years, the last section of the book, dealing with the period since the end of the Second World War, has been revised and updated from time to time. Since a claim to have dealt with one's subject 'up to the present day' must always be out of date, I have decided with this edition to draw a line at the end of 1989. The close of a decade is not usually of significance in itself, but on this occasion it may be an appropriate finishing-point, since the last months of 1989 were a time of upheaval for the world at large, and within it for the world of publishing. It was clear that whatever the 1990s might hold, they would not be merely a continuation of the eighties.

My aim in this study is primarily informative, but is necessarily also critical, since one must choose for discussion a relatively small amount of material from a very wide field. While I have tried to see children's literature in its historical and social contexts, my standards are essentially literary. Children's books are part of literature, just as children are part of humanity. A good book for children must be a good book in its own right.

Where the works of the past are concerned, I have long had faith in the sifting process of time — 'time' being shorthand for the collective wisdom of a great many people over a long period. The capacity to survive, I have always thought, is a good test of a book; and while the earliest children's books are mainly of historical interest, I have tried in previous editions, when I came to the late nineteenth and twentieth centuries, to concentrate on work that was in print and likely to remain so. This criterion has become almost impossible to apply. Good books are going out of print at an alarming rate. Among those newly appearing, it gets harder and harder to predict which few will stay the course; so many are published, and the time within which they must establish themselves is so short. Books that might once have been nursed along for years will be quickly dropped if they do not sell in profitable numbers.

So, although it is only realistic to take some account of availability, I have felt free to discuss books which are not currently in print if I think them to be of sufficient interest. I have given proportionately more space to the period since 1945 than to previous periods; this reflects the acceleration of publishing for children since the end of World War II and allows for some wastage. Obviously my choices can be mistaken, and in any case omission from this study does not imply an adverse view; there are many books I would have liked to include had space permitted it, and no doubt there are many good ones that I have not come across. I hope I have not missed any potential classics.

The arrangement is broadly chronological. I have grouped books of a kind together, for convenience in discussion and comparison, but I do not regard classification by genre as important. It must often be arbitrary, and the best books tend to resist pigeonholing. And I have not laboured too hard to allocate books to age-groups. Children are individuals, and are not all ready for the same book at the same time. I have given brief biographical information about major writers of the past, but not usually about contemporary or very recent ones.

I am sorry that foreign-language books have had to be left out, even where translations are available. Children's literature is an international field. But one cannot do everything in one book. The territory to be covered is large already, and it has not seemed wise to wander outside it. I have also, after some hesitation, omitted popular series-books and other material of insignificant literary merit. Ephemeral matter produced to catch a market can be highly entertaining, and may well be important to the educationist, sociologist or social historian. But, for better or worse, this is a study of children's literature, not of children's reading-matter. The books that are worth discussing, and that one hopes will survive, are those that have engaged the whole heart and skill of writer or artist.

Cambridge, April 1990

J.R.T.

PART ONE

Before 1840

1

The beginnings

BEFORE there could be children's books, there had to be children — children, that is, who were accepted as beings with their own particular needs and interests, not merely as miniature men and women. This acceptance is a fairly recent development in Western social history. The Greek and Roman civilizations took little account of children except as creatures to be trained for adult life. Plato, it is true, had some liberal ideas on education, but they were never put into effect. And classical literature has nothing that can be called a children's book in the sense of a book specially written to give pleasure to children. *(Aesop's Fables* were primarily folk-tales.)

In England, from the Roman withdrawal to the Norman Conquest and for many years afterwards, the monasteries were the chief refuges of learning and the monks were the teachers of such children as learned to read. Books, before the introduction of printing, were rare and precious, and the writing of books to amuse children would have been an economic as well as a psychological impossibility.

In medieval and early Tudor England, the poor man's child (unless he could get his foot on the educational ladder, which led into the Church) was likely to labour long hours from an early age. The children of tradesmen and of the middle and upper classes were commonly put out to apprenticeship or page service, and none too gently treated. Those who were of good family might well be bartered in marriage before they reached their teens. A great many children of all classes died young.

I do not know of any survival from the age of manuscript that can be called a children's story. But there were manuscripts that embodied *lessons* for children: especially the 'courtesy books' which flourished in the fifteenth century. Their advice was often given in rhyme, so that it could more easily be remembered. 'Symon's Lesson of Wisdom for All Manner Children,' which forms part of *The Babees' Book,* includes these exhortations:

> Child, climb not over house nor wall
> For no fruit nor birds nor ball.

Child, over men's houses no stones fling
Nor at glass windows no stones sling,
Nor make no crying, jokes nor plays
In holy Church on holy days.
And child, I warn thee of another thing,
Keep thee from many words and wrangling.
And child, when thou goest out to play
Look thou come home by light of day.
And child, I warn thee of another matter,
Look thou keep thee well from fire and water . . .
Child, keep thy book, cap and gloves
And all things that thee behoves,
And but thou do, thou shalt fare worse
And thereto be beat on the bare erse.[1]

This was instruction, not entertainment. But although stories were not being written for children there was a vast amount of story material in general circulation which must have reached them by one means or another. There were the legends and romances of Troy, King Arthur, Guy of Warwick, Bevis of Hampton, St George, and all the miscellaneous assortment known as the *Acts of the Romans*. There were *Aesop* and *Reynard the Fox*. There were the stories and ballads of Robin Hood and Randolph Earl of Chester and many others. Above all, though scorned by the literate, there were the humble folktales, passed down by word of mouth from generation to generation. All these were common property; no distinction was made between stories for adults and for children. Sir Philip Sidney, as late as the reign of the first Queen Elizabeth, refers in his *Apology for Poetry to* 'a tale which holdeth children from play and old men from the chimney corner'.[2] It would not have occurred to him that the children should have been listening to something suitable for their tender years while the old men in the corner cackled over riper material. A tale was for all.

It could thus be said that the prehistory of children's literature has two branches: the material that was intended specially for children or young people but was not story, and the material that was story but was not meant specially for children. The first English printer, William Caxton, had a foot on each branch. By 1479 he had published *The Book of Courtesye;* but his first book of all was the *Recuyell of the Historyes of Troy* in 1474, and he also printed *Aesop* and *Reynard* and the *Morte Darthur*. His successor, Wynkyn de Worde, issued a translation of the Acts of the Romans.

During the century after Caxton, the old stories continued to

'This fable showeth that he is wyse whiche fayneth not to desyre that thynge the which he may not have': from 'The foxe and the raysyns' in Caxton's *Fables of Aesop* (1484)

circulate, but with the advance of the Renaissance educated people began to look more to Europe and the rediscovered classics. Tales like those of Bevis of Hampton began to seem outdated, and only fit for the uneducated and for children. From the mid sixteenth century also, the Puritans, now increasing in numbers and strength, attacked the old material as being ungodly and corrupting.[3] Hugh Rhodes, in his *Book of Nurture* (1554), urged that children should be kept from 'reading of feigned fables, vain fantasies, and wanton stories and songs of love, which bring much mischief to youth.' This plea, which in one form or another has echoed vainly down the centuries, clearly implies that such material did find its way into children's hands. And the commercial possibilities of 'feigned fables and wanton stories' were soon to be realized by the producers of chapbooks: crudely-printed booklets that were sold for a copper or two by pedlars up and down the country from the seventeenth century onwards.

But books produced specially for children until the end of the seventeenth century were nearly all schoolbooks or books of manners or morals. The courtesy books had put the emphasis on civilized behaviour, but as the Puritan influence grew the stress fell more heavily on religion and morals.

The Puritans were certainly aware of children, but were

aware of them in a rather special sense: as young souls to be saved, or, more probably, damned. They therefore directed a good deal of literature at young people with the aim of rescuing them from hellfire. One of the leading Puritan writers was James Janeway, who published in 1671 *A Token for Children, being an Exact Account of the Conversion, Holy and Exemplary Lives, and Joyful Deaths of Several Young Children.* Addressing his young readers in a preface, Janeway says:

> You may now hear, my dear Lambs, what other good children have done, and remember how they wept and prayed by themselves, how earnestly they cried out for an interest in the Lord Jesus Christ: you may read how dutiful they were to their parents, how diligent at their book, how ready to learn the Scriptures and their catechisms . . . how holy they lived; how dearly they were loved; how joyfully they died.

The stories are of saintly children who died young in a rapture of prayer. This clearly was the highest fate the author could conceive for them. He exhorted his readers: 'If you love your parents, if you love your souls, if you would escape hellfire, and if you would go to Heaven when you die, do you go and do as these good children.' The book was popular for many years, and reprints continued into the nineteenth century.

Another publication of the 1670s, *A Looking-Glass for Children,* contains a verse warning, by Abraham Chear, in the person of a young girl who contemplates her own appearance:

> When by spectators I am told
> What beauty doth adorn me,
> Or in a glass when I behold
> How sweetly God did form me,
>
> Hath God such comeliness bestowed
> And on me made to dwell.
> What pity such a pretty maid
> As I should go to Hell!

The great work to come from a seventeenth-century Puritan writer was John Bunyan's *The Pilgrim's Progress* (1678), discussed in the next chapter. It was not intended as a book for children, though it came to be regarded as one. The book which Bunyan did write specially for children − *A Book for Boys and Girls* (1686), later reissued as *Divine Emblems* − is unlikely to be eagerly read by them today. It has a rugged sternness that goes beyond even Janeway's. This, for instance, is how Bunyan writes 'upon Death':

> Death's a cold Comforter to Girls and Boys
> Who wedded are unto their Childish Toys:

More grim he looks upon our Lustful Youth
Who, against Knowledge, slight God's saving Truth:
But most of all he dismal is to those
Who once professed the Truth they now oppose.
Death has a Dart, a Sting, which Poyson is,
As all will find who do of Glory miss . . .

It would be wrong to suggest, however, that the 'good godly books' of the Puritans totally dominated the English scene. The old tales were still told and could even be found in print. And many books of social and moral instruction were written in less intense and less feverish tones than those of the Puritans.

In the new American colonies, Puritan attitudes were naturally pervasive, since freedom to follow their own (Puritan) religion and way of life was the colonists' main aim. Books in the early years came largely from England. John Foxe's *Book of Martyrs*, first published in 1563, with its fierce indictment of Papism and gruesome accounts of violent death, was considered highly suitable for children in England and New England alike. A happier importation, when its time came, was *The Pilgrim's Progress*. Janeway's *Token* was also well known, and was reprinted in Boston in 1700 with the addition, by the eminent and fearsome divine, Cotton Mather, of *A Token for the Children of New-England, Or, Some Examples of Children in whom the Fear of God was remarkably Budding, before they dyed, in several Parts of New-England. Preserved and published for the Encouragement of Piety in other Children*. In succeeding years the pious last words of many more godly children were published and continually reprinted.

But the dominant book for children in colonial America was the *New England Primer*. Basically the *Primer* was a combined ABC and catechism. It was also however a miscellany, containing pictures and verses; and in an age when children had little else to read they must have pored over it for many hours and obtained from it some degree of entertainment.

The *Primer* contained a famous sequence of alphabetical rhymes, each with accompanying woodcut, which began with the pithy dogma

> In Adam's fall
> We sinnèd all

and continued through to

> Zaccheus he
> Did climb a tree
> His Lord to see.

The problem of X was triumphantly solved:

> Xerxes the Great did die,
> And so must you and I.

All the verses were changed from time to time, place to place, edition to edition, except the first, which sternly endured.

A In *Adam's* Fall
   We Sinned all.

B Thy Life to Mend
   This *Book* Attend.

C The *Cat* doth play
   And after flay.

D A *Dog* will bite
   A Thief at night.

E An *Eagles* flight
   Is out of fight.

F The Idle Fool
   Is whipt at School

The *New England Primer*
(1727 edition)

There was also the lengthy exhortation to his children of Mr John Rogers, the 'first Martyr in Queen Mary's Reign', who 'was burnt at Smithfield, February the fourteenth, 1554. His Wife, with nine small Children, and one at her Breast, following him to the Stake, with which sorrowful Sight he was not in the least daunted.' A woodcut illustrates this occasion. The book contains a number of verses, some of them hardly encouraging:

> I in the Burying Place may see
> Graves shorter there than I;
> From Death's Arrests no Age is free,
> Young Children too may die.

Some editions also have woodcuts of animals and birds, with rhymed captions; and there is a lively dialogue between Christ, Youth and the Devil, in which Youth, having succumbed to the Devil's wiles and sought too late to repent, is consigned by Christ to death and damnation:

> When I did call, thou wouldst not hear
> But didst to me turn a deaf ear;

And now in thy calamity
I will not mind nor hear thy cry;
Thy day is past, begone from me
Thou who didst love iniquity . . .

This, clearly, is a Christ of harsh Puritanism rather than 'gentle Jesus, meek and mild'.

The *New England Primer* also came to incorporate the catechism originally published as *Spiritual Milk for Boston Babes in either England: Drawn out of the Breasts of both Testaments for their Souls' Nourishment, but may be of like Use to any Children*, by John Cotton. The dates and places of first publication, both of the *Primer* and of *Milk for Babes*, are uncertain. The latter is believed to date from the 1640s; the *Primer* probably originated in England under another title in the reign of Charles II, but it was well established as the *New England Primer* by 1690, and eventually made its way back to England under that title. Its American sales over the 150 years to 1830 have been estimated at six to eight million.[4] Another well-known work of Puritan New England was Cotton Mather's *A Family Well Ordered, or An Essay to render Parents and Children Happy in one another* (1699). In the second part of the book, addressed to children, Mather declares that

The Heavy Curse of God will fall upon those Children that make Light of their Parents . . . The Curse of God! The Terriblest Thing that ever was heard of; the First-born of Terribles! . . . *Children*, if you break the Fifth Commandment, there is not much likelihood that you will keep the rest. Undutiful Children soon become horrid Creatures, for Unchastity, for Dishonesty, for Lying, and all manner of Abominations . . . And because these undutiful Children are Wicked overmuch, therefore they Dy before their Time . . .

Children, if by Undutifulness to your Parents you incur the Curse of God, it won't be long before you go down into Obscure Darkness, even into Utter Darkness: God has reserved for you the Blackness of Darkness for ever.

The idea that wickedness could lead to early death was a common one, though it appears to be at odds with the inferences to be drawn from Janeway's *Token*. Yet the Puritan preachers cared deeply about children, as can be seen from Benjamin Colman's *Devout Contemplation on the Meaning of Divine Providence, in the Early Death of Pious and Lovely Children* (1714). Colman is concerned to explain the fact that the 'abundance of the Children of Men, and of our most hopeful, pious and promising Children do Die Young . . . What brittle and tender Things are our Babes, and what Multitudes die in Infancy!'

But even in New England the Puritans did not have it all their own way. Cotton Mather wrote in his diary on 27 September 1713:

I am informed that the Minds and Manners of many People about the Countrey are much corrupted by foolish Songs and Ballads, which the Hawkers and Peddlars carry into all parts of the Countrey. By way of antidote, I would procure poetical Compositions full of Piety, and such as may have a Tendency to advance Truth and Goodness, to be published and scattered into all Corners of the Land. These may be an extract of some, from the excellent Watts's Hymns.[5]

The excellent Watts's *Hymns and Spiritual Songs* had been published in 1707; in 1715 came the first of the innumerable editions of his *Divine Songs* for children. They were extremely popular in the American colonies as well as in England, and the well-known *Cradle Hymn* ('Hush! my dear, lie still and slumber') won a place in later editions of the *New England Primer*. Watts's attitudes in fact reflect a softening of the old

Woodcut from Bunyan's *Divine Emblems*
(1724 edition)

harsh Puritanism. It is enlightening to compare his verses on the bee with those of Bunyan, less than thirty years earlier. To Bunyan the bee's most notable attribute was its sting:

The Bee goes out, and Honey home doth bring;
And some who seek that Honey find a Sting.
Now wouldst thou have the Honey and be free
From stinging, in the first place kill the Bee.

This Bee an Emblem truly is of Sin,
Whose Sweet unto a many Death hath been . . .

The lesson drawn by Dr Watts is quite different:

How doth the little busy bee
Improve each shining hour
And gather honey all the day
From ev'ry opening flower.

How skilfully she builds her cell,
How neat she spreads the wax,
And labours hard to store it well
With the sweet food she makes.

In works of labour or of skill
I would be busy too,
For Satan finds some mischief still
For idle hands to do.

The difference in outlook between Bunyan and Watts is profound. By the early eighteenth century new ways of thought and new attitudes to children were gaining ground. The belief that children were naturally sinful went with an old-fashioned fundamentalism; it was giving way to a view, based on the New Learning and on rational theology, that a child began life in a state of innocence. He was, quite literally, a different creature.

2

Mr Locke and Mr Newbery

IN 1693 — according to a modern writer, Penelope Mortimer — the English philosopher John Locke 'published his *Thoughts Concerning Education* and invented the Child'.[1] The first part of this statement is incontrovertible. The second is a wild exaggeration, but like many wild exaggerations it has some truth in it. Locke's *Thoughts* were the work of a powerful and original mind, and even where they were not new they gave expression and weight to important ideas of the time. Locke saw the mind at birth as a blank page on which lessons were to be impressed. He advocated much milder ways of teaching and bringing up children than had been usual in England. He believed they could be 'cozened into a knowledge of their letters . . . and play themselves into what others are whipped for.' And the child that had learned to read, he thought, should be given 'some easy pleasant book, suited to his capacity . . . wherein the entertainment that he finds might draw him on and reward his pains in reading . . . and yet not such as should fill his head with perfectly useless trumpery, or lay the principles of vice and folly.' But Locke found there was a grave shortage of books that were easy and pleasant without being useless trumpery. All he could recommend, outside the Scriptures, were *Aesop* and *Reynard the Fox*.[2]

It is remarkable that the only two books which Locke could approve had both been put into print by Caxton before 1500. In Locke's eyes, nothing of value for his purpose had been published in the succeeding two hundred years. Curiously, just before and just after his words were written, three adult books appeared which were to become children's literature by adoption, though none of them was written to fulfil his prescription. These were John Bunyan's *The Pilgrim's Progress* (1678), Daniel Defoe's *Robinson Crusoe* (1719), and Jonathan Swift's *Gulliver's Travels* (1726). Undoubtedly Locke had in mind younger children than might be expected to read these books for themselves; but their success, together with Locke's indication of a vacancy, may have helped to bring about the realization that such a thing as a juvenile market was a possibility.

Although *The Pilgrim's Progress* is allegorical, it is impossible even for an adult to read about Christian's journey to the Celestial City in any other way than as a story. The passages through the Slough of Despond and the Valley of Humiliation, the fight with the monster Apollyon, the loss of Christian's comrade Faithful in Vanity Fair, the crossing of the River of Death: these are actual and vivid events, as real in their own way as the mass of detail with which Defoe built up Robinson Crusoe. It may be noted that the themes of all these three books – the dangerous journey, as in *The Pilgrim's Progress;* the desert island, as in *Robinson Crusoe;* and the miniature or other imaginary world, as in *Gulliver* – have served for innumerable later books, both children's and adult, and are by no means worn out.

The 1740s are commonly regarded as the decade in which both the English novel and the English children's book got under way. It seems clear that the beginnings of both are connected not only with new ways of thought but also with the rise and growing refinement of the middle classes in the eighteenth century. The 'Glorious Revolution' of 1688, when William and Mary replaced James II on the English throne, was the country's last revolution: it established the parliamentary system of government which has been continuous from then to now. A growing number of people had the time, the money, the education and the inclination to be readers of books. Middle-class life was growing more domestic, centred upon the home and the family rather than on the bustle of the street or the great house. Children were coming into their own: ceasing to be dressed like little adults, calling their parents 'Papa' and 'Mamma,' and leading more sheltered and perhaps more innocent lives.

This was also the time when publishing began to develop in its modern direction. Up to the eighteenth century there were booksellers rather than publishers: the bookseller both published and sold the work (and quite possibly printed it, too). The first use of the word 'publisher' in its modern sense recorded by the Oxford English Dictionary is in 1740, although the demarcation line was to remain confused for at least another half century. But once the novel, which broadly speaking was sophisticated fiction for adults, began to replace the tale, which was unsophisticated fiction for everybody, there was a logical gap for the children's book to enter.

Samuel Richardson's *Pamela* may be said to mark the

opening of this gap. Richardson (1689-1751), a master-printer who turned author at the age of fifty, was always interested in education. In 1740 he produced an edition of *Aesop* intended specially for children. At the same time he was at work on a 'complete letter-writer' in which he was to offer hints on conduct. This developed into the epistolary novel *Pamela, or Virtue Rewarded,* which was described as being published 'in order to cultivate the principles of virtue and religion in the minds of the youth of both sexes.'

To us it is clear that in spite of the author's intention to instruct the young, the line of development from *Pamela* is towards the modern adult novel. *Pamela* does not now seem either suitable or attractive matter for young readers. It ran to four volumes (but was outrun by the same author's later works, *Clarissa* in seven volumes and *Sir Charles Grandison* in eleven.) It tells of the trials of a poor girl who spends most of her time repelling the advances of her rich young employer, Mr B. Her reward for so stoutly defending her virtue is that Mr B, having failed to gain possession by dishonourable means, falls back on honourable ones and marries her. This seems less edifying to us than it did to Richardson and his contemporaries.

Abridged versions of *Pamela* and her successors were soon published, 'familiarized and adapted to the capacities of youth.' But it is hard to imagine the younger children, even in an age when books were scarce, reading Richardson. Dr Johnson said aptly enough that anyone trying to read Richardson for the story would hang himself with impatience.[3] To find something for the younger readers it is best to turn to the publications of John Newbery.

Newbery was the friend and sometimes the employer of Johnson and of Oliver Goldsmith; and he was an admirer of 'the great Mr Locke', to whom tribute is paid in those terms in the preface to his first publication for children, the *Little Pretty Pocket-Book* (1744). The year after publishing the *Pocket-Book,* Newbery opened a children's bookshop in St Paul's Churchyard which he was to run for twenty-two years. (It continued, under his heirs and successors, for well over another century.) Here Newbery not only sold children's books but published and wrote them. He died rich, but made most of his money from a separate occupation as patent-medicine promoter.

The late Harvey Darton, whose *Children's Books in England* (1932) is still the most authoritative study of the subject over the period up to Queen Victoria's death, refers boldly to 'Newbery the Conqueror'. According to Darton, the year 1744, when the first Newbery children's book was published, was 'a date comparable to the 1066 of the older histories'.[4] This was undoubtedly written with tongue in cheek, and Newbery was not in fact the first in the field. As early as 1694 (the year after Locke's *Thoughts)*, one 'J.G.' had published *A Play-book for Children*, 'to allure them to read as soon as they can speak plain'; and, probably in 1702, 'T.W.' issued *A Little Book for Little Children*, 'wherein are set down, in a plain and pleasant Way, Directions for Spelling, and other remarkable Matters. Adorn'd with Cuts.' But these, and others like them, were directly concerned with teaching children to read and spell.

Closer to Newbery in date and approach was Thomas Boreman, who brought out from 1740 onwards a series of tiny books, the size of a snapshot, which he called *Gigantick Histories*. Then there was a Mrs Cooper of Paternoster Row who issued *The Child's New Plaything* (second edition 1743), and there was Mr J. Robinson of Ludgate Street, who sold the *Little Master's Miscellany*, first published in 1743. Books for little masters and misses had arrived, and would soon multiply. John Newbery was not the only person to see their commercial possibilities. But of all the early children's publishers he was by far the best known and most successful, and did most to set the trade going.

John Newbery (1713-67) was the son of a Berkshire farmer. He became the owner of a printing business in Reading while still in his twenties, by marrying the widow of the previous owner. In 1743 he moved to London, and the following year he brought out the book which marked the Newbery Invasion:

According to Act of Parliament (neatly bound and gilt): A Little Pretty Pocket-Book, intended for the Instruction and Amusement of Little Master Tommy and Pretty Miss Polly, with an agreeable Letter to read from Jack the Giant-Killer, as also a Ball and a Pincushion, the use of which will infallibly make Tommy a good Boy and Polly a good Girl. To the whole is prefixed a Letter of Education humbly addressed to all Parents, Guardians, Governesses, &c, wherein Rules are laid down for making their Children strong, healthy, virtuous, wise and happy . . .

The book cost sixpence and the ball or pincushion twopence extra. One side of the ball or pincushion was red, the other black, and the idea was that pins were to be stuck in one side or the other to record the good or bad deeds of the child who owned it. The book itself contained pictures, rhymes and games; eventually we see the good boy in a coach and six and the good girl getting a gold watch. Newbery, like Richardson, tended to reward virtue in a material way.

The device of the ball or pincushion is in accordance with Locke's ideas of teaching by play rather than the whip. (Locke himself had suggested that spelling could be taught with alphabet dice, and Newbery had issued in 1744 a spelling and counting game played with a set of fifty-six squares.) But the key word on the title-page of the *Pocket-Book* is 'amusement'. Little Master Tommy and Pretty Miss Polly were not only to be instructed; they were to be entertained.

In the next few years Newbery published at least thirty titles for children. Some, like the *Little Pretty Pocket-Book,* were miscellanies; some, of which the most famous was *Goody Two-Shoes,* were fiction; others, such as *Tom Telescope's Philosophy of Tops and Balls* (sub-titled 'The Newtonian System of Philosophy') were educational. Newbery's characters and imaginary authors include Woglog the Giant, Tommy Trip, Giles Gingerbread (the boy who lived on learning), Nurse Truelove, Peregrine Puzzlebrains, Primrose Prettyface and many others of similar name. There is no doubt that Newbery himself wrote some of the books, though it will never be known which ones were his. Like other booksellers of the day, he employed a number of hacks ready to turn their hands to any task. But Dr Johnson remarked that 'Newbery is an extraordinary man, for I know not whether he has read or written more books';[5] and Goldsmith describes in *The Vicar of Wakefield* how Dr Primrose was assisted by

a traveller who stopped to take cursory refreshment. This person was no other than the philanthropic bookseller in St Paul's Churchyard, who has written so many little books for children: he called himself their friend, but he was the friend of all mankind. He was no sooner alighted but he was in haste to be gone, for he was ever on business of the utmost importance, and was at that time actually compiling materials for the history of one Mr Thomas Trip. I immediately recollected this good-natur'd man's red pimpled face . . . and from him I borrowed a few pieces, to be paid at my return.[6]

Whatever else he may have been, Newbery was an astute business man with an eye on the main chance. ('Trade and Plumb-cake for ever. Huzza!' is the caption to the frontispiece of *The Twelfth-Day Gift, 1767,* and it might well have been his own slogan.) But the publishing business, though successful, was not the reason why he died rich. Soon after coming to

London he bought the selling rights of Dr James's Fever Powder, which under Newbery's promotion became the most famous nostrum of the day. It was the star performer in what became a long list of proprietary medicines, and is mentioned in several of the Newbery children's books (for among Newbery's accomplishments was a mastery of the art of the puff). It was always followed by marvellous cures – though Goody Two-Shoes' father, unlucky man, was 'seized with a violent Fever in a Place where Dr James's Powder was not to be had', and that was the end of him. The formula of the famous powder was handed down through five generations of the Newbery family. I am told by the successors to the Newbery business that the powder went on being made until the Second World War, when the formula, so closely guarded for so long, was destroyed in the London blitz. The powder is believed to have been based on antimony. In its heyday two centuries ago it had the confidence of the highest in the land. It also cured distemper in cattle.

In advertising, too, John Newbery had original ideas. He offered at the beginning of 1755

Nurse Truelove's New Year Gift, or the Book of Books for Children, adorned with Cuts and designed as a Present for every little Boy who would become a great Man and ride upon a fine Horse; and to every little Girl who would become a great Woman and ride in a Lord Mayor's gilt Coach. Printed for the Author, who has ordered these books to be given gratis to all little Boys at the Bible and Sun in St Paul's Churchyard, they paying for the Binding, which is only Twopence each Book.

This early example of the Amazing Free Offer was satirized by a writer in *The World* in March 1755 who, 'not to be outdone by this public-spirited gentleman,' offered three volumes of *The World* 'gratis, at every bookseller's shop in town, to all sorts of persons, they paying only nine shillings for the bindings'.[7]

But it should not be supposed that Newbery was a rogue. He had a reputation for fair dealing, and Sir John Hawkins, the first biographer of Dr Johnson, described him as a man of 'a good understanding and great integrity'.[8]

Collectively the Newbery books are important in the development of children's literature, but individually the only title with much significance is *Goody Two-Shoes*. This has often been attributed to Oliver Goldsmith, but it could equally well have been written by Newbery or by one or more of the writers in his stable. The title itself is still familiar, and pantomimes under

THE
HISTORY
OF
Little GOODY TWO-SHOES;
Otherwise called,
MRS. MARGERY TWO-SHOES.
WITH
The Means by which she acquired her
Learning and Wisdom, and in conse-
quence thereof her Estate; set forth
at large for the Benefit of those,

Who from a State of Rags and Care,
And having Shoes but half a Pair;
Their Fortune and their Fame would fix,
And gallop in a Coach and Six.

See the Original Manuscript in the *Vatican*
at *Rome,* and the Cuts by *Michael Angelo.*
Illustrated with the Comments of our
great modern Critics.

The THIRD EDITION.
LONDON:
Printed for J. NEWBERY, at the *Bible* and
Sun in St. *Paul's-Church-Yard,* 1766.
[Price Six-pence.]

Goody Two-Shoes: from John Newbery's edition of 1766

the name of *Goody Two-Shoes* have been performed in
England in the past decade. But few of us are familiar with the
story. Its description on the title-page is:

> The History of Little Goody Two-Shoes, otherwise called Mrs Margery
> Two-Shoes, with the Means by which she acquired her Learning and
> Wisdom, and in consequence thereof her Estate; set forth at large for
> the Benefit of those
>
> > Who from a state of Rags and Care
> > And having Shoes but Half a Pair
> > Their Fortune and their Fame would fix
> > And gallop in a Coach and Six.
>
> See the Original Manuscript in the *Vatican* at *Rome,* and the Cuts by
> *Michael Angelo.* Illustrated with the Comments of our great modern
> Critics.

The promise of a coach-and-six is typical Newbery, and the
remarks about the Vatican and Michelangelo are more of his
little jokes. (At the back is a 'letter from the printer' saying that
the copy can go back to the Vatican, 'and pray tell Mr Angelo
to brush up the cuts.') The dedication is 'to all young Gentlemen and Ladies who are good or intend to be good', from
'their old friend in St Paul's Churchyard.'

Goody Two-Shoes' parents are turned off their farm by a
grasping landlord and soon afterwards die: her father from a
fever untreated by the vital powder and her mother from a
broken heart. She and her brother Tommy wander the

hedgerows living on berries. Tommy goes to sea; Goody Two-Shoes (so nicknamed because of her delight on becoming the owner of a pair of shoes) manages to learn the alphabet from children who go to school, then sets up as a tutor, and eventually becomes principal of a dame-school. There is a good deal about her work as a teacher, and her efforts to stop cruelty to animals; eventually she marries a squire, and at the wedding a mysterious gentleman turns up. 'This Gentleman, so richly dressed and bedizened with Lace, was that identical little Boy whom you before saw in the Sailor's Habit.' In other words it is brother Tommy, who has of course made his fortune at sea. And so Goody Two-Shoes, now rich, becomes a benefactor to the poor, helps those who have oppressed her, and at last dies, universally mourned.

The Newbery books are dead now, and apart from modern facsimiles there are very few copies still in existence. Even in 1881 Charles Welsh, one of Newbery's successors, could write that they were 'as scarce as blackberries in midwinter, for what among books has so brief a life as a nursery book?' But the name of Newbery is kept very much alive by the annual award of the John Newbery Medal by the American Library Association for the most distinguished children's book of the year. And there is nothing eccentric in the choice of an eighteenth-century Englishman to give his name to this American honour, for Newbery was as much the ancestor of modern American children's literature as of British. Dr A. S. W. Rosenbach, in the preface to the catalogue of his famous collection of early American children's books, said plainly that

the first really important name in the history of American children's literature is that of the famous English publisher John Newbery . . . for it was his children's books which were imitated and pirated in this country, and which gave the first genuine impetus to the development of books written for the young as distinct from books written for grown-ups and considered suitable for children.[9]

3

Rousseau and the lady writers

THE PURITAN grip was stronger in the American colonies than in England, and not so soon relaxed. In the early eighteenth century, besides the *Bible* and the *New England Primer*, the staple items of approved reading were Bunyan's *The Pilgrim's Progress*, Watts's *Hymns* and *Divine Songs*, and Janeway's *Token for Children* with American additions. There were many other memoirs of pious children, admonitions from solemn and forbidding divines and legacies of advice from father to son or mother to daughter.

But not all was austerity; Defoe and Swift soon crossed the Atlantic, and there were the chapbook versions of such old stories as *The Seven Giants of Christendom* and *Valentine and Orson*. To judge from the number of surviving editions, *The Babes in the Wood* and *Tom Thumb* seem to have sold particularly well. Sometimes it was possible to combine dreadful warnings with sensationalism, as in the English chapbook — extremely popular in America — of *The Prodigal Daughter*, who makes a bargain with the Devil to poison her parents. This transaction presented a challenge which early illustrators happily accepted.

Between the pieties and the pedlars' unconsidered trifles there was ample room for the little books of John Newbery, his competitors and successors. The printer who is particularly associated with their introduction to America was Isaiah Thomas of Worcester, Massachusetts (1749-1831). His method was simple piracy; so far as I know he never paid a penny for the use of all this commercially valuable material. In his defence it could be said at least that he was making available the most appealing children's books of his day.

For most of the eighteenth century America was of course still colonial, and the cultural capital was London. There was virtually no American writing for children, though printers were active, especially in Boston and Philadelphia. Thomas and his competitors would often change minor details in English books in order to Americanize them: London town became Boston town, and the reward for the good little girl in *Nurse Truelove's New Year's Gift* (a Newbery title) was to ride in the

The Devil and the Disobedient Child, from an
eighteenth-century American edition of
The Prodigal Daughter

Governor's gilt coach, instead of the Lord Mayor's coach as in
England. Similarly, a few years later, Jacob Johnson of Philadelphia, founder of what was to become the publishing house of
Lippincott, adapted an advertising rhyme of a Newbery
successor, John Harris, which began:

> At Harris's, St Paul's Churchyard,
> Good children meet a sure reward.

Johnson made it read:

> At Johnson's store in Market Street
> A sure reward good children meet.

The rest of the rhyme is worth quoting. It goes:

> In coming home the other day
> I heard a little master say
> For ev'ry three-pence there he took
> He had receiv'd a little book,
> With covers neat, and cuts so pretty,
> There's not its like in all the City;
> And that for three-pence he could buy
> A story-book would make one cry;
> For little more a book of riddles;

> Then let us not buy drums or fiddles,
> Nor yet be stopt at pastry-cooks,
> But spend our money all in books;
> For when we've learnt each book by heart
> Mamma will treat us with a tart.[1]

It is an interesting advertisement, in either an American or an English context, because in each case the bookseller is wooing the child directly: it is *his* threepence they're after. He has the dignity of the paying customer.

For most of the century after John Newbery's death there seem to have been two rather muddy streams of children's literature: the didactic and the commercial. As in Newbery's own output, the two streams are not entirely separate. A typical list of juvenile publications in the second half of the eighteenth century will yield its quota of Newberyish titles, mainly anonymous: *Letters between Master Tommy and Miss Nancy; The Juvenile Auction,* by Charley Chatter; *Tea-Table Dialogues between Miss Thoughtful, Miss Sterling, Miss Prattle, etc.; The Top Book of All for Little Masters and Misses; Drawing-School for Little Masters and Misses; The Picture Exhibition, containing the Original Drawings of 18 Little Masters and Misses.* These titles were clearly meant for the rising respectable middle-class, and all its little masters and misses.

Sometimes a superficially didactic aim was used as cover for sheer fun, as in a little book which was published eight years after John Newbery's death by his nephew Francis: *Vice in its Proper Shape; or, the Wonderful and Melancholy Transformation of several Naughty Masters and Misses into those Contemptible Animals which they most Resemble in Disposition, Printed for the Benefit of all Good Boys and Girls.*

Inside, this is referred to as a 'diverting Account', and so it is; the diversion is more evident than the instruction. Master Jack Idle is transmogrified into an ass; Master Anthony Greedyguts into a pig ('kind Death was pleased to dispatch him in the twelfth year of his Age, by the help of a dozen penny Custards'); Miss Dorothy Chatterfast into a magpie; little Monsieur Fribble into a monkey; Miss Abigail Eviltongue into a serpent; and Master Tommy Filch into a wolf. (The end of this tale is marked with a 'mournful and terrifying Howl'.)

Vice in its Proper Shape was reprinted by Isaiah Thomas at Worcester in 1789. Two years earlier Thomas had issued another title, published in England by Newbery's successors, in which the pill was equally small by comparison with the sugar coating. This was *The Juvenile Biographer,* supposedly written by an eleven-year-old 'Little Biographer'. The book gives an account of certain young ladies and gentlemen who are characterized by their names: there is, for instance, Master Simon Lovepenny, whose

principal Study, or at least that which pleased him most, was casting Accounts, and he had learned many intricate Interest Tables by Heart. Thus far he was undoubtedly a good Boy . . . If he at any time lent any little Fellow a Penny for a Week, he always took a Farthing Interest.

Of Master Jemmy Studious, the author fears that 'by his sticking so very close to his Books, he may hurt his Constitution'; and goes on to remark, in tones worthy of E. Nesbit's self-congratulatory Oswald Bastable:

I hope my little Readers will not imagine that I am jealous of Master Jemmy's Abilities, and fearful that he may rival me in writing such little Books as this:— No, though I am but a little Fellow, I have a great Soul, and am above all Thoughts of Jealousy. I will therefore say no more about it.

This kind of material was on a different level altogether from that of the chapbook publishers, whose trade remained, as Darton says, in a state of 'busy stagnation: a perpetual marketing of old stuff without change even in its appearance'.[2]

John Newbery had led a movement up the market which his successors and their competitors continued. Before long a superior didactic strain began to be heard. By the end of the eighteenth and the beginning of the nineteenth centuries, the writing of children's books in England was beginning to rank as an occupation for gentlewomen.

The ladies ranged from the mildly pious to the sternly moralistic. There were those such as Anna Letitia Barbauld, Lady Fenn, Priscilla Wakefield, Dorothy and Mary Jane Kilner, and Mary Elliott, who saw no harm in giving children instruction mixed with a little lukewarm enjoyment, and perhaps earning themselves an honest guinea in the process. There were also the successors in spirit to the fierce old Puritans: notably Mrs Trimmer and Mrs Sherwood. But the best remembered of all the women writers of this period, Maria Edgeworth, though no less didactic, sprang from a different and more intellectually motivated group – the English followers of Rousseau.

The influence of Jean-Jacques Rousseau (1712-78) on English-language children's literature is comparable with that of Locke. His important work in this context – not of course a children's book – is *Émile* (1762), which in effect is a programme for bringing up a boy. Locke had wanted a rational and more liberal approach to education; Rousseau wanted a totally new one. Rousseau was all for naturalness and simplicity, the language of the heart, the ideal of the Noble Savage. Where better to find and cherish an unspoiled nature than in the child?

Émile is brought up in the country; he runs around tree-climbing and leaping brooks, in the company of his tutor, whom he regards as a friend. He does not read books, which obviously are not natural and which might contaminate his mind; although when he is in his teens Rousseau allows him just one volume: *Robinson Crusoe*. Except that he is always to ask the use of what he is doing, Émile is to have no moral teaching until he is fifteen. By then his body will be strong and active, his mind unclouded by prejudice. He will be ready to grow up into the Ideal Adult.

Even now, there is something exhilarating about this programme, however unpractical it may seem. In its day it had a profound effect, not least on some of the writers for children. They conveniently forgot Rousseau's ban on books, and (as Florence Barry says in *A Century of Children's Books*) 'quickly rose to the demand for a new sort of fable, wherein the child of nature, walking in the shadow of the Perfect Parent (or tutor) acquired a measure of wisdom and philanthropy beyond his years'.[3] Such tales, inspired by *Émile,* are (Florence Barry adds) 'a satirical comment on the writing of books to prove that books are useless.'

The French followers of Rousseau, such as Armand Berquin, Mme d'Epinay and Mme de Genlis, are outside the scope of this study. But a prominent and enthusiastic English supporter was the eccentric Thomas Day (1748-89), who wrote in the light of Rousseau's teaching the most famous of the late eighteenth-century didactic works for children, *Sandford and Merton* (1783-89).

Day was a gentleman of independent means who resolved 'to devote his talents to humanity'. In organizing his own life he went far beyond Rousseau, attempting to find a wife worthy of his high ideals by training up a young girl from an orphanage; the project was unsuccessful, however, and in the end he married an heiress.

Day had come, like Locke, to the conclusion that there was 'a total want of proper books' to be put into children's hands when they learned to read. In *Sandford and Merton* he collected a number of little stories 'likely to express judicious views of nature and reason', and fitted them into a framework, which was the friendship and education of Harry Sandford, a farmer's son, and Tommy Merton, the spoiled child of a rich merchant.

Harry saves Tommy's life, and Mr Merton decides that the two boys shall be taught together by the local clergyman, Mr Barlow. Mr Barlow (clearly a disciple of Rousseau and Day) tells them edifying stories and, by way of relief, conducts Socratic dialogues with Tommy; the lesson most often taught is of the goodness of what is simple and natural, and the viciousness of wealth. The stories tell, for instance, of the rich and the poor man cast on a savage shore, where the poor man quickly proves his true superiority; of the fat dog Jowler and the lean dog Keeper, with a similar moral; of the Spaniards Alonzo and Pizarro in South America where Alonzo farms (usefully) and Pizarro seeks gold (uselessly). And so on. In spite of some lapses, Tommy is much improved in character by the end of the third and last volume. As he says to Harry at their final leavetaking:

To your example I owe most of the little good that I can boast; you have taught me how much better it is to be useful than rich or fine — how much more amiable to be good than to be great. Should I be ever tempted to relapse, even for an instant, into any of my former habits, I will return hither for instruction, and I hope you will again receive me.' Saying this, he shook his friend Harry affectionately by the hand and, with watery eyes, accompanied his father home.

Day's great friend and fellow-Rousseauite was Richard Lovell Edgeworth (1744-1817), who in his time had four wives and fathered twenty children, among them Maria Edgeworth (1767-1849). Maria collaborated with her father in a manual of *Practical Education* (1798) which was very influential in its day. The Edgeworths opposed such elaborate toys as coaches and dolls' houses, preferring simpler ones which gave the child something to do; and they were far ahead of their time in recommending that children should be taught science.

Maria Edgeworth was the author of many determinedly didactic stories for children and young people — often with a utilitarian emphasis which clearly derives from Rousseau. Her most famous story is one that shows her least attractive side. This is 'The Purple Jar', included first in *The Parent's Assistant* (1796), and later in *Early Lessons* (1801). A little girl named Rosamond longs for the purple jar in the chemist's window, and begs her mother to buy it for her instead of a pair of shoes. She soon realizes that the jar is useless; it isn't even purple, for its colour comes from an unpleasant-smelling liquid. Meanwhile her shoes grow worse and worse until at last she can 'neither run, dance, jump nor walk in them'. The story ends with Rosamond hoping she will be wiser another time. Its values now seem questionable. We are inclined to sympathize with Rosamond in wanting the purple jar, and to feel it was up to her mother to buy shoes for her anyway. (They are not poor, and are accompanied to the shop by a servant.)

A much better story, which is equally but less offensively didactic, is that of *Simple Susan,* an artless country girl who triumphs through sheer goodness over the wiles of a grasping attorney. Here our doubts about the message arise from the suspicion that in real life the attorney would have triumphed over Susan. Yet this is a charming story, highly readable and told in beautiful clear prose. Most extraordinary of all is 'Waste Not, Want Not', also from *The Parent's Assistant,* which recounts the remarkable consequences that ensue from careful Ben's saving the string around his parcel while thriftless Hal 'cut the cord, precipitately, in sundry places'.

Perhaps the most repellent piece of English Rousseauism came from Mary Wollstonecraft (1759-97), here seen as a writer for children but better known as an early propagandist for the rights of women. Her book was *Original Stories from Real Life, with Conversations calculated to regulate the Affections and form the Mind to Truth and Goodness.* It was first published in 1788 and reissued in 1791 with illustrations by William Blake. Two little girls, Mary and Caroline, are brought up by an all-knowing tutor, a Mrs Mason, who reproves them at frequent intervals for their various misdeeds and tells them cautionary stories. At one stage Mary and Caroline quarrel over a pet bird, and in the mêlée it gets trodden on. Mrs Mason then relates the sorry tale of Jane Fretful, who not only throws a stool at a pet dog, causing it to die in agony, but also breaks her mother's heart and, having impaired her own constitution by continual passions, hastens to her end, 'scolding the physician for not curing her. Her lifeless countenance displayed the marks of convulsive anger.' At one point in the book, one of the little girls says, 'I declare I cannot go to sleep. I am afraid of Mrs Mason's eyes.' Mrs Mason is indeed a most unlovable character.

Mary Wollstonecraft later married William Godwin, and was the mother of Mary Shelley, wife of the poet Shelley and author of *Frankenstein.* Godwin (1756-1836) ran a children's bookshop for some twenty years from 1805, and published among other things Charles and Mary Lamb's *Tales from Shakespeare* (1807). Charles Lamb, we know, was none too keen on the solemn women writers, for he complained in 1802, in a letter to Coleridge, that

> *Goody Two-Shoes* is almost out of print. Mrs Barbauld's stuff has banished all the old classics of the nursery; and the shopman at Newbery's hardly deigned to reach them off an old exploded corner of the shelf, when Mary asked for them. Mrs B's and Mrs Trimmer's nonsense lay in piles about. . .
>
> Damn them! — I mean the cursed Barbauld Crew, those Blights and Blasts of all that is Human in man and child.[4]

Mrs Barbauld (1743-1825) seems hardly to merit so fierce a malediction. In 1781 she had published *Hymns in Prose for Children,* written in the belief that a child should see God's presence in all things. A few years later she collaborated with her brother, John Aikin (1747-1822), in *Evenings at Home,* which was a staple of children's reading in the first half of the nineteenth century. It appeared in six volumes (subsequently combined into one) between 1792 and 1796. They were divided into an evening's reading for each of thirty evenings. The mixture varies, but a typical evening contains a dialogue, a traveller's tale, a brief instructive story, a fable and a poem. The stories are often reminiscent of Day and Maria Edgeworth. 'The Power of Habit', for instance, features two brothers, James and Richard. Their father dies and leaves them a little money; Richard makes his way with the aid of this and his own efforts, but James gambles away his inheritance, joins the Army, goes to the West Indies, and soon dies of a fever.

The most interesting item in *Evenings at Home* is 'The Trial', by Dr Aikin, which describes the investigation into the breaking of the windows of Dorothy Careful, 'Widow and Dealer in Gingerbread'. Henry Luckless is accused, but new evidence appears which proves that the guilty party is really Peter Riot. This is an early example of the whodunnit.

Lamb's other target, Sarah Trimmer (1741-1810) was the author of the *History of the Robins,* discussed in a later chapter. She was a belligerent moralist and educationist of conservative views who noted that children's books had 'multiplied to an astonishing and alarming degree, and much mischief lies hid in them.' She was fair game.

Mrs Trimmer also believed that 'the greatest injury the youth of this nation ever received was from the introduction of Rousseau's system'[5] — a considerable exaggeration, since 'Rousseau's system' had made little headway in England. Like many other English people, she was alarmed by the French Revolution, and from 1802 to 1806 she ran a publication called *The Guardian of Education* to fight both Jacobinism and Rousseauism. She was however anxious that the lower orders should be helped and instructed, so long as they were not led to forget their place, and she was an early supporter of the Sunday School movement.

Mrs Trimmer thus had much in common with her contemporary Hannah More (1745-1833), who was concerned in establishing schools where the populace could learn to read, but after the French Revolution became increasingly worried about what might result from this ability. Miss More launched in the 1790s the Cheap Repository Tracts, which children as well as adults read in their millions. These were little stories with a strong moral, about such characters as Betty Brown the Orange Girl, Tawny Rachel the Fortune Teller, and the Cheapside Apprentice. The most famous was *The Shepherd of Salisbury Plain* (1798), in which this humble individual, struggling to keep alive a sick wife and several children in his leaky cottage, accepts with what now seems maddening resignation the burdens laid upon him by the social order and the will of God.

But the most formidable of the didactic women writers was still to come. This was Mrs Sherwood, born Mary Martha Butt (1775-1851), whose *History of the Fairchild Family* (1818) was clearly designed to strike the fear of hellfire into every child's soul. Mrs Sherwood spent some years in India, as the wife of an Army officer, and while there wrote *Little Henry and his Bearer* (1814), which tells how a little boy converted his Indian servant to Christianity. *The Fairchild Family* was published soon after her return to England, when she was in her early forties.

It is a family story in which every chapter has its moral lesson. Again and again we see the Fairchild children, Henry, Lucy and Emily, doing naughty things, being sharply pulled up and punished by their parents and warned where such conduct will inevitably lead them. For example, Henry is locked all day in a little room at the top of the house without food, for having stolen an apple and lied about it. At last Mr Fairchild goes to release him:

'Henry,' said Mr Fairchild, 'you have had a sad day of it; but I did not punish you, my child, because I do not love you, but because I wished to save your soul from hell.' Then Mr Fairchild cut a large piece of bread and butter for Henry, which he was glad of, for he was very hungry.

If there was the danger of hellfire, however, there was always the hope of heavenly reward; thus Mrs Fairchild, giving sixpence to a poor woman, quotes: 'he that giveth to the poor lendeth to the Lord, and the Lord will pay it again.'

A macabre incident is a visit to the cottage in which Mr Fairchild's old gardener Roberts has just died. 'You never saw a corpse, I think?' says Mr Fairchild. 'No, Papa,' answers Lucy, 'but we have great curiosity to see one.' So off they go:

> When they came to the door they perceived a kind of disagreeable smell, such as they had never smelt before; this was the smell of the corpse, which having been dead now nearly two days had begun to corrupt . . . the whole appearance of the body was more ghastly and horrible than the children expected . . . At last Mr Fairchild said, 'My dear children, you now see what death is; this poor body is going fast to corruption. The soul I trust is in God; but such is the taint and corruption of the flesh, by reason of sin, that it must pass through the grave and crumble to dust . . . Remember these things, my children, and pray to God to save you from sin.'
>
> 'Oh, Sir!' said Mrs Roberts, 'it comforts me to hear you talk!'

In another passage the children are taken to see the gibbeted body of a man who murdered his brother, and Mr Fairchild points out that the two brothers, 'when they first began to quarrel in their play, as you did this morning, did not think that death, and perhaps hell, would be the end of their quarrels.'

It now seems to us unspeakably cruel to threaten children with damnation for faults which are common to all and which are almost impossible to eradicate. But *The Fairchild Family* (which the author extended at intervals until 1847, though some of the more horrific passages were left out of later editions) was a nineteenth-century bestseller, and was still being reprinted in the early part of this century.

4

Fact and fancy

ON ONE QUESTION, people of all shades of enlightened eighteenth-century opinion were agreed: they did not approve of fairy stories. The humble folk-tales had indeed been kept out of respectable print ever since printing began. In Tudor and Stuart times, the literate part of the population had looked on them as peasant crudities. The Puritans had objected to them because they were untrue, frivolous and of dubious morality. To the Age of Reason they appeared uncouth and irrational: the French courtly revival associated with the names of Perrault and Mme D'Aulnoy had no strong echo in England. The writer of *Goody Two-Shoes* complained that 'People stuff Children's Heads with Stories of Ghosts, Fairies, Witches, and such Nonsense when they are young, and so they continue Fools all their Days.' Jean-Jacques Rousseau did not find fairy tales or even fables useful. The extreme position against fairy tales is probably that taken up by a lady who wrote to Mrs Trimmer's *Guardian of Education:* 'Cinderella,' she said, 'paints some of the worst passions that can enter into the human breast, and of which little children should if possible be totally ignorant; such as envy, jealousy, a dislike to mothers-in-law and half-sisters, vanity, a love of dress, etc., etc.'[1]

In general, anything that smacked of impossibility, absurdity, unbridled fancy was alien to eighteenth-century ways of thought. The lady writers at the end of the century were at pains to dissociate themselves from the idea of any such licence. Their literal-mindedness indeed could be formidable. Mary Jane Kilner, in her foreword to *The Adventures of a Pincushion* (late 1780s), pointed out to her young readers that inanimate objects 'cannot be sensible of any thing which happens, as they can neither hear, see, nor understand; and as I would not willingly mislead your judgement I would, previous to your reading this work, inform you that it is to be understood as an imaginary tale.'

If imagination stood at such a discount, was it really necessary to admit it into children's reading at all? Samuel Griswold Goodrich (1793-1860), the first American to write systematically for children, thought not. From childhood Goodrich – better known by his pseudonym of Peter Parley — had been horrified by such tales as *Little Red Riding-Hood* and *Jack the Giant-Killer,* which he thought were

calculated to familiarize the mind with things shocking and monstrous, to cultivate a taste for tales of bloodshed and violence; to teach the young to use coarse language and cherish vulgar ideas; to erase from the young heart tender and gentle feelings and substitute for them fierce and bloody thoughts and sentiments.[2]

In conversation with 'that amiable and gifted person' Hannah More, he formed the idea of Peter Parley's tales of travel, history, nature and art, the aim being 'to feed the young mind upon things wholesome and pure, instead of things monstrous, false and pestilent'.[3] So in 1827 appeared *Tales of Peter Parley about America,* the first of a long series. Goodrich believed in writing for children as if one were talking to them, and his style was often avuncular or garrulous. *Tales about America* begins:

Here I am! My name is Peter Parley! I am an old man. I am very gray and lame. But I have seen a great many things, and had a great many adventures, and I love to talk about them. I love to tell stories to children, and very often they come to my house, and they get around me, and I tell them stories of what I have seen, and of what I have heard.

The book consists mainly of American history, rather rambling and with many digressions. It was followed the next year by *Tales of Peter Parley about Europe,* and so on through a wide range of places and subjects. Over the next

Peter Parley's Christmas Tales,
illustrated by William Croome

thirty years, Goodrich wrote about 120 books for children and forty for 'my early readers, advanced to maturity'. Sales of genuine Parleys totalled at least seven million, and there were extensive piracies and imitations, particularly in England.[4]

Goodrich had thought highly of Hannah More's *Cheap Repository Tracts*. Religious tract societies were established in England in 1799, and in New York and New England at about the same time, with the aim of furthering an education based on religion. These societies were much concerned with children's reading, and they too distrusted fiction. The Tract Society of New York, forerunner of the American Tract Society, in an undated leaflet issued about 1820, declared that 'Books of mere fiction and fancy are generally bad in their character and influence . . . Beware of the foul and exciting romance. Beware of books of war, piracy and murder. The first thought of crime has been suggested by such books.'[5] Sunday School unions were also being formed at this time, and in their early days much of the literature of both movements was crude but vigorous and to the point. A booklet issued by the American Sunday School Union in Philadelphia soon after its foundation in about 1825 is called *The Glass of Whiskey*, and begins:

There is a bottle. It has something in it which is called whiskey. Little reader, I hope you will never take any as long as you live. It is a poison. So is brandy, so is rum, so is gin, and many other drinks. They are called strong drink. They are so strong that they knock people down and kill them.

The book tells of Hugh, who is given drink as a small child and eventually becomes a confirmed drunkard; and of another little boy who drinks from a jug of rum, becomes drunk, falls over, and lies there until he dies.

The movements in both countries soon had to recognize the appeal of fiction, however, and decided that they could only beat it by joining it. Together they were responsible for a sub-literature of great piety, great quantity, and singularly uninspiring quality. The American Sunday School Union, suspiciously aware that children's books were still being imported in great numbers from England, made a stipulation for would-be writers that their books must not only be 'clearly and absolutely of a moral and religious character', but must also be 'American and for American children'.[6] This latter requirement, coming at the point it did in the development of American writing for children, could have had valuable results; unfortunately it did not inspire work of any interest. The other great organization, the American Tract Society, decided to enlist authors 'of some reputation and experience.' Again the results were not impressive, although the society did manage to get three books (not the ones for which he is now remembered) from Jacob Abbott.[7]

Abbott (1803-79) was a well-known figure in his day. He was variously preacher, professor, school principal and educationist, as well as writer of something like 180 books. These included the series of Rollo books, appearing from 1834 onwards — *Rollo Learning to Talk, Rollo Learning to Read,* and so on — in which a little boy learns to cope with the tasks and duties of daily life, broadening his horizons as he grows older. Then there were the Lucy books, designed to be 'entertaining and useful to the sisters of the boys who have honoured the Rollo books with their approval', and the Jonas books, intended 'not merely to interest and amuse the juvenile reader, but to give him instruction, by exemplifying the principles of honest integrity and plain practical good sense, in their application to the ordinary circumstances of childhood'.

The strangest of these, and to my mind one of the oddest books ever written for children, was *Jonas a Judge, or Law Among the Boys* (1840), in which a boy named Jonas, who has studied for some months in a lawyer's office, sorts out for a group of smaller boys, on strictly legalistic lines, their squabbles involving such matters as consideration, binding promise, testimony, warranty of title, tenure and possession. It is a curious idea, but Abbott makes a remarkably good job of putting difficult legal concepts into very simple words.

The *Franconia Stories,* ten little books published between 1850 and 1853, were Jacob Abbott's main contribution to American children's literature, though he did not place any special value on them himself. Unlike the Rollo, Lucy or Jonas books, these were unalloyed fiction, though they were of course gentle, wholesome fiction, with nothing about them of 'the foul and exciting romance'. The stories present scenes from the lives of children in a New England village. The principal child characters include Phonny, a cheerful, energetic, thoughtless small boy; his cousin Malleville, a delicate small girl; Wallace, a university student; and Antoine Bianchinette, known as Beechnut, the hired lad who works around the house. The children are real children, the country real country, the incidents such as could really happen. The author has a precise sense of the ways in which children's minds can work; he understands how Malleville, invited to see the schoolhouse and wanting to do so, nevertheless says 'No' to the invitation because she is afraid. There is a splendid passage of gentle comedy when Malleville, in bed as a patient, gets up at night, covers up her sleeping attendant, and goes downstairs to make a hearty supper.

But it is Beechnut — resourceful, inventive, a born leader and knowing it, patient but tough with the younger children, and a master at making the punishment fit the crime — who is the most memorable character in the *Franconia* books. Maybe Beechnut is the last representative of the Rousseau-Day-Edgeworth instructional line; but if he is a tutor figure he is the most likeable tutor figure of all.

The hand of the instructor lay heavily however on children's reading in the early years of the nineteenth century, both in America and England. Catherine Sinclair, in her preface to *Holiday House* (1839) observed that

while every effort is used to stuff the memory, like a cricket-ball, with well-known facts and ready-made opinions, no room is left for the vigour of natural feeling, the glow of natural genius, and the ardour of natural enthusiasm. It was a remark of Sir Walter Scott's many years ago, to the author herself, that in the rising generation there would be no poets, wits or orators, because all play of the imagination is now carefully discouraged, and books written for young persons are generally a mere dry record of facts, unenlivened by any appeal to the heart, or any excitement to the fancy.[8]

Miss Sinclair (1800-64) wanted to write about 'that species of noisy, frolicsome, mischievous children which is now almost extinct.' *Holiday House* offers a remarkable and cheering contrast both to the severities of such as Mrs Sherwood and to the factual pedestrianism of the Parleys. True, Miss Sinclair had a strong moral purpose, and her Harry and Lucy have an unco' guid elder brother Frank, whose inevitable death-bed extends over many pages. But her children are human, and they have a delightful if facetious uncle David who connives at their misdeeds and who tells them a 'Nonsensical Story about Giants and Fairies'. In this splendid and inventive story-within-a-story occurs the Giant Snap-'em-Up, who often ate for dinner

an elephant roasted whole, ostrich patties, a tiger smothered in onions, stewed lions, and whale soup; but for a side dish his greatest favourite consisted of little boys, as fat as possible, fried in crumbs of bread, with plenty of pepper and salt.

The inclusion of a story about giants and fairies — creatures that had been little loved by the intelligentsia of many successive generations — is itself a minor sign of the times. At last the fairy tales were coming out from under their cloud. There is no doubt that their emergence into respectability has a relationship with the Romantic movement, the rise in esteem of imagination after its long repression by reason, the replacement to some degree of classical influences by German and Nordic ones, and the atmosphere in which classical architecture gave way to Gothic. In Germany, modern fairy tales (Kunstmärchen) were much in favour among the early nineteenth-century Romantic writers.

In 1802 William Godwin had declared himself in favour of imagination and Perrault's stories; and in 1809 Godwin appears to have had a hand in the *Popular Fairy Tales* issued by one Benjamin Tabart.[9] But the two great fillips to the fairy tales in

Hans and his brutal brothers:
drawing by Richard Doyle from
The King of the Golden River

England were given by the successful translations of Grimm in 1823-6 and of Hans Andersen by Mary Howitt in 1846. In America in 1819, Washington Irving retold the old tales of *Rip Van Winkle* and *The Legend of Sleepy Hollow,* and in 1832 published his *Legends of the Alhambra.* In England in 1838-40 came E. W. Lane's version of the *Arabian Nights,* previously available in chapbook and adult editions, but now put into a form which was found suitable for children. John Ruskin wrote his splendid modern fairy tale *The King of the Golden River* in 1841, though it was not published until ten years later. And, in deliberate reaction against 'Peter Parleyism', Henry Cole (better known today as a moving spirit behind the Great Exhibition of 1851 and as the man who introduced the Christmas card to Britain) revived a great number of the old fairy tales in *Felix Summerly's Home Treasury* (1841-9). Many other stories and collections appeared, and from the mid-century onward fairy tales were generally acceptable, although Samuel Goodrich was still fulminating against them in his autobiography, *Recollections of a Lifetime,* as late as 1857. Complaints of unsuitable (usually meaning 'frightening') material have continued to crop up from time to time, especially about Grimm, but the old arguments against fairy tales as being immoral or contrary to reason have lapsed.

With *Holiday House* and *Felix Summerly* we are in Queen Victoria's reign and on the verge of the modern age in children's literature. The didactic story is by no means finished, but new kinds of book are beginning to be written. In the 1840s Captain Marryat publishes his children's adventure stories, pointing the way to Ballantyne, Kingston, Robert Louis Stevenson and Henty. In the 1850s, *Tom Brown* and *Eric* introduce the boys' school story, while Miss Charlotte M. Yonge's domestic stories for girls lead up towards Louisa Alcott's *Little Women* in the following decade. In the 1860s come two great fantasies, the perfect *Alice* and the imperfect but remarkable *Water Babies.* Mark Twain's *Tom Sawyer* and the best-loved of animal stories, Anna Sewell's *Black Beauty,* are to follow in the 1870s.

In the mid-nineteenth century, in fact, after a hundred years or more of fitful and unspectacular progress, children's literature was making a breakthrough. One can offer a few guesses at the reasons. First, it was a generally energetic and enterprising time. Then, the world's English-speaking populations – still of course mainly concentrated in the United States and Britain – were growing and becoming more literate, and this was helping to provide the essential economic base for a flourishing children's literature. Adult fiction was in a state of rapid development, and this was echoed in children's books. Publishing itself was becoming ever more respectable: the smalltime catchpenny publisher was by no means extinct, but the new publisher with modern attitudes and methods and professional status was coming along rapidly. Good writers were increasingly ready to give of their best for children. And the market itself was going up in the world: John Newbery had priced most of his books at a few coppers, but *Alice in Wonderland* was sold at 7s. 6d. (the equivalent of something like £18, or $30, today) at which price it was an immediate and lasting success.

The main streams into which children's literature now divides will be looked at in more detail in the succeeding chapters.

PART TWO

1840-1915

5

Nineteenth-century adventures

THE VICTORIAN English-speaking world was very much a man's world. In the reading classes — that is, mainly middle and above — it was man's work and pleasure, or at any rate man's dream, to build a nation or empire, win wars, pioneer newly-won territories, or develop industrial or commercial wealth. Woman's place remained in the home; the feminine virtues were piety, domesticity, sexual submission and repression. Books for boys and girls reflected this division. For boys there was the life of action on land and at sea: the world of the 'boy's adventure story' (still often so described in book catalogues). For girls there was a different kind of fiction, considered suitable for the gentler sex, which will be discussed in the next chapter. Happily there is no doubt that girls read and often preferred the so-called boys' books; less happily, this meant they had to read about young heroes, not young heroines.

Frequently the adventure stories could also be described as historical fiction; there is no clear division, and nearly all the best-known writers went to history at one time or another for their subjects. It is pointless to separate 'historical' from 'pure' fiction in the works, say, of Stevenson, Ballantyne, Henty and Marryat. The Victorian adventure story has in fact a dual origin. Of its two great influences, one is *Robinson Crusoe;* the other is the historical novel as established by Sir Walter Scott.

Robinson Crusoe, though not written for children, filtered through to the schoolroom well before the end of the eighteenth century, and was often found in truncated chapbook versions. It gave rise to innumerable imitations and variations, conveniently described by the French term 'Robinsonnades'. Everyone knows, even if not everyone has read, J. D. Wyss's *Swiss Family Robinson,* introduced into England by Godwin in 1814. Captain Marryat, who did not think much of Wyss's geography or seamanship, wrote *Masterman Ready* on the same theme in 1841; and among many other Robinsonnades are Mayne Reid's *English Family Robinson* (1851), Fenimore Cooper's *Mark's Reef* (1847) and R. M. Ballantyne's *The Coral Island* (1857). The first Canadian children's book of any importance, written by Catharine Parr Traill and published in 1852, was called *Canadian Crusoes;* and the Crusoe theme is also characteristic of early Australian children's stories.

The influence of Sir Walter Scott's novels was equally pervasive. Scott has been out of fashion for years: far fewer modern students of English literature are interested in him than in Jane Austen, George Eliot, the Brontës or Dickens. But Scott was immensely popular in his day and for long afterwards, and had a much greater effect than might be supposed from the amount of critical attention paid to him today. There can be no doubt that his novels helped to set the trend of the nineteenth-century adventure story. Defoe and Scott are not the only begetters, but they are among the most important.

James Fenimore Cooper (1789-1851) was often described as the American Walter Scott. He wrote historical novels and two sea adventure stories, one of them in direct competition with Scott; but the books for which he is remembered, and which found their way to the children's shelves, were the five 'Leatherstocking Tales'. These deal with the adventures in the wilderness, and among the Indians, of the white hunter Natty Bumppo. Cooper wrote about Indians with respect and sympathy, though apparently without first-hand knowledge of tribal life.

The Leatherstocking books are concerned with the conflict of wild and civilized, not only of Indians and Whites; and Natty Bumppo is not the simple hero of a Western yarn. But the books can be — and I suspect usually are, with a bit of skipping — read as robust straightforward adventure stories. The most popular is *The Last of the Mohicans* (1826); the others are *The Pioneers* (1823), *The Prairie* (1827), *The Pathfinder* (1840) and *The Deerslayer* (1841).

The first historical adventure stories to be written specially for children were those of the Englishman Captain Marryat (1792-1848). After a vivid career at sea, Marryat had started by writing novels for the general public, notable among them being *Peter Simple* (1834) and *Mr Midshipman Easy* (1836). Then Marryat deliberately crossed the border from adult to children's fiction and produced his 'Juvenile Library' (which he sometimes referred to as his 'little income'). Besides *Masterman Ready,* previously referred to, he wrote *Settlers in Canada* (1844), *Children of the New Forest* (1847) and *The Little Savage* (1849), the last of which was finished after his death by his son Frank. All these books have Crusoesque elements, even *Children of the New Forest,* which however is primarily a historical novel on the Cavaliers-and-Roundheads theme.

But Marryat's natural breeziness was often overlaid by didacticism when he wrote for children. Though his children's books have their attractions, and have stayed the course well, they have many preachy and wearisome passages. As Harvey Darton truly says, *Mr Midshipman Easy* was the real boys' book, in spite of a few passages to which a censor might object.[1] Its most likeable aspect is the presentation of the hero: the author mocks Jack Easy's youthful waywardness but at the same time sympathizes with it. There is an air of decency and generosity about the book, as well as a deep love of the Navy and the seafaring life.

It is a short step from *Mr Midshipman Easy* to the work of the 'real' boys' writers: the writers for young England in its Victorian heyday of discovery and conquest. Robert Louis Stevenson, who had no great sense of mission himself, acknowledged the inspiration of 'Kingston, and Ballantyne the brave'.[2] W. H. G. Kingston (1814-80) had his day, but it has gone by. He was the author of *The Three Midshipmen* (1862) and a great many other titles (he is credited with one hundred and seventy-one books in forty-two years). A letter written by G. K. Chesterton about 1890, when he was sixteen, remarks that 'my brother is intent upon *The Three Midshipmen* or *The Three Admirals* or *The Three Coalscuttles* or some other distinguished trio by that interminable ass Kingston'.[3]

'Ballantyne the brave' was born in Edinburgh in 1825, and when he was sixteen went to Canada in the service of the Hudson's Bay Company at a salary of twenty pounds a year. He wrote his first (adult) book while stationed at one of the loneliest outposts of Empire: a 'fort' in the far North-west where he was in charge of one Indian and one horse, and the mail came twice a year. In 1847 he came home to join the family printing firm (which had printed Sir Walter Scott's novels); nine years later, at the age of thirty-one, he published his first children's book, *The Young Fur-Traders* (1856). The first edition came out with the title *Snowflakes and Sunbeams* — a perfect Victorian namby-pamby title, diametrically opposed to the spirit and content of the book, and one which was quickly dropped. Ballantyne then wrote *Ungava* (1857), which had a similar setting, and followed it in the same year with *The Coral Island*, his best-known story. Like Kingston, he was immensely prolific, and wrote over one hundred books in forty years.

The Coral Island is a first-person narration, and it begins briskly, for Ballantyne gets his hero born, brought up, and sent to sea, his two companions introduced, the ship wrecked, and the three lads cast ashore on their island, all in a mere eighteen pages – a length which was nothing to a Victorian novelist. Threesomes are popular in the classical adventure story, and here the threesome consists of the narrator, a quiet, thoughtful lad, rather lacking in humour; the leader, Jack Martin, 'a tall strapping broad-shouldered youth of eighteen, with a handsome, good-humoured, firm face'; and Peterkin Gay, 'little, quick, funny, decidedly mischievous, and about fourteen years old'. From an author's point of view, this is a very practical threesome to work with; its members provide a three-cornered contrast in character and approach to life, and distinguish themselves clearly from each other without calling for any outstanding subtlety. And we may note that Ballantyne stands back a little from the narrator, in order to get the benefit of him as a character and not just as a mouthpiece – a sophisticated technique for that day and for boys' writing.

The first half of the book is devoted largely to telling how the three boys manage to keep alive, what they eat and drink and wear, and how they make themselves at home. This is in the Crusoe tradition; it is also full of intrinsic interest. There is some deep psychological factor here; we all wonder how we would manage if ever we had to fend entirely for ourselves; consequently the reader-identification in a good desert-island story can be unusually intense. The latter part of the book is inferior, though it has a great deal of action: clashes with savages, the narrator seized by pirates (one of whom repents with his last gasp), and finally a quixotic expedition to rescue a black girl who is being forced to marry a heathen against her will whereas she wants to marry a Christian chieftain. An important feature of the latter part of the book is that missionaries are at work spreading Christianity in the South Seas, and it is quite clear to the author that this is a great civilizing as well as Christianizing mission. Today hardly any children's writer would venture to put the Christian religion in the forefront of his picture, any more than he would the old imperialism. That kind of confidence is gone.

The English name which is probably identified above all others with the Victorian adventure story is that of G. A. Henty (1832-1902). Beginning in the Crimea, Henty had thirty years of intermittent travel and adventure as a war correspondent, in days when a war correspondent's life was hard and perilous and when, as Henty himself said, a good seat on a horse was an essential qualification. He wrote seventy-odd boys' books, as well as a few adult novels.

Henty had a horror of any lad 'who displayed any weak emotion and shrank from shedding blood, or winced at any encounter'. His heroes are all cast in the same mould: they are straightforward, extroverted young Philistines. Charlie Marryat, in *With Clive in India* (1884) is a fair example:

Charlie Marryat's muscles were as firm and hard as those of any boy in the school. In all sport requiring activity and endurance rather than weight and strength he was always conspicuous . . . He had a reputation for being a leader in every mischievous prank; but he was honourable and manly, would scorn to shelter himself under the semblance of a lie, and was a prime favourite with his masters as well as his schoolfellows.

Nothing is said about Charlie's academic attainments. But Henty himself could have claimed to serve the cause of education, for according to his biographer G. M. Fenn he 'taught more lasting history to boys than all the schoolmasters of his generation'.[4]

Military history was Henty's speciality, and the hero's adventures were frequently grafted on to actual events. Our hero is always of officer status, and often has a faithful attendant of lower rank who follows him through thick and thin. The simple public school-and-empire-building code requires some use of moral blinkers. Henty is not hypocritical, and often admits British misdeeds and failures; nevertheless for him it is a case of 'my country right or wrong'. Charlie Marryat receives large presents from Indian potentates and grows rich with plunder; clearly Henty does not see this wealth as ill-gotten. In this book there is a single reference to 'the low hovels of the black town', but no sign of interest in the conditions of the native population. Occasionally Henty shows concern over people's sufferings — for instance in a chapter of *Cornet of Horse* (1881) entitled 'The Sad Side of War', though the setting there is European. It must have been hard in his day to see 'natives' as people. For him, broadly, the only good native is a loyal native (i.e. loyal to Britain).

'The expedition was launched by greed and decorated with murder and treachery, and concluded by luck rather than righteousness.' So wrote Harvey Darton about the plot of *Treasure Island* (1883).[5] If this had been pointed out to Robert Louis Stevenson, he would undoubtedly have smiled and

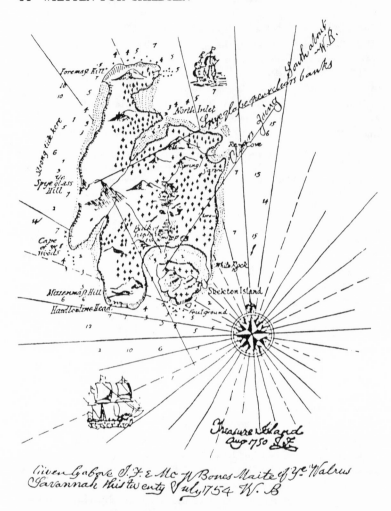

Robert Louis Stevenson's map of Treasure Island, which he drew
himself, and described as the chief part of his plot

shrugged his shoulders. He had jettisoned, without a thought,
all the moral attitudes which previous writers for children
thought it proper to maintain. The total liberation from
didacticism is one of *Treasure Island*'s outstanding features (as
Darton well realized). Darton detected a strain of the Penny
Dreadful, and indeed there is such a strain running through
much of Stevenson's work: *Dr Jekyll and Mr Hyde* is surely
the greatest Penny Dreadful of all.

Robert Louis Stevenson was born in Edinburgh in 1850, the

son of a lighthouse-builder; he was a delicate only child and much doted upon by his parents. Their deep possessive love gave rise to dreadful and hurtful family troubles. Stevenson was wayward, was slack at the university, and developed a liking for low company (as a refuge, no doubt, from his parents' awesome respectability). He could not accept his parents' rather narrow religion, and this was a great grief to them; moreover, he had no wish to follow his father's profession of engineer. And his father, Thomas Stevenson, had great contempt for what he called 'the devious and barren paths of literature'.

Stevenson married Fanny Osbourne in 1880. By then he was beginning to make a modest income from his writing, but he was still subsidized by his father. When his father died in 1887, he felt no longer tied to his homeland; he went off to California, where his wife came from, and after making two Pacific cruises settled in Samoa. He died in 1894 of a cerebral haemorrhage, when he was just 44.

Treasure Island was written in Scotland. In August 1881, R.L.S. was staying at a cottage in Braemar, Perthshire, with his parents and his stepson, Lloyd Osbourne. The Scottish August weather was cold, wet and windy. To keep the boy amused, Stevenson drew a map of an imaginary island, colouring it elaborately and calling it 'Treasure Island'. From there it was quite a short step to writing a story about it. Soon he was reporting progress in a letter to his friend W. E. Henley:

Will you be surprised to learn that the book is about buccaneers, that it begins in the 'Admiral Benbow' public house on the Devon coast, that it's all about a map, and a treasure, and a mutiny, and a derelict ship, and a current, and a fine old Squire Trelawney, and a doctor, and a sea-cook with one leg, and a sea-song with the chorus 'Yo-ho-ho and a bottle of rum' (at the third *Ho* you heave at the capstan bars) which is a real buccaneer's song, only known to the crew of the late Captain Flint . . . that's the kind of man I am, blast your eyes. Two chapters written, and have been tried on Lloyd with great success . . . A chapter a day I mean to do; they are short. No women in the story; Lloyd's orders . . . It's awful fun, boys' stories. You just indulge the pleasure of your heart, that's all; no trouble, no strain . . . just drive along as the words come![6]

The most obvious qualities of *Treasure Island* are its sheer speed, colour and excitement. This is what happens when a first-rate writer, just coming to the peak of his powers, applies himself with boyish enthusiasm to a work that sweeps him away and has swept nearly all readers away ever since. It is a limited aim pursued with great power. Then, it is the creation of a world — a world of the author's own that carries absolute conviction. The characters are vividly drawn, especially that of Long John Silver, who is something new in boys' fiction and perhaps in any fiction: the villain with something heroic about him. There is also the haunting person of Ben Gunn the castaway, and in the early chapters are the dreadful rum-ridden Captain Billy Bones and the menacing blind man Pew.

Treasure Island rode roughshod over what had previously been the rules for children's writing, and left the rules so that they could never be the same again. The blurring of the usual black-and-white of right and wrong has already been noted. 'Our' side − Squire Trelawney, Dr Livesey and the rest − is not particularly in the right; Long John Silver is by no means a sheer villain; the blood flows freely and impartially. Stevenson has shown a lordly disregard for the moralists. Well might he say of *Treasure Island* that 'it seemed to me as original as sin'.[7]

Two or three years later, Stevenson wrote a historical romance, *Kidnapped* (1886), set in the Highlands after the '45 rebellion. This ranks as a classic in its own right. To my mind it has nothing like the magic of *Treasure Island,* though it does have a fine swashbuckling character in Alan Breck Stewart. *Catriona* (1893) is a sequel to *Kidnapped,* and is less exciting but more romantic.

With Rider Haggard (1856-1925) we are back on the borderline between children's and adult literature. Most of Haggard's books, to my mind, lie on the other side of the border, but *King Solomon's Mines* (1885) must be mentioned, since Haggard admitted that he was inspired to write it by the success of *Treasure Island,* and it was issued by the same publishers in a binding designed to make it look like a companion volume.

The heroes of *King Solomon's Mines* are a threesome in the classic pattern. Allan Quatermain, the narrator, is a veteran elephant-hunter in South Africa; his companions are Sir Henry Curtis, a splendid rugged leader-of-men, and Captain John Good, a stoutish dandified man with an eyeglass who is a slightly comic character. The book has two main themes: a search for treasure in the legendary King Solomon's Mines in a remote land beyond desert and mountains; and the restoration of an African ruler to his throne against the opposition of a tyrant usurper and a wicked witch who appears to be hundreds of years old.

King Solomon's Mines is vivid and powerful. The secrets of its success, I think, are first the idea of the Quest; secondly the

Lost Country, another theme which always stirs the imagination; thirdly, the heroic crossing of desert and mountain barriers (more potent symbols); and finally the time-mystery of the old witch Gagool, a living embodiment of evil. *King Solomon's Mines* is a triumph of the exotic.

At the end of the nineteenth century the adventure story in Britain was returning, much enriched, to its position of seventy or eighty years before; the best books were being written not for children but for adults, though children were welcome to read them. Conan Doyle and John Buchan, Anthony Hope and the H. G. Wells of *First Men on the Moon* were and are enjoyed both by boys and by great big boys.

America had its opposite numbers to the successful British boys' writers: equally prolific, equally popular, and by now possibly even more outdated. Harry Castlemon (Charles Austin Fosdick, 1842-1915) wrote fifty-eight adventure stories, and knew very well what he was about: 'Boys,' he said, 'don't like fine writing. What they want is adventure, and the more of it you can get into 250 pages of manuscript, the better fellow you are'.[8] Oliver Optic (William Taylor Adams, 1822-97) wrote twice as many books as Castlemon: the Army and Navy series, the Starry Flag series, and very many others. Louisa May Alcott thought little of them, describing them as 'optical delusions', and asking (in *Eight Cousins*): 'Is it natural for lads from fifteen to eighteen to command ships, defeat pirates, outwit smugglers, and so cover themselves with glory that Admiral Farragut invites them to dinner, saying: "Noble boy, you are an honor to your country!"?'[9]

The invariable combination of bravery with moral uplift resulted in a succession of stereotyped and priggish heroes, occasionally redeemed by the sheer absurdity of their remarks. The hero of Optic's *The Sailor Boy, or Jack Somers in the Navy* (1865) refuses to gamble with a shipmate, who thereupon calls him a 'little snivelling rat-catcher', and asks:

'Why didn't you bring your ma with you to keep you from falling overboard?'

'Because I can take care of myself, and because I want to keep my mother out of bad company,' replied Jack sharply.

It is always interesting to know people's reasons for not taking Mother along when joining the Navy.

Castlemon and Optic are of little significance today: partly

Drawing by E.W.Kemble, from *The Adventures of Huckleberry Finn*

because their talents were less remarkable than their output, partly because their books reflect a conventional idea of adventure rather than the real thing. Adventure for Americans was not the same as for the British. To the Victorian Englishman it was something you found overseas; increasingly it was connected with the building of that empire on which the sun has now set. But the great American adventure was the making of America. It is unfortunate that the successive waves of immigration and the westward thrust of the frontier did not at the time inspire children's books of any real merit. But there is more justification than merely the wording of their titles for considering *The Adventures of Tom Sawyer* and *The Adventures of Huckleberry Finn* under the heading of adventure stories. These books showed that adventure did not have to be sought at the other side of the world; it was as near as your own backyard. Adventure did not happen only to stiff-upper-lipped heroes of superior social status; it could happen to ordinary people, even to inferiors like Huck and to mere chattels like Jim. And the Mississippi River as a setting was spacious enough to accommodate any story – even the great American novel.

Samuel Langhorne Clemens (1835-1910) was apprenticed to a printer but became a river pilot and later a writer. He took his pseudonym from the leadsman's call he had heard daily on the Mississippi: Mark Twain. His three best books – *Tom Sawyer* (1876), *Life on the Mississippi* (1883), and *Huckleberry Finn* (1884) are all based on his early life on and beside the river. Twain's humour and attitudes were 'Western' or at any rate 'frontier', as distinct from the European-mindedness of the East.

It is generally agreed that *Tom* is a lesser work than *Huck,* although it is more than just a prelude and May Hill Arbuthnot declared confidently in *Children and Books* that 'most children like *Tom* better'.[10] The most convincing of Tom's adventures are the small adventures of a real boy in a small town; the melodramatic episode involving body-snatching and murder in the graveyard juts out awkwardly from the rest of the book, and one does not really believe in the treasure. But the character of Huck Finn is a triumph; it seems natural and obvious that Mark Twain should make him the hero of the later book. The main theme of *Huckleberry Finn* is of course the journey of Huck and the runaway slave Jim; and, as has often been pointed out, the river voyage, with its variety, its endless succession of incident, its triumphs and setbacks, its humour and suffering, can be seen as an emblem of life.

Huckleberry Finn has one characteristic in common with the otherwise dissimilar *Treasure Island:* its author had not the least interest in reinforcing the conventional morality. But although Mark Twain denied that his narrative had a moral, it has a good deal of moral irony: as for instance in the workings of Huck's conscience over his wickedness in 'stealing a poor old woman's nigger', and in a laconic dialogue about a steamboat accident:

'We blowed out a cylinder-head.'
'Good gracious! Anybody hurt?'
'N'm. Killed a nigger.'
'Well, it's lucky, because sometimes people do get hurt.'

Subsidiary to the great adventure of America itself, there was in the second half of the nineteenth century the individual adventure of making one's way in life; making good. This in part was what America was all about. In theory at least, the way to the top was open to the poorest street-lad or unlettered immigrant who was willing to work hard and use his initiative. There was no stultifying assumption that 'the rich man in his castle, the poor man at his gate' were locked into place by the Divine Will: 'God made them high or lowly, and ordered their estate.' Becoming rich through hard work has not always been a fashionable ideal; but it was inspiring, and legitimately inspiring, in late-nineteenth-century America, and its prophet, in books for young people, was Horatio Alger, Jr. (1834-99). Beginning with *Ragged Dick* in 1868, Alger wrote more than a hundred books, mostly in series of six. As a writer he was insignificant, but as a phenomenon he was astonishing, and although his books are no longer read his name remains an American household word.

Ragged Dick is the prototype Alger hero, and his story is typical of almost all Alger stories. He is a dirty, ill-clad shoe-black who sleeps rough. But he gets a chance: in this case, the job of showing well-dressed Frank round New York City. Dick starts washing, takes a room, learns to read and write, puts money in the savings bank, and is on the way to success. Dick is capable and cheerful, and in his urchin days has a salty wit.

'You won't be a boot-black all your life,' [somebody tells him].
'No,' said Dick; 'I'm goin' to knock off when I get to be ninety.'

The gift of repartee seems to disappear when eventually he becomes Richard Hunter Esquire, respectable and dull.

In spite of the difference in their positions, Dick has much in common with a Henty hero; for 'he was above doing anything mean or dishonorable. He would not steal, or cheat, or impose on younger boys, but was frank and straightforward, manly and self-reliant. His nature was a noble one, and had saved him from all mean faults.'

Ragged Dick was followed by *Phil the Fiddler, Paul the Peddler, Tattered Tom* (a girl), *Mark the Match Boy* — inspired by a youngster who told Alger he was 'a timber merchant in a small way, sellin' matches' — and a succession of similar Alger-figures. Alger, who knew what it was to live in dingy lodgings and lack the price of a meal, genuinely cared about the situation of the New York street lads, and for some time had a room in the Newsboys' Lodging House, where he became acquainted with Fat Jack, Pickle Nose, Cranky Jim, Tickle-me-Foot, Soggy Pants, One Lung Pete, Toothless and Jake the Oyster.[11] And in *Phil the Fiddler (1872)* he exposed the 'padrone system', under which immigrant Italian children were sold into beggary, thieving and prostitution in American cities.

If the Alger success-stories seem far-fetched, it should be remembered that Andrew Carnegie, John D. Rockefeller, Henry Ford, Joseph Pulitzer and many others made their way to wealth from humble origins. Alger naturally did not think in terms of the establishment of great foundations; to him success meant simply money and respectability. His morality was commercial morality: honesty was the best policy, but you must beware of sharpers and never trust a stranger. Curiously, affluence when it came was not always the result of hard work. Assistance of the rich-uncle kind was sometimes required, and

Title page of *Rufus and Rose* (1870), the sixth and last book in the *Ragged Dick* series by Horatio Alger, Jr.

it was not unusual for Alger heroes to be rightful heirs to large fortunes, or richly rewarded for brave deeds, or handsomely adopted. And they did not always climb swiftly to the summit; their achievements were often more modest. Paul, in *Paul the Peddler* (1871) and its sequel *Slow and Sure* (1872), progresses only 'from the street to the shop'. He finishes as proprietor of a men's outfitters. 'At the end of two years he took a larger shop and engaged two extra clerks. Prompt in his engagements, and of thorough integrity, he is likely to be even more prosperous as the years roll on.'

Exotic settings are not inherently more original, or even more interesting, than city streets; but one end-of-century writer who used them seems to me to be now much under-rated. This is Thomas L. Janvier (1849-1913). *The Aztec Treasure-House* (1890), about a lost city ruled by an ancient, formidable priest-king, is a powerful piece of work with strong resemblances to *King Solomon's Mines,* but is excelled by *In the Sargasso Sea* (1898), an outstanding story now unaccountably neglected. This is a novel about a man on his own: trapped in a seemingly-endless jam of wrecks and tangled weed, far from any living soul but surrounded by dead ships and dead men. No doubt there are echoes of Defoe in the account of how the hero — who is yourself, for you are compelled to identify — makes his way out of the maze, overcoming setback after setback, and above all enduring. But *In the Sargasso Sea* has a living nightmare quality that is entirely its own. There is an unforgettable passage telling how the narrator discovers an ancient slave ship with its hold full of chained skeletons; and another — highly wrought, but not in its context overwritten — which describes the heart of the wreck-jam: the oldest, most rotten ships of all, illuminated at night by phosphorescent light, 'as though a desolate sea-city were lying there dead before me, lit up with lanterns of despair'.

Whether the heart of the Sargasso Sea really could be like this is not important; Janvier's descriptions are feats of imagination, not reportage. *In the Sargasso Sea* is a book that deserves to live.

Among early children's books with Australian settings, stories of pioneering adventure and hardship in a new country were, not surprisingly, prominent. William Howitt (husband of the Mary Howitt who translated Hans Andersen and wrote 'The

Spider and the Fly') lived there for two years and wrote *A Boy's Adventures in the Wilds of Australia* (1854), which included much accurate description of the country and its wildlife. In 1869 Richard Rowe wrote *The Boy in the Bush*, a set of episodes rather than a novel, introducing subjects which have long been staples of writing about Australia: snakes, drought, an old convict, a gold rush. *Tom's Nugget: a Story of the Australian Goldfields*, by J. H. Hodgetts, and *From Squire to Squatter*, by Gordon Stables, both published in 1888, were among many stories of immigrants who had to make their way and win acceptance. But often, according to H. M. Saxby in his *History of Australian Children's Literature*, the writers of children's books on Australia were only visitors, 'and some would appear never to have set foot in the land at all, so distorted is their picture of local conditions.' The interminable Kingston wrote *Twice Lost: a Story of Shipwreck and Adventure in the Wilds of Australia* (1881) and *Australian Adventures* (1884); but his descriptions were even more incredible than his plots.

6

Domestic dramas

VICTORIAN GIRLS may have yearned for the world of action; but that was not the world they were destined to enter. Boys were expected to develop in a manly way, girls in a womanly. ('Manly' and 'womanly' were much-used and highly-approved terms.) Books were expected to assist the process. Girls' literature – wrote Edward Salmon in 1888 –

enables girls to read something above mere baby-tales and yet keeps them from the influence of novels of a sort that should be read only by persons capable of a discreet judgement . . . While it advances beyond the nursery, it stops short of the full blaze of the drawing-room.[1]

As the century went on, there were increasing glimpses of the broader horizons beyond the drawing-room window; and there is no doubt that girls read the popular novelists as well as their brothers' adventure stories. But it remained the function of girls' books to glamorize, to make more acceptable and less narrow, the circumscribed life of the virtuous girl and woman. Novels that achieved the right combination of romance and uplift could be immensely successful. *The Wide, Wide World* (1850), by Elizabeth Wetherell (Susan Warner, 1819-85), went through thirteen American and several English editions in its first two years. This is a sentimental, religiose story which begins with a long, long leavetaking between the heroine Ellen and her mother, who is going abroad to die. Ellen is sent to live in the country with a rigid, outspoken aunt; meets a saintly friend, Alice, who is too saintly to survive to the end of the book; and becomes adoptive sister to Alice's brother John, who looks at the end as though he will finish up as something more than a brother.

To be as popular as *The Wide, Wide World* was over many years, a book must have something more than length and piety; and, apart from its vast scope for tears and identification, I think it is the account of Ellen's life in the country with the crusty but not altogether unlovable Aunt Fortune – Ellen has to rough it a good deal, and wash under the pump – that makes this book successful. And although virtuous friend Alice is a bloodless figure, human nature breaks in, in the shape of a bad girl, Nancy, who says it is no use trying to teach her to be good; 'you might as well teach a snake not to wriggle.' In 1853 came the same author's *Queechy*, in which, after nine years and 500 pages of vicissitudes, a young American girl marries an English gentleman and becomes mistress of a stately home. *Queechy* too was highly popular, although Miss Charlotte M. Yonge did not approve of it, feeling that books like this had 'the very grave and injurious effect of leading little girls to expect a lover in any one who is good-natured to them'.[2]

Another hugely successful book, both in America and England, was Maria Cummins's *The Lamplighter* (1854). Its heroine Gerty is a wild child, dragged up by a brutal woman in a Boston slum. After she has thrown a brick through this woman's window, Gerty defends herself to the inevitable virtuous young lady who has befriended her: 'Did anybody ever drown your kitten? Did anybody ever call your father Old Smutty? If they had, I know you'd hate 'em just as I do.' This is a book with an intriguing start and some promising characters. But the plot deteriorates into a concoction of mysteries of identity, rival suitors, misunderstandings, pride and snobbery, deathbeds, and faithful separation duly rewarded. And the fate of fierce, impulsive Gerty is what has come to be called a cop-out: she grows into a beautiful, pious, uninteresting young woman and marries her childhood sweetheart Willie, who by now has made his way in the world.

Among British writers for girls at this time, the best known was Miss Charlotte M. Yonge (1823-1901). Miss Yonge was the daughter of an Army officer turned country gentleman, and lived all her life in her native village of Otterbourne, in Hampshire. Of all Victorian women she was perhaps the most Victorian: impeccably virtuous, conscientious, fruitful in good works, knowing her place, and knowing woman's place too — for in spite of her own considerable talents she 'had no hesitation in declaring my full belief in the inferiority of woman, nor that she brought it upon herself' (in the person of Eve).[3] For more than forty years she edited a magazine for girls with the title, which now sounds unfortunate, of *The Monthly Packet*. Her views were entirely conventional and conservative.

In the third chapter of *Little Women*, Jo is found by her sister Meg in the attic, 'eating apples and crying over *The Heir of Redclyffe*'. This was Charlotte Yonge's best known, and almost her first book, published in 1853; it is a romantic novel intended for the general reader, though it was popular with older girls and was considered quite safe.

Miss Yonge wrote a long series of family chronicles, as well as many historical novels and a good deal of other material, including Sunday School rewards. Her family stories are her most interesting work, and *The Daisy Chain* (1856) is the best of them. It is about the numerous children of Dr May, who lose their mother in a carriage accident and have to rely on their own resources for their upbringing. The heroine Ethel is a careless, clumsy girl, not pretty. She is eager to learn Latin and Greek, though after the accident she finds it her duty to give up these studies. (Renunciation was an important principle to Miss Yonge; for as she said, 'self-denial is always best, and in a doubtful case the most disagreeable is always the safest.') Ethel and her brothers and sisters are all living people, and *The Daisy Chain* is the most important forerunner of *Little Women*.

The life and work of Louisa May Alcott (1832-88) have been written about endlessly, and undue brevity here will no doubt be forgiven. She was the daughter of the unworldly if brilliant philosopher and educationist Bronson Alcott and of his necessarily practical wife Abba May. The March sisters and 'Marmee' were portraits of her own family, and *Little Women* (1868) was based largely on incidents in their own lives. It was

Frontispiece by J.Priestman Atkinson to
an 1889 edition of *The Daisy Chain*

a gifted editor, Thomas Niles of the Boston firm of Roberts Brothers, who persuaded Louisa May to write a girls' story when she would rather have produced 'a fairy book'. She noted in her journal: 'I plod away, though I don't enjoy this sort of thing. Never liked girls or knew many, except my sisters; but our queer plays and experiences may prove interesting, though I doubt it'.[4]

When it was finished, she and her editor both thought it rather dull, but *Little Women* was an immediate success and was followed by *Little Women, Part 2* (better known in England as *Good Wives)* in 1869, and by half a dozen books that dealt with the March family of later years, as well as some about other characters. The last of the *Little Women* series, *Jo's Boys,* appeared in 1886. I have not read all the later books, and what I have read failed to hold me; it is, however, on the two parts of *Little Women* that Louisa May Alcott's reputation rests. The qualities that account for its success are obvious: truth, warmth, simplicity, intimacy. The Marches are a real family you might have known. Jo March, based on the author herself, is the obvious inspiration of many a later heroine, and the very name of Jo still seems to bear her imprint.

There is some sermonizing in *Little Women;* but there is also human reaction against sermonizing. (When Jo has been indulging in it, her friend Laurie asks, 'Are you going to deliver lectures all the way home?' Jo says, 'Of course not; why?' Laurie says, 'Because if you are, I'll take a bus.') Laurie, I fear, has never seemed quite like masculine flesh and blood to me. I suspect that he is the nice girl's dream-boy-next-door: handsome, attentive, and unlikely to attempt anything more dangerous than holding hands. Yet the dismay still felt by readers when they realize that Miss Alcott will not let Jo marry him suggests that I am in the minority, and that most readers see them both as real people. There is no point in adding to speculation on Miss Alcott's motives for keeping Jo and Laurie apart; but does Jo cop out by accepting the staid Professor Bhaer? It could be argued that she cops out sooner than that, for at the end of *Little Women* she is improved to the extent that she 'neither whistles, talks slang, nor lies on the rug as she used to do.' Already that is not the real Jo; the Jo we remember is the one who does these unladylike things.

Little Women marks not only an increased truth-to-life in domestic stories, with children seen as people rather than examples of good and bad; it also marks a relaxation of the stiff and authoritarian stereotype of family life persisting from the still recent times when the Fifth Commandment came first and the earthly father was seen quite literally as the representative of the heavenly one. ('Henry,' said Mr Fairchild to his son, 'I stand in place of God to you, whilst you are a child.') This mellowing was necessary before the family story, of which *Little Women* is the first great example, could come into its own. A relationship between rulers and subjects had to be replaced by one of mutual affection. The family story could not work in an atmosphere of repression or of chilly grandeur. The key characteristic is always warmth.

The heavy Victorian father was of course no myth — though not all Victorian fathers were heavy — and often his womenfolk would gladly accept and reinforce his authority. Charlotte Yonge had a very strict girlhood and was bullied abominably by her father, but she did not resent it, and seems to have regarded it as a natural accompaniment of male superiority. In the United States, Martha Finlay's Elsie Dinsmore, as late as 1867, will do nothing that is not in obedience to Father's will: 'I cannot disobey Papa,' she says, 'even if he should never know it, because that would be disobeying God, and He would know it.' At one point the reason Papa gives Elsie for not allowing her to do something is 'because I forbid it; that is quite enough for you to know.'

With *Elsie Dinsmore,* Martha Finlay (1828-1902) launched Elsie as a little girl of eight on her tearful career, which was continued with *Elsie's Girlhood, Elsie's Womanhood, Elsie's Widowhood* (the author killed off her husband, to the luxuriant grief of the readership) and, among many other titles, *Grandmother Elsie.* Elsie must be a strong contender for the title of the most goody-goody heroine in the whole of fiction. At the age of eight she had

clear and correct views on almost every subject connected with her duty to God and her neighbour; was very truthful, both in word and deed, very strict in her observance of the Sabbath . . . very diligent in her studies, respectful to superiors, and kind to inferiors and equals; and she was gentle, sweet-tempered, patient and forgiving to a remarkable degree.

Her fictional career reads as though one of those pious children of earlier days had somehow missed its triumphant death. The first book tells how Elsie, by sheer goodness and obedience, wins a place in the heart of her stern, cold Papa. Elsie's father strikes one as singularly unlovable; he treats her with monstrous unfairness and even more monstrous indifference, until eventually he shows the beginnings of concern for her by cutting down her diet and giving orders that she is to have bread and milk for breakfast instead of meats, hot rolls and coffee. However, one is bound to agree with him when he complains that Elsie cries too easily. In the first book alone she has reached her sixth bout of sobbing by page 14, and is in tears again on pages 21, 22, 41, 43, 46 (twice), 48, 55, 57, 60, 63, 65 (tears of happiness), 68, 80, 90, 91, 92, 96, 104, 107, 109, 115, 129, 132, 133, 151 154, 155, 157, 158, 160, 162, 163, 164, 166, 170, 171, 172, 173, 174, 176, 188 (twice), 204, 207, 209, 215, 217, 223, 227, 232, 233, 234, 237, 239, 242, 248, 249, 258, 291 and 316.

Elsie is not only good but extremely beautiful, and heiress to an enormous fortune. (May Hill Arbuthnot described her as 'a prig with glamour'.[5]) To post-Freudians her relationship with Papa seems ambiguous; even when she grows up he is always sitting her on his knee, fondling her, stroking her hair and covering her with kisses. In *Elsie's Girlhood* (1872) she slips aside from him awhile and falls in love with a young man; but he turns out to be highly unsuitable, and Papa soon sends him packing. In the end she marries a friend and contemporary of Papa — this being, one can hardly help thinking, the next best thing to marrying Father himself. The fascinating thing about Elsie is that although she is so pure, and the tone of the books is religious and uplifting, the reader nevertheless can wallow in emotion and sensuality while contemplating those beautiful large soft eyes, forever filling with tears; that slender frame forever being clasped to Father's breast for kisses and fondlings. This perhaps is the literary equivalent of 'tonic wine', which you can drink without guilt but which is quite highly alcoholic. Jane Manthorne, in her Hewins-Melcher Lecture to the New England Library Association in 1966, bracketed Martha Finlay with Susan Warner and Maria Cummins as 'the lachrymose ladies', and suggested that 'they brought to the starved, arid lives of women and girls a blend of familiar realities and necessary dreams.'[6] The English novelist G. B. Stern, writing about Elsie in the 1930s, remarked that 'what Grandma read when she was a little girl makes the case-histories at the back of Havelock Ellis look like white muslin polka-dot with a light blue sash.'[7]

Happily it is Jo March rather than Elsie Dinsmore who sets the fictional pattern for American girlhood in the later nineteenth century, though the more-or-less willing acceptance that lively girls must grow into sweet submissive women continues. At twelve, Katy Carr, in Susan Coolidge's *What Katy Did*

(1872) has 'always so many delightful schemes rioting in her brains, that all she wished for was ten pairs of hands to carry them out', and when she's grown up she means to do something grand:

> 'Perhaps it will be rowing out in boats and saving people's lives, like that girl in the book. Or perhaps I shall go and nurse in the hospital, like Miss Nightingale. Or else I'll head a crusade and ride on a white horse, with armour and a helmet on my head, and carry a sacred flag. Or if I don't do that, I'll paint pictures, or sing, or scalp — sculp — what is it? you know — make figures in marble.'

Alas, poor Katy. In *What Katy did Next* (1886) she is just a nice young lady, 'so nice all through, so true and sweet and satisfactory'; and she falls contentedly in love with a tall, bronzed, good-looking naval officer.

Gypsy Breynton, in the *Gypsy* series by Elizabeth Stuart Phelps which began in 1866, is another appealing and vigorous heroine: 'There was not a trout-brook for miles where she had not fished. There was hardly a tree she had not climbed . . . Gypsy could row and skate and swim, and play ball and make kites, and coast and race and drive and chop wood.' The trouble with these promising heroines of the 1860s and 1870s is that there isn't anywhere for them to go or anything for them to become, except perhaps writers. Jo March would have liked to go to college; so would Gypsy, but there's no question of it, and she has to content herself with keeping brother Tom on the straight and narrow path when he goes to Yale.

But in real life the active young woman of the upper middle class was not to be held down. Vassar College, offering women a broad education in full intellectual equality with men, had opened in 1865 (and it was not the first American women's college). The new-model young woman had found her way into fiction by 1882, when Lizzie W. Champney, in *Three Vassar Girls Abroad,* showed three charming if somewhat serious young bluestockings — younger sisters, conceivably, to Henry James's Isabel Archer — setting out on their European travels. These three, who demonstrate 'the absurdity of a chaperone for earnest American girls', are well aware that 'there are two kinds of girls, girls who flirt and girls who go to Vassar College.'

Continuing their travels *in Italy* (1885) and *at Home* (1887), the three Vassar girls — not always the same three — remain unashamedly studious and artistic, and have no doubts about their right to a career. In *Three Vassar Girls in South America* (1885), intrepid Victoria Delavan says 'Shoo!' to a jaguar.

Fortunately there is a gentleman standing near by with a gun.

For younger children, Sophie May (Rebecca Clarke, 1833-1906) wrote the popular *Little Prudy* books from 1863 onwards. These are artless but pleasing stories about the everyday sayings and doings of a little girl. In the first book, for instance, Prudy, fired with enthusiasm about going to Heaven, climbs up three ladders, balances on the topmost beam of the house, and shouts down that she's almost there. (Her parents think this is all too true.) Then — at four — she thinks she'll poke a knitting needle right through Nannie's ear, because it will look so funny sticking out at the other side. When she plays doctor, Prudy examines her little sister Dotty and diagnoses the 'pluribus unum'. And so on. There are six books in the *Little Prudy* series, and Sophie May went on to write the *Dotty Dimple* series and the *Flaxie Frizzle* series.

The poor — as distinct from merely hard-up — family made its appearance in *The Five Little Peppers and How They Grew*, by Margaret Sidney (1881). This was the first of a series, estimated to have sold at least a million copies,[8] about the loyal and resourceful family life centring around widowed Mrs Pepper, who 'with a stout heart and a cheery face', works away at tailoring and mending in order to pay the rent of the Little Brown House.

The first notable Australian family story, *Seven Little Australians*, came in 1894 from Ethel Turner (1872-1958), who suggested in her foreword that anyone who wished to read of model children should 'betake yourself to *Sandford and Merton* or similar standard juvenile works', and added:

In England and America and Africa and Asia the little folks may be paragons of virtue; I know little about them. But in Australia a model child is — I say it not without thankfulness — an unknown quantity . . . There is a lurking spirit of joyousness and rebellion and mischief in nature here, and therefore in children.

The little Australians of Miss Turner's title are the six children of Captain Woolcot by his first (dead) wife and the seventh, a baby nicknamed the General, by his new young girl-wife Esther. Two at least of the Woolcots — lively thirteen-year-old Judy and fat greedy untruthful Bunby (six) — are attractive characters; and there is also Meg, initiated at sixteen into the painful mysteries of tight-lacing. But the shadow of the stern father still lies over this story. Captain Woolcot — than whom only Mr Dinsmore can be firmly pronounced less lovable — is ready at any time to take a horsewhip to his sons or banish a daughter to boarding school; and any pleasure the reader may take in the children's ingenious activities is undermined by the certainty of Father's displeasure.

Rebecca of Sunnybrook Farm, by Kate Douglas Wiggin (1903) and *Anne of Green Gables,* by L. M. Montgomery (1908) are stories of remarkable similarity: each is about an imaginative small girl who comes to live with a pair of elderly folk, brings new interest to their lives, and grows from childhood into lovely young womanhood. Both authors write well and with occasional dry wit about small-town life; both seem deeply in love with their central character. Geographically the books are not far apart: one set in Maine, one across the Canadian border on Prince Edward Island. Even the titles have a similar ring. Rebecca came first; but red-haired loquacious Anne, with a strong line in page-long eloquence, is no mere carbon copy.

Rather more evidently than Rebecca, Anne exemplifies the ugly-duckling-into-swan theme which has such obvious attraction for young girls. Sheila Egoff, in *The Republic of Childhood* gives Anne a reluctant pass-mark, but remarks that 'the increasingly sentimental dishonesty of [the author's] succeeding books tends to destroy the first'.[9] I have the advantage of not having read any of this author's other books, and can say of Anne, with Miss Egoff, but less grudgingly: 'Her I can accept.' Surely one has to like a child who can decline an invitation by explaining that 'it is my duty to go home to Miss Marilla Cuthbert. Miss Marilla Cuthbert is a very kind lady who has taken me to bring up properly. She is doing her best, but it is very discouraging work.'

Among the late-Victorian English lady writers, Mrs Ewing (Juliana Horatia Ewing, 1841-85) was one of the most respected in her day and for some time after it. She married an Army officer, and the Army provided the background for two of her stories: *Jackanapes* (1884), in which the son of an officer who died at Waterloo grows up to give his own life for a comrade on the battlefield, and *The Story of a Short Life* (1885), in which a crippled boy meets his early death in a way that surely would have won James Janeway's approval. *A Flat-Iron for a Farthing* (1872) is a somewhat low-tension story of a small boy and his growth to manhood. *Jan of the Windmill* (1876), with its clanking clumsy plot, seems to me to read like inferior George Eliot. Mrs Ewing also wrote two 'country tales': *Lob-*

Lie-by-the-Fire (1874) and *Daddy Darwin's Dovecot* (1884). These and other books add up to a varied and respectable output, but none of them seems to me to have the essential vitality that will carry a book on through changing times and tastes.

Mrs Molesworth, who was born as Louisa Stewart in 1839 and lived until 1921, scored a century of children's books, some of which remained popular for many years. Among those known to me, *The Cuckoo Clock* (1877) is the most appealing. It is about a little girl named Griselda who goes to live with her two old-maid aunts in an old-fashioned house in an old-fashioned town. She finds life dull, and grows bored and querulous. But she enters a fantasy world by talking to the cuckoo in the clock, and the cuckoo takes her on a series of magic trips, finally leaving her with a real-life friend: a little boy who has come to live near by.

Griselda is a real child, not the least bit goody-goody; but the most interesting character is the cuckoo. He is a fairy, or at any rate 'a fairyfied cuckoo'; but he is apt to be crotchety and he continually tells Griselda off — thus anticipating E. Nesbit's Psammead. The magic adventures are described as if they actually happened, and will be accepted in this spirit by younger readers; but to an older child the thought will soon occur that these could be the dreams or imaginings of a lonely little girl; and when Griselda herself says at the end that 'the way to the true fairyland is hard to find, and we must each find it for ourselves', the hint is there for those who are ready for it. *The Tapestry Room* (1879) has a similar ambiguity. Do Hugh and Jeanne really enter the castle in the tapestry and make their way to the fantasy land beyond it, or is it all a dream? It is impossible to say; the author deliberately leaves her readers guessing.

Frances Hodgson Burnett has sometimes been grouped as one of a trio with Mrs Ewing and Mrs Molesworth; but she was a much more powerful writer than the other two, and her books have deservedly lasted better. She was born as Frances Hodgson in Manchester in 1849, and emigrated with her family to America, where in 1873 she married Dr Swan Burnett. Her second son Vivian, born in 1876, was the original of Fauntleroy in *Little Lord Fauntleroy* (1885), her first children's novel. She became immensely successful as a writer both for adults and children, travelled widely, mixed (to her own enormous satisfaction) in exalted circles, lived for some years in England, and finally returned to America to a splendid house which she had built for herself on Long Island. She died in 1924.

Mrs Burnett's reputation suffered for a long time from the notoriety of *Little Lord Fauntleroy* − as did that of the book's illustrator, Reginald Birch. Harvey Darton refers to it as being supreme among the namby-pamby books, and adds that it 'ran through England like a sickly fever. Nine editions were published in as many months, and the odious little prig in the lace collar is not dead yet.'[10] But this is not really fair comment: Cedric Errol is neither odious nor priggish. He is a likeable, unaffected little boy in a back street in New York, who is found to be the heir to an earldom, and who has some embarrassment in breaking the news to his friend Mr Hobbs, the stoutly-republican grocer at the corner shop. He reminds Mr Hobbs that he has said he wouldn't have any aristocrats sitting around on *his* biscuit barrels.

'So I did,' returned Mr Hobbs stoutly. 'And I meant it. Let 'em try it, that's all.'

'Mr Hobbs,' said Cedric, 'one is sitting on this box now.'

And he is duly apologetic. The point of the story is that the only true nobility is within oneself. Because Fauntleroy is a brave, decent, considerate little fellow, he makes the transition from back street to castle without difficulty: he treats his formidable grandfather the Earl of Dorincourt with exactly the same respect as Mr Hobbs. At one point a rival claimant to the title appears, and Fauntleroy is unworried: he would be neither better nor worse if he were to revert from riches to rags. Eventually (and here the story is conventional) he softens the heart of the fierce old Earl, makes him kinder to his tenants, and reconciles him to the sweet patient daughter-in-law (Fauntleroy's mother) whom he had refused to receive.

A Little Princess (1905, but originally published in a shorter version as *Sara Crewe* in 1887) is a *Fauntleroy* in reverse. Sara, the rich and favoured pupil at Miss Minchin's Seminary for Young Ladies, is suddenly found to be poor and is promptly demoted to being little better than a skivvy in a garret. The moral is exactly as in *Fauntleroy:* that true nobility lies within oneself. Sara, in adversity, can bring herself to behave with the magnanimity of a princess, and therefore she *is* a princess. The author cannot resist restoring Sara's fortunes at the end of the book, but in this case it is the proper ending; justice is done.

Mrs Burnett's last important book, *The Secret Garden,* was published in 1910 − twenty-five years after *Fauntleroy.* Much

Drawing by Reginald Birch from
Little Lord Fauntleroy

had happened to her, both as woman and as artist, in the years between. There is an interesting growth of complexity from the one-dimensional *Fauntleroy,* through the more subtle *Little Princess,* to the rich texture of *The Secret Garden.* And there is a corresponding increase in depth of the central child characters. Fauntleroy simply and effortlessly *is* a hero; Sara Crewe is shown by circumstances to be a heroine; but Mary Lennox in *The Secret Garden* has to struggle all the way to achieve a true heroine's status .

Mary Lennox is (at least to begin with) quite *un*likeable. She is a spoiled child from India who goes to live in her uncle's house on a Yorkshire moor. Left to her own devices, she finds that there is a small deserted garden, locked and neglected for many years; and together with a country lad named Dickon she brings it round, bringing herself round in the process. Then she finds that her young cousin Colin, a supposed invalid, also lives in the house, unwilling to use his limbs. Mary, Dickon and the garden between them restore him to happy and healthy life.

There is something about *The Secret Garden* that has a powerful effect on children's imaginations: something to do with their instinctive feeling for things that grow, something to do with their longing for real, important, adult-level achievement. Self-reliance and cooperation in making something are the virtues that Mary and Colin painfully attain. These are not Victorian virtues. The Victorian ideal was that children should be good and do as they were told.

> Christian children all must be
> Mild, obedient, good as He

wrote Mrs Alexander, in *Once in Royal David's City*, unconsciously moulding Jesus in the image of her own time. It was no part of this ideal that children should be self-reliant, constructive, inner-directed. Perhaps it required somebody like Mrs Hodgson Burnett, who was no simple Christian (she dabbled in various unorthodoxies, and *The Secret Garden* contains clear indications of belief in some kind of Life Force) to bring forward this new, significant and potentially subversive doctrine.

7

Imagination rehabilitated

IN THE EARLY nineteenth century, as was pointed out in Chapter 4, imagination emerged from the long imprisonment it had suffered in the name of reason; and the old fairy tales, which had circulated mainly by word of mouth and in the humbler forms of print, began to find their place in 'approved' children's literature. Their returning march was to continue all through the century; and they were joined by the modern fairy tale and fantasy.

It may be useful at this point to define, undogmatically, a few terms which are often confused: myth, legend, fairy tale, folk tale, fantasy. Myths are about creation; why the earth and sea and sky are as they are; who runs the world, and how. Myths explain. Legends are about the achievements of real, half-real or imaginary heroes; about battles long ago. Fairy tales, ancient or modern, are stories of magic, set in the indefinite past and incorporating traditional themes and materials; they may be about giants, dwarfs, witches, talking animals, and a variety of other creatures, as well as good and bad fairies, princes, poor widows and youngest sons. Folk tales are the traditional tales of the people. They are often fairy tales, but they do not have to be; 'folk' indicates the origin, 'fairy' the nature of the story.[1]

Fantasy, for my purposes, is a modern form, belonging to the age of the novel. It is extremely various; it may involve the creation of new worlds, or it may require no more than a single derangement of physical possibility, such as a time shift, in the world we know. Drawing a line between modern fairy tale and fantasy can be difficult; I am inclined to look on a sustained piece of work as fantasy, even if it makes use of fairy-tale elements, because I think it is a characteristic of the fairy tale that it is brief. But to decide the point at which a short story becomes a long one is no easier than to decide the point at which a short piece of string becomes a long one. In English-language children's literature, fantasy has tended to be a British speciality; newer countries have gone in more for stories of contemporary life. The important nineteenth-century fantasies are almost all British, and British dominance has continued, though becoming much less marked.

The tales of Perrault, Grimm and Hans Andersen were all available in English by the middle of the nineteenth century. Among the more important of the many Victorian translations, revivals and retellings which follow the publication in the 1840s of *Felix Summerly's Home Treasury* were Anthony Montalba's *Fairy Tales of All Nations* in 1849 and Sir George Dasent's *Popular Tales from the Norse* (Asbjörnsen and Moe) in 1859. Joel Chandler Harris's *Uncle Remus* stories − tales from the plantations, largely talking-beast stories of African origin − appeared in America in the early 1880s (and, a century later, were brilliantly retold by the black writer Julius Lester in a 'modified contemporary southern black English' which replaced the original dialect and made them accessible to a general audience.) Andrew Lang began his ever-extending spectrum of 'coloured' fairy books with *The Blue Fairy Book* in 1889, and Joseph Jacobs collected and retold his English, Celtic and Indian tales between 1890 and 1894.

Aesop, buttressed by its appended 'morals' and by the approval of such authorities as John Locke, had never shared the disgrace of the popular tales; nor had Greek myth and legend, which were backed by the general prestige of the classics. In 1808 Charles Lamb produced his *Adventures of Ulysses,* based on Chapman's Homer. By 1851 the movement

Brer Rabbit, of the *Uncle Remus*
stories, as seen by A.B.Frost

of taste from classical to Gothic had gone so far that Nathaniel Hawthorne, writing to his publisher about his plan to retell stories from Greek legend in *A Wonder Book for Boys and Girls*, explained that he would 'aim at substituting a tone in some degree Gothic or romantic . . . instead of the classical coldness which is as repellent as the touch of marble'.[2] The twelve stories which make up *A Wonder Book* (1852) and its successor *Tanglewood Tales* (1853) are set in a modern framework; they are supposedly told by a young student to a group of children who are allotted the fanciful 'fairy' names of Primrose, Periwinkle, Sweet Fern and others. This is a Mid-summer-Night's-Dreamy touch; but Hawthorne's direct, informal retellings do not strike a modern reader as notably 'Gothic or romantic'. Today it seems that Hawthorne's frame-work has tarnished, but the stories in it glow as brightly as ever.

Predictably, the acceptance of fairy tales, in an age so much concerned with morality as the Victorian, had to be accom-panied in some quarters by proof that fairy tales did children moral good. An article written by Charles Dickens in 1853 was much quoted in their defence. Dickens credited fairy tales with nourishing in the child's heart such qualities as 'forbearance, courtesy, consideration for the poor and aged, kind treatment of animals, the love of nature, abhorrence of tyranny and brute force'.[3] This seems questionable. But even Dickens felt that his old illustrator George Cruikshank went too far in his *Fairy Library* (1853-4), which turned four well-known fairy tales into propaganda for total abstinence. In Cruikshank's *Cinderella*, when it is proposed to celebrate the wedding of Cinderella and the Prince by making the fountains flow with wine, the Fairy Godmother objects that the use of strong drink is 'always accompanied by ill-health, misery and crime'. And, after some discussion:

'My dear little lady,' exclaimed the King good-humouredly, 'your arguments have convinced me; there shall be no more fountains of wine in my dominions.' And he immediately gave orders that all the wine, beer and spirits in the place should be collected together and piled upon the top of a rocky mound in the vicinity of the palace, and made a great bonfire of on the night of the wedding: — which was accordingly done, and a splendid blaze it made.

Cruikshank did not include in his story any comments from the populace.

As the fairy tales came back into favour, it was natural that modern writers should feel tempted, not only, like Cruikshank, to emend, but to write new ones of their own. Often they did not fully realize what they were up against, for the old folk stories had stood the test of a great deal of time and were not so easily outshone as the modern writers expected.

The modern fairy tale may be said to begin with 'Uncle David's Nonsensical Story' in Catherine Sinclair's *Holiday House.* John Ruskin pronounced weightily in favour of fairy stories, as well he might, being the author of *The King of the Golden River.* In 1855 the novelist W. M. Thackeray published his 'extravaganza' or 'fireside pantomime', *The Rose and the Ring,* set in the imaginary countries of Paflagonia and Crim Tartary. This is a facetious piece of work, parts of which are directed over the head of the child reader; but the episode in which the porter Gruffanuff is turned into a brass door-knocker has the authentic fairy tale mixture of humour and horror. There is little merit in Charles Dickens's *The Magic Fishbone,* which originally was one of four stories making up *A Holiday Romance* (1868); it could hardly have survived without the recommendation of Dickens's name. The Dickens story which children have always loved, though it was written for the general reader and not specially for them, is 'A Christmas Carol', from the *Christmas Books* (1834-5).

The swing of opinion in favour of the fairies was a strong one, and it was not long before the appearance in children's literature of nostalgia − of a recurrent kind similar to the longing for an idealized Merry England − for a land fit for fairies to live in. In the preface to *The Hope of the Katzekopfs* (1844), a fantasy-with-a-moral which was once popular but has had its day, Francis Paget complained about 'the unbelief of this dull, plodding, unimaginative, money-getting, money-loving nineteenth century'. And after telling a set of eight fairy stories in *Granny's Wonderful Chair* (1857), Frances Browne remarked sadly that fairy times were long ago:

Great wars, work and learning have passed over the world since then, and altered all its fashions . . . The fairies dance no more. Some say it was the hum of schools − some think it was the din of factories that frightened them; but nobody has been known to have seen them for many a year, except, it is said, one Hans Christian Andersen, in Denmark.

Acceptance of fantasy depended on much the same conditions as the acceptance of fairy tales. It needed an atmosphere in which it was agreed that children could without harm be given stories which not only were not literally true but were actually impossible. This acceptance, when it came, meant freedom at last for the imagination of the children's writer to soar. But early flights were tentative; it took time for authors to feel their wings.

Even the late Georgians had allowed one kind of story that could technically be classed as fantasy: the life story of some creature or thing which (as young readers were conscientiously reminded) was not *really* capable of telling the tale: a dog or mouse or monkey, a pegtop or pincushion. One of the best of early Victorian children's books, Richard Hengist Horne's *Memoirs of a London Doll* (1846), belongs to this genre, though it is much less moralistic than its predecessors, and of greater literary merit. Its narrator, Maria Poppet, is (says Margery Fisher in her introduction to the 1967 reissue[4]) 'neither child nor adult but, consistently, doll'. But the spirit of the book is not the spirit of fantasy; it is really a panorama of London life, or such aspects of it as might be expected to appeal to a child – the Lord Mayor's Show, the Zoo, the Christmas pantomime. Horne (1802-84) was a friend of William and Mary Howitt. He went to Australia with William Howitt in 1852, stayed on there when Howitt came back, and wrote no more for children.

The decade in which fantasy took wing was the decade of *Alice's Adventures in Wonderland* and *The Water Babies:* the eighteen-sixties. These two books were both published in London by the rising house of Macmillan. Their authors were both in Holy Orders: they were the Reverend C. L. Dodgson (1832-98), otherwise known as Lewis Carroll, and the Reverend Charles Kingsley (1819-75).

Alice had its origin in a river trip which young Mr Dodgson made with the daughters of the Dean of his Oxford college, 'all in the golden afternoon' of 4 July 1862. He began telling a story to amuse his young friends; during the next few months he wrote it down, and in 1864 he produced for Alice a handwritten book, illustrated by himself, which he called *Alice's Adventures under Ground.* The extended, definitive version, *Alice's Adventures in Wonderland,* with the famous illustrations by John Tenniel, appeared after many delays and difficulties in time for Christmas, 1865 (though dated 1866). Kingsley's *Water Babies* appeared in instalments in *Macmillan's Magazine* in 1862-3, and was issued in book form in the latter year.

The similarities between the two authors may be striking, but are less striking than the differences. Kingsley was an active, aggressive, masculine man, one of the original 'muscular Christians', busy in a dozen fields, an early rebel and supporter of the Chartists, a hearty extrovert, the father of a family. Dodgson was a shy, retiring introvert, a conservative, and (apart from some donnish spikiness) a conformist; he spent his life in the shelter of his college, and the only human company he really enjoyed was that of little girls.

Dodgson derived his pseudonym from his first two names, Charles Lutwidge. Lutwidge is the same as Ludwig, of which Lewis is the Anglicized version, and Carroll is another form of Charles. He met Alice, the little daughter of Dean Liddell of Christ Church, in 1856, and in the same year took up photography, at which he became extremely good. His portrait of Alice shows a lovely dark elfin child with a fringe. It was for her, not the demure little blonde of Tenniel's drawings, that he wrote his masterpiece.

Comment on books as well known and as much discussed as the two *Alices* may well seem superfluous; and I shall keep it brief. *Alice in Wonderland* was published in 1865, when Dodgson was thirty-three; *Through the Looking-Glass* came out in 1871, when he was nearly forty.

Superficially the books resemble each other closely. In each, Alice meets a succession of fantastic characters, and each ends with a big set-piece: the trial scene in *Wonderland* and the banquet in *Looking-Glass*. But the striking difference is that for better or worse *Looking-Glass* is much more contrived than *Wonderland*. The earlier book was based on actual stories told to children; the later one was written at leisure to please the author himself. The machinery used to begin *Wonderland* is very simple and casual; Alice follows the White Rabbit down a rabbit-hole and the story is under way. *Looking-Glass* begins more elaborately with Alice's climbing through the mirror and with the reversal of normal processes at the other side of the glass, which is worked out in considerable detail. *Wonderland* has no obvious formal structure; its incidents follow each other quite casually, like a dream sequence. *Looking-Glass* is based on the tight pattern of a game of chess.

There is no point in trying to prove that either is the better book. *Wonderland* has probably always been more popular. One tends to have the impression that it contains the best characters, but this is arguable. True, it has the Mad Hatter and the March Hare and the Cheshire Cat and the Duchess; but *Looking-Glass* has Humpty Dumpty and the White Knight and Tweedledum and Tweedledee and the Red Queen. Both books

At this moment her foot slipped, and splash! she was up to her chin in salt water. Her first idea was that she had fallen into the sea : then she remembered that she was under ground, and she soon made out that it was the pool of tears she had wept when she was nine feet high. "I wish I hadn't cried so much!" said Alice, as she swam about, trying to find her way out

Alice in the pool of tears: one of Lewis Carroll's own
illustrations from *Alice's Adventures under Ground*

are of perennial interest to adults. They are the source of many familiar quotations, and they have often been interpreted in symbolic or psychological terms. I have heard them described as 'children's books for grown-ups' – to which it could be replied that the best children's books can be appreciated at more than one level.

Late in life Lewis Carroll wrote *Sylvie and Bruno* (1889) and *Sylvie and Bruno Concluded* (1893): a long, muddled and sentimental pair of books which have good things in them but as a whole are almost unreadable. The original Alice lived until 1934; she was able to join in celebrating the Lewis Carroll centenary in 1932, and wrote her name in a copy of *Alice* for Queen Elizabeth II. To all appearances she was (like Keats's Fanny Brawne) a perfectly ordinary person, and it was quite by chance that she sparked off a masterpiece of English literature.

Charles Kingsley took a second in mathematics and a first in classics at Cambridge, was ordained, and in 1842 became curate of Eversley, Hampshire, where he was to stay, though with many excursions, for the rest of his life. In 1844 he married, and in the same year he became Rector and set about energetically reforming the parish – opening schools and a lending library, starting a mothers' club, lending villagers the money to buy pigs, and even starting some small-scale farming experiments.

In 1848 Kingsley was fascinated by the Chartists, with whom he felt a great deal of sympathy. He joined with F. D. Maurice, J. M. Ludlow and others to form the Christian Socialist movement. In spite of this, he was in many ways a bluff Englishman of his period. He saw the British as superior to the lesser breeds, he was for class distinction and for fox-hunting, he was anti-intellectual ('Be good, sweet maid, and let who will be clever'), he was violently Protestant, he saw art as representation and thought photography a distinct improvement upon painting. Eventually he gravitated towards the Establishment: he became chaplain to the Queen in 1859, was Regius Professor at Cambridge from 1860 to 1869, and when he died he was a Canon of Westminster.

Kingsley wrote several novels, including *Westward Ho!* (1855), a long historical romance which was often read by young people, though not specially intended for them. He also retold three Greek legends in *The Heroes* (1856). In 1862 he began writing *The Water Babies* for his fourth and youngest child, Grenville. Its hero, Tom, is a little chimney-sweep who runs away, is drowned in a river, and becomes a water-baby: the water-babies being 'all the little children whom the good fairies take to, because their cruel mothers and fathers will not; all who are untaught and brought up heathens, and all who come to grief by ill-usage or ignorance or neglect.'

Tom swims down-river to the sea, and is taken by the other water-babies to their home at St Brandan's Isle, otherwise Atlantis. Here the fairies Bedonebyasyoudid and Doasyouwouldbedoneby teach him to be good. He regresses and becomes covered with prickles; the author comments that this was quite natural, 'for you must know and believe that people's souls make their bodies, just as a snail makes its shell.' To be cured of his prickles, Tom is brought a schoolmistress, a beautiful little girl named Ellie whom he had met on land, and she teaches him 'what he should have been taught at his mother's knee.' In the last part of the story Tom swims off on a quest which is completed when he finds his old master Grimes and helps him to repent of his wickedness.

The first chapters of *The Water Babies*, where Tom is a chimney-sweep, are splendid. There is no doubt that Kingsley could have written a first-class realistic story for children had he chosen to do so. Then there is a change of gear into fantasy as Tom enters the water. The second section, in the river, is also very fine in a different way. The watery passages are sensuous and poetic, and are written out of expert, loving naturalistic knowledge. In the later sections the story unfortunately grows ever more wild and woolly; Kingsley becomes entangled in his symbolisms and comes near to destroying his own work.

The main theme of *The Water Babies* is redemption. Tom is working out his own salvation, and the strongest symbolism is that of being washed free from sin. At the child's level, *The Water Babies* is a combination of adventure and fantasy with a clear moral tone. It is a pity that the story contains a good deal of dross. This is one of the few cases in children's literature where an edited version, such as the one made by Kathleen Lines in 1961, is preferable to the original text.

The *Alice* books and *The Water Babies* have their resemblances, which are by no means superficial. Both are interspersed with verses good enough to have a life of their own. The *Alice* books contain, among others, the 'Lobster Quadrille', 'Jabberwocky', and 'The Walrus and the Carpenter'. In *The Water Babies* are 'When all the world was young, lad', 'Clear and cool', and that sentimental masterpiece 'I once had a sweet little doll, dears'. In the *Alice* books real life is often turned upside down, while *The Water Babies* frequently offers a reversal, or reflection, of life on land. Both authors (but Carroll more often and more interestingly) delight in absurd logic.

But in the last analysis the contrasts between these two great fantasies of the 1860s outweigh the resemblances. In *The Water Babies* we have a powerful but imperfect piece of work, a marred masterpiece. The *Alice* books are on a greatly restricted scale but are finished works of art. And these characteristics reflect those of the two authors. One was a man of vigorous social purpose — indeed, a man of many different and urgent purposes which were often tangled up together. The other was remote, spiky and tortuous, but — at least so far as the child readers were concerned — had the sole aim of giving pleasure.

8

The never-lands

THE *Alice* books and *The Water Babies* mark the true beginning of the age of fantasy in children's literature, but it could be argued that the most powerfully imaginative of all the Victorian fantasy writers was George MacDonald (1824-1905), a Congregational Minister who turned author. *At the Back of the North Wind* (1871) is the story of little Diamond, son of a coachman, and his two parallel lives: one of harsh reality in working-class London (with many hints of Dickens and Mayhew); the other a dream-life in which he travels with the North Wind, which appears to him as a beautiful woman with streaming black hair and splendid bosom. In the end Diamond dies, and finds peace 'at the back of the North Wind'. The story is a full and complex religious allegory. I did not like it myself as a child, finding it cold and frightening. As an adult I have re-read it with respect but still with rather little pleasure.

The Princess and the Goblin (1872), is also religious allegory, but to me is much more appealing. The young Princess Irene lives in a castle on a mountain; at the top of the castle, up a staircase that is hard to find, lives her mysterious, aged but beautiful grandmother; underneath, a malicious tribe of goblins are tunnelling through the mountain towards the castle's foundations, aiming to seize Irene and make her the wife of their prince. A miner's son, Curdie, with whom Irene has strange adventures underground, saves both her and the royal household, though he can only do so with the supernatural help of the mysterious grandmother. The sequel, *The Princess and Curdie,* published eleven years later, is disturbing. After defeating the forces of decay and evil in Irene's father's capital city, Irene and Curdie marry and become queen and king; but they have no children, and after their death the capital sinks into still greater iniquity, until 'one day at noon, when life was at its highest, the whole city fell with a roaring crash' and was wiped from the face of the earth for ever. The author has clearly been condemning the state of civilization in his own day, and his conclusion is savagely pessimistic. This book and *North Wind,* though both have elements of greatness, seem to me to be flawed in various ways, and possibly

Diamond finds a nest in the North Wind's hair: an
illustration by Arthur Hughes from *At the Back of
the North Wind* (1871)

disturbing for some children. But these objections do not apply
to *The Princess and the Goblin,* which is a splendid story,
carrying entire conviction.

MacDonald wrote a number of shorter stories, including the
strange, almost mystical *The Golden Key,* about a quest for 'the
country whence the shadows fall', and *The Light Princess,* in
which a princess's lightness of mind – she cares not a whit
about anything or anybody – is matched by a lightness of
body, so that she is liable to float away in the breeze. The
story tells how by falling in love she acquires gravity. These
two remarkable tales were collected, with others, in *Dealings
with the Fairies* (1867), and more recently in *The Light
Princess and other tales* (1961).

George MacDonald was an intensely serious writer. The
'dealings with the fairies' which mainly influenced E. Nesbit

(1858-1924) were of a lighter nature. Thackeray, in *The Rose and the Ring*, and Andrew Lang, in *Prince Prigio* (1889) and *Prince Ricardo* (1893), had made humorous use of fairy tale materials; and in *The Good Little Girl* (1890) F. Anstey had achieved a simultaneous burlesque both of fairy tale and moral tale, for the jewels that fall from little Priscilla's lips every time she makes a particularly improving remark turn out to be all fakes. F. Anstey (Thomas Anstey Guthrie, 1856-1934) influenced Nesbit more directly still with *The Brass Bottle,* in which a young man is granted wishes which invariably land him in difficulties — an idea that Nesbit undoubtedly borrowed for *Five Children and It.* Another humorous fairy tale was *The Reluctant Dragon*, in Kenneth Grahame's *Dream Days* (1899), and here again E. Nesbit paid the author the sincerest form of flattery by writing, shortly afterwards, a series of dragon stories.

To split E. Nesbit's work down the middle and consider it in separate chapters as family stories and fantasy would be awkward and pointless — especially as some of her best books were both. She drew in fact on two traditions: on the one hand the light modern fairy tales and fantasies just mentioned, and on the other hand the family stories of Charlotte M. Yonge, Louisa Alcott, Mrs Ewing and Mrs Molesworth. From Mrs Molesworth indeed she may be said to have borrowed with both hands, for there can be no doubt that the cuckoo in *The Cuckoo Clock* was an ancestor of the Psammead.

Though E. Nesbit came from a middle-class family, and in her time earned a great deal of money, she knew poverty and insecurity. When she was a girl, her widowed mother lost most of her money; and in early married life her husband Hubert Bland lost his capital through an absconding partner (as did the Bastable children's father in *The Treasure Seekers),* and she had to work hard to support the family. Her first children's book, *The Story of the Treasure Seekers,* was published in 1899, when she was forty-one years old. Before this, she had written a great many adult magazine stories, verses and articles — none of which were of any special merit — and had even tried public reciting and hand-colouring Christmas cards. The Bastable children's efforts to raise money to help the shaky family finances were thus an echo of her own struggle.

The Bastables first try actually digging for treasure, then they try being detectives, selling poems, rescuing a princess, borrowing from a moneylender and answering an advertisement that says that 'any lady or gentleman can easily earn two pounds a week in their spare time'. These various attempts either fail to come off or else succeed in some quite different way from the one intended. In the end the family's troubles are solved by the discovery of a rich uncle, a device which was used by a great many Victorian writers, and which may generally be taken as an indication that no real solution was possible.

The principal character in *The Treasure Seekers* and its sequels is Oswald, the eldest Bastable boy, who is the narrator. In creating Oswald, Nesbit surely showed a touch of genius. Oswald does not say that he is the narrator; he only says that the narrator is 'one of us', and he refers to Oswald in the third person; but even to a child it is obvious that it is Oswald who is telling the story from the number of puffs and the amount of self-congratulation that he manages to get in. 'Oswald', he says, 'is a boy of firm and unswerving character'; and again, 'Alice was knitting by the fire; it was for Father, but I am sure his feet are not at all that shape. He has a high and beautifully formed instep, like Oswald's.'

In the second Bastable book, *The Wouldbegoods* (1901), the thread that links the episodes together is the society formed by the children for doing good deeds. Their good deeds, however, by a convincing childish rationalization, usually turn out to be pieces of glorious naughtiness. There is a third Bastable book, *New Treasure Seekers* (1904), which shows a slight falling-off; and after that Nesbit dropped the Bastables, successful as they were. Artistically this was a praiseworthy decision; too many successful characters in fiction have been kept running too long and have become bores.

The three Bastable books are purely family stories; there is no magic in them. E. Nesbit wrote a second group of three books which are also about a family of children but which introduce magical creatures as well: the Psammead in *Five Children and It* (1902) and *The Story of the Amulet* (1906); and the Phoenix in *The Phoenix and the Carpet* (1904). The Psammead, or sand fairy, is a round fat furry creature with its eyes on the ends of horns, like a snail; the Phoenix is the well-known fabulous bird, and it appears when a strange egg is accidentally dropped into the fire. Both the Psammead and the Phoenix can grant wishes. But they are not mere wish-granting machinery; they are characters in their own right. So much is this so that the children, whose surname is never given, are much less strongly characterized than the Bastables; they are almost kept in the background.

In *Five Children and It,* the wishes which are granted by the Psammead bring nothing but trouble. Thus the children wish for a vast amount of gold but find they cannot spend it in the shops; they wish for wings and get stranded on top of a church tower, and so on. But it is the Psammead itself that steals the show: the Psammead, which is bad-tempered, which is frightened of getting wet, which has to blow itself up to grant a wish and finds it dreadfully tiring. The silly vain Phoenix in *The Phoenix and the Carpet* is almost equally successful. *The Story of the Amulet* is a more serious piece of work. It is concerned with time: the children have a half amulet through which they can step into the past, and they seek to reunite it with its missing other half. The book displays yet another Nesbit gift: that of making the past come vividly alive.

E. Nesbit's best period was brief, and ends, to my mind, with *The Railway Children* (1906). Of the books which followed it, *The Enchanted Castle* (1907), *The House of Arden* (1908), and *Harding's Luck* (1909) all have their admirers. There are later books still, but they are generally acknowledged to be inferior. It is arguable that even *The Railway Children* is not on the level of Nesbit's best work. It is none too tidily organized, it is too sentimental for the present-day taste, and the long arm of coincidence reaches all over the place. But the vital warmth of E. Nesbit is strong in *The Railway Children;* it is a much-loved book among British children and a favourite choice for film and television versions.

Peter Pan, as everyone knows, is the boy who wouldn't grow up. Properly speaking, the actual title *Peter Pan* belongs to J. M. Barrie's play, which was first staged in 1904 and has been performed year after year with enormous success. The book came later, and exists in several versions, some of which are not by Barrie himself. Barrie's own adaptation, *Peter and Wendy,* was published in 1911. The play, with its brilliantly stagey incidents and characters, has delighted many thousands of children and adults. The book, considered on its own, is less satisfactory.

There is no doubt that Barrie created two or three vivid and memorable characters: Captain Hook, with the hook in place of his lost hand, and the ticking crocodile, and possibly Peter Pan himself, though it is doubtful whether the idea of a boy who never grows up has much appeal to children. Children expect and want to grow up. The profound effect that *Peter Pan* has had on parents is illustrated by the fact that the name Wendy, now quite common, was invented by Barrie.

But much of the time the author is winking over the children's heads to the adults, and putting in jokes that to children are meaningless — as for instance in Captain Hook's preoccupation with good form (in a *real* children's story, what would a pirate chieftain care for good form?) or in the parody of a military commentator analysing Hook's battle with the Indians — 'To what extent Hook is to blame for his tactics on this occasion is for the historian to decide', and so on. There is a taste of saccharine about some parts of the book; notably Wendy's mothering of the lost boys. I believe also that the kind of fantasy in which the children's nurse is a dog and in which Father banishes himself to the dog-kennel is a different sort of fantasy from that of the Never Never Land, and the two do not mix. All in all, *Peter and Wendy* is not a very good book; I am sure it benefits unduly from the fame of the play.

Rudyard Kipling's *Puck of Pook's Hill* was published in the same year as E. Nesbit's *Amulet* (1906), but whereas *The Story of the Amulet* took people from the present into the past, *Puck of Pook's Hill* brings people from the past into the present. Two children, Dan and Una, unintentionally summon up the figure of Puck — otherwise Robin Goodfellow, the spirit of old England — and he in turn introduces to them people who have lived on and fought for the piece of Sussex soil where they live.

The theme is the continuing nature of England, conceived as ever-present in its four dimensions of space and time. Kipling's time machinery is primitive compared with Nesbit's. He was more concerned that the past should blend and blur with the present than that the mechanism should whirr and click efficiently. *Puck of Pook's Hill* and its sequel, *Rewards and Fairies* (1910), are among the most attractive of Kipling's books, and show the better side of his patriotism.

The work of the American writer and artist Howard Pyle (1853-1911) has been highly praised by some good judges. In *Pepper and Salt* (1886), *The Wonder Clock* (1888), and *Twilight Land* (1895) Pyle retold old tales from a variety of sources in his own distinctive style. Among much else achieved in an industrious career, he also re-created *The Merry Adventures of Robin Hood* (1883), and reshaped Arthurian legend in

The·Merry·Friar·carrieth·
Robin·across·the·Water :·.

Illustration by Howard Pyle from *The Merry Adventures
of Robin Hood* (1883)

four stout volumes, beginning with *The Story of King Arthur
and his Knights* in 1903.

Pyle was his own illustrator, and was undoubtedly a designer
of high ability; his books form individual and visually satisfying
wholes. But I cannot share American enthusiasm for him as a
writer. The reason is partly personal: I find conscious archaism

uncongenial, and Pyle's work strikes me in the same way as imitation medieval or Tudor architecture; it does not properly belong either to its own time or to the one it imitates. This perhaps is an unduly puritanical attitude; it can be maintained that artists of all kinds are perfectly entitled to work in styles of the past if their talents so impel them. But there is more to it than that; for, as with pseudo-Tudor buildings, I feel that again and again the details are not quite right. In *The Merry Adventures of Robin Hood* the young Robin, aged eighteen, meets a party of foresters, of whom one accosts him:

'Halloa, where goest thou, little lad, with thy one penny bow and thy farthing shafts?'
Then Robin grew angry, for he was mightily proud of his skill at archery.
'Now,' quoth he, 'my bow and eke mine arrows are as good as thine; and I'll hold the best of you twenty marks that I hit the clout at three-score rods.'
At this all laughed aloud, whereat Robin grew right mad. 'Hark ye,' said he; 'yonder, at the glade's end, I see a herd of deer, even more than three-score rods distant. I'll hold you twenty marks that I cause the best hart among them to die.'

With the best will in the world I cannot believe in this, or many other passages, as English dialogue of any period. Pyle's Arthurian books I find totally impenetrable. To my mind, his writing is at its best in his fantasy *The Garden Behind the Moon* (1895), a sad and often moving allegory which is strongly reminiscent of George MacDonald. Unfortunately it does not have MacDonald's imaginative force and has not withstood the erosions of time.

I hesitate to say that Howard Pyle's books are overrated in the United States; it is not wise to make condemnatory pronouncements about work that one finds unsympathetic and therefore hard to assess fairly. But I do not hesitate to say that L. Frank Baum (1856-1919), the author of *The Wizard of Oz,* has been shockingly underrated by American authorities on children's literature. He got not a single line in all the 688 double-column pages of the last edition of *Children and Books* to appear in May Hill Arbuthnot's lifetime, and only one rather disdainful reference in the *Critical History of Children's Literature* by Cornelia Meigs and others. I cannot help wondering whether some unconscious snobbery was involved: a partiality for Pyle, the cultured Easterner making use of Old World materials, contrasted with a feeling that fantasy was too lofty and refined a genre for a newspaperman from the Middle West.

To an outsider it seems that the unabashed American-ness of the *Oz* books makes them all the more original and attractive. As Edward Wagenknecht said in 1929, 'it is in *The Wizard of Oz* that we meet the first distinctive attempt to construct a fairyland out of American materials'.[1]

'Tell me,' [says a princess in *Ozma of Oz* (1907)] 'are you of royal blood?' 'Better than that, ma'am,' said Dorothy. 'I come from Kansas.'

The characters who join Dorothy in the first book, *The Wizard of Oz* (1899) are the Scarecrow, who wants brains instead of straw, the Tin Woodman, who wants a heart, and the Cowardly Lion, who wants courage. These creatures are quite new and, in the phrase of a little girl quoted by Baum in his introduction to *Ozma of Oz*, 'real Ozzy'. They are not human, but they are in quest of important human attributes. Baum went on inventing and developing 'real Ozzy' creatures. In *The Land of Oz* (1904) the Tin Woodman, promoted to emperor, has had himself nickel-plated, and we meet Mr H. M. Woggle-Bug; H. M. stands for Highly Magnified. *Ozma of Oz* introduces Tiktok the wind-up machine man, and the Hungry Tiger, who is restrained by conscience from eating living creatures, and acknowledges himself to be 'a good beast, perhaps, but a disgracefully bad tiger'.

There are frequent satiric or speculative passages in the *Oz* books: rarely subtle, often intelligent, sometimes naive. *The Emerald City of Oz* (1910) contains Baum's blueprint for Utopia. There is neither money nor property in Oz; people enjoy work as much as play, and everyone is proud to do what he can for his neighbours. With *The Emerald City* Baum tried to end the series, but the children would not let him. He wrote fourteen *Oz* books, and the series was continued by Ruth Plumly Thompson after his death. Undoubtedly it went on too long, but this had not been his intention. Time, rather than the children's book Establishment, will decide about the *Oz* books; and perhaps time has gone some way towards deciding already, for they have remained popular with children, and a sizeable Oz cult has grown up among adults. The name of Oz, by the way, was taken from the O-Z drawer in a filing cabinet.

9

The world of school

THE school story sprang into prominence with the publication in 1857 and 1858 of Thomas Hughes's *Tom Brown's Schooldays* and F. W. Farrar's *Eric, or Little by Little*. It flourished in Britain — though not so much in the rest of the English-speaking world — for the remainder of the Victorian era, and in a reduced way for some years afterwards. As recently as the mid-1960s it was possible for an observer with an eye on the choir-school stories of William Mayne and on novels by Antonia Forest and Mary K. Harris to think he detected signs of renewed vigour. But the revival has not continued — not, at least, in the shape of the classical, high-Victorian and post-Victorian boarding-school story. An aura of privilege based on class and money hangs about the boarding school and tends to make it appear an unacceptable setting. In recent years there have in fact been many books in which school is a focal point; but almost invariably the school is a day school, and going to school is part of daily life. There is no need, in looking at present-day fiction, to consider the school story as a separate genre.

The older type of boarding-school story is another matter. It had interesting features and fictional advantages. A boarding school is in many ways a self-contained world in which boys or girls are full citizens. At home, a young person is a subordinate member of the family; it is a parent, not a child, who is the householder, the citizen, the decision-maker, the person responsible to the law. At school the boy — it was commonly though by no means always a boy — is standing on his own feet; he must hold his own among his contemporaries; he is responsible for himself. The school story thus gets over one of the first problems of any realistic literature for children: how to make the characters full participants in the life of their community.

And school is a world in which personal politics are always in full swing. Leadership and discipline and rivalry are the everyday issues of the school story. Who is to captain the team? Is the unruly group to be brought under control, and if so, by whom? How is the odd-boy-out to be fitted into the community? The clash between authority and the individual is the stuff of a great deal of drama, and for young people the school is an ideal setting in which to show it. At home, parental authority is only one strand in the subtle mesh of the parent-child relationship; but at school there is a natural and accepted opposition between what pupils are supposed to do and what they will do if they get the chance.

Then, school life is full of live moral issues: the familiar problems like bullying, cribbing and sneaking, and the less familiar but more interesting ones that arise out of conflicting loyalties to the group, to one's friends and to oneself.

Before *Tom Brown* and *Eric*, there had been a few scattered books with school settings, but no school stories as we understand them. Sarah Fielding's *The Governess*, in the seventeen-forties, and Charles and Mary Lamb's *Mrs Leicester's School* (1809) are collections of individual stories fitted for convenience into a school framework. They are now of interest only to the specialist; so is Harriet Martineau's *The Crofton Boys* (1841), a somewhat harrowing didactic work whose hero is crippled for life at an early stage in the proceedings. The true beginning of the school story comes with *Tom Brown;* and the setting, most appropriately, is Dr Arnold's Rugby, at the dawn of the great age of the British public (that is, private) school.

Thomas Hughes (1823-96) was himself an Old Rugbeian, a pupil and admirer of Dr Arnold; he was also a Christian Socialist, associated with F. D. Maurice, Charles Kingsley and others. Hughes wanted *Tom Brown* to be a 'real novel for boys – not didactic, like *Sandford and Merton* – written in a right spirit, but distinctly aiming at being amusing'.[1]

The story of *Tom Brown's Schooldays* is episodic; there is no closely-knit plot. We see Tom first at home, then going through the trials of a new boy at Rugby; he is initiated into football and other school activities; he is bullied, but bears it bravely; he gets into scrapes with his friend Harry East and acquires a reputation as a rather reckless, irresponsible fellow. The turning-point in his school life is when a timid new boy, Arthur, is put under his wing. This gives Tom a sense of responsibility and makes a man of him; he comes good, as we have always known he will, and in the last chapter we see him:

a strapping figure, nearly six feet high, with ruddy tanned face and whiskers, curly brown hair and a laughing, dancing eye. He is leaning forward with his elbow resting on his knees, and dandling his favourite bat, with which he has made thirty or forty runs today, in his strong brown hands. It is Tom

Brown, grown into a young man nineteen years old, a praepostor and captain of the eleven, spending his last day as a Rugby boy, and let us hope as much wiser as he is bigger since we last had the pleasure of coming across him.

The air of the book is generally on the hearty side; it exudes muscular Christianity. Tom Brown has much in common − and not accidentally − with Fielding's Tom Jones, though his morals are more Victorian. The characterization of the book is variable. Tom is quite convincing as a cheerful, decent, happy-go-lucky English boy, often in trouble but growing up to be a Christian gentleman; but he is fundamentally dull, for all that. His friend East is another open, honest, somewhat reckless fellow, but more of an individualist, unable to be serious for long and impervious to exhortation − an attractive character whose eventual conversion by Tom and Dr Arnold does not quite ring true. Dr Arnold himself is an important character, and we get the sense of the presence of a great man, but only because the author's admiration is so very plain: we do not get a portrait of the Doctor which itself would convey his greatness. Hughes, who admitted that he was 'not much of a thinker', was not close to Arnold, and seems to have had little understanding of his ideas.

In *Tom Brown* we are moving towards the belief in team sports as the great character-builder. Arnold himself was not a 'hearty', and would have been shocked by the promotion of team-spirit as a way of life. But British society, and the building of the Empire, required team-spirit more than individual virtue, and Hughes's misinterpretation helped the Arnold revolution to find its way into a new channel. Edward C. Mack and W. H. G. Armytage suggest in their biography of Hughes that *Tom Brown* 'made the modern public school'.[2] This may be too sweeping, but there is truth in it. The high Victorian idea of the public school spirit is summed up in a stanza from the school song 'Forty Years On':

> God give us bases to guard and beleaguer,
> Games to play out, whether earnest or fun,
> Fights for the fearless and goals for the eager,
> Twenty and thirty and forty years on!

The other great early school story − F. W. Farrar's *Eric, or Little by Little* − runs counter to the developing public-school ethos. Here we are primarily concerned with the moral fate of the individual. School is a background, though a vivid one, against which this individual drama is played out; team-spirit is of no great importance, and indeed the hero's prowess at games is seen largely as a snare – the snare of easy popularity.

Farrar was born in 1831 and went to King William's College on the Isle of Man, which is the original of Rosslyn School in *Eric*. He was an undergraduate at Cambridge and afterwards a master at Harrow. He was only twenty-seven when he published *Eric*. Later he became Headmaster of Marlborough, was an extremely popular preacher and writer, and finished his career as Dean of Canterbury, dying in 1903.

Farrar's Christianity was of quite a different kind from Hughes's. The Christianity professed and preached by Hughes was a sensible man's everyday religion. But Farrar was an intense, a passionate Christian. His story tells, with enormous involvement, how Eric Williams – a boy of noble soul, fine appearance and high promise – fights a running and mostly losing battle with the temptations of evil. The phrase 'little by little' describes the progress of his decline. It is all summed up in a verse prefaced to chapter eight:

> We are not worst at once; the course of evil
> Begins so slowly and from such slight source
> An infant's hand might stop the breach with clay;
> But let the stream grow wider, and Philosophy
> Aye, and Religion too – may strive in vain
> To stem the headlong current!

From connivance in the use of a crib and irreverence in the school chapel, Eric sinks through swearing and smoking to drinking spirits in a low pothouse, assaulting a master, and stealing pigeons from a loft. Eventually his sins are such that only a beautiful and repentant death can atone.

After being out of print for many years, *Eric* was reissued in England in 1971. It is by our standards – and apparently was by Victorian masculine standards – a preposterous book: preposterous in its morality, its manners, and its tear-jerking. Nevertheless it deserves attention. It is powerful and readable. It is the work of a born writer as well as a born preacher. And it is the projection of a view of life in which everything matters. If you were a passionate Puritan, your life could never be dull. You were faced with moral choices, which could easily become crises, every day of the week. If you failed to rise to the occasion – and the failure might be nothing greater than the telling of an untruth to save trouble, or some minor duty neglected – then you were on the slippery road to ruin. It is this knowledge that life is real and earnest, this profound conviction that things really matter, that is lacking in so many individual lives today. Preposterous as it is, *Eric* shows us an outlook, a whole way of thinking and feeling, that we may not otherwise easily come into contact with.

The nearest American equivalent to Tom Brown is young Tom Bailey, whose schooldays at 'Rivermouth' (based on Portsmouth, New Hampshire) are the main subject of the autobiographical *Story of a Bad Boy* (1870), by Thomas Bailey Aldrich. This is in fact the story of 'not such a very bad boy'; the author chose his title to distinguish himself from 'those faultless young gentlemen who generally figure in narratives of this kind'. But, he remarks, 'I may truthfully say I was an amiable, impulsive lad, blessed with fine digestive powers, and no hypocrite.' (There is an essay to be written on the importance of being Tom: to be Tom is to be thoroughly masculine, wholesome, cheerful, well-meaning if thoughtless, and in general a good fellow.) In spirit at least, Aldrich's book is quite close to *Tom Brown's Schooldays*. Its air of rather smug yet likeable old-boy nostalgia is not easily matched in our century.

There are other American school stories of the period, among them Edward Eggleston's *Hoosier School Boy* (1883), and a little later the school-and-sport stories of Ralph Henry Barbour. In Canada James de Mille wrote his *B.O.W.C.* (Brethren of the White Cross) series, including *B.O.W.C.: a Book for Boys* in 1869 and *The Boys of Grand Pré School* in 1870; and from Australia came one of the best of early girls'-school stories in Louise Mack's *Teens: a Story of Australian School Girls* (1897). But the genre remained above all British, and the master of the classical, high Victorian school story was the Englishman Talbot Baines Reed (1852-93).

Most of Reed's books first appeared as serial stories in the *Boy's Own Paper*, which was dedicated to the provision of wholesome, healthy, boyish literature, in contrast to the penny dreadfuls. He was thus working within limits which would prevent him from doing anything very unconventional even if he wanted to. His best-known story, *The Fifth Form at St Dominic's,* published in book form in 1887, carried a foreword by the *Boy's Own Paper* editor claiming that there was a 'breeziness about it calculated to stir the better life in the most sluggish'.

Understandably, Reed left such difficult issues as emotional attachments untouched. He was content to produce solid, readable and not oppressively didactic stories on acceptable themes. In *The Fifth Form at St Dominic's,* the main issue is one of suspected dishonesty in the competition for an important academic prize; in *The Willoughby Captains* (1887) it is the position of a boy who is made head of a 'bad' house. Reed handled complicated plots and sizeable casts with great professionalism; yet the writing of school stories was only one of his many activities. He ran a family business, wrote a history of typefounding and many essays and articles, and was the first secretary of the Bibliographical Society; and he was only forty-one when he died. In a postscript to the 1971 edition of *The Fifth Form at St Dominic's,* Brian Alderson says that his books were the works of 'a man who knew how to be both serious and humorous, and who was strong, but at the same time innocent and affectionate'.[3]

Frank Eyre, in his study of *British Children's Books in the Twentieth Century* (1971), suggested that Reed had brought the school story to 'a perfection of unreality that later writers could only copy'; and added that 'Kipling introduced new ideas in *Stalky and Co,* but these were not of a kind that practitioners in the older form could follow'.[4] It is true that in its later manifestations the school story seemed to grow ever more stereotyped. Eventually, in the hands of conventional second-rate practitioners, it became, like the detective novel in the 1930s, so limited and artificial that both practitioners and readers grew bored with it. But by the time this stage was reached the school story was already dead so far as the best writers were concerned. And Kipling, with his new ideas, must take some of the blame, for it was he who introduced the serpent into the Old School Eden. After the knowingness of *Stalky* it was difficult ever again to assert the innocent values of the classical school story.

Stalky (1899) was deliberately tough and unsentimental. From the first paragraph onward, it is clear that this was meant to be the real lowdown on school life. The story is set in the United Services College in North Devon, which Kipling himself had attended. Many of the characters and episodes are based on fact. The heroes are three boys who share a study: Stalky, who is the brains of the outfit, a cool, ingenious fellow; M'Turk, who is a patrician; and Beetle, a giglamped bookish boy whom the others tolerate because his literary abilities amuse them and sometimes come in useful. Beetle is Kipling. And *Stalky and Co* and *Eric* are on quite different planes. It is *Stalky* that deals with the real, unregenerate, deplorable yet

No. 1.—Vol. I.   SATURDAY, JANUARY 18, 1879.   Price One Penny.
[ALL RIGHTS RESERVED.]

MY FIRST FOOTBALL MATCH.
BY AN OLD BOY.

I t was a proud moment in my existence when Wright, captain of our football club, came up to me in school one Friday and said, "Adams, your name is down to play in the match against Craven to-morrow."

I could have knighted him on the spot. To be one of the picked "fifteen," whose glory it was to fight the battles of their school in the Great Close, had been the leading ambition of my life—I suppose I ought to be ashamed to confess it—ever since, as a little chap of ten, I entered Parkhurst six years ago. Not a winter Saturday but had seen me either looking on at some big match, or oftener still scrimmaging about with a score or so of other juniors in a scratch game. But for a long time, do what I would, I always

seemed as far as ever from the coveted goal, and was half despairing of ever rising to win my "first fifteen cap." Lately, however, I had noticed Wright and a few others of our best players more than once lounging about in the Little Close where we juniors used to play, evidently taking observations with an eye to business. Under the awful gaze of these heroes, need I say I exerted myself as I had never done before? What cared I for hacks or bruises, so only that I could distinguish myself in their eyes? And never was music sweeter

"Down!"

Front page of the first number of *The Boy's Own Paper* (1879),
with a school story by Talbot Baines Reed

entertaining young male animal. Beside the bad characters of *Stalky* – bad characters who are heroes – the good characters of *Eric* shine with a pale, unearthly light. Stalky and his friends are much more convincing and much more attractive. Yet a good deal of *Stalky* makes uneasy reading today. The exploits of Study Number Five occasionally take place in the worrying twilight zones of human conduct in which Kipling seems a peculiarly blinkered guide. There is, for instance, the episode called 'The moral reformers'. Stalky and Co find that two big boys have been bullying a little one. They manage by a trick to get the bullies trussed up and helpless. Stalky tells them that 'now we're goin' to show you what real bullyin' is'; and there is an eight-page description in grim and gloating detail of how the bullies are tortured in their turn. Counter-bullying is not really any more admirable than bullying; it seems morally obtuse, at the least, to report it with gleeful approval.

Another episode in *Stalky* – probably the best known of all – is the one where the gentleman afterwards known as the 'Jelly-bellied Flag-flapper' comes to give a patriotic address to the school, and the boys are very properly nauseated.

In a raucous voice he cried aloud little matters like the hope of honour and the dream of glory that boys do not discuss even with their most intimate equals; cheerfully assuming that, till he spoke, they had never considered these possibilities. He pointed them to shining goals, with fingers which smudged out all radiance on all horizons. He profaned the most secret places of their souls with outcries and gesticulations.

On the face of it, the handling of this episode is a fine and strong part of the book, and one must suppose that it was brave of Kipling to condemn flag-flapping, especially at the time of the Boer War. Doubts begin to stir when it is stated on the next page that the universal opinion in the dormitories was that the speaker must have been born in a gutter and bred in a board-school. And by the end of the book it is made clear that the real objection is simply to his vulgarity. Stalky and his friends will do brilliantly well under fire and will kill Fuzzy-wuzzies just as well as the flag-flappers. Stalky's noncon-formism is no more than an admired version of conformism. Or perhaps the truth is even worse than that. Kipling worships the power of Empire while kicking away its ideals. And although the ideals of the Empire-builders may have been naive, they were sincerely believed in by great numbers of well-meaning people. To fawn on the power and reject the ideals is squalid.

If *Stalky* could be considered in isolation it would be enough to say that it is an unpleasant, though vigorous, piece of work. But there is no isolation in literature, and *Stalky* had far-reaching effects. P. G. Wodehouse (1881-1975) fortunately escaped them, and wrote a number of school stories (notably *Mike* in 1909) in which the Code is much the same as in

Talbot Baines Reed's books or even in *Tom Brown*. But it was growing difficult for an intelligent writer to produce a school story for boys. Kipling had damaged the genre by making it appear naive; and the First World War was to demonstrate with incomparably greater cruelty the inadequacy of its simple values. 'God give us bases to guard or beleaguer: Games to play out, whether earnest or fun' – it was magnificent but it was not war; it had nothing to do with life and death in the trenches.

10

Articulate animals

ANIMAL stories may be divided for convenience into two main kinds: those about humanized animals and those about animals as such. Examples of the former are young children's books such as those of Beatrix Potter and Alison Uttley, where the animals talk, wear clothes, visit each other and have a family life like our own. The most distinguished of British humanized-animal books would be generally agreed to be the Beatrix Potter books and Kenneth Grahame's *The Wind in the Willows*. In the other kind of animal story – as written, for instance, by Ernest Thompson Seton or Henry Williamson or John and Jean George – the animal is presented, as nearly as possible, in its animal nature.

Both types of story have their merits, and both have their difficulties. The author who tries to portray a real animal from within is up against the basic fact that we do not and cannot know what it feels like to be an animal. True, the more the author knows about the animals he is writing about, the better qualified he will be to attempt that perilous imaginative leap into the animal mind. But the procedure must still be speculative. Perhaps in the last resort all the writer can do is to stretch his own imagination and those of his readers.

The humanized-animal story also has its risks: it can easily degenerate into sentimentality and whimsy, and even into falsehood, as when we tend to distinguish between 'good' animals – usually meaning nice furry ones – and 'bad' animals, which are slimy or snappy and generally uncuddleable.

In fiction, the humanized or semi-humanized animal has a long tradition behind it. In the great collections of folk tales, such as the Anansi stories of Africa and the West Indies, there is often confusion between men and animals – Anansi himself is now one, now the other – and the animals have broadly human attributes which, however, are modified by their animal characteristics. Western folk tales are full of humanized animals. Often in the old tales there is a loose camaraderie or even cousinship between man and animals – an earthy acceptance perhaps that we and they are not so very different. We can see this assumption of kinship working in a naive way every day among small children. The animals they see around them are not clearly differentiated from people. It would not surprise them if an animal spoke to them in the street. My youngest child, when she was three years old, looked at a magazine picture of a mother kangaroo with its baby in its pouch and asked: 'Where's the daddy kangaroo? Is he waiting for them in the car?' In her world a kangaroo could drive a car quite easily.

In children's literature – that is, work deliberately written for children – animals were given a good start by the pioneer publisher, John Newbery. In about 1760 he brought out *A Pretty Book of Pictures for Little Masters and Misses; or Tommy Trip's History of Birds and Beasts,* which contains 'a familiar description of each in verse and prose, to which is prefixed the History of Tom Trip himself, of his dog Jouler, and of Woglog the great Giant'. Jouler, by the way, is no ordinary dog, because 'Tommy, when he has a mind to ride, pulls a little bridle out of his pocket, whips it upon honest Jouler, and away he gallops – tantivy!'

Even at the end of the eighteenth and beginning of the nineteenth centuries, when literal-mindedness in writing for children was most insisted on, animal stories with an element of fantasy managed to be written and approved. Mrs Trimmer, that redoubtable opponent of the fairy story, wrote her *Fabulous Histories,* later called *The History of the Robins* (1786), in which, as she said, 'the sentiments and affections of a good father and mother are supposed to be possessed by a nest of redbreasts.' I suspect that Mrs Trimmer was trying to have it both ways, for she went on to say that young readers should be taught to consider her stories 'not as containing the real conversations of birds (for that it is impossible we should ever understand) but as a series of *fables* intended to convey moral instruction applicable to themselves, at the same time that they excite compassion and tenderness for those interesting and delightful creatures on which such wanton cruelties are frequently inflicted, and recommend *universal benevolence.'*

Mrs Trimmer's baby robins were called Robin, Dicksy, Pecksy and Flapsy: names which could easily have come out of a modern children's book. And four little mice in Dorothy Kilner's *Life and Perambulations of a Mouse* (1783) were Nimble, Longtail, Softdown and Brighteyes. Animal stories appeared intermittently in publishers' lists during the first half of the nineteenth century, but there is nothing which is of any real interest today. In 1861 came Ballantyne's *Dog Crusoe,* an adventure rather than an animal story; and Holme Lee's *True Pathetic History of Poor Match* (a terrier) appeared in 1863. But the first animal story of major importance was Anna Sewell's *Black Beauty* (1877).

Anna Sewell (1820-78) was lamed as a child and lived the quiet life of a semi-invalid. *Black Beauty* was her only book, and she wrote it in the last years of her life 'to induce kindness, sympathy and an understanding treatment of horses'. It is the story, told by a horse in the first person, of the ups and downs of his life: mostly downs, for although Black Beauty is well born and well bred he descends through a series of mishaps and chances to being a London cabhorse (and he could have sunk lower: to pulling a coal cart, for instance). Happily in the end he finds a good home and lives out his days in comfort.

The author is constantly concerned to put over her message; and from one point of view – which was probably her own – the whole book is a treatise on the care of horses, illustrated with numerous examples. But clearly a book does not survive on account of its message – particularly in a case like this, where the message has been largely outdated since the motor-vehicle succeeded the horse. I think *Black Beauty* survives partly through its successful appeal to compassion in children and partly because the story carries conviction, in spite of some absurdly un-equine remarks in the horse's narration. And Miss Sewell proved her independence of mind, as well as her sincerity and courage, by condemning war and fox-hunting – two institutions which right-minded people were supposed to accept without question.

Black Beauty had an unashamed and extremely popular imitator in Marshall Saunders's *Beautiful Joe* (1893) – a book which now seems to caricature the worst features of its original. It is told in the first person by a dog, who explains that 'I have seen my mistress laughing and crying over a little book that she says is the story of a horse's life, and sometimes she puts the book down close to my nose to let me see the pictures.' Joe, formerly kicked and beaten by a brutal owner, has been rescued early in the book and now belongs to gentle Miss Laura; but the lesson on kindness to animals goes on, and on, until Joe brings his story to a close: 'Goodbye to the boys and girls who may read it; and if it is not wrong for a dog to say it I should like to add, "God bless you all."'

Marshall Saunders was a Canadian; but the serious Canadian

contribution to the animal story was something very different from this riot of anthropomorphism. Within a few years two Canadians, Ernest Thompson Seton (1860-1946) and Charles G. D. Roberts (1860-1943), were to pioneer the realistic animal story, or wild-animal biography. This is a field of writing in which Canada has continued to excel: perhaps not surprisingly, since it is a country in which the wilderness looms geographically and psychologically large.

Roberts, best known in his lifetime as a poet, was the more eminent literary figure, but Seton now looks more important as a writer of animal stories. Sheila Egoff, in *The Republic of Childhood*, says it is 'difficult, and probably pointless, to try to decide which of his stories Seton particularly intended for children, for of all types of writing the realistic animal story makes perhaps the least distinction in the age of its readers'.[1]

Seton was an artist and naturalist, founder of the Woodcraft Movement, and at one time Chief Scout of America. His animal biographies, beginning with a group of stories collected as *Wild Animals I Have Known* in 1898, were based on intimate personal knowledge and were mostly in short story or short novel form. In the latter form he had a fine shaping ability. *Monarch the Big Bear* (1904) parallels the course of a bear's life with the course of a river, using such chapter-heads as 'The Freshet', 'Roaring in the Canyon', 'The Ford', 'The Deepening Torrent' and 'The Cataract'; and the action, beginning quietly, is correspondingly intensified all the way along. In contrast, *The Biography of a Grizzly* (1900), which begins with the bear Wahb as a cub and ends when the aged, ailing creature plods to its death, swells into action in the middle and fades to a dying fall. Seton matched his style to the movement of his story; and he displays the quiet assurance of the man who knows what he is talking about:

There are bears that eat little but roots and berries; there are bears that love best the great black salmon they can hook out of the pools when the long 'run' is on; and there are bears that have a special fondness for flesh. These are rare; they are apt to develop unusual ferocity and meet an early death. Gringo was one of them, and he grew like the brawny, meat-fed gladiators of old . . .

Seton's stories usually ended tragically; that was part of their truth to life in the wild. Roberts was equally well aware of 'Nature red in tooth and claw'; but his best known story, *Red Fox* (1905), finishes with the animal hero's 'final triumph over the enemies of his kind' — notably man — to find freedom in the wilderness. Sir John Fortescue's *Story of a Red Deer*

'The Cat that Walked by Himself', from Kipling's
Just So Stories (1902)

(1897) is an English animal biography of some merit and
staying power — a paperback edition appeared in 1971 — but
its mixture of anthropomorphism and realism seems to me
unsatisfactory. Fortescue's class-ridden animal society, complete
with rural accents, is amusing but does not sort well with the
tragic and moving conclusion in which the old stag is hunted
to its death. The American Jack London produced a great deal
of varied, energetic writing in a varied, energetic life; most of
it was not intended to and is never likely to appeal to children,
but his realistic story of dogs and men, *Call of the Wild* (1903)
tends nowadays to find its place among children's books.

Rudyard Kipling's *Jungle Books* (1894-5), and especially the
Mowgli stories, must rank among the best loved of all English
children's books. Mowgli, it will be remembered, is a boy who

is found in the jungle by wolves, grows up with the wolf pack, becomes friendly with Baloo the bear and Bagheera the panther, and kills the tiger Shere Khan. Rejected by men, he returns to the jungle as its master, but in the end he feels the irresistible call to 'make his lair with his own blood', and leaves the jungle for good.

To children, the Mowgli stories are absorbing, exciting and wish-fulfilling tales. A child reader is bound to identify himself with Mowgli, who not only has the marvellous privilege of living among the animals but is clearly their superior, since they cannot meet his eye and they acknowledge him as their leader. To readers of any age the animal characters such as Baloo and Bagheera, and Akela the old leader of the wolf pack, are appealing. They speak in their own distinctive and slightly poetic language. Baloo and Bagheera call Mowgli 'Little Brother' and address him as 'thou', and they use such terms as 'the red flower' for fire. It is an acceptable convention which gives the animals a necessary dignity. There are strange, impressive risings to the occasion, as on the proclamation of the Water Truce in time of drought, when all animals, even those who normally prey on each other, may drink in peace from such water as there is.

To adults it may seem evident that there is a profound ambiguity. The contrast of man and animal is crucial to the story, but to put Kipling's animals beside those of a Seton or a Roberts is to see that he is not attempting anything like their kind of naturalism. The world of the jungle is in fact both itself and our own world as well: the human jungle. The Law of the Jungle — of which Kipling gives specimen clauses — appears really to indicate how *men* must fend for themselves in a dangerous world: how they must hunt together and must be bold, but bold in obedience to their leaders. In his own disconcerting way, Kipling is as didactic as any Victorian moralist. Underlying these brilliant stories of life among the animals is his own code of masculine behaviour.

Besides the Mowgli stories, the *Jungle Books* contain several other tales, mostly set in India. These include the story of the mongoose, Rikki-tikki-tavi, which was my own childhood favourite. Kipling drew on his experience of India and knowledge of its lore, as well as on his own endlessly fertile imagination. And he wrote for younger children his own beast-fables, or perhaps more accurately beast-myths, in the *Just So Stories* (1902). These tell how the camel got his hump, the leopard his spots, and so on. They are rolling, rich, and resounding: much more effective when told aloud than they look on the page; and no one who has ever known them forgets how the rhinoceros got his folded skin and bad temper from the Parsee's cake-crumbs, or how the Elephant's Child spanked his grown-up relations (a great and subversive favourite with children, this). And there are phrases handed down in families like small heirlooms: 'a man of infinite-resource-and-sagacity', 'satiable curtiosity', 'more-than-oriental splendour', and above all perhaps 'the great grey-green, greasy Limpopo River, all set about with fever-trees'.

The animals in *The Wind in the Willows* (1908) are much farther along the road to humanization than are Mowgli's friends in the jungle, or even the horses in *Black Beauty*. To all intents and purposes they are — to borrow a phrase from May Hill Arbuthnot — 'ourselves in fur';[2] though we must remember that Kenneth Grahame, like his contemporary Beatrix Potter, had been a patient observer of the ways of small animals.

Grahame lived from 1859 to 1932, and for ten years was Secretary of the Bank of England, though according to his contemporaries he did not exert himself unduly. He published *The Golden Age* in 1895 and *Dream Days* in 1898 — both books being evocations of childhood, though not written for children. *The Wind in the Willows* appeared in 1908, the year in which he retired from the Bank.

The central characters in *The Wind in the Willows* are the creatures who live on the river bank: especially, in the opening chapters, the Mole and the Water-Rat. They lead a pastoral, golden-age, dream-days kind of life, packing picnic hampers and messing about in boats — a thoroughly human idyll. But not far from the river bank is the Wild Wood, inhabited mainly by rather undesirable animals such as stoats and weasels; and beyond the Wild Wood is the Wide World, with which the river-bank animals, if they have any sense, have nothing to do. Mole and Rat are sensible fellows; but their eccentric friend Toad goes off into the Wide World, dashing around in power-ful motor-cars and getting himself put in prison, with the result that the stoats and weasels take possession of his ancestral home. In the end Toad escapes and comes to his senses; with the help of the august Badger the river-bank animals rout their enemies; Toad Hall is retaken and the old Arcadian life is resumed.

Rat and Mole paddling upstream: a drawing by E.H.Shepard
from the 1931 edition of *The Wind in the Willows*

There are three strands in *The Wind in the Willows*. The
most substantial part, and the one that children usually enjoy
most, is the Toad narrative. Toad's adventures on the road, his
imprisonment and his escape in washerwoman's clothing, the
train chase and the triumphant recapture of Toad Hall are
humorous and exciting stuff. The second strand is formed by

the four river-bank and Wild Wood chapters in which Toad does not appear. Here the hero is the Mole, who finds daily toil a bore (just as Grahame did) and throws it all up in favour of a life of idleness and good fellowship. These are the chapters that give the book its idyllic atmosphere.

The third strand consists of the two important chapters inserted by Grahame into the finished draft of the book: 'Wayfarers All' and 'The Piper at the Gates of Dawn'. In 'Wayfarers All', the Water Rat, first watching the swallows fly south and then meeting a seafaring rat, feels the call of the south, the urge to set off for exotic places; but the Mole catches him just in time, drags him back into his house, and holds him down until the attack has passed. It is a curious episode, since after all Mole himself has given up his settled way of life for ever. In 'The Piper at the Gates of Dawn', Rat and Mole go looking for the lost cub of Otter, little Portly, and are drawn by sweet irresistible music to an island in the river where they meet the great god Pan, who has Portly curled up asleep between his hooves. This chapter is written in a mystical style and spirit, and from it the author's own credo may be deduced.

The Wind in the Willows has an unmistakably pre-1914 air and can arouse in adults a nostalgia (possibly misleading) for a time that few people now alive can remember. It is however a great deal more than a mere period piece. Peter Green's biography, *Kenneth Grahame* (1959), contains a long and fascinating analysis. Not everyone will agree with all Green's findings, but there is no doubt that Grahame's masterpiece has hidden depths of which the author himself could hardly have been aware. This is one reason why it is so satisfying at all ages. Quite small children will enjoy the adventures of Toad; the river-bank passages and the two inserted chapters will appeal successively as they grow older; and even the adult at the tenth or twelfth reading will realize that he has not yet got to the bottom of this subtle and complex work.

11

Writers in rhyme

POETRY wanders unconcerned across the vague and shifting border between children's books and just plain books. A great deal of lyric poetry lies open to young readers, and children's poetry anthologies normally include a high proportion of verse that was written without any special thought of a child readership. This is not surprising, since in one respect at least the poet's eye and the child's eye work in the same way. The gift of seeing and feeling things afresh, as if they had never been seen or felt before, is traditionally a quality of the lyric poet; it is also a childlike quality. There is of course much poetry that is adult in the sense of being beyond the range of a child's response; the compiler of an anthology for children is likely to pass it by, and to seek out poems that lie within the area which children and adults share. And this area is not so narrowly restricted as might be thought. Themes like love and death are not necessarily excluded; for children can grasp imaginatively a great deal that in literal terms they cannot understand.

Nevertheless, a sizeable amount of poetry, and a vastly greater quantity of verse which does not qualify for that description, has been written specially for children. It is worth discussion, for it constitutes a recognizable body of work, and indeed it is surprising to realize how much has been produced for children by good poets, and how much of it is still alive and enjoyable − by adults as well as by children.

The beginnings run parallel with the beginnings of prose literature for children. On the one hand are song, ballad, nursery rhyme: the oral tradition, long considered unworthy of formal record. On the other hand is instructional material, undoubtedly meant for children but not in any serious sense creative literature. It was common for the old courtesy books to be rhymed, as an aid to memory − particularly useful in times when you could not expect everybody to have a copy of the book. It was also well understood that verse could sugar the instructional pill.

Verse written for utilitarian purposes is unlikely at any time to have much literary merit, though there are occasional exceptions. A partial one comes in the *Booke in Englyssh metre of the great marchaunt man called Dyves Pragmaticus, very pretye for chyldren to rede,* which was written by Thomas Newbery (not to be confused with John Newbery two centuries later) and published in 1562-3. Interestingly, this was designed not to instruct in morals or manners but to help children 'rede and write Wares and Implements in this worlde contayned'. It is best taken in small quantities: for example,

> I have Suchet, Surrip, Grene Ginger and Marmalade,
> Bisket, Cumfecte and Carraways as fine as can be made,
> As for Poticary and Grocery, I have all that trade
> You shall se of all thynges, come hether to me.
>
> I have here to sell fine Needells and Thimbels
> Nayle pearsers, smalle podde Chyselles and Wimbels
> Blades, and for weavers fine Shuttells and Brembils,
> What do you lacke, friend? come hether to me.
>
> I have inkyll, Crewell and gay Valances fine,
> Pannes to warme Bedde, with gyrte corde and lyne,
> The money is your owne, and the ware is myne,
> Come see for your love, and come bye of me.

Here the evocative names of the wares, and the unmistakable tones of the salesman, make the verses still pleasing, if not exactly literature. Even the grave Puritans did not disdain verse as a vehicle of enlightenment; and Isaac Watts, in the (post-Lockean) preface to his *Divine Songs* (1715) is still emphasizing its instructional value:

There is a greater Delight in the very Learning of Truths and Duties this way. There is something so amusing and entertaining in Rhymes and Metre, that will incline Children to make this part of their Business a Diversion . . . What is learnt in Verse is longer retain'd in Memory, and sooner recollected. The like Sounds and the like number of Syllables exceedingly assist the remembrance.[1]

These beliefs indeed still underlie such modern forms as the safety-first slogan and the television jingle.

Dr Watts can be identified, far more confidently than can the first publisher or writer of fiction for children, as the first children's poet. The immense popularity of the *Divine Songs,* of which six or seven hundred editions were published in England and America during the succeeding two centuries, was due not to the didactic purpose but to the limpid simplicity and memorability of the verses. They were known in every respectable Georgian and Victorian nursery; Lewis Carroll parodied several of them in *Alice in Wonderland;* and even today most of us know more of them than we realize. 'How doth the little busy bee', 'Let dogs delight to bark and bite' — these and many other lines are still familiar.

In the three quarters of a century after the *Divine Songs*, the most important writer of verse for children to achieve print was Mother Goose. The earliest known nursery-rhyme collection was *Tommy Thumb's Song Book*, which was published by Mrs Cooper of Paternoster Row in 1744 and contained 'Sing a Song of Sixpence', 'Hickory Dickory Dock', 'Baa Baa Black Sheep', and other well-known rhymes. Better remembered today is *Mother Goose's Melody*, which contained some fifty nursery rhymes and twenty pages of songs from Shakespeare. It was 'illustrated with Notes and Maxims, Historical, Philosophical, and Critical', which in fact were facetious.

This book is hard to date. The notes have been attributed to Oliver Goldsmith, which would imply publication by John Newbery, but I do not know of any supporting evidence. *Mother Goose's Melody* was on the lists of Newbery's successors, and must have appeared in England some time before Isaiah Thomas's first American edition in about 1785. The genealogy of Mother Goose is dubious, and likely to remain so. The old nursery rhymes are of considerable but obscure antiquity, as are many of those chanted by children in their games.[2] Mother Goose as a name seems to have come into English from Perrault's *Contes de ma Mere l'Oye*, which, confusingly, were fairy tales, not nursery rhymes. Undoubtedly the old lady is of a composite constitution; the only certainty is that there was no truth in the Bostonian claim that she was a Mistress Goose, or Vergoose, of Boston.

Watts, best known today for his hymns, was a minor but genuine poet; he has been called 'one of the more imaginative poets of the early eighteenth century'.[3] The next poet of any significance to write for children was a very major poet. William Blake's intention in writing his *Songs of Innocence* (1789) was clearly expressed in the introductory poem, 'Piping down the valleys wild', which concludes:

> And I made a rural pen,
> And I stain'd the water clear
> And I wrote my happy songs
> Ev'ry child may joy to hear.

Reversing the familiar process by which work intended for the general reader finds its way to the children's list, the *Songs of Innocence* have found their place as part of the general heritage of English poetry. This is right and proper, although in poem after poem Blake is unmistakably addressing himself to children. The movement of the *Songs of Innocence* out of accepted children's literature probably has much to do with their natural pairing with the *Songs of Experience*. These came five years later and contained less of the joy of childhood; brightness had fallen from the air. Yet I would hesitate to say that the elusive border between children's and general literature passes between the *Songs of Innocence* and the *Songs of Experience;* in fact the Blake poem which above all others stirs the imagination of children is in the latter book: 'Tyger, Tyger, burning bright . . .'

Blake was an obscure writer in his day; as Harvey Darton put it, 'he was only a grubby old eccentric, communing with God in a back garden'.[4] Much more influential and widely read were Ann and Jane Taylor (1782-1866 and 1783-1824). They were the principal authors of *Original Poems for Infant Minds,* which was published in 1804 and contained the sentimental, immensely popular 'My Mother':

> Who fed me from her gentle breast
> And hushed me in her arms to rest
> And on my cheek sweet kisses pressed?
>   My Mother.

In stanza after stanza of identical termination, a tribute converts itself gradually into a promise:

> When thou art feeble, old and grey
> My healthy arm shall be thy stay
> And I will soothe thy pains away,
>   My Mother.

Sixty years later this was described as 'one of the most beautiful lyrics in the English language'.[5] To a present-day adult it seems a bad poem, but it is a good bad poem. It is difficult to read or hear the whole of it and not be moved by its lush sincerity. Ann Taylor, who wrote it, also wrote 'My Father' in similar vein; and her admiring contemporaries added, among others, 'My Sister', 'My Daughter', 'My Son', 'My Uncle', 'My Governess', 'Our Saviour', and 'My Tippoo' (a dog):

> When first a puppy Tippoo came,
> Companion of each childish game,
> Who on my heart held stronger claim
> Than Tippoo?

The Taylors went on to write *Rhymes for the Nursery* (1806) and *Hymns for Infant Minds* (1808). Among their verses, Jane's 'Twinkle, twinkle, little star' was parodied by Lewis Carroll and is still well known. Their success was probably responsible for the appearance in 1809 of Charles and Mary Lamb's *Poetry for Children* – written to order, as Charles Lamb said, by an old bachelor and an old maid.[6] This was in the same vein and did not do particularly well, or deserve to – though it has occasional felicities, such as a little gem of the mock-heroic called 'Feigned Courage'.

Several of the Taylors' poems, like 'Meddlesome Matty', were cautionary verses, and helped to establish a sub-genre in which English ladies like Elizabeth Turner and Mary Elliott were active, sometimes with unintentionally hilarious results. American ladies could write cautionary verses too, as Miss A. Howland demonstrated in her *Rhode Island Tales* (1833). The story of Lydia and the razor is typically instructive. Lydia's uncle gives her his razor to take care of, and silly Lydia cannot resist trying it out on her little sister:

> 'Dear Abby,' she said,
> 'This beautiful thing only see;
> Sit down here directly and hold up your head,
> And I'll shave you as nice as can be.'
>
> Little Abby consented, and straight they begin
> Their dangerous play with delight,
> But oh! the first stroke brought the blood from her chin
> And they both screamed aloud with affright.
>
> At the sound of their voices their mother appeared
> And well might such figures amaze her,
> For the littler girl was with blood all besmeared
> And the other was holding a razor.

Lydia is reprimanded, and promises to shun such dangerous playthings in future. There is nothing to suggest that it might have been criminal negligence on Uncle's part to give a child his razor.

One of the most remarkable publishing successes of the early nineteenth century was William Roscoe's *The Butterfly's Ball* (1807), which appeared as an attractive, square-shaped little book with one couplet and one picture to each page. It begins:

> Come take up your hats and away let us haste
> To the Butterfly's Ball and the Grasshopper's Feast;

and its account of the rural jollities of the insects and their friends is notable, not for any special poetic merit but for a

Drawing by William Mulready from *The Lion's Masquerade*, by Mrs Dorset (1807)

total absence of ulterior motive; it is all just for fun. Roscoe, a Member of Parliament and busy public man, never tried to cash in on what appears to have been a casual triumph; but the publishing world showed, not for the first or last time, that it knew a bandwagon when it saw one. In the next year or two there followed, from various writers, *The Peacock's At Home, The Lion's Masquerade, The Elephant's Ball, The Butterfly's Funeral, The Court of the Beasts, The Eagle's Masque, The Fishes' Feast, The Fishes' Grand Gala, The Horse's Levee, The Jackdaw's At Home, The Lobster's Voyage, The Rose's Breakfast, The Water-King's Levee, The Wedding Among the Flowers, The Butterfly's Birthday, The Council of Dogs, The Lion's Parliament,* and *The Tyger's Theatre.*

In the United States, a somewhat similar phenomenon to the success of *The Butterfly's Ball* was that of Clement C. Moore's *A Visit from St Nicholas* (1823):

> 'Twas the night before Christmas, when all through the house
> Not a creature was stirring, not even a mouse . . .

Moore's galloping anapaests have stayed the course, and his poem, unlike Roscoe's, is universally known and popular today. Robert Browning's *Pied Piper of Hamelin* (1842) has also survived and seems still firmly established.

The great writers of nonsense verse for children, who have never been surpassed, are Edward Lear (1812-88) and Lewis Carroll. Lear's *Book of Nonsense,* by the Old Derry down Derry who loved to see little folks merry, was published in 1846. It was a book of limericks. Lear's great nonsense stories in verse came much later, with *Nonsense Songs* (1870), including 'The Jumblies' and 'The Owl and the Pussy-Cat', and *Laughable Lyrics* (1877), among which are 'The Pobble who has no Toes' and 'The Dong with the Luminous Nose'. Carroll's best-known verses are mostly in the *Alice* books. Those in *Wonderland* (1865) are largely parodies; Carroll's more original verses are in *Looking-Glass* (1871).

Two of these − 'The Walrus and the Carpenter', with its logical absurdity, wild invention, and satire on sanctimonious hypocrisy; 'Jabberwocky' with its superb word-coinages − are among the most brilliant nonsense verses in the English language. Yet Lear was a poet, in a sense in which the word cannot quite be applied to Carroll. As Lear's biographer, Vivien Noakes, truly says, his development as a nonsense writer 'is increasingly away from pure nonsense into sad and moving poetry'.[7] There is an imaginative richness, but in the later work

The Jumblies at sea, as Edward
Lear himself saw them

also a growing melancholy, in Lear's stories of wandering and travel in distant, exotic, and surely unhappy lands.

Christina Rossetti (1830-94) told an original fairy story in verse in *Goblin Market* (1862), using an individual, flexible verse style that changes subtly with the movement of the story. The goblins' tones at the start are light and tempting:

> Come buy our orchard fruits,
> Come buy, come buy;
> Apples and quinces,

> Lemons and oranges . . .
> Damsons and bilberries,
> Taste them and try:
> Currants and gooseberries,
> Bright-fire-like barberries,
> Figs to fill your mouth,
> Citrons from the South,
> Sweet to tongue and sound to eye;
> Come buy, come buy.

It is a tale of two sisters: Laura eats the goblin fruit and nearly dies, but Lizzie defies the goblins and wins the 'fiery antidote' to save her. In 1872 Christina Rossetti published *Sing-Song,* a book of rhymes for young children: brief, neat, quiet, with haunting undertones.

Robert Louis Stevenson's *Child's Garden of Verses* (1885) is written as if by a child in the first person, and was indeed drawn from Stevenson's memories of his own childhood. In several of the poems one can see the child, already absorbed in longings for travel and adventure, who will grow up to write romantic and exotic books and will finish his life in the South Seas:

> I should like to rise and go
> Where the golden apples grow;
> Where below another sky
> Parrot islands anchored lie,
> And, watched by cockatoos and goats,
> Lonely Crusoes building boats . . .

At times the child's-eye view is fresh and clear; elsewhere there is a shifting of perspective — humorous or nostalgic — between the author as child and the author as man. The sense of time elapsed and irrecoverable is strongest in the fine concluding poem:

> As from the house your mother sees
> You playing round the garden trees,
> So you may see if you will look
> Through the windows of this book
> Another child, far, far away
> And in another garden play.
> But do not think you can at all
> By knocking on the window call
> That child to hear you. He intent
> Is all on his play-business bent.
> He does not hear, he will not look,
> Nor yet be lured out of this book.
> For, long ago, the truth to say
> He has grown up and gone away,

> And it is but a child of air
> That lingers in the garden there.

The American Eugene Field seems to be rather out of favour these days, even in his own country. A selection of his poems called *Lullaby Land* was made and introduced by Kenneth Grahame in 1897, and was well named, for there is in the poems a curiously recurrent emphasis on going to sleep. The best known is the dreamy, vague, but still appealing 'Wynken, Blynken and Nod'. Field also wrote 'The Duel', about the gingham dog and the calico cat who ate each other up. He and James Whitcomb Riley (1849-1916) were disparagingly described by May Hill Arbuthnot as 'newspaper poets';[8] but Field at least has been found fit for higher purposes than to wrap up the supper, and Riley is still remembered, if only for 'Little Orphant Annie':

> The gobble-uns'll git you
> Ef you
> Don't
> Watch
> Out!

Another American writer of verse for children, Laura Richards, was born in the same year as Eugene Field but outlived him by half a century. Her main collection, *Tirra Lirra*, was not published until 1932; it included poems dating back to the nineteenth century, but even so this does not seem the place to consider it. The English poet Walter de la Mare, born in 1873, also lived long into the next century, and will be discussed in a later chapter. Hilaire Belloc (1870-1953) fits in more comfortably here because his *Bad Child's Book of Beasts* (1896), *More Beasts for Worse Children* (1897), and *Cautionary Tales* (1908) looked back to the moral versifiers of the eighteenth and nineteenth centuries. The works of these writers were still to be found in the late Victorian and Edwardian nursery. Belloc saw them off with good-humoured parody:

> Your little hands were made to take
> The better things and leave the worse ones:
> They also may be used to shake
> The Massive Paws of Elder Persons.

For the sad but risible tale of string-chewing Henry King, or of untruthful Matilda who found that 'every time she shouted "Fire!" they only answered "Little liar!",' modern children are indebted indirectly to Isaac Watts, Ann and Jane Taylor, and their imitators.

12

Pictures that tell a story

ILLUSTRATION is older than the printed book, and the woodcut is older than movable type. The early printers had no difficulty in combining text with pictures, although their technical means were very limited. Caxton's edition of *Aesop's Fables* was illustrated with 186 woodcuts. And the woodcut, though challenged by copper and steel plate engraving from the seventeenth century onwards, continued to be a dominant means of book illustration until late in the nineteenth century. It is still used quite often in picture books today, but woodcuts are now reproduced lithographically rather than directly from the wood block.

The early history of picture books and illustration shows a familiar division: on the one hand vigorous and popular material which was not specially meant for children but which they presumably saw and enjoyed; on the other hand material designed for children but not very creative or pleasurable. The great hand-drawn picture-books of the Middle Ages included, most notably for the present purpose, the Bestiaries. The monks saw the animal creation as being in a sense God's picture-book, from which lessons about faith and works could be drawn. The bestiaries could not make the full transition into print, because printing was unable to match the pictorial glories of manuscript, but their influence persisted strongly. Edward Topsell's splendid *Historie of Four-footed Beastes* (1607) owed them a great deal, both in the extraordinary beasts included and in the qualities ascribed to actual ones. The bestiarists, like the early cartographers, tended to be fairly accurate about what was well known and close to home, but to grow wilder and wilder towards the edge of the map, where roamed (so to speak) such creatures as dragons, hippogriffs and manticoras.

These excesses were modified with the passage of time and the growth of knowledge, but there are distinct traces of the bestiaries — and some of their time-honoured mis-statements — in natural history books of the eighteenth century; and many items of bestiary lore are well known and half believed today.

The *Orbis Pictus,* or *Visible World,* of John Amos Comenius, which appeared in an English translation in 1658-9, is commonly regarded as the first picture-book to be designed specially for children, although the purpose of this 'Picture and Nomenclature of all the chief Things that are in the World, and of Man's Employments therein' was solely to teach. So long as the aim was instruction, even the Puritans did not object to illustration; Janeway's *Token for Children* itself was 'adorn'd with Cuts'. The chapbooks, without any such lofty aim, were usually illustrated by crude but emphatic woodcuts. And the books for little masters and misses of John Newbery, his contemporaries and successors, could boast of their 'cuts so pretty'. Leigh Hunt, in *The Town* (1848), wrote of his childhood love for the 'little penny books . . . rich with bad pictures' that came from Newbery's in St Paul's Churchyard; and added that 'we preferred the uncouth coats, the staring blotted eyes and round pieces of rope for hats of our very badly drawn contemporaries to all the proprieties of modern embellishment'.[1]

The master of the woodcut, Thomas Bewick (1753-1828), and his brother John (1760-95) both produced books for children among their other work. Thomas Bewick illustrated in 1771 *The New Lottery Book of Birds and Beasts;* and in 1779 *A Pretty Book of Pictures for Little Masters and Misses; or, Tommy Trip's History of Beasts and Birds* (a variation on a Newbery title of the early 1760s), and the two brothers collaborated in *Select Fables* (1784). Thomas edited and illustrated his own *Fables of Aesop and others* in 1818.

William Blake's *Songs of Innocence* (1789) was an extraordinary production in every way. It was written, designed, engraved on copper, printed, bound and hand-coloured by Blake himself. Blake also made water-colour drawings for an edition of Bunyan's *The Pilgrim's Progress;* they are in his visionary mood and successful in themselves, although not in the spirit of the text. His engravings for Mary Wollstonecraft's *Original Stories from Real Life* (1791 edition) are very poor, however; and altogether this gloomy production must be one of the least prepossessing works that can ever have resulted from the labours of two exceptionally talented people.

As might be expected, most of the major nineteenth-century illustrators in England and America worked on children's books at one time or another. Earliest among them was William Mulready (1786-1863), whose drawings for Roscoe's *Butterfly's Ball* in 1807 and its successors (see page 108) must have had much to do with its remarkable success. The 1823

The elves and the shoemaker: engraving by George Cruikshank
from the 1823 edition of *Grimm's Fairy Tales*

English edition of *Grimm's Fairy Tales* was a landmark in
more ways than one, and the illustrations by George Cruikshank (1792-1878), though they now seem extremely small for
the size of their subjects and the amount of detail they contain,
are full of life and character, and in keeping with the spirit of
the text. Cruikshank was a prolific artist, now probably best
known to the layman as the first illustrator of Dickens. Richard
Doyle (1824-1883), who drew the famous *Punch* cover which
stayed in use for more than a century, illustrated in Gothic
style John Ruskin's *King of the Golden River* (1851) (see page
35), another story of historical importance as well as intrinsic
interest. Arthur Hughes (1832-1915), as illustrator, is associated
above all with George MacDonald; most notable probably are
his mysterious drawings for *At the Back of the North Wind*
(1871), in which little Diamond seems to be — and the reader
may feel himself to be — about to drown in the great waves of
the North Wind's hair (see page 77.)
    Of all Victorian illustrations, those of John Tenniel (1820-
1914) for the *Alice* books are by far the best known. The

American artist Henry C. Pitz, in *Illustrating Children's Books* (1963), described Tenniel as 'a good workmanlike illustrator, above average but scarcely inspired'. But Pitz acknowledged that Tenniel was the ideal artist for this assignment, and said that 'Carroll's texts brought out his best and resulted in a definitive collaboration'.[2] Of this there can be no doubt. Many artists have now illustrated the *Alice* books in many styles, but (with the exception perhaps of Arthur Rackham) their efforts seem little more than curiosities. The Carroll texts and Tenniel illustrations are inextricably woven together.

Arthur Rackham (1867-1939) made his reputation before the First World War, though he went on illustrating all through the

An Arthur Rackham silhouette, from the edition of Charles
Dickens's *A Christmas Carol* which he illustrated

inter-war years, and the list of books that he illustrated or re-illustrated is a long one. He was not one of my own childhood favourites; I was frightened by his sinister creatures and (above all) by his gnarled, groping trees. While acknowledging him to have been a good artist with strong individual vision, I still do not find his work enjoyable; but this no doubt is a personal reaction caused by too-vivid recollection of the old shudders. Even his *Mother Goose* (1913) has its alarming moments: Jack Sprat casts a menacing shadow on the wall, and the man, wives and cats coming from St Ives have a disturbing air of witchcraft. And well might Miss Muffet be frightened by the outsize spider that sits down beside her in Rackham's version.

American children's-book illustration in the nineteenth century had not yet come into its own. For the earlier illustrators there were of course not a great many children's books to illustrate. The prolific F. O. C. Darley (1822-88) is remembered in this context mainly for his drawings in mid-century editions of the Washington Irving stories. Winslow Homer (1836-1910), a more distinguished artist, unfortunately did not illustrate any children's book of real importance, though his work appeared in such magazines as *Our Young Folks* and the *Riverside Magazine*. (The children's magazines, further discussed in the later part of this chapter, were important outlets for the work of artists as well as writers.) The earthy humour of E. W. Kemble (1861-1933) won him as a young man the commission at Mark Twain's request to illustrate *Huckleberry Finn,* for which he received the then enormous fee of two thousand dollars (see page 48). Another artist with a strong sense of humour, A. B. Frost (1851-1928), illustrated Joel Chandler Harris's *Uncle Remus* stories (see page 68) and was one of many noted contributors to the magazine *St Nicholas*. Reginald Birch (1856-1943), an American born in England, also did much work for *St Nicholas*. He had a long and honourable career, but his reputation never recovered from the odium of having illustrated *Little Lord Fauntleroy*.

The outstanding late-nineteenth-century American figure is Howard Pyle. Illustrating his own books, Pyle took immense pains to integrate text and picture, often with much laborious hand-lettering and with deserved success (see page 82). One has to admire his industry as illustrator no less than as writer. For me, the trouble with Pyle the artist is content rather than form. His work has been described by such adjectives as hearty, healthy, clean, cheery and honest;[3] but I have to confess myself unconvinced by his depiction of those merry old times which I suspect to have been somewhat less merry, and a good deal less wholesome, than Pyle's drawings would imply.

Book illustration is one thing; the picture-book, in which pictures play at least an equal and usually a leading part, is another. Although it has scattered precursors, the modern picture-book dates effectively from the last third of the nineteenth century, and owes as much to the British engraver and printer Edmund Evans (1826-1905) as to any individual artist. Colour printing — taking over gradually from the hand-tinting by squads of children which had been used in many children's books of the early nineteenth century — had been fairly common, if crude, since the 1840s. Evans brought it to as fine an art as was then possible, and in addition found artists whose work was worthy of his craftsmanship. The 'quality'

Drawing by Randolph Caldecott from *John Gilpin's Ride* (1878)

picture book in colour was his conception, and it was he who led the first three great picture-book artists – Walter Crane, Randolph Caldecott and Kate Greenaway – to work in this field.

Having discovered and interested the young Walter Crane, Evans produced for two successive London publishers from 1865 onwards a long series of Crane's 'toy books', or nursery picture books, mostly based on alphabets, Mother Goose rhymes, or fairy tales. Crane (1845-1915) was most successful as a designer and decorator of books; his style, highly composed and somewhat static, is seldom at its best when he uses strong colours or tries to show rapid action. Among his nursery books, the most appealing of those known to me is *The Baby's Opera* (1877), in which simple music for old nursery rhymes is worked into an overall design of gentle, somewhat mannered but pleasing elegance.

Randolph Caldecott (1846-86) was already an established artist when he was urged by Evans in the late 1870s to begin the series of picture-books by which he is now best known. He offers a strong contrast to Crane: his style is spare and wiry, and he is first-class in scenes of action. His *John Gilpin* (1878) is still the best of the many illustrated versions of Cowper's poem. Nobody else has matched Caldecott's picture of Gilpin in mid-ride, clinging desperately to the horse's mane as geese fly, almost audibly squawking, from under its hooves, dogs chase after it, and passers-by stare in bewilderment from the roadside. And Caldecott's rustic dancers in *Come Lasses and*

Lads (1884) look as if they might dance right out of the page.

As well as being picture-book artists, Crane and Caldecott were illustrators of other people's books, Crane being particularly associated with novels by Mrs Molesworth and Caldecott with Mrs Ewing.

Kate Greenaway (1846-1901) was the daughter of an engraver, and was a painstaking but only moderately successful freelance artist until in 1877 she took a set of drawings, accompanied by her own verses, to Edmund Evans, who decided at once to make a book from them. This was *Under the Window* (1878), and its success astonished everyone. Evans had boldly printed 20,000 copies to sell at six shillings — a large edition at what was then a high price. They were sold so

Drawing by Kate Greenaway from *The Pied Piper of Hamelin* (1888)

quickly that copies were changing hands at a premium before there was time to reprint. Kate Greenaway's name and style became almost instantly familiar, not only in Britain but in America and on the Continent of Europe. Her later work included a second book of her own verses, *Marigold Garden* (1885); a *Mother Goose* (1881), an edition of Ann and Jane Taylor's verse, *Little Ann and other poems* (1882-3), and a magnificent picture-book version of Browning's *Pied Piper of Hamelin* (1888).[4]

Kate Greenaway's verses are innocuous, ordinary, and of no significance away from the pictures; but the pictures are an endless delight – clear, fresh, innocent, individual. Anyone can recognize Kate Greenaway children. They are always cool, neat and self-possessed, and one is convinced that they will never get dirty or come to any harm. On one page of *Under the Window* three tiny children are rowing in a flooded field in what look like bathtubs. They are calm and happy, and obviously in no danger whatever; it is a sweet dream of childhood. The Greenaway costumes belong, with modifications, to the earlier part of the century. Miss Greenaway did not follow contemporary fashion in children's dress; it followed her. Her young ladies, in *The Language of Flowers* (1884) and elsewhere, are as lovely and innocent as her children. They obviously never need to blow their noses or perform any of the grosser physical functions. They are the immortals of the broad, smooth lawns and the rich flower-beds; it is unendingly late May, the trees are in bloom, the clear girlish laughter ripples out to eternity, and there is honey for tea forever.

Kate Greenaway often put quite large numbers of children into a picture; she had a fondness for arranging them in lines or clusters or in the patterns of play, and perhaps she had also a shrewd understanding that children love detail and enjoy illustrations that can be pored over rather than taken in at a glance. Palmer Cox (1840-1928) is not on the same artistic plane as Kate Greenaway, and his verse is dreadful doggerel, but his *Brownie* collections beginning with *The Brownies: Their Book* in 1887 and continuing for the next quarter-century, show an even more obvious grasp of the importance of detail. The Brownies – described as 'imaginary little sprites who are supposed to delight in harmless pranks and helpful deeds' – are multitudinous, busy and varied, always in perilous situations but never coming to any harm; and you can follow individual Brownies – monocled dude, kilted Scotsman, policeman with truncheon – from picture to picture through book

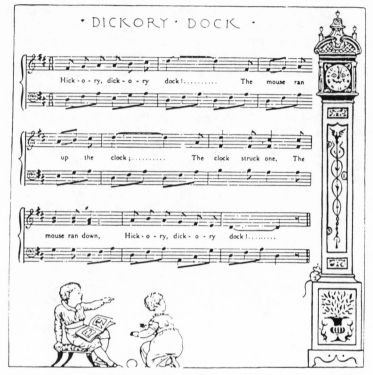

A page from *The Baby's Opera*, by Walter Crane

after book. They were highly popular in their day, and a few years ago made a welcome reappearance in paperback.

L. Leslie Brooke (1862-1940) was a genial humorous artist of strong appeal if no great subtlety, and was another who paid proper attention to detail. The jaunty animals who were entertained in *Johnny Crow's Garden* (1903) and at *Johnny Crow's Party* (1907) combined with crude but easily remembered rhymes to make these two books a pair of long-lived nursery favourites. *Johnny Crow's New Garden,* nearly thirty years later (1935) showed the lion 'with the very same tie on' and the other guests remarkably unchanged. Brooke's homely approach was effective with familiar tales and nursery rhymes, too; witness his Three Bears, with the Great Huge Bear and Middle Bear watching fondly as Little Small Wee Bear stands on his head; and his Little Pig sitting down contentedly if improbably to roast beef, with napkin tied round neck.

Helen Bannerman's *Story of Little Black Sambo* (1899) has become controversial in recent years. The question of 'racism' in books will be referred to later in this study. At this point *Little Black Sambo* must be mentioned as a picture-story book of scant artistic merit but of instant appeal to large numbers of small children. It has always seemed to me that the story rather than the pictures accounted for its success. The tale of Sambo, his fine clothes and the tigers has everything that is needed. It is ingeniously repetitive-with-differences; the small hero comes out on top, the conclusion is absurd but satisfying, and the whole thing is so intrinsically pictorial that it needs little help from the artist. Even with Mrs Bannerman's own crude illustrations it could not miss.

The outstanding writer and artist of picture-story books at this time was of course Beatrix Potter (1866-1943). The story of her life is well known: the lonely town child with a passion for natural history and a longing for the country; the still-isolated young woman who wrote the first version of *Peter Rabbit* in a letter to her ex-governess's child; the author who would have married her publisher against the wishes of her rich stuffy parents, had he not suddenly died; the creator over twelve years or so of a score of small masterpieces for small children. And then marriage at the age of 47, and the willing transformation of shy Miss Potter into the shrewd and increasingly crusty countrywoman Mrs Heelis.

There is something formidable and a little disconcerting about Mrs Heelis, who discouraged all curiosity among her compatriots, described an appreciative article about her work as an artist as 'great rubbish, absolute bosh!', and sent a 'somewhat acid' letter to Graham Greene when he wrote a critical essay on her books.[5] Yet the horny shell of Mrs Heelis can be seen as having grown protectively over the vulnerable Miss Potter. Among the letters of Beatrix Potter, one has always seemed to me to be extremely touching: the one written to Millie Warne, her would-have-been sister-in-law, in which she said that Jane Austen's *Persuasion* had always been a favourite with her, and that when Norman Warne proposed, 'I thought my story had come right, with patience and waiting, like Anne Elliot's did'.[6] (But Norman Warne died.) And it pleases me that in later years Mrs Heelis always had time for visiting Americans — partly because of what her biographer Margaret Lane calls 'the serious and intelligent American attitude towards children's literature'.[7] To a lady from Boston she wrote: 'I always tell nice Americans to send other nice Americans along'.[8]

Graham Greene's essay on Beatrix Potter[9] was written no doubt with tongue in cheek; his references to her 'vintage years in comedy' and 'the period of the great near-tragedies' are not to be taken too seriously; but behind his gentle satire there obviously lies a genuine respect for her work. Greene considered *The Roly-Poly Pudding* (1908), of which the title was later changed to *The Tale of Samuel Whiskers,* to be her masterpiece. But there seems no point in drawing up an order of precedence. Preferences among the best twelve or fifteen of the books are apt to be personal. The firm ring of the words, the precise composition and characterization of the drawings, the dry humour and the decisive and satisfying conclusions are common to them all. They differ in their individual nature but they are alike in excellence and they are all parts of a body of work that has a country-grown flavour and firmness.

Ideally, in a study of this kind, one would wish to deal adequately with the great children's magazines, whose heyday began in the 1860s. In the extremely small space available it is only possible to point out that the magazines offered enormous encouragement to good writing for children, and the thriving state of English-language children's literature during their best years owed a great deal to their influence. Among many others, America had the long-running *Youth's Companion,* founded in 1827, the short-lived but excellent *Riverside Magazine* (1867-70), *Our Young Folks* (1865-73) and Harper's *Young People* (1879-99). All of these had their distinguished contributors; but the magazine whose reputation outshone them all was *St Nicholas,* which began under the editorship of Mary Mapes Dodge in 1873.

Mrs Dodge (1831-1905) was an author of some talent — she wrote *Hans Brinker, or The Silver Skates* (1865), a respectable but by now time-tarnished story of childhood in Holland — and an editor of genius, with the twin gifts of discovering new writers and coaxing work out of established ones. The list of contributors to *St Nicholas* includes Louisa May Alcott, Thomas Bailey Aldrich, Frances Hodgson Burnett, Susan Coolidge, Emily Dickinson, Lucretia Hale (with the *Peterkin Papers,* in which the resourceful Lady from Philadelphia gave injections of common sense to a family much in need of it), Rudyard Kipling, Jack London, Howard Pyle and Mark Twain.

England could not match *St Nicholas,* but in its best days the *Boy's Own Paper,* founded in 1879, published work by R. M.

Ballantyne, G. A. Henty and Jules Verne, and all the school stories of Talbot Baines Reed. *Aunt Judy's Magazine* (1866-85) was initially edited by Mrs Margaret Gatty, the mother of Mrs Ewing; and most of Mrs Ewing's stories appeared in its pages. *Good Words for the Young* (1868-77) was edited for a time by George MacDonald and serialized *At the Back of the North Wind;* and *Young Folks,* which ran under a succession of different titles from 1876 to 1897, published Robert Louis Stevenson's *Treasure Island.*

The turnover of young readers is rapid; they grow up; and while this benefits a book, which can hope to find new readers and does not need to retain the old, it makes life very hard for a children's magazine. A magazine is constantly losing readers by natural wastage, and needs to run fast to stay in the same place.

The revered old magazines like *St Nicholas,* the *Boy's Own Paper* and the *Youth's Companion* survived the First World War, and had a nostalgic hold on the affections of older people; but they could not grip the rising generation in the radio, film and television age (which bore harder generally on magazines than books). They ran on gallantly if wearily for many years: the *Youth's Companion* until 1929, *St Nicholas* until 1939, the *Boy's Own Paper* until 1967; but they all failed in the end. Marianne Carus's *Cricket,* founded in 1973, has made the best attempt so far to carry on the torch.

In children's literature, the years leading up to the First World War were the last of the English ascendancy, already challenged by the growing amount of American talent. While England can still claim, in proportion to its population, to produce as many good writers as the United States, it is a smaller country and cannot expect to regain its old dominant position.

The last years of the old peace were rich years. More talent was going into children's books than ever before. Robert Louis Stevenson and his successors had raised the adventure story to a higher status than it had known before or has known since. Rudyard Kipling was at the peak of his powers in the last decade of the nineteenth century and the first of the twentieth; and he was a writer of international reputation among adults, not a 'mere' children's writer. E. Nesbit, also at her peak, had excelled in both family and fantasy stories. Kenneth Grahame had produced *The Wind in the Willows* in 1908, and Frances

Hodgson Burnett *The Secret Garden* in 1910. Walter de la Mare's first collections of poems had appeared. Edmund Evans and the great picture-book artists — Crane, Caldecott, Greenaway — had accomplished their revolution; and Beatrix Potter had already done all her best work.

It was a splendid array of talent. The Victorian-Edwardian era ended gloriously. After the war, nothing was quite the same.

From Kate Greenaway's *Marigold Garden*

PART THREE

1915-1945

13

Fantasy between the wars

IN BRITAIN especially, the enormous wound of the First World War took many years to heal. It was not only that (as C. Day Lewis put it) 'lost in Flanders by medalled commanders, the lads of the village are vanished away'.[1] Britain lost an appalling and disproportionate number of its best men — and also the children they would have had. And the psychological shock of the war was immense.

The effect was deeply felt in children's literature as elsewhere. The decade after the war was the dreariest since at least the middle of the nineteenth century. The loss of actual writers is of course incalculable. Walter de la Mare and John Masefield and A. A. Milne and Arthur Ransome survived the war; but we cannot know how many were killed who might have written works to compare with theirs. In the war years themselves, active service and paper shortage drastically cut down the amount of new writing and also left a backlog of old titles to be reprinted; afterwards there was a great expansion in quantity but a sad lack of quality. The 1920s in children's literature were a backward-looking time. Old books were reissued, the trade in cheap 'rewards' flourished exceedingly, and there was a huge output of second, third and tenth rate school and adventure stories.

A depressing feature of the decade in Britain was the general lack of interest in children's books. This was in sorry contrast to the United States, where rapid advances were taking place. Library work with children — pioneered by Caroline Hewins, Anne Carroll Moore and many others — had expanded greatly during the opening years of the new century, and by 1920 was an important and well-established part of public library service. Specialist training courses for children's librarians had been organized at the Pratt Institute in New York since 1898 and at Pittsburgh since 1900. The first children's editor was appointed by Macmillan of New York in 1919, and other American publishers followed in the next few years. The yearly Children's Book Week began in 1919. In 1922 Frederic Melcher presented, through the American Library Association, the first John Newbery Medal for the most distinguished contribution to American literature for children. In 1924 Anne Carroll Moore began to edit a weekly page of criticism of children's books in the *New York Herald Tribune*, and in the same year the specialist *Horn Book* magazine was founded in Boston. In emulating these developments, Britain lagged years behind.[2]

Producing a favourable environment for children's literature is not of course the same thing as producing children's literature itself. It takes time to have its effect, and even then may encourage the worthily second-rate more than the first-rate, which appears at its own will and not that of anybody else. American children's books of the twenties do not now look as impressive as one might have hoped for in the circumstances; and some of the early Newbery Medal winners, though still in print, strike one as embalmed books rather than living ones. But over the years both children and writers, inside and outside the United States, have cause to be thankful for American institutional support. Without it, many authors in more than one country would have had to decide whether they wished to write or to eat.

In England the best work of the post-war decade was mainly in poetry, or fantasy, or poetic fantasy. Of the decade's leading writers, Walter de la Mare and Eleanor Farjeon may be regarded above all as poets; but they also contributed much to children's literature in prose.

Walter de la Mare (1873-1956) left school when he was fourteen and worked for twenty years for an oil company before becoming a full-time writer. His life was uneventful and he only once left England. Before the war he had already written *The Three Mulla-Mulgars* (1910), later renamed *The Three Royal Monkeys,* a poetic animal-fairy-tale which has always had its devotees, though it is something of a minority taste. In the 1920s his stories began appearing, now in ones and twos and now in collections. *Broomsticks (1925)* was the most important collection. It contained, among much excellent material, the story of 'The Three Sleeping Boys of Warwickshire', which I believe to be the best of all modern short fairy-tales — for a fairy-tale it is, though it is set in the relatively recent past, a mere two or three hundred years ago. Old Noll, the miserly chimney-sweep, has three young apprentices and hates them bitterly because, beaten and half-starved though they are, they are still as blithe as the birds. One night he shuts their souls out from their bodies while they are at dreamplay in the moonlight; whereupon they fall into a fifty-three-year sleep which lasts until a young girl kisses their cold mouths and brings them back to life. It is a simple story but absorbing and beautifully told; and although it has familiar fairy-story ingredients it also has a dimension of human sympathy which the old folk-tales often lack. The best of de la Mare's tales were brought together in his *Collected Stories for Children* (1947).

Eleanor Farjeon (1882-1965) described her own books as 'a muddle of fiction and fact and fantasy and truth', and confessed that 'seven maids with seven brooms, sweeping for half a hundred years, have never managed to clear my mind of its dust of vanished temples and flowers and kings, the curls of ladies, the sighing of poets, the laughter of lads and girls'.[3] Her prose work for children mostly took the form of tales, and the quotation indicates its flavour more effectively than a brief description could do. *Martin Pippin in the Apple Orchard* (1921), a ring of romantic stories woven round the figure of the countryman who is also a wandering minstrel, was originally regarded as an adult book, but gravitated to the children's list in 1952. It then seemed well suited to the needs and tastes of young girls beginning to grow up. But the world has gone on turning, and for better or worse the Arcadia of Martin Pippin and the country maidens has come to seem far out of touch with the milieux of modern adolescence. *Martin Pippin in the Daisy Field* (1937) is an undoubted children's book and has worn better. It contains among others the happy tale of little Elsie Piddock, who skips for ever to save the children's playground. *The Little Bookroom* (1955) is Eleanor Farjeon's own choice from among the stories of many years, and is the best introduction to her work.

No English poetic fantasy is more poetic, or more fantastic, than Carl Sandburg's *Rootabaga Stories* (1922). And Sandburg (1882-1967) was not a European-orientated East Coast writer; his territory was the American heartland. The Rootabaga Country is where the railroad tracks change from straight to zigzag and the pigs have bibs on. It is a wild, imagined country; at the same time it is undoubtedly prairie country, wide and spacious. Sandburg's happy inconsequent stories are full of light and air, full of absurd characters like Gimme the Ax and Bimbo the Snip, Poker Face the baboon and Hot Dog the tiger. They are comic, inventive, repetitive, accumulative, and wonderful-sounding, clearly meant for reading aloud; and they evoke visual images too. The story of the White Horse Girl and the Blue Wind Boy, who set off together to find the place where the white horses come from and the blue winds begin, is a poem that has strayed into prose. The recurrent colours of the *Rootabaga Stories* are blue and silver: the blue and silver of a fine bright morning with a little light cloud. I am told they have been highly successful with modern American children of about eight to ten, especially when well read aloud. Hardly any British child can know them, but they are included in the *Sandburg Treasury* (1970), which became available in Britain.

The *Rootabaga Stories* are modern American fairy tales. There are also modern American folk tales about the more-than-lifesize heroes of pioneering days. These are true folk material in the sense that they were told aloud, heard, remembered, embellished and passed along by tough outdoor workers who often had little entertainment except that of telling the tales: loggers, cowboys, the men who pushed out the railheads. The stories began to reach print in children's books in the 1920s and 1930s. Esther Shephard, with *Paul Bunyan* (1924), was the first of several writers to record the astonishing feats of the great lumberjack; and in 1937 James Cloyd Bowman recounted some tall tales about *Pecos Bill, the Greatest Cowboy of All Time*. I do not know of any children's book featuring John Henry, the mighty Negro construction worker, 'born with a hammer in his hand', before Irwin Shapiro's *John Henry and the Double-Jointed Steam Drill* (1945). In 1965 Ezra Jack Keats made one of his best picture-books out of John Henry's achievements: *John Henry,* subtitled *An American Legend.*

The 'Doctor Dolittle' books of Hugh Lofting (1886-1947) were a fantasy that had its roots in Flanders mud; for Lofting served in the trenches in the First World War, and the idea of the doctor who learns animal languages came to him from his reflections on the part that horses were playing in the war.

If we made the animals take the same chances we did ourselves, why did we not give them similar attention when wounded? But obviously to develop a horse surgery as good as that of our Casualty Clearing Station would necessitate a knowledge of horse language.[4]

The famous doctor began in letters home to Lofting's children, and the dozen books which began with *The Story of Doctor Dolittle* in 1920 tell of his travels and adventures, in which he makes use of his communicative skills and other remarkable qualities, returning from time to time to his base

'It's a case of flat feet': Dr Dolittle diagnoses the problem of
a fox cub that cannot run fast enough for its own safety: a
drawing by Hugh Lofting from *Doctor Dolittle's Circus*

in the quiet English village of Puddleby-on-the-Marsh. The
Doctor's animal friends include Dab-Dab his duck-housekeeper,
Chee-Chee the monkey, Polynesia the parrot, and the memor-
able Pushmi-Pullyu with a head at each end.

Edward Blishen contrasted the Dolittle stories with 'classics
of perfection and completeness', and remarked that 'in their
rambling amplitude, their very unevenness, they are like life
itself, and children can live in them, in a most generous
sense'.[5] Lofting himself tired of Doctor Dolittle, and at one
stage tried to leave him on the moon, but like other writers
before him he was forced to relent and bring the departed
hero back. Dolittle is a character of profound innocence,
almost a saint; but he is a good man who, unlike many good
characters in fiction, remains lovable – partly because even a
child can perceive and smile at his unworldliness. The later
stories carry an increasing burden of Dolittle's (and Lofting's)
worries about where the world is going. In *Doctor Dolittle's
Return* (1933), for instance, we have the Doctor, back from the
moon, fearing that 'all life faces a losing game down here with

us', and preoccupied with ways of forming 'a new and properly balanced world'.

Hugh Lofting has been accused of being 'a white racist and chauvinist';[6] and undoubtedly there are parts of the Dolittle books that are now found offensive. Prince Bumpo, who is black and begs the Doctor to turn him white, and King Koko, who is usually either sucking a lollipop or using one as a quizzing-glass, have become notorious. Today it is all too evident that Lofting, who was born in England although he spent most of his adult life in the United States, shared the insensitivity of many Englishmen of his day to whom all foreigners were funny and those of a different colour were doubly funny. Lofting's lapses illustrate the extreme difficulty of escaping accepted attitudes, for he was far from being a crude imperialist, and he once wrote:

If we make children see that all races, given equal physical and mental chances for development, have about the same batting averages of good and bad, we shall have laid another very substantial foundation stone in the edifice of peace and internationalism.[7]

It is sad that a writer with such excellent intentions should have got himself into such posthumous trouble. I hope that in time Lofting will be forgiven, for assuredly there was no malice in this worried, sincere, well-meaning man. It is a rare individual who can rise above the general insensitivities of his own day, and none of us can tell what unsuspected sins we may be found guilty of in fifty years' time.

In Australia fantasy has often been attempted but has never been the most successful type of writing for children. The first notable Australian fantasy was published in 1918, and for many years was undoubtedly the best. This was *The Magic Pudding*, by Norman Lindsay (1879-1969); and it is a solid, strongly-flavoured fantasy whose recipe is (it seems to me) uniquely Australian. The pudding runs around on legs; he can be steak-and-kidney or boiled jam roll or apple dumpling, just as you wish; you can cut away at him for as long as you like and he will never get any less. Naturally he grumbles a bit at leading such a life; and at one point he sings in a very gruff voice:

> O who would be a puddin',
> A puddin' in a pot,
> A puddin' which is stood on
> A fire which is hot . . .
>
> I hope you get the stomach ache
> For eatin' me a lot.

> I hope you get it hot,
> You puddin'-eatin' lot.

The pudding belongs to Bunyip Bluegum and his friends Bill Barnacle the sailor and Sam Sawnoff the penguin. They have to defend him against professional pudding-snatchers, and that is what the story is all about. It is firmly related to the stomach (for which most children have a proper regard) and it is thickly stuffed with corny verses and nonstop knockabout humour.

The spectacular British success of the 1920s was scored by A. A. Milne's *Winnie-the-Pooh* (1926) and its sequel *The House at Pooh Corner* (1928). Like the Christopher Robin verses, the *Pooh* books have had their ups and downs in general esteem. In the early years they were much in vogue among adults. Later they were condemned by some as being smug, bourgeois and whimsical. But I have not heard this kind of comment recently, and I found when my own children were small that one of the pleasures of parenthood was that of reading the *Pooh* stories aloud and realizing afresh how good they were and how much they were enjoyed.

A. A. Milne was born in 1882, educated at Westminster and at Cambridge, and from 1906 to 1914 was on the staff of *Punch,* of which he became assistant editor. He fought in France during the war, and at the same time managed to write his early plays; his first big success was *Mr Pim Passes By* in 1920. Milne had married in 1913, and he records in his autobiography *It's Too Late Now* that in August 1920 his collaborator (i.e. his wife)

produced a more personal work. We had intended to call it Rosemary but decided later that Bill would be more suitable. However, as you can't be christened William — at least, we didn't see why anybody should — we had to think of two other names, two initials being necessary to ensure any sort of copyright in a cognomen as often plagiarised as Milne. One of us thought of Robin, the other of Christopher; names wasted on him who called himself Billy Moon as soon as he could talk and has been Moon to his family and friends ever since. I mention this because it explains why the publicity which came to be attached to Christopher Robin never seemed to affect us personally but to concern either a character in a book or a horse which we hoped at one time would win the Derby.[8]

Milne wrote all his four books for children — the two *Pooh* books and the two books of verses — between 1924 and 1928, when Christopher Robin (or Billy Moon) was small. In 1929 he

Pooh and Piglet tracking the Woozle: a drawing by E.H.Shepard
from *Winnie-the-Pooh* (1926)

made a play, *Toad of Toad Hall*, from *The Wind in the
Willows*: it is excellent Milne but doubtful Grahame, though
Grahame seems to have approved of it. Milne then decided he
had done all he wished to do in children's writing. He
continued for some time to be a successful playwright for
adults, and lived until 1956.

The characters in *Winnie-the-Pooh* and *The House at Pooh
Corner* are humanized toys rather than humanized animals.
They were the inhabitants of Billy Moon's nursery, and it was
Mrs Milne's idea to bring them to life. Pooh has only one

bearlike characteristic, which is that he likes honey. Piglet has one piggy characteristic, which is that he likes Haycorns. Otherwise the characterization is quite arbitrary: Tigger (the tiger) is bouncy, Eeyore the donkey is gloomy, Rabbit is an organizer, and so on; and none of these qualities has anything to do with animal nature. Of them all:

> Pooh is the favourite, of course, there's no denying it, but Piglet comes in for a good many things which Pooh misses, because you can't take Pooh to school without everybody knowing it, but Piglet is so small that he slips into a pocket, where it is very comfortable to feel him when you are not sure whether twice seven is twelve or twenty-two. Sometimes he slips out and has a good look in the inkpot, and in this way he has got more education than Pooh, but Pooh doesn't mind. Some have got brains and some haven't, he says, and there it is.[9]

The setting of the *Pooh* books is the Hundred-Acre Wood, a self-contained Arcadia, inconspicuously presided over by Christopher Robin, to whom the inhabitants can go for help at need as if to a grown-up. The books consist of a series of episodes, of which the recollection remains pleasurable after a score of readings: Pooh and Piglet trying to trap a Heffalump, for instance; and the Expotition to the North Pole; and Eeyore's birthday, when he gets a Useful Pot to put things in and also a burst balloon, being something to put in a Useful Pot; and the tracking of a Woozle round the spinney by its footprints in the snow. (This last story generates superior giggles in children, as the two silly animals go round and round the spinney discovering at each circuit that the Woozle has been joined by more companions.)

Apart from any nostalgic pleasure, the adult returning to the *Pooh* books is bound to appreciate the sheer grace of craftsmanship. Milne was a most accomplished professional writer. He was a happy lightweight, and used to say merely that he had the good fortune to *be* like that. In children's as in adult literature, the lightweight of true quality is a rare and welcome phenomenon. The *Pooh* stories are as totally without hidden significance as anything ever written – which is why they were such a perfect vehicle for the American Professor F. C. Crews's satire on the academic industry, *The Pooh Perplex* (1963). Professor Crews assembled a set of ponderous essays on various 'aspects' of Pooh by imaginary academic critics. Had he directed this battery on *The Wind in the Willows* his satire would have misfired, for there are indeed many layers of meaning to be found in that remarkable book. But for all his rotundity Pooh – bless him – is one-dimensional.

Two 'toy' stories that were contemporary with the *Pooh* books and survived alongside them for many years were *The Velveteen Rabbit* (1922) and *Poor Cecco* (1925) by Margery Williams Bianco (1881-1944). *The Velveteen Rabbit* is concerned with the magic by which toys become real – they become real when a child has loved them enough – but seems to me to be confusing at the end, when the Velveteen Rabbit, condemned to destruction for being 'a mass of germs', is transformed by a fairy into a living rabbit. This is a different kind of magic, and puts a different meaning on the phrase 'becoming real'. And there's a touch of sentimentality which, though not gross, is enough to flaw the book.

Poor Cecco is a better book than *The Velveteen Rabbit*. It is about a community of toys, living in a house and garden whose human inhabitants never appear and are clearly quite unimportant. Poor Cecco (we are not told why he is 'poor') is a wooden horse; there are also, among others, Bulka and Tubby, the much-worn rag puppies; Gladys and Virginia May, the rather affected young-lady dolls; and the mean and greedy Money-Pig. And when Poor Cecco and Bulka go off to see the world and have adventures, they come back with a new member of the family, resourceful wooden Jensina (whose shoes are very comfortable because they're painted on her feet). These toys, like Pooh and his friends, had their origins in the toys of the author's own child. They are, I think, more like toys and less like people than the inhabitants of the Hundred Acre Wood; they move and talk as one might expect toys to move and talk, and as a child might pretend they could. They are, so to speak, very *lifelike* toys, and as easy to love as real ones.

Almost at the opposite pole from the 'toy' fantasy of the Milne and Bianco books is John Masefield's *The Midnight Folk* (1927), which is a great seething cauldron of magic and adventure. Masefield (1878-1967) ran away to sea as a boy, did various humble jobs in America, and returned to England to be a journalist and writer. He was Poet Laureate from 1930 until his death, and wrote many poems and stories about the sea. *The Midnight Folk* may be regarded as his first children's book, though his adventure stories, like those of Anthony Hope, Rider Haggard and John Buchan, belong to the old tradition which drew no line between the reading of young people and adults.

The hero of *The Midnight Folk* is a boy named Kay Harker, who lives a lonely and rather wretched life in a country house, looked after by a governess, a cook and a maid. His black cat Nibbins, who has been a witch's cat, draws him into a quest to recover the treasure of Santa Barbara, which was entrusted to his great-grandfather Captain Harker and was never seen again. The quest is conducted in opposition to a coven of witches led by one Abner Brown, whose grandfather was a mutineer on Captain Harker's ship. It is a fine, full-blooded story which moves at a great pace and compels belief. Among the characters is the dreadful but to my mind enchanting old woman Miss Piney Trigger, daughter of one of the mutineers, whom Kay flies to see on a magic horse. He finds her sitting up in bed:

Propped up by pillows, a wicked old woman in a very gay dressing-gown was reading a sprightly story, at which she was laughing. Beside her on the table was a bottle of champagne: she sipped a glass of the wine from time to time. In her mouth was a long cigarette-holder containing a lighted cigarette.

Before long this shocking old soul is singing:

'I'll live to the age of a hundred and eight,
And then I'll go courting to find me a mate;
I'll live to the age of a hundred and nine,
And finish my bottle whenever I dine;
I'll live to the age of a hundred and ten,
When I'll mount on my horse and go courting again.

'Deuce take these lily-livered times! I'll have a devilled bone to my breakfast as long as I've a gum in my mouth. Cheer up, my lads, there's shot in the locker still.'

Eight years later, Masefield followed up *The Midnight Folk* with *The Box of Delights,* of which Kay Harker is again the hero, though now a few years older. This is another rich mixture of magic and adventure, making ingenious use of the time dimension.

Two American fantasies for younger children which both appeared in 1930 were Elizabeth Coatsworth's *The Cat who Went to Heaven* and Anne Parrish's *Floating Island.* Elizabeth Coatsworth's book, which won the Newbery Medal, was not published in England until 1949, but then established itself successfully and went through several impressions. This story of the poor artist, his housekeeper, and the little cat Good Fortune which finds the blessing of the Buddha has a delicate, catlike air, and captures exactly the oriental spirit — at least as we in the West conceive it to be. Into the narrative are woven, neatly and intricately, a series of Chinese legends. It is also interspersed with the 'songs of the housekeeper', which unfortunately are insipid stuff. They could have been plain and homely without being as feeble as this:

> Dear Pussy, you are white as milk,
> Your mouth's a blossom, your coat's silk
> What most distinguished family tree
> Produced so great a rarity?

There is a bathetic echo here of Blake's *Tyger:* 'What immortal hand or eye Could frame thy fearful symmetry?'

Floating Island is about the shipwrecked Doll family. The island is so named by Mr Doll, who doesn't quite understand the difference between islands and ships. Having survived many adventures, the family decide they must look for rescue, because 'dolls can never be happy for very long unless children are playing with them.' The book is dated by its determinedly bright, talking-down-to-the-children tone of voice; but it is full of ideas, and an ingenious use of (skippable) footnotes offers a poetry of sea and sand, flowers and fishes to those who find it acceptable.

Fantasy however was not an important part of American writing for children in the 1930s, and even in England it slipped back a little from the leading position it had held in the previous decade. *Mary Poppins* (1934) was the first of a series by P. L. Travers which has many devotees, especially in America. The magic nursemaid with the turned-up nose and the flowery hat, who can slide *up* the banisters, to cite the least of her achievements, was memorably portrayed by the artist Mary Shepard, and afterwards improbably glamorized in a long loud film version. The humour is partly that of paradox – that a mere nursemaid should be so godlike in her powers and attitudes – but mostly comes from a comic and inventive use of magic. Mary Poppins is clearly not a contemporary figure, and her setting – a supposedly hard-up suburban household which nevertheless manages to employ cook, housemaid and gardener as well as Mary Poppins herself – now seems as remote as Samarkand. The American popularity of these books may owe something to, and may even propagate, illusions about English domestic life.

Alison Uttley's *A Traveller in Time* (1939) has proved itself a stayer, going through many reprints. It tells of the experiences of a young girl, Penelope Taberner, at Thackers, an ancient farmhouse in Derbyshire; a foreword makes it clear that the setting is that of the author's own childhood and suggests that she had similar experiences. In fantasy (or perhaps in dream; the distinction here is slight) Penelope slips in and out of a past time: that of the imprisoned Mary Queen of Scots. She becomes involved in the Babington plot to free the Queen, but knows from the history books that it must fail. The story as told doesn't build up much tension — perhaps for the very reason that we already know the outcome of the conspiracy. The positive quality of the book is a profound and loving sense of place, and of the endurance of that place in time, as Penelope/Alison dreams her way back and forth between Thackers then and Thackers now. The farmhouse as she knows it in her own lifetime has long absorbed that ancient upset, and remains safe, serene, the warm and perfect place where honest country folk wait to welcome you home.

Patricia Lynch published *The Turf-Cutter's Donkey* in 1934, and also wrote many Irish tales in which magic is hardly separable from everyday life; *My Friend Mr Leakey*, by J. B. S. Haldane (1937), was an ingenious mixture of magic and science; *The Ship That Flew*, by Hilda Lewis (1939), carried modern children into the distant past. The most remarkable fantasy of the 1930s, however, was J. R. R. Tolkien's *The Hobbit* (1937). When he wrote *The Hobbit,* Tolkien was Professor of Anglo-Saxon at Oxford, an authority on Beowulf and the northern sagas; and some years later he wrote a saga of his own, *The Lord of the Rings* (1954-5), which interlocks at a crucial point with *The Hobbit.*

Professor Tolkien did not believe that fairy-story (which he defined in a way that would include his own books) should be specially associated with children:

If fairy-story as a kind is worth reading at all it is worthy to be written for and read by adults. They will, of course, put more in and get more out than children can. Then, as a branch of a genuine art, children may hope to get fairy stories fit for them to read and yet within their measure; as they may hope to get suitable introductions to poetry, history and the sciences.[10]

This last sentence seems to show where Tolkien would have placed *The Hobbit*: it is 'a branch of a genuine art' and at the same time an introduction to wider realms of fantasy which include *The Lord of the Rings*. In style and manner *The Hobbit* is undoubtedly a children's book, though adult readers are not excluded. *The Lord of the Rings* belongs to general rather than children's literature, though children in turn are not excluded. Hobbits are little people about half our height (a large hobbit can ride a small pony). As described in *The Hobbit,* they are

inclined to be fat in the stomach; they dress in bright colours (chiefly green and yellow); wear no shoes, because their feet grow natural leathery soles and thick warm brown hair like the stuff on their heads (which is curly); have long clever brown fingers, good-natured faces, and laugh deep fruity laughs (especially after dinner, which they have twice a day when they can get it).

Bilbo Baggins is a peace-loving hobbit who has no wish to be a hero; all he wants is to stay quietly at home; but he is persuaded to try to destroy the dragon Smaug, who guards an ill-gotten treasure in a great cavern in a hillside, and who terrorizes the people near by. Bilbo wins in the end, because although he is peaceable by nature he has great courage and persistence.

Tolkien revised *The Hobbit* after World War II to make it fit in better with *The Lord of the Rings.* The most memorable chapter is one called 'Riddles in the Dark', in which Bilbo encounters the loathsome creature Gollum on the shores of an underground lake, and emerges with the ring which Gollum had cherished as his 'birthday present' and his 'precious'. In *The Fellowship of the Ring* (first of the three parts of *The Lord of the Rings*) the importance of this incident becomes clear. The ring is a great ring of power, the Master-ring, the One; and it was made by Sauron, the Dark Lord:

> One Ring to rule them all, One Ring to find them,
> One Ring to bring them all and in the darkness bind them
> In the Land of Mordor where the Shadows lie.

To prevent Sauron from recovering the ring and dominating all with his evil power, Bilbo's nephew Frodo must cast it into the Cracks of Doom in Orodruin, the Fire-mountain; that is the matter of *The Lord of the Rings.* Professor Tolkien denied that it had any inner meaning; it is a story. It is very long (though Tolkien said it was too short[11]) and requires of the reader a deliberate suspension of our normal time-scale, rather like the mental adjustment required in order to read a long medieval poem. You must put out of your mind any thought of being in a hurry.

The Lord of the Rings has been a prolonged success with adult and perhaps above all with student audiences. One of the most common graffiti in the English-speaking world is FRODO LIVES. And a few years ago you could buy in the United States buttons which said: TOLKIEN IS HOBBIT-FORMING.

14

History and brass tacks

THE BEST American fiction for children between the wars ran largely to historical and period stories. A high proportion of these, naturally, related to America's own past. Favourite themes were European settlement of the East Coast, the War of Independence, and the drive to the West; and the points of view — naturally again in view of the authors' backgrounds, for which they were not responsible — tended to be those of the white Anglo-Saxon. Cornelia Meigs's *Master Simon's Garden* (1916) was the forerunner of much that was to come. The garden planted by Simon Redpath in a New England village is obviously symbolic of a colony in the New World; as Master Simon says, 'I have planted a garden here in the wilderness, and I must abide to see what sort of fruit it bears.' At the same time the garden represents a belief in love and beauty, in contrast to the surrounding wilderness of bleak religious intolerance. Using Simon Redpath's garden as a link, the story moves on through several generations, and the tone at the end is inspirational; the author declares that 'each generation has something new to add, some record of danger faced, of hardship endured, of work well done for the good of all.'

Master Simon's Garden — high-minded, painstaking, and just a shade dull — was a long way distant in spirit from the period adventure stories, set in the age of sail, of Charles Boardman Hawes (1889-1923). Rich-textured and eventful, crammed with swash and buckle, *The Mutineers* (1920) and *The Dark Frigate* (1923) can now be seen to be late examples of the high adventure story as practised by Robert Louis Stevenson and others at the end of the nineteenth and start of the twentieth centuries. The tradition they represented was a more robust and red-blooded one than that which *Master Simon's Garden* was helping to initiate; but the future lay with the literary successors of Miss Meigs. The feebler productions of the twenties and thirties have by now of course faded away from memory and from the library shelves; those that have survived have done so through vigour and vitality rather than good intentions.

Rachel Field's *Hitty, Her First Hundred Years* (1929)

presents, through the eyes of a doll, an American historical panorama. Hitty, made 'with a pleasant expression' out of mountain-ash wood in Maine in whaling days, survives a century of change and adventure to finish up, with plenty of good years still ahead of her, in a New York antique shop. Hitty was (and I presume still is) a real doll, found in a shop in Greenwich village, and was present at the award of the Newbery Medal to her author. Rachel Field (1894-1942) was poet, playwright and artist, and wrote the adult novel *All This and Heaven, Too.* Her books for children include, besides *Hitty*, the historical novel *Calico Bush* (1931), which describes a year in the life of a French girl bound as servant to a family from Massachusetts settling in Maine in the mid eighteenth century.

A move from Massachusetts to open up new lands in Maine is the underlying theme also of *Away Goes Sally* (1934): the first of a series of five books by Elizabeth Coatsworth. A quarrel between Uncle Joseph, who wants to go, and Aunt Nannie, who insists on staying put, is ingeniously resolved when Uncle Joseph builds a house on runners, which he gives to Nannie so that she may 'travel to the district of Maine and yet never leave your own fire'. And the substance of the book is the journey (based on fact) through white winter landscapes to Maine. The book excels in its description of country life and ways, and manages at times to convey a most satisfying serenity. In the second book, *Five Bushel Farm* (1939), a new house is built; and the later ones show Sally's horizons expanding as she grows up. Miss Coatsworth's *Here I Stay* (1938) once more has a Maine background; it is about an early nineteenth-century girl who stays on, after her father's death, on the land they have farmed together. This is a story of loneliness, danger, courage and inner resource, and it is unashamedly aristocratic in feeling; its heroine is of no common clay. The book was published in Britain, better late than never, thirty-four years after its first appearance; and Leon Garfield, reviewing it in the *Guardian* with tongue gently in cheek, described it as 'a dignified, beautiful book that I recommend heartily to dignified, beautiful girls'. It was in fact originally written as an adult novel.

The eight books by Laura Ingalls Wilder (1867-1957) which began with *Little House in the Big Woods* (1932) and concluded with *These Happy Golden Years* (1943) look westward with the pioneering Ingalls family. They follow Laura's early life from a child of not yet five to her marriage at eighteen to

Almanzo Wilder. The series is fiction only because it is shaped and distanced by the third-person narration and is told in the manner of story rather than autobiography. Everything it describes actually happened; not even the names are changed. It gives a picture of a simple, hard and extraordinarily happy life in the third quarter of the last century.

The Ingallses, moving westward from Wisconsin through Minnesota to South Dakota, are poor in the sense that they have only basic possessions and hardly any money, but they are rich in everything that really matters; and the books make it clear without ever bothering to spell it out that happiness depends hardly at all on what you own. Laura's doll, when she is a little girl of four, is only a corncob wrapped in a handkerchief. It is a marvellous thing to be given a rag doll for Christmas; and this same rag doll, called Charlotte, is carefully packed in Laura's trunk when she marries, fourteen years later.

Life in the big woods, on the prairie, on the banks of Plum Creek, and by the shores of Silver Lake, is adventurous and yet safe, because Pa Ingalls is always there, able to make or mend or manage anything, knowing just how to cope with a bear or a blizzard, and finding time in the evening to sing and play his fiddle; because Ma is there, too, able to create a home from the most unpromising materials. The author understands how every job about the house and farm is done, and can describe it in a clear and absorbing way. One of the eight books, *Farmer Boy* (1933), leaves the Ingalls family to look at the childhood of Almanzo, whom Laura will marry. Almanzo's father is a prosperous farmer in northern New York State, and the Wilders' life is a good deal less elemental than the Ingallses'; but 'boughten stuff' is still the exception. What you need you make. Almanzo's clothes come from the backs of his father's sheep; it is Mother who dyed the wool for his coat, Mother who wove and shrank the cloth and made it up.

The best of all the books is *The Long Winter* (1940), which tells how the Ingalls family survive through month after month, blizzard after blizzard, on open prairie with no trains getting through and no supplies.

Even after Laura was warm she lay awake listening to the wind's wild tune and thinking of each little house in town, alone in the whirling snow with not even a light from the next house shining through. And the little town was alone on the wide prairie. Town and prairie were lost in the wild storm which was neither earth nor sky, nothing but fierce winds and a blank whiteness.

They come close to starvation; eat coarse bread made from wheat ground in a coffee mill; make sticks of twisted hay for the fire; become thin, pale, lethargic. Two young men come to the rescue by driving through the snow in search of a lone farmer who still has wheat. At long long last Laura hears the Chinook, the wind of spring. The train gets through and they celebrate Christmas in May.

Like the other books, but more deeply and impressively, *The Long Winter* is about family solidarity, the warmth of love opposed to the hostile elements. The story intensifies until at last there is the one enemy, winter; the one issue, survival. The writing is clear, plain, and as good as bread.

Carol Ryrie Brink's *Caddie Woodlawn* (1935) looks westward, too. A Newbery medal winner which was reprinted more than thirty times in its first thirty years, it is subtitled *A Frontier Story*. It covers a year in the life of Caddie – aged eleven at the start – who runs wild with her brothers when she is not helping around the Wisconsin farm. Most of the book narrates everyday incidents, but there are excitements too: when a prairie fire threatens the schoolhouse and when there are fears of an Indian massacre. As with *Master Simon's Garden,* the climax is inspirational. Caddie's father has the chance of inheriting a title and estates in England, but only if he will renounce America. (The author seems not to have known that a title cannot be bequeathed on conditions, or indeed bequeathed at all.) The decision is made by family vote to turn this opportunity down, and we leave Caddie philosophizing in the golden light of late afternoon. 'Her face was turned to the west. It was always to be turned westward now, for Caddie Woodlawn was a pioneer and an American.'

Esther Forbes's *Johnny Tremain* (1943), set in Boston at the start of the Revolutionary War, also has its inspirational note: 'We fight, we die, for a simple thing. Only that a man can stand up.' Unlike *Caddie Woodlawn,* it is a true historical novel, concerned with actual historical events; and it seems to me (though not for this reason) that it has true classic quality. I have the impression that the author may even have known she was writing a classic; for *Johnny Tremain* has an air of absolute sureness and solidity; like one of its redoubtable New Englanders it knows where it is going and knows it will be treated with respect.

The story is of a young apprentice silversmith, prevented by injury from following his craft, who becomes involved with the organizers of the rebel movement. Johnny plays a minor, quite believable rôle in the rising, by carrying messages and gathering intelligence from British officers and their servants. He does not take part in the actual fighting, and is no standard 'young hero'. Cocky at the start in 'the pride of his power', he has to be taken down a peg; but he matures in the course of the story, which takes him from the ages of fourteen to sixteen.

A feature of the book is its strong pictorial quality. The best set pieces not merely are colourful but have a powerful sense of historical occasion, as in the description of the 'great scarlet dragon' of the British brigade, seen first with its head resting on Boston Common, and later marching off on its thousands of feet. The book's main fault is a slight lack of cohesion between its two components: the personal story of Johnny, the smart apprentice whose expectations are dashed by injury, and the broad general subject of the rebellion. The first few chapters might be the start of quite a different kind of book. But the strengths far outweigh this weakness. And there is a fine sense of fair play in the recognition that men of all persuasions are good, bad and indifferent; in the willing acknowledgement that the crowds who sullenly watch the scarlet dragon are all Englishmen, fighting for English liberty.

English historical novels of the inter-war years seem, in retrospect, unexciting. The one lively innovation was made by Geoffrey Trease when, as a young man, he introduced the radical, 'committed' historical story. *Bows Against the Barons* (1934) presents Robin Hood as a leader of the people against their oppressors. The first chapter is headed, sarcastically, 'Merrie England', and opens with a peasant lad being lashed by a fat-bellied bailiff and then dunned for tithes by a beady-eyed priest. 'The masters,' readers are told, 'were the masters. The peasants must obey and be whipped and work again, till death brought time for resting.' And when treachery brings Robin Hood to his death, a follower spits savagely, 'So they got him in the end. They always do.' *Comrades for the Charter*, published in the same year, is about the abortive working-class Chartist campaign of 1839, a year 'dark with the misery of the people, starving upon tiny wages to make a few rich men even richer'.

There is no law of literature to say that a historical novel must be fair to all sides; but the best ones usually are (which does not mean that they have to be neutral). The breadth of mind and sensitivity of perception needed to write a good historical novel can hardly coexist with narrow prejudice. Putting the early Trease books beside *Johnny Tremain*, one

cannot help seeing how they suffer from their naive partisan-
ship. But Trease has (rightly, I think) allowed them to reappear
virtually unchanged in later editions, while admitting that 'if I
were writing *Bows Against the Barons* now, I would write it
rather differently'.[1]

By the time he wrote *Cue for Treason* (1940), his best novel
up to that time, Trease was less concerned with the heavy-
handed punching home of a message. *Cue for Treason* opens
in Cumberland with a popular movement against enclosures,
but soon shifts by way of a company of strolling players to
Shakespeare's London. The hero, Peter Brownrigg, becomes an
actor and makes friends with Kit Kirkstone, a girl who is
pretending to be a boy in order to play girls' parts. Together
they help to foil a plot against the Queen's life. It is all richly
improbable; but it is a strong, exciting story, and rich
improbability can be more nourishing than thin verisimilitude.

Geoffrey Trease's new-style historical novels reflected in part
a wider down-to-brass-tacks approach which − surprisingly,
perhaps − was as evident in England as the United States. In
Britain it began with Arthur Ransome's *Swallows and Amazons*
series, starting in the early 1930s. Ransome did not write the
kind of story we now look on as 'realistic'; but, unlike the hack
writers and some of the literary fantasists of the previous
decade, he did write seriously and without condescension
about the real lives of real children. His books gave a new
direction and impetus to English children's writing.

Arthur Ransome (1884-1967) was the son of a university
professor, went to school at Rugby, and left to work in a
publisher's office. Later he became a special correspondent
successively of the old *Daily News* and *Manchester Guardian,*
and travelled to many parts of the world, including Russia and
China. He was also a writer of books and essays − it did not
please him to settle into a fixed job − and he had been a
published author for a quarter of a century when *Swallows
and Amazons* appeared. That was in 1930, when he was forty-
six years old.

Ransome was an open-air man, and for all his travels he was
as happy in the Lake District or East Anglia as anywhere else.
He loved boats and fishing, and he loved to be on holiday. The
Swallows and Amazons books are all about holidays. They are
also books about the children's own activities: grown-ups are
kept firmly in the background, with the partial exception of a

Drawing by Arthur Ransome for his own *Swallows and Amazons* (1930)

favourite uncle, 'Captain Flint', who apparently was modelled on Ransome himself.

There are twelve *Swallows and Amazons* stories; they appeared over a period of eighteen years, from 1930 to 1947, but the timespan they cover in the characters' lives is only about five years. There are three main sets of characters. First there are the Walker children – John, Susan, Titty and Roger – whose father is in the Navy. The Walkers are the Swallows, so named from the sailing dinghy of which they have the use. Then there are the Amazons — also named after their boat — who are Nancy Blackett and her younger sister Peggy. Finally there are the Two Ds, Dick and Dorothea Callum, who enter the series at the fourth story, *Winter Holiday* (1933).

Eight of the twelve books are set either in the Lake District or East Anglia, and deal in a practical way with the kind of adventures that children lucky enough to have boats and trusting parents might reasonably expect to have. Two books, *Peter Duck* (1932), and *Missee Lee* (1941), stick out from the rest of the series; they are exotic, rip-roaring and improbable and are set in distant waters. These are supposed to be stories invented by the Swallows and Amazons themselves, as distinct from the ones that 'really' happened: that is, there are two separate fictional planes, and *Peter Duck* and *Missee Lee* are more fictional than the rest. In *We Didn't Mean to Go to Sea* (1937) the Walkers drift out to sea from Harwich in a friend's cutter and finish up by sailing it to Holland. Ransome was so anxious to get his facts right that he carried out this man-oeuvre himself. The last book of all is *Great Northern?* (1947), in which all the children and 'Captain Flint' take part, and in which a pair of rare diving birds found nesting in the Hebrides are defended against an unscrupulous egg-collector.

With the Lake District books especially, I suspect that the main appeal to children must be that of identification: of imagining oneself to be among this fortunate group who can actually sail dinghies on Windermere and spend nights camping on an island in the middle of the lake. The author's attention to detail is a great help here. He explains so authoritatively how everything was done — whether it was a matter of seamanship or pitching camp or catching trout or cookery — that the reader is convinced that it actually happened, and almost that he or she was there at the time.

The values of the *Swallows and Amazons* series are such as to meet with the approval of conscientious middle-class parents. There is a clear — and to most such people a welcome — preference for country over town, and for manpower or wind-power over mechanization. It is entirely appropriate that these decent and sensible books should have been written by a stalwart of the old *Manchester Guardian*. Yet in some ways their scope is limited. Faced with a million words about the Walker children and their friends, we may wonder if they could really be so consistently right-minded; we may wish we could see them in a living relationship with their parents, instead of having the parents mainly as understanding figures in the background; we may even wish they were not always on holiday.

Ransome seems in fact to have deliberately avoided any serious approach to problems of personal relationship. 'Captain Flint' as a benevolent uncle is a very simple figure; the Blacketts' dreadful Great Aunt belongs strictly to fiction. The older children, though well into their teens before the series ends, maintain a sexless comradeship which does not quite accord with the facts of adolescence. And on the whole there are rather few insights; rather few of those moments when the reader is pulled up in sudden awareness that life is richer or stranger than he had realized.

Many others of the most interesting books of the thirties were, like Ransome's, about families and their real-life activities; and enormous pains were taken to get the facts exactly right. Noel Streatfeild (1895-1986), who wrote perceptively and often about family life, published her first children's book, *Ballet Shoes,* in 1936. This was virtually the beginning of a new genre, the 'career novel', and Miss Streatfeild followed it up with books which had tennis, the theatre, films and skating as their backgrounds. All were based on detailed personal research, and so was *The Circus is Coming* (1938), her best-known and possibly her best pre-war book. In it, two children, Peter and Santa, gradually fit themselves into the super-family of the circus.

Eve Garnett, in *The Family from One-End Street* (1937), wrote about characters who belonged frankly to the urban working class. Jo Ruggles is a dustman and his wife Rosie a washerwoman; they have seven children and they live in a small old terrace house near the town centre. The book consists of a series of homely episodes from their daily life. Lily Rose, the eldest child, helps with the washing and burns a petticoat; Kate, the second, wins a scholarship to the grammar school and loses her precious hat; James stows away on a barge and nearly gets loaded into the hold of a sea-going ship. Mr Ruggles finds some money, is honest and gets a reward; and this leads to the final episode, a set-piece in which the whole family goes to London on a Bank Holiday outing.

There is a warm sense of family solidarity which is the most attractive characteristic of the book and may account for its long-lasting popularity with children. Nevertheless it seems to me to be too condescending to be altogether commendable. Mr and Mrs Ruggles are seen from above and outside. Even their names, and the choice of their occupations as dustman and washerwoman, make them seem slightly comic. People from higher up the social scale are terribly nice to the Ruggleses; and the Ruggleses know their place.

Ruth Sawyer's Newbery Medal-winning *Roller Skates* (1936) now gives an adult reader a similar sense of unease to that engendered by *The Family from One-End Street*, although in this case the heroine is at the other side of the social divide. Lucinda, at ten, has been left for a year in New York while her parents are in Europe. Skating around the city, she makes friends with Mr Gilligan the cab-driver and Patrolman M'Gonegal and Tony the son of the Italian fruit-stall man. This shows how democratic she is. But Lucinda has it both ways, because she is also a lady. At the end of the book she is a bridesmaid at a wedding, and the bride whispers in her ear: 'I think you're going to grow up to be someone rather distinguished some day. I'm going to be proud to remember always that you were one of my bridesmaids.' Lucinda is high-spirited, friendly, affectionate, responsive, everything; in a different way she is almost as perfect as Elsie Dinsmore.

Elizabeth Enright (1909-68) made her name with *Thimble Summer* (1938), another Newbery winner. It is a slight, episodic story of a girl's summer on a mid-Western farm. Contemporary in setting at the time it was written, the book has motor-cars in it, and a fair with a Ferris wheel (which, as you might expect from a fictional Ferris wheel, gets stuck); but the life it describes is still far from cosseted, and occasionally recalls the *Little House* books. The heat and dust of the Wisconsin farm stay in the memory more than Garnet Linden's actual adventures, and there are many small, precise touches, as when Garnet gets home to the farm after an outing and kicks her shoes off: 'the dust was soft as velvet under her feet, and she could feel each one of her toes rejoicing.' In *The Saturdays* (1940), Miss Enright introduced the Melendy family, about whom she later wrote three more books. Living in New York City, where an allowance of fifty cents a week doesn't go far, the Melendy children form the Independent Saturday Afternoon Adventure Club and pool their resources, so that each child in turn can 'do something really good'. And the resulting adventures have far-reaching and pleasant consequences.

There is a confusing similarity of name between Elizabeth Enright and Eleanor Estes, both of whom started to write family stories at about the same time. Even the names of their fictional families begin with the same initial. Mrs Estes is above all the author of *The Moffats* (1941), *The Middle Moffat* (1942) and *Rufus M* (1943). Both writers seem happier with the episodic, loosely-linked chain of stories than with the fully-structured novel; both are good at capturing the exact 'feel' of everyday life. In *The Moffats,* nine-year-old Janey reflects that her big sister Sylvie never plays cops and robbers any more,

and some day she would probably get married. Then who would take care of her chilblains and sing her to sleep, Janey wondered, giving the stone a terrific kick which lodged it between a tree and a fence.

She stopped and worked at it with her toe. Finally it bounded out and she kicked it hard straight in front of her.

'Besides,' she thought, 'nothing ever divides into threes's well's fours.'

The Estes style is simpler, more (apparently) artless than Enright's; the child's eye at the centre of the story is more evident; and it is notable that the point of view is almost always that of the younger members of the Moffat family, Janey and her small brother Rufus. While all suggestions about reading ages must be tentative, one would expect the Melendy stories to appeal to somewhat older children — ten up, perhaps — than the Moffats, who can be appreciated very satisfactorily by eight and nine year olds.

Robert McCloskey's *Homer Price* (1943) is homely and episodic, too, but is in a different tradition: that of the Tall Tale. Homer lives about two miles outside Centerburg, in the Midwest, where Route 56 meets Route 56A; his father owns a tourist camp and gas station, and Homer does odd jobs around the place. So far, so credible. But the six stories that make up the book are wild as well as hilarious. Homer and pet skunk Aroma capture a gang of robbers; Homer and friends meet the Super-Duper from the comics and find he can't even get his car out of a ditch; the doughnut machine at Uncle Ulysses' lunch-room just won't stop making doughnuts; Uncle Telemachus and the Sheriff, competing for the hand of Miss Terwilliger, amass what are probably the two biggest balls of string in the history of the world. McCloskey's own jaunty drawings capture the spirit of the thing exactly; and he went on to write *Centerburg Tales* in 1951, introducing the master tall-taleteller Grampa Hercules.

Homer, unfortunately, has not established himself in England; perhaps he is too American. And perhaps Richmal Crompton's William is too English to cross the Atlantic successfully in the other direction. The thirty-odd *William* books, beginning with *Just William* in 1922, were at their best in the 1920s and 1930s, although new ones continued to appear until their author's death in 1969 at the age of 78. Miss Crompton did not set out to write for children, but was not the first or last author to see her work find its own place in the children's list. William was promptly adopted by his contemporaries, perhaps because he was the daredevil that every small boy likes to think himself: always getting into scrapes, and often scoring off the grown-ups in the process of getting out of them. The *William* stories offer to young readers a happy blend of identification and condescension; they can at the same time imagine themselves to be William and yet see him from the outside as a small boy doing ridiculous and laughable things. William in fact is a most effective character – though not particularly lifelike, for no real boy could have his mixture of imagination and eloquence with extreme naivety.

The first few *William* books – those written in the 1920s and early 1930s – have a good deal of merit, and it would be wrong to put them on a par with long-running sequences which have no merit at all. Later the author's invention began to flag, and the adult characters (never her strongest point) grew sketchier and less convincing. But William kept going. Born at the age of eleven, he remained eleven for all the forty-seven years of his life. Never did a boy's twelfth year hold so many birthdays, so many Christmases, so many unwilling visits to aunts, so many tangles with beery tramps or eccentric spinsters, so many ingenious schemes gone so far awry, so many reluctant washings of so dirty a face. Five words will suffice for William's obituary notice. He had a full life.

Realism of the rougher kind was not common in children's books of the inter-war years. There was a prevailing feeling that this was something that ought not to be inflicted on children. One genre in which harsh facts of life were bound to emerge, however, if the writer was honest, was the naturalistic animal story. The Canadian Roderick Haig-Brown (1908-76), in the preface to *Ki-yu: a Story of Panthers* (1934; British title *Panther*) went out of his way to meet criticism of the 'bloody and cruel' killings scattered through the pages of his book. Haig-Brown pointed out that 'no wild animal is cruel, or kind either for that matter', and expressed his conviction that 'nothing in nature, so long as it is honestly observed and honestly described, can harm the mind of a child. Almost all the ills of the human race may be traced to the fact that it has strayed too far from nature and knows too little of the natural order of things. Conceal from children, if you will, the baseness of man. But let them read and understand the ways of animals and birds, of water and wind and earth; for these things are pure and true and unspoiled.'

There is material here for any amount of argument. *Ki-yu* is a fierce animal-biography in the Seton tradition, and is itself almost pantherlike in its prowling power. It is no more shaped than most lives of men and animals are shaped; Ki-yu hunts and kills, mates and fights, and his death comes not at the hands of David Milton, the hunter who has pursued him for years, but from a pack of wolves that finds him wounded and closes in on him: 'Long savage teeth tore the hide from his flesh, tore his flesh from his bones, crushed and scattered the bones while the marrow in them still lived.' I agree on the whole with Haig-Brown's views quoted above; but words like 'pure and true and unspoiled' have appreciative connotations that hardly seem appropriate for the pitiless workings of natural selection; and *Ki-yu*, though an impressive story, is a singularly bleak one.

The inter-war period was a good one for animal stories. Will James's *Smoky* (1926) is an animal biography of a very different kind from *Ki-yu*: the story of a cow-horse told by a cowboy. There is a striking resemblance to *Black Beauty*, in spite of the total contrast of setting; for Smoky, stolen from the range, finds himself kicking and bucking in rodeos, then is sold in turn to a livery stable and a cruel vegetable-salesman before being rescued to end his days in peace. Will James wrote in a cantering cowboy style which at first sight seems barely literate; but he knew what he was doing. A man with less of the craftsman in him could never have been so cunningly casual.

Dhan Gopal Mukerji (1890-1936) was an early Indian writer for children in English; and among other books about men and animals in the Indian jungle he wrote *Kari the Elephant* (1922), *Hari the Jungle Lad* (1924), and *Ghond the Hunter* (1928). Mukerji also wrote the Newbery-Medal-winning *Gay-Neck* (1927), the story of a carrier pigeon, beginning in India and moving to wartime France. Mary O'Hara's *My Friend Flicka* (1941), which was published as an adult novel but has found a junior audience, is 'of men and animals' too; a boy's struggle to break in a half-wild filly is combined with a father-son conflict. Joseph Wharton Lippincott's *Wilderness Champion* (1944) centres on the excellent idea of a dog that is torn between staying with a human master and running wild with wolves in the mountains of Alberta. Marjorie Rawlings wrote *The Yearling* (1938) about a boy and a deer; Eric Knight wrote *Lassie Come Home* (1940), about the homing journey of a collie from Scotland to Yorkshire; Phil Stong injected some humour into a genre not generally noted for it with *Honk, the Moose* (1935). And young children still enjoy Munro Leaf's *The Story of Ferdinand* (1936), about the bull who would rather smell flowers than fight.

15

Craftsmen in two media

ONE MAJOR twentieth-century poet did his best work for children, and dominated the field of children's poetry in the first half of the century. This was Walter de la Mare (1873-1956). His *Songs of Childhood* appeared in 1902, and *Peacock Pie* in 1913 (but not until 1917 in the States). New poems were added in several collections, notably *Poems for Children* (1930) and *Bells of Grass* (1941). Finally de la Mare included most of his poems for children or about childhood in *Collected Rhymes and Verses* (1944).

De la Mare's special quality as a poet is one that is widely desired and rarely possessed; an ability to recapture the childlike vision, to show things in words as they feel to a child. His craftsmanship was excellent to a degree that may have harmed his reputation in the long run. He could be and sometimes was more melodious than any other English poet except perhaps Tennyson, and it is easy to retain on the ear an impression of silvery delicacy rather than of force or substance. The corrective to this is to read *Peacock Pie* (the best book of all) and to note how often he is humorous, how often robust — look at *The Ship of Rio* — and how he is perfectly capable of bouncy rhyme and down-to-earth diction if that is what the subject demands. He can manage the quick short line:

> Ann, Ann!
> Come! Quick as you can!
> There's a fish that *talks*
> In the frying-pan.

and the long one that holds itself up by subtle internal supports:

> Tom sang for joy and Ned sang for joy and old Sam sang for joy;
> All we four boys piped up loud, just like one boy;
> And the ladies that sate with the Squire — their cheeks were all wet
> For the noise of the voice of us boys, when we sang our Quartette.

De la Mare always rings true emotionally; he is never self-conscious, saccharine, coy or condescending — all of which are ways of being out of true. His effect on lesser verse-writers probably has not always been good, but a poet is not to be blamed for his emulators and imitators. I do not believe he is over-rated.

I am not so sure about Eleanor Farjeon (1881-1965), whose outstanding personal qualities may have caused her work to be valued too highly in her lifetime. She was prolific, and there were many collections of her verses, which were often rolled forward from one book to another. Her own choice from a wide span of her work was made in *The Children's Bells* (1960). She wrote many fairy poems, poems of time and place and of the seasons. All were graceful and some were more than graceful; for instance, 'It was Long Ago', recalling an incident from the earliest misty edge of memory; or 'Cotton', which reflects Eleanor Farjeon's special feeling for young girlhood. Yet already it seems that time may be closing gently over much of her work.

Rose Fyleman (1877-1957) is remembered for a single line: 'There are fairies at the bottom of our garden!' Her arch little verses were highly popular in the 1920s, and she produced several 'fairy' collections, all of which are out of print as I write. She must however be given the credit for having induced A. A. Milne to try writing verse for children. He tells the story in his autobiography:

Rose Fyleman, starting a magazine for children, asked me, I have no idea why, to write some verses for it. I said that I didn't and couldn't, it wasn't in my line. As soon as I had posted my letter, I did what I always do after refusing to write anything: wondered how I would have written it if I hadn't refused. One might for instance have written:

There once was a dormouse who lived in a bed
Of delphiniums (blue) and geraniums (red),
And all the day long he'd a wonderful view
Of geraniums (red) and delphiniums (blue).[1]

So he did write, and his writings grew into a book, *When We Were Very Young* (1924), which was followed by *Now We Are Six* (1927). In my own household, when my children were young and living at home, a great deal of Milne — like much of Lear and Belloc — was known by heart and recited on the slightest provocation. 'The King's Breakfast' — 'I do like a little bit of butter to my bread!' — was probably the greatest all-round favourite, and 'King John's Christmas', 'The Little Black Hen', and 'Disobedience' ('James James Morrison Morrison Weatherby George Dupree') all had their partisans. Milne has been accused with some justice of sentimentality, especially in the notorious 'Vespers' ('Little Boy kneels at the foot of the bed'); but he could be realistic, too, and he was realistic in his comment on his own verses: whatever else they lacked, he said, they were technically good.[2] So they are; and children and many adults do like verses that trip well off the tongue.

Laura Richards (1850-1943) was the daughter of Julia Ward Howe, who wrote the Battle Hymn of the Republic. She contributed to *St Nicholas* in its early days, but her main collection, *Tirra Lirra,* did not appear until 1932, when she was over eighty. It includes work dating back to the previous century, as well as new rhymes. Much of what she wrote was nonsense verse. *Eletelephony* — about the elephant that tried to use the telephant, but unfortunately got his trunk entangled in the telefunk, and found that the more he tried to get it free the louder buzzed the telefee — is especially popular. My personal favourite is Little John Bottlejohn, who was wooed by a mermaid and won.

Elizabeth Madox Roberts (1886-1941) is remembered for her unpretentious, un-cute verses about children's everyday experiences in *Under the Tree* (1922). Child's-eye-views of people and animals are more than commonly convincing, and there are some interesting perspectives:

> The ants are walking under the ground
> And the pigeons are flying over the steeple,
> And in between are the people.

Yes, that places us, precisely.

Stephen Vincent Benet (1898-1943) and his wife Rosemary (1898-1962) wrote *A Book of Americans* (1933), which presents verse profiles of a number of historical and not-quite-historical figures. An unexpected and moving poem is on Nancy Hanks:

> If Nancy Hanks
> Came back as a ghost,
> Seeking news
> Of what she loved most,
> She'd ask first
> 'Where's my son?
> What's happened to Abe?
> What's he done? . . .
> Did he grow tall?
> Did he have fun?
> Did he learn to read?
> Did he get to town?'

When Nancy Hanks died she was thirty-four years old and her son, Abraham Lincoln, was nine.

The most influential poet and critic of his day, T. S. Eliot

(1888-1965), made his contribution to children's literature with *Old Possum's Book of Practical Cats*, which was published in 1939 and, nearly half a century later, inspired the enormously successful musical, *Cats*. 'Old Possum' was a nickname given to Eliot by his fellow-poet Ezra Pound. Most readers will have their favourite cats, with the Jellicles probably heading the list; but the most practical cat of all, and the most elusive, is Macavity the mystery cat, who has 'broken every human law, he breaks the law of gravity' and who ensures that when the crime squad reaches the scene 'Macavity's not there.'

The pioneer picture-book artists had been mainly British: Crane, Caldecott and Greenaway; Potter, Rackham and Brooke. And the first picture book to look forward unmistakably to the twentieth century in its graphic style was also the work of a British artist. This was the William Nicholson *Alphabet*, which

C.B.Falls: *ABC Book* (1923)

appeared in 1898 – a quarter of a century before the famous *ABC* of Charles Falls, with its full-page woodcuts of animals and birds, printed in strong, solid colours. (Curiously, both Nicholson in Britain and Falls in the States were distinguished poster-designers.) Nicholson was also the creator of two splendid picture books: *Clever Bill* (1926) and *The Pirate Twins* (1929), both of which marry brief brilliant texts with bold bright drawings. Clever Bill is the toy soldier who runs so fast that when Mary leaves him behind in the excitement of going on a visit he is there to meet her train at the other end. As for the Pirate Twins, Mary finds them on the beach, takes them home and baths and feeds and teaches them; but they're very naughty, and one fine day they steal a boat and sail away. 'We have gone for ever. Don't worry. Back soon,' says their farewell note; and they always come back for Mary's birthday.

Between the wars the balance swung sharply westward. With few exceptions, the artists who became prominent in those years were American. But many of them, though American citizens, had been born on the Continent of Europe, and their work was enriched by European flavours. Miska Petersham (1888-1960) was trained in Hungary. With his wife Maud he made Margery Clark's *Poppy Seed Cakes* (1924) – a book of short realistic tales with a Russian atmosphere – into a splendid picture-story book and a design landmark, whose illustrations in vivid red, gold and blue were completely integrated with the text. The Petershams' *Miki* (1929), with a Hungarian setting, had a similar, almost crude homeliness and earthiness, reminiscent of folk art; but there was an unexpected lyric touch and total colour-change in a swift-moving black-and-blue picture of warriors in the Milky Way. Later work by the Petershams, including *The Christ Child* (1931) and their award-winning *The Rooster Crows* (1945), seems to me to have become more conventional and less interesting.

Wanda Gág (1893-1946) was born in Minnesota, but 'grew up amidst Old World customs, songs and folklore',[3] and her work had a peasant humour. Her Grimm (*Tales from Grimm,*

The very old man, the very old woman, and the homely
kitten: from Wanda Gág's *Millions of Cats*

1936) is totally unfrightening; her people are round and reassuring. Wanda Gág created one of the unchallenged picture-book classics in *Millions of Cats* (1928), about the very old man and the very old woman who wanted a cat for company, and how the very old man found a hillside covered with cats:

> Cats here, cats there,
> Cats and kittens everywhere,
> Hundreds of cats,
> Thousands of cats,
> Millions and billions and trillions of cats.

But the cats bit and scratched and clawed each other and at last ate each other up – all except one homely little kitten which was just right for the very old couple. *Millions of Cats* is entirely in black and white, and offers the plainest proof that colour is not essential to a successful picture-book. Indeed, while Wanda Gág was able almost to repeat the success of *Millions of Cats* with *The Funny Thing* (1929) and *Snippy and Snappy* (1931), her later *Nothing At All* (1941), which had the same format but used colour, shows a total loss of cutting edge.

Ludwig Bemelmans (1898-1962) was born in Austria, but went to America in 1914 and enlisted in the U.S. Army in the First World War. His *Madeline* (1939) and its successors sometimes have a scandalously slapdash air, but they are full of life and movement and ideas; and Madeline, smallest of the 'twelve little girls in two straight lines' who plague the life of poor Miss Clavel, is a formidable little character.

Virginia Lee Burton (1909-68) is best known as author-illustrator of *Mike Mulligan and his Steam-Shovel* (1939) and *The Little House* (1942). The latter, about the little house in the country which is gradually surrounded and dwarfed by the advancing city, until rescued at last and towed away in one piece to deeper country, is one of the most affectionate and likeable of picture-books. (But the Little House, though spelled with initial capitals and referred to as 'she', is somewhat lacking in personality, to say nothing of architectural distinction. And can the happy ending be permanent, or will the city catch up once more?) A similar loving approach, giving life to inanimate creatures, was successful in *Maybelle the Cable Car* (1952), a celebration of the survival in San Francisco of that admirable mode of transport; but Virginia Burton's painstaking work as designer and illustrator of the *Song of Robin Hood* (1947), in which she did a separate drawing for each of nearly

500 stanzas, was not successful in proportion to the labours of the artist.

Dr Seuss (Theodore Seuss Geisel) is not the greatest of artists; I have heard the remarkable animals he draws described as 'boneless wonders'; but his early books *And to Think that I Saw it on Mulberry Street* (1937) and *The 500 Hats of Bartholomew Cubbins* (1938) were ingenious developments of original and truly visual ideas. In *Mulberry Street,* a boy builds up in his mind's eye (and on the page) a marvellous picture of what he has seen on the way home from school, only to have it shattered by Father's interrogation on

Drawing by Dr Seuss from *And to Think that I Saw it on Mulberry Street*

his arrival. Bartholomew Cubbins' self-replacing hats, in an unlikely fairy-tale situation, are an embarrassment that almost proves fatal, but the fortunate flowering of the last few of the 500 brings him safely to a happy ending. To me these remain the most appealing of the numerous Dr Seuss books.

James Daugherty and Robert Lawson — both vigorous draughtsmen — and Edgar and Ingri Parin d'Aulaire, whose work often seems to me to be curiously naive and somewhat static, are among other American artists who made their reputation during this period, and who have their admirers.

Among British artists, E. H. Shepard (1879-1976) became known principally for his illustrations to the A. A. Milne books (see page 134). Shepard's delineations of Christopher Robin and his toys are as definitive as Tenniel's Alice; they are part of our whole conception of the characters and undoubtedly played a great part in the books' success. According to Milne,

Pooh and Piglet and the rest had been given 'that twist in the features which denotes character' by the affection of their owner, and Shepard 'drew them as one might say from the living model'.[4] Shepard was still busy around the time of his ninetieth birthday, producing coloured versions of these illustrations and the ones he did for *The Wind in the Willows*. His daughter Mary Shepard achieved for Mary Poppins almost what her father did for Pooh.

Kathleen Hale's long series of books about *Orlando the Marmalade Cat* began in 1937. Their packed, vivid pictures have an air of lively and colourful extravaganza. Orlando's varied adventures are told in text as well as picture, and there is verbal as well as visual humour. In *Orlando, His Silver Wedding* (1944) one sees the *Daily Mews* being read, and an advertisement on a bus invites passers-by to 'buy our book on Etticat'. In one of the later titles, *Orlando and the Water Cats* (1972), the puns are in French, for the Water Cats are derived from Chat-eau, and their chateau is looked after by Chat-Elaine. This is an idea that has also occurred to the French cartoonist Siné.[5]

Mervyn Peake (1911-68) is one of the many artists who have tried to produce a 'different' Mother Goose, and one of the few who have actually done so. His *Ride a Cock-Horse* (1940), which was reissued in 1972, makes the familiar world of the old nursery rhymes seem strange and new: new in its way of looking and feeling, not in any incongruous modernity. Several of its characters are grotesque or strangely remote: the fine lady on a white horse would never even hear you if you called to her; the king in his counting-house, in 'Sing a Song of Sixpence', is a miser in an economy crown, momentarily distracted from his calculations by the intrusion of birds and song. But Peake can be tender, too, as in the mother-and-child frontispiece or the candle-lit mystery of 'How Many Miles to Babylon?'

The one British illustrator of international eminence to become known in the years leading up to the Second World War was Edward Ardizzone (1900-1979), whose style — at the same time traditional and highly individual — is unmistakable. Ardizzone's child characters are presented gently, affectionately and sympathetically, but he is not soppy; as author-artist he celebrates courage and self-reliance. He began his well-known series of picture-story books about seafaring Tim with *Little Tim and the Brave Sea Captain* in 1936. The Tim books have plenty of action and not too many words; and they display a

Edward Ardizzone drawing from *Tim's Last Voyage* (1972)

mastery of technique so effortless as to be almost unnoticeable. Cartoon-style 'balloons' − an endearing Ardizzone characteristic − add immediacy and sudden sharp glimpses of character.

The books continued after the war. *Tim All Alone* (1956) was the first winner of the Kate Greenaway medal. In 1972 came *Tim's Last Voyage* in which, after a wreck on the Goodwin Sands, Tim promised his mother not to go to sea again until he was grown up. We learn at the end of the book, however, that in time Tim will become a fine sailor and captain of a great ship; and there on the last page is a picture of a grown-up, manly Tim in uniform, looking everything that England expects. And though Tim's seagoing days are over, children will no doubt continue adventuring with him for years to come.

Ardizzone created several other picture books, featuring

among their characters Lucy, Ginger, Paul (the hero of the fire) and Nicholas (of the fast-moving diesel). He also made excellent picture books out of texts by other writers, among them Mary Lavin's *The Second-Best Children in the World* (1972) and fine new editions in 1973 and 1974 of Graham Greene's *The Little Fire Engine, The Little Train, The Little Steam Roller* and *The Little Horse Bus.*

As illustrator he worked with many of the leading writers of the day. Among those in the children's-book field with whom he was particularly associated were Eleanor Farjeon *(The Little Bookroom,* 1955, and other titles) and James Reeves (some twenty titles, beginning in 1952 with *The Blackbird in the Lilac).*

PART FOUR

1945-1989

16

The turbulent years

THE four and a half decades from 1945 to 1989 were years of turbulence rather than tranquillity. They were years in which, above all, the world faced the threat of the Bomb. For the first time, humanity was in a position to exterminate itself, and to do so in a singularly horrible manner. The balance of terror held, however, throughout the period; and at the end of the 1980s came developments of breathtaking size and speed which appeared to be breaking down the rigidities of the Cold War and making early nuclear catastrophe unlikely. It was impossible, as the nineties opened, to predict what was going to happen next. But the Bomb had not gone away; the danger that sooner or later nuclear weapons would fall into extreme or irresponsible hands had not diminished. Other threats to the future were perceived: growing populations, dwindling energy resources, damage to the environment, the rapid spread of Aids.

There was no major war, but conflicts seethed all over the world, and the electronic media brought them instantly and vividly into people's homes. Terrorism became commonplace. The gap between rich and poor nations showed no sign of closing. In the advanced western countries, poverty remained, though on a far less desperate scale than in the Third World. The United States lived through the Korean and Vietnam wars, through racial turmoil and political scandals. Britain ceased to be a Great Power and suffered relative economic decline; the British Empire was dismembered, though its ghost lingered on in the form of the Commonwealth. Old certainties broke down; the bulwarks of religion and family life were weakened. Groups that had been denied their place in the sun began to assert themselves.

For individuals in the West who had earning power there was growing prosperity; the 'haves' began to outnumber the 'have-nots'. Ownership of cars, refrigerators and washing-machines became the norm rather than the exception. It was the age of consumerism, of the computer, of television. TV became the dominant cultural medium, and American culture the dominant influence. New movements, new ideas, new fads tended to cross the Atlantic from west to east, though there was a modest continuing counter-flow both of 'high' and 'pop' culture.

On its smaller scale, children's literature reflected changes in the wider world. The Bomb itself did not feature to a great extent, but its shadow was there. Writers and editors of children's books came to accept that the world is a perilous place in which nobody can lead a protected life. Although for younger children the winds must still be tempered, older children's fiction moved away from the secure worlds of tradition; 'tell it like it is' became the motto.

This development did not begin at once. After the recovery from wartime shortages, the 1950s were a peaceful era in children's books. America had what Ann Durell, a distinguished editor, has described as 'the Indian summer of the Eisenhower years', when 'society was dominated by a sort of mid-Atlantic bourgeoisie that felt it had saved the world for democracy and had thus earned the right to perpetuate forever the sociological and cultural values of Edwardian England'. The children's book world in the United States was solidly Anglophile, and, Miss Durell added, 'it seemed that almost any book published in London would have an American edition sooner or later'.[1] Protectiveness extended to an unwritten ban on lying or stealing − unless punished − on drinking or smoking, sexual suggestiveness and bad language. Drugs were not even over the horizon.

In Britain, the decade was a hopeful one. Publishing houses were at last appointing children's editors with standing and ambition, and building up 'quality' lists. Oxford University Press, for instance, before and during the Second World War, had published the much-execrated books about the intrepid airman Biggles by Captain W. E. Johns. Now Biggles was dropped, and under the successive editorships of Frank Eyre, John Bell and Mabel George the Oxford children's list achieved extraordinary prestige. Other major publishers also raised their standards. Puffin Books had been established by Penguin during the war, and with Eleanor Graham as editor became the world's first major children's paperback imprint. Conditions were right for a renaissance, and it came with the emergence of a new wave of writers headed by Rosemary Sutcliff, Philippa Pearce and William Mayne, and such artists as Brian Wildsmith and Charles Keeping.

The 1960s seemed at first to be continuing the reign of peace and prosperity. Institutional support for children's books was increasing on both sides of the Atlantic. American publishers had the boost of Title II (of President Johnson's Elementary and Secondary Education Act, 1965) which made huge funds available for book purchase. The books themselves still tended to preserve the traditional values. Family life was exemplified in the reassuring pages of Eleanor Estes, Elizabeth Enright, the early Madeleine L'Engle (as in *Meet the Austins*) and many others. As late as 1964, the then-new edition of May Hill Arbuthnot's *Children and Books,* the Bible of American children's-literature teachers, observed:

> It is in the family that the child learns his first lessons in the laws of affectionate relationships . . . The status of the mother and the father in the family circle provides a child with his first concepts of the woman's role and the man's role in life, and often determines his consequent willingness or unwillingness to accept his own sex. Books such as *Caddie Woodlawn* can help in this necessary process of growing up, for tomboy Caddie, despite her love of boys' games and adventures, gradually learns to appreciate her woman's role.[2]

This pronouncement was greatly modified in the succeeding (1972) edition, revised by Zena Sutherland after Mrs Arbuthnot's death.

In Britain, the rise of the 'quality' children's book in the 1950s and early 1960s had several consequences. One, an excellent one, was that many talented authors, some of them already established as writers for adults, were attracted into the field. Another was that people, notably educators, who had previously shown little interest in children's literature began to take notice of it. They were not always delighted with what they found. A long-running controversy brewed up in the late fifties and continued through the sixties over the so-called reluctant reader. There were complaints, not unfounded, that children's books and their authors were 'too middle class' and that there were not enough books about life as it was known to less privileged children. This deficiency was to a great extent remedied as the sixties went on and writers themselves began to come from a wider social spectrum; but the complaint was succeeded by a new and more political one: that children's books were reinforcing the existing social structure rather than working towards a new one.

The sixties were the years when everything happened. The key phrase of the decade was coined in February 1960 by the British Prime Minister, Harold Macmillan, when he referred in a speech in South Africa to a 'wind of change' that was blowing through the African continent. The context of the phrase 'wind of change' was rapidly broadened to extend to any powerful movement for radical change; and in the sixties many winds were beginning to blow. In August 1963 the Rev. Martin Luther King led a march to Washington and spoke the famous words: 'I have a dream that one day this nation will rise up and live out the true meaning of its creed: we hold these truths to be self-evident, that all men are created equal.' In 1967 the first Black Power conference was held. Black Americans were on the move.

In 1965, in a seminal article in *Saturday Review* on 'The All-White World of Children's Books', Nancy Larrick complained of 'the almost complete omission of Negroes' (she did not use the word 'black') 'from books for children'. Integration, she went on, 'may be the law of the land, but most of the books children see are all white'.[3] Incorporation of the black experience into children's literature is discussed in a later chapter of the present study. There had in fact already been a good many American children's books about racial minorities, but they were by white writers and they tended to imply that a black or brown child was a white child under the skin. This was well-meant but not what was needed. A search by editors for black writers, and a great deal of soul-searching by white ones, were positive outcomes of the new consciousness; a less welcome outcome over the succeeding years was a determined sniffing-out of alleged racism in what often amounted to a witch-hunt.

An article with almost as great an impact as Nancy Larrick's appeared in *School Library Journal* for January 1971: 'A Feminist Look at Children's Books' by the 'Feminists on Children's Media', an anonymous collective of women. The authors studied award-winning and recommended books, which, they found, 'fell or were pushed by our merciless analysis' into various, mainly undesirable categories: the plain Sexist Book, the Cop-out Book, in which after a show of independence the girl character adjusts to the stereotyped role of women, and so on.[4] The campaign against sexism in children's books was now in full swing in the United States, though it was slow to take off in Britain. I commented on it in a column in the *Guardian* in January 1972 and got no response at all, whereas a column at that time attacking or defending Enid Blyton would have brought shoals of letters. A year or two later I was to receive inquiries almost daily from anxious mothers who wondered whether I could recommend *any* non-sexist books for their daughters to read.

Yet in many ways the most significant phenomenon of the sixties and early seventies was a less spectacular one: the accelerating loss of confidence on the part of the parental generation. Traditionally, as was assumed by May Hill Arbuthnot in the passage previously quoted, the parental role was to guide and set an example to the children; parents were the repositories of society's wisdom and experience, the benefits of which they would hand on to the succeeding generation. But in the turbulent world of the 1960s, parents were no longer sure that they embodied the wisdom of the ages. They had not, after all, built a safe, ordered world for their children to come into.

Along with wars, racial and sexual tensions and fear of the Bomb came recognition of a great deal of hypocrisy on the part of the middle generation. High divorce rates, the sometimes almost casual break-up of marriages, cynicism and self-seeking in business and professional life − these were adult, not childish or teenage phenomena. Adults did what they liked, and it was up to children to face the consequences. In the past there had been − among the white middle classes, at least − an unwritten social contract between children and parents. The children gave, if not total obedience, at least a willing allegiance, respect and cooperation; the adults provided a stable home and emotional security. This contract was increasingly breached on one side and was beginning to be breached on the other. A teenage culture was growing up, of which the basis was in part positive − the recognition of adolescence as a springtime in which one has boundless energy, growing independence and a great capacity for enjoyment − and in part negative: a rejection of adult values. And younger children were growing, not directly towards adulthood but towards this new intervening status.

Authors were now writing into, and about, a world which had changed since their own younger days. One result, in the late sixties and early seventies, was a spate of teenage novels by writers whom I described as 'aunts in miniskirts', tackling with determined understanding the fashionable problems of the day. Farther down the age range, children were expected to face in fiction the harsh realities of divorce, illness and death, as well as war and holocaust. The happy two-parent white family ceased to be the fictional norm. Not only were there one-parent families and broken homes; parents slid rapidly down the moral slope. In young-adult books particularly, parents were more and more likely to be useless or positively vicious, reaching bottom probably with the collection of no-good and alcoholic parents populating the novels of Paul Zindel.

The social and political pendulum, having swung a long way in one direction between the mid-fifties and the late-sixties, had to swing back. The backward swing was impelled by the ten-year recession that struck much of the world in the early seventies. Unemployment rose; it was no longer easy to drop out of society and drop back in again. The result, in the English-speaking countries, was not revolutionary fervour but a drift towards conservatism and orthodoxy. This did not immediately affect the content of children's books, though it did encourage a conservative backlash against anti-racist and anti-sexist groups, and there were attempts at book-banning from the Right and complaints of the subversion of traditional values and of law and order.

The recession did, however, sharply affect the economics of children's book publishing on both sides of the Atlantic. Hardcover books, still the bedrock, are sold mainly to school and public libraries. In the seventies, library budgets were cut, yet book production costs rose remorselessly. Obviously fewer books could be bought. Libraries did their best to keep on buying new books, but tended not to replace their stocks of old ones. Publishers cut down the length of their initial printing runs, thereby increasing unit costs still further. At the same time, high interest rates and warehousing charges meant that a rate of sale that formerly justified a reprint was now insufficient. These trends have continued, at least in Britain. A report published by the Book Trust in 1989 showed a ten-year decline in the purchasing power of public libraries, and noted that librarians struggling to preserve their book funds had 'a near impossible task when faced with the requirements for capital expenditure and for the maintenance of opening hours and access to libraries'.[5]

A drastic effect of recession was thus the crumbling of backlists. Traditionally, children's books were published for the long term, and, if they were any good, could be expected to stay in print for years; but the new pattern of publishing meant early death for those that were not generating sufficient profit. Inevitably, this made it more difficult for writers to establish themselves in the children's field, since in order to prosper it is necessary to build up a list of titles in print and achieve steady sales over a long period. A further effect of the decline in the library market was that publishers became more dependent on sales in the bookshops – and also in supermarkets and any other outlet they could find – with the result that they were on the whole selling to less informed purchasers than the librarians. There was more demand for shelf appeal and less for literary quality. The concentration of publishing into fewer hands, and the build-up of big conglomerates, frequently operating on both sides of the Atlantic, has meant growing emphasis on 'the bottom line,' and has intensified these effects. At the time of writing, fiction for older children and teenagers seems to be suffering most as a result of the swing from library to bookshop sales: in part perhaps because parents and relatives will buy books for younger children but hesitate to guess what older ones will like. And the price of a new book, especially in hardback, bears little relation to the pocket money of the potential reader himself or herself. The library – if it has funds – can offer a choice for all tastes and keep young people reading.

In Britain especially, the flow of new writers in the late fifties and the sixties was followed as the seventies went on by a relative dearth. By the mid-1980s new talent had become so scarce that the appearance of one exceptionally gifted young writer – Janni Howker – put the children's book world into a state of excitement. Too high a proportion of the worthwhile children's books of the eighties came from writers whose reputations were already made. Later in the decade there were signs of an upturn, but it was precarious. The world recession had lifted, but Britain's economic outlook was once again in doubt, and the general atmosphere was somewhat gloomy.

Happily, the other major English-speaking and book-producing countries were in a more cheerful state. The United States, where children's literature has stronger institutional support, avoided many of Britain's ups and downs, and the emergence and recognition of talent proceeded more steadily. At the end of the decade, children's publishing and bookselling were doing well – specialist children's bookstores were said to be the fastest-growing sector of the American retail market – and there was an air of optimism. Canadian writing and publishing for children had lagged behind until the mid 1970s, but in the 1980s were catching up rapidly, helped by generous state support. Australia had already for many years produced a remarkably high number of good children's books and writers, and continued to do so, while high levels of interest and support and excellent bookstores helped to sustain an enthusiastic atmosphere.

Writers and publishers outside the United States and Britain still have difficulty however in getting their books onto the international circuit. Children's book publishing still revolves largely round a New York-London axis. In present circumstances one has to hope that books of sufficiently high quality will make their way eventually to the lists of major American or British publishers, or both; but the shortage of books from many parts of the English-speaking world suggests that this cannot be relied on.

Among the genres of children's literature, historical fiction unfortunately seems to have lost ground. It suffers in some quarters from a self-fulfilling belief: 'children don't like historical fiction, so we will not offer it to them'. Fantasy has held its place, though it is no longer true – if it ever was true – that it is the realm of all the highest talents. Realism, for long the dominant mode in the United States, has come increasingly to the fore in Britain. As between Britain and the United States, I have the impression that the balance has shifted; that more American books for children and young people have been successfully published and sold in Britain than previously, while in contrast the going has become much harder for British writers in the United States. I regret the latter development but not, on the whole, the former. Fifteen or twenty years ago, even interested adults in Britain were frequently unaware of American children's literature; it would be hard for them to be unaware today.

The effects of television and the video-cassette on children's reading are uncertain. Studies have produced conflicting results. There is no doubt that more child-hours are spent on watching than on reading, but it is of course fallacious to suppose that the child who sits in front of the television set for thirty hours a week would otherwise spend the time reading good books. The head of BBC children's television, Anna Home, has pointed out more than once that the adaptation of a book for TV results in an instant increase in demand for the book. But this is of course demand directed at a small number of books, not at books in general.

In Britain especially, the status of the children's writer remains low, and, whether as a cause or a consequence, writers lack the stimulus of informed critical attention. Children's book reviewing in newspapers and magazines is starved of space and is often of poor quality; and while there is now a fringe of academic interest in children's literature, little is published on the subject that displays outstanding judgment or percipience. Pressures to stamp out alleged racism and sexism have abated, partly perhaps because they have served the useful part of their purpose in increasing the necessary sensitivities of writers and publishers, and partly because the public has grown bored with the wilder absurdities of the pressure groups.

The present scene in Britain, though probably not elsewhere in the English-speaking world, is less inspiring than it was when I hopefully claimed, in the first edition of this book a quarter of a century ago, that we were living in a golden age of children's literature. But I do not wish to sound too pessimistic. There are still a few British publishers who will bring out books because they are good, even while knowing they are not going to make much money. Interest in children's literature in schools and colleges of education is still growing, though it has not reached American, Canadian or Australian levels. School bookshops thrive; so do the children's book groups formed by parents. Paperback publishing for children – spearheaded for much of the period by the dynamism of Kaye Webb at Puffin – has expanded greatly, and whereas 'quality' books in hardback are sometimes alleged to sit unread on the library shelves, these same books in soft covers are bought to be read, and frequently read to pieces. And there is something of a boom in 'babylit', as concerned young parents – young enough to have grown up on good contemporary books themselves – seek to set the newest generation on the reading track. That is hugely encouraging. Mother's or father's knee is where it all begins.

The chapters that follow will try to trace the main lines of children's fiction, poetry and picture-books over the four and a half decades.

17

Britons and their past

IN Britain at least, historical fiction has traditionally had high standing among children's books. A review in *The Times Literary Supplement* in April 1972 began by declaring that 'the historical novel for children has for many years set a standard by which other writing has been judged'.[1] This seemed a somewhat grandiose claim even then, but it is significant that it could be seriously made in a serious journal. If today the children's historical novel does not have the prestige it used to have, this is not because of literary inadequacy, for the standard has in fact remained high. The explanation, I think, lies in a change in adult perceptions of children's needs.

To middle-class adults a generation ago, thinking mainly of middle-class children who were being academically educated, history required no justification; it was part of the essential furniture of the mind. In recent years there has been a point of view from which history lacked 'relevance' for the contemporary child. 'All about dead people and Hottentots' was a complaint made about history two or three years ago in a televised discussion of traditional education; and it received some support as well as being opposed. To me this complaint seems misguided; we do not know who we are or where we are unless we know something of other times and places. And while the phrase 'historical fiction' may not ring excitingly in children's ears, I do not believe that individual books, if otherwise appealing, will be resisted on the ground of being set in the past. As always, a great deal can be achieved by adult enthusiasm. Enjoyment cannot be prescribed, but it can be communicated. For myself I remain convinced that historical fiction is an important genre, and one that can give reward and pleasure to young readers.

In Britain, since the end of the Second World War, one name has stood out above the rest: that of Rosemary Sutcliff. Her major books have combined compelling narrative power with the exploration of important and absorbing themes. She began her writing career in the early 1950s with some rather guileless books for younger children, but found her true voice with *The Eagle of the Ninth* (1954), in which a young Roman centurion,

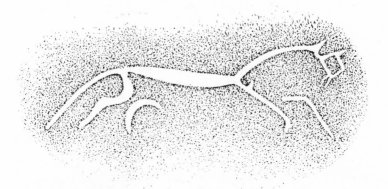

The White Horse of Uffington: illustration by Shirley Felts
from Rosemary Sutcliff's *Sun Horse, Moon Horse*

invalided out of the army, sets off into wild northern Britain
on a mission to find out what happened to his father's lost
legion. This was the first book of a sequence, set in Roman
Britain, which continued with *The Silver Branch* (1957) and
The Lantern Bearers (1959).[2]

The last of these, in which a young Roman officer decides to
stay on in Britain after the legions have gone, is crucial. The
Romans who remain are struggling to carry what light they can
into the dark ages that will follow. In *Dawn Wind* (1961), we
are in the darkness; the hero Owain is a boy whose family
have been killed in the Saxon invasions and who becomes a
Saxon thrall. But the book ends on a note of hope when Einon
Hen the Welsh statesman speaks to Owain not only of 'the last
gleam of a lantern far behind' but also of 'the hope of other
light as far ahead'. He looks to a new union of Saxons and
Britons: 'it is not the dawn as yet, Owain, but I think the dawn
wind stirring'.

These four books are themselves part of a larger sequence,
extended over a considerable body of work, whose subject is
the making of Britain. It goes back in time to the Bronze Age
in *Warrior Scarlet* (1958) and forward to *The Shield Ring*
(1956), in which Norseman meets Norman, and *Knight's Fee*
(1960), where the Norman Conquest is over and Normans too
are beginning to lose themselves in a common identity. And
Miss Sutcliff moves sideways, as it were, from Roman Britain
in *The Mark of the Horse Lord* (1965), in which Phaedrus the
gladiator first impersonates, then becomes identified with, the

leader of the Gaelic 'horse people'. Peoples mix, conquerors are absorbed, and all along, timeless and patient, from *Warrior Scarlet* through to *Knight's Fee* two thousand years later, are the Little Dark People, who endure and survive.

This sequence seems to me still to constitute the basic structure of Miss Sutcliff's work, though from time to time she has added to it or filled it out. Among her later books, I particularly admire *Sun Horse, Moon Horse* (1977), which offers an explanation of the white horse carved into the hillside at Uffington in Berkshire, and which has a hero who is artist as well as chieftain and, ultimately, sacrifice. And *Frontier Wolf* (1980) showed its author still in vigorous possession of the powers that went into *The Eagle of the Ninth* a quarter-century earlier. Alexios Flavius Aquila, kin to the Marcus Flavius Aquila of *The Eagle*, is sent in disgrace to command a rough irregular unit of frontier scouts, recruited from among the tribesmen in northern Britain.

Looking along the lines, Alexios saw men, long and rangy for the most part, clad in greasy and weatherworn leather tunics and cross-gartered breeks, even their iron-bound caps three parts hidden under the snarling head of the wolfskin cloak each man wore pulled forward over it . . . They stood easily, feet a little apart, and looked back at him out of hardbitten wind-burned faces, rogues' faces, some of them, cautious or reckless, cunning or blank, all of them careful to give nothing away. But in them all, binding them together, something that was different from the oneness of other army units. Maybe it was the oneness of the wolf pack. Alexios did not know.

Alexios has to win the confidence of this unpromising mob, and eventually to lead them in a long, fierce, fighting retreat, at the end of which the ragged remnants are declaring that if he cared to set up as Emperor they'd be right behind him.

Rosemary Sutcliff's view of early British history was formed some years ago, and would be disputed by many modern historians – a thought that does not worry me, since different interpretations can all contain their own truth, and in any case she is less an analyst of the past than a writer who brings it to pulsing life. Her heroes have mostly been cast in a traditional mould: brave, intensely honourable, full of officer-like qualities. Women are not usually important in her books: the fierce physical action she describes with such power has generally been a masculine rather than a feminine field. An exception is *Song for a Dark Queen* (1978), which tells the story of Boudicca, queen of the Iceni in eastern England, who led a revolt against the Romans and was defeated. A later book, *Flame-Coloured Taffeta* (1986), has a less spectacular heroine in Damaris, an eighteenth-century farmer's daughter, who helps a mysterious, injured young man to escape capture in a coastal area where smuggling is a regular trade.

This book and *Bonnie Dundee* (1983) are set in later times than those of Miss Sutcliff's previous work, and both of them involve, in very different ways, the ill-fated Jacobins. *Bonnie Dundee* portrays, through the eyes of an old man who was once a follower, that charismatic but ambiguous hero John Graham of Claverhouse, Earl of Dundee. Dundee was 'bloody Clavr'se' to the Presbyterian Covenanters he oppressed, but 'bonny' to Walter Scott, who gave him the epithet properly belonging to the city whose name he bore. He died in 1689 at Killiecrankie, where he won a fruitless victory for the deposed King James. Miss Sutcliff, it has been pointed out, 'will always put down her harp for a battle',[3] and Killiecrankie gives her full scope. She also explores once more, to powerful effect, the theme of loyalty, with which she has been concerned throughout her work.

A less known but not less successful book than Rosemary Sutcliff's full-length novels is *The Truce of the Games* (1971). In this she succeeds in one of the hardest tasks a writer for children can tackle: to make a historical story comprehensible and attractive to the younger readers – down to eight or thereabouts – who have little experience of life or sense of historical time, and who may also have limited reading skills. Amyntas is from Athens, Leon from Sparta; their cities are at war, but there is a truce for the Olympic Games, during which the two boys become friends as well as rivals. But their friendship cannot last beyond the time of truce. And they are almost of military age – a fact that lies behind Leon's words on parting: 'The gods be with you, Amyntas, and grant that we never meet again.'

The upright young protagonists of the traditional historical novel for the young have fallen out of favour in recent years. There has been a growing tendency to replace them with heroes (or heroines) of humbler social status and with a greater share of ordinary human fears and weaknesses. The 'radical' historical novel had been introduced by Geoffrey Trease in the 1930s. By the start of the Second World War Trease had, in his own words, 'got the propagandist urge out of his system'.[4] In the post-war years he continued to be in the vanguard of historical writing for children, and contributed a good deal to the outmoding of 'gadzookery' and the modern insistence on authenticity rather than colourful romanticism. Established and prolific writers tend to become part of the scenery; Trease ceased to excite the commentators and came to seem a little old-fashioned. Yet 1989 saw him, as the doyen of British children's writers, celebrating his eightieth birthday, his fifty-fifth year as a published writer, and his imminent century of books. *Follow My Black Plume* (1963), *The Red Towers of Granada* (1966) and *Popinjay Stairs* (1973) are among the more notable of his later historical novels.

Trease should not be confused with another prolific writer of similar name, Henry Treece (1911-66). Treece wrote twenty-five historical novels for young people in the last twelve years of his life; and they were by no means the whole of his literary output during that time. He was much concerned with the long period of strife and confusion in Europe between, roughly, the Roman invasion of Britain and the Norman Conquest; and he returned again and again to the Vikings, in such novels as *Viking's Dawn* (1955), *Viking's Sunset* (1960) and *The Last of the Vikings* (1964). In *Man with a Sword* (1962), Treece fleshed out the shadowy figure of Hereward, leader of the resistance against William the Conqueror. To me his books have often seemed more admirable than enjoyable; there is so much in them that is harshly bleak and violent.

Barbara Willard's historical novels have been inspired by a feeling for place as much as period — the place being the Sussex wealden country where she herself lives. She was already a veteran writer when she began the sequence known as the Mantlemass novels; but this sequence is undoubtedly her prime achievement. Mantlemass is a manor farm in the Ashdown Forest, and the novels are mainly about the members of two intertwining families, the Mallories and the Medleys, who successively hold it from the Crown. They are more yeomanry than gentry, though there runs through them a slight, mysterious strain of royal blood. The time-span of the sequence is from the end of the Wars of the Roses in 1485 until the English civil war in the mid seventeenth century, when the house is burned down.

The series began with *The Lark and the Laurel* (1970) and continued with *The Sprig of Broom* (1971), *A Cold Wind Blowing* (1972), *The Iron Lily* (1973) and *Harrow and Harvest* (1974). It then seemed complete, but the author went back and filled in some gaps with *The Eldest Son* (1977), *A Flight of Swans* (1980) and *The Keys of Mantlemass* (1981).

A major theme of the series is the impact of public events on private lives: the people of Mantlemass are affected willy-nilly by the overthrow of Richard III and the plottings against his successors, the dissolution of the monasteries, the religious swings of the mid sixteenth century, the troubles with Spain, the Armada, and finally the civil war. At the same time, the sequence is a deeply loving, though unsentimental, portrayal of people and place in constant interaction; of the complex relationships between contemporaries and between the generations; of the influence of work and landscape and the passage of time and of the seasons. There is a perpetual concern with continuity, with cause and effect: 'Lord, we are tied, all of us, to the long strange past – and no way to cut the string, that I can ever see,' says Roger Medley, near the end of *Harrow and Harvest* and of the whole long story.

Peter Carter's *The Sentinels* (1980) is a notable example of the endeavours of recent historical novelists to reconstruct events of the past in what may have been a harsh or even murky reality, rather than in heroic style. The year is 1840; Britain has outlawed slavery, and a Royal Navy anti-slavery patrol is now trying to stamp it out by blockading the Slave Coast of West Africa and intercepting the slavers. The story is told mainly over the shoulder of John Spencer, 'gentleman volunteer' in a sloop-of-war, HMS *Sentinel.*

Considering the infamy of the slave trade, the aim is unquestionably admirable; but on board the *Sentinel*, as always and everywhere, motives are mixed. The seamen and their officers are men following a dangerous trade, and most of them are by no means angelic. There is money involved, since freed slaves and captured ships mean bounty: 'O Lord, send us down six great big slavey-ships – without any guns!' prays a waggish member of John's crew. But Captain Murray of the *Sentinel* is a religious and upright man, a firm believer in the cause; and alongside the physical battles against slave-runners there are conflicts within the ship. Ultimately I think Carter's book is a celebration of the old Royal Navy, with all its brutality, its loyalty and bravery:

all the ships and all the men on them; the good, the bad, the indifferent, the heroes and the villains, there for whatever motives; greed, glory, three meals a day and a damp hammock, yet all fulfilling their role under the red ensign their lords and masters in England have sent to fly along the hot and fever-ridden coasts of Africa.

Peter Carter's novel may be seen as complementary to the excellent American novel *The Slave Dancer,* by Paula Fox, discussed in the next chapter. The scene and the year are the same, but Fox's story is presented from the point of view of a boy on a slave ship which is trying to dodge the Navy. Interestingly, Carter's and Fox's central figures are each cast ashore with a slave after almost drowning, and in each case a friendship results, though the friendships cannot continue into later life. While *The Sentinels* has not the harsh poetry, the emotional and psychological penetration of Paula Fox's book, it is a fine piece of work.

The ending of slavery was not a tidy, stroke-of-the-pen business. Marjorie Darke's *The First of Midnight* (1977) is set in a late eighteenth-century Bristol where, although there is no such thing as a slave in England itself, the slave trade is still a mainstay. The ex-slave Midnight still has a master who beats him and from whom he runs away; and, by a neat moral irony, the girl Jess who befriends and loves him, though she is born free, is sold three times over for a few shillings a time in the first few pages. As in the Fox and Carter novels, friendship − in this case love − ends in parting, for essentially the same reason. Midnight yearns for Africa, and must go.

Jill Paton Walsh contributed to children's literature one of the best historical novels of the 1970s in *The Emperor's Winding-Sheet* (1974), about the siege of Constantinople and its final fall to the Turks in 1453. The emperor is the last Constantine; his winding-sheet is the city itself; his tragedy is that of a city, an empire, a civilization. *A Chance Child* (1978) illustrates the difficulty and ultimate unimportance of classification by genre, for it combines history with fantasy and realistic writing in the moving story of a neglected contemporary child who wanders away through time to join his fellows who suffered in the Industrial Revolution. In *A Parcel of Patterns* (1983), Jill Paton Walsh tells the dreadful but heroic story of the Derbyshire village of Eyam, which isolated itself to prevent the spread of the Plague and lost three-quarters of its population. Though a tragedy, this is in part a love story, with its fragile moments of happiness, and with beautiful evocative descriptions of landscape and the natural world contrasting with the sterile darkness of disease and death.

Hester Burton has written several adventure stories and romantic novels with solidly researched historical settings. Among them is *Time of Trial* (1963), in which an old radical bookseller, at the outset of the nineteenth century, stands up for 'the ancient liberty of Englishmen to speak and write what we will'. This is, I think, a fine novel − thanks partly to Mr

Pargeter the bookseller, absurdly innocent yet happy and wise in his way, and still more to the heroine, his daughter Margaret, a spirited young lady who is also a girl of honest flesh and blood.

Ann Schlee, who had written three previous historical novels, surpassed them with her fourth: the quiet and poignant *Ask Me No Questions* (1976), in which a Victorian girl, finding children starving and sick of the cholera in the nearby baby-farm (an asylum for pauper children) finds also that the grown-ups around her don't want to know about it. Susan Price, in *Twopence a Tub*, published in 1975 when she was only 19, wrote about the desperate hardships of two related mining families in a Midland pit strike in 1851. And Clive King, a published writer for more than twenty years and author of the perennially popular *Stig of the Dump*, produced a rousing historical adventure story with a perky, resourceful young hero in *Ninny's Boat* (1980), a novel about post-Roman voyagers to Britain.

The names of other British writers of historical fiction may well occur to informed readers. I have omitted some authors because their work seems to me to lack a sense of immediacy. A historical novel, starting as it does at a backward remove in time, has a special need of richness, vitality, and above all the power to draw the reader into the middle of things, rather than leave him watching as if through a pane of glass. Accuracy of historical detail is not enough. The past must be made new, made *now*.

In an article in the *Horn Book* in 1972,[5] Jill Paton Walsh distinguished the true historical novel — one that is 'wholly or partly about the public events and social conditions which are the material of history, regardless of the time at which it is written' — from the non-historical book with a setting in the past, for which she proposed the name 'costume novel'. This is a useful distinction, although in my ears the phrase 'costume novel' has a pejorative ring which I think was not intended.

Presumably most of Leon Garfield's books would come under this heading, since although they are set in and around the eighteenth century they have little direct concern with 'public events and social conditions'. Leon Garfield's eighteenth century is a setting designed by himself, making free and highly personal use of such period materials as appeal to his imagination. *Smith* (1967) is about a twelve-year-old pickpocket from 'the tumbledown mazes about fat St Paul's'. Mixed motives of greed and pity bring Smith into strange partnership with a blind magistrate; together they unmask villainy and regain a fortune for its rightful owners. The ambitious *The Drummer Boy* (1970) sets innocent hero Charlie, honest serving-wench Charity and sad ambiguous surgeon Mister Shaw into contrast with the bloody glory of the battlefield and the cold, poisonous grandeur of General Lawrence and his daughter Sophia.

In these and other stories published up to 1970, Garfield's preoccupations are consistent: again and again there are puzzles of identity, contrasts of genuine and false feeling, and unmaskings of apparent good as evil or evil as good. *The Strange Affair of Adelaide Harris* (1971) develops a comic gift which was implicit, and sometimes explicit, in the earlier books. Garfield, like Dr Johnson or his revered Dickens, is a Londoner of letters, but here he may be said to be on holiday in Brighton, where Dr Bunnion has his Academy for the Sons of Gentlefolk and Merchants. The staff of the Academy, with their wives, children and pupils, are propelled at ever-increasing speed through a maypole-dance of events until, with a series of final flourishes, the innumerable complexities of the plot are unwound and the mild hero and classics master, Mr

'I rather fancy I am entitled to — satisfaction': a drawing by Fritz Wegner from *The Strange Affair of Adelaide Harris*, by Leon Garfield

Brett, is found happily paired with the pretty daughter of the arithmetic master. Of all the Garfield books up to the late 1980s, this and its sequel *Bostock and Harris* (1979) are perhaps the most purely enjoyable. The comedy comes like sandpaper in every grade from fine to coarse: from sweet malicious dialogue to the emptying of chamber-pots on people's heads.

First impressions of Garfield's work are apt to be dominated by the spectacular Garfield style – highly-coloured, energetic, exuberant, crammed with audacious images. He has a wonderful way with similes, which he scatters around like brilliant litter. This style may have tended to draw attention away from the growing depth and resonance of later novels. *The Prisoners of September* (1975) is a sombre and searching book, and incidentally a 'true' historical novel. The great public event on which it hangs is the French Revolution, and its central incident arises from the massacre of 'enemies of the people' in a Paris prison in 1792 (hence the title.) It is a tale of two friends, not two cities. Both are drawn into the turmoil; one takes the way of daylight and the other, driven by a perverted idealism, the way of darkness. But at the end there is reconciliation, the flowering of greater love than before, and the beginning of atonement and redemption.

The Pleasure Garden (1976), *The Apprentices* (1976-8) and *The Confidence Man* (1978) are concerned with religious issues and are profoundly influenced by the Bible, which Garfield declared in 1976 to be a richer source of inspiration than the Norse and Celtic mythologies then in fictional vogue.[6] *The Pleasure Garden* is set in an eighteenth-century London commercial pleasance – a place of dreams and pretences where the old can pretend to be young, the ugly to be beautiful and the poor to be rich. All is well until, hideously, murder intrudes. It looks almost as if Garfield has rewritten the Fall. Here is his *Paradise Lost,* and perhaps also his *Paradise Regained,* for at the end the Garden is still in business; Eden is still open to the innocent, even the seedily innocent. In *The Confidence Man* (1978), a mysterious Black Hussar turns out to be a rogue and charlatan; yet he leads a band of people, persecuted for their religion, to their promised land in the New World. As a saviour he is created by faith, especially that of the young protagonist, Hans Ruppert. At the end, Hans, disillusioned, no longer believes in him, or in God, and demands from God a miracle, a parting of the waters. And the waters are parted, by a young Indian boy with a paddle. If it's a miracle, it's a very simple one performed through simple human agency; and one implying that an unprincipled rogue, too, might be serving the purposes of God.

The Biblical influence can also be seen in the cycle of twelve stories known as *The Apprentices* (1976-8). In the first of these, *The Lamplighter's Funeral,* a link-boy significantly named Possul shines his light into London's darkest corners. *The Cloak* centres on the pawning of a cloak with the embroidered text 'I know that my Redeemer liveth' (an audacious but not facetious pun). In *Moss and Blister*, a baby is delivered in the inn yard at Christmas, and the midwife's assistant believes she is to officiate at the Second Coming; but it turns out that for a very good reason it cannot be so. *Tom Titmarsh's Devil* turns on the banning of the mysterious Mr Match's book 'Thine is the Kingdom', which wrestles with the problem of evil.

After all this, many readers were relieved when Garfield returned to what they saw as his mainstream with *John Diamond* (1980), a story about a boy's adventures in the crowded, perilous streets of eighteenth-century London. There is in fact a danger of reading too little into *John Diamond,* for which the text could be taken from *Julius Caesar:* 'The evil that men do lives after them.' Only the innocent goodwill of the young hero, son of the evil-doer, can put the evil to rest.

The December Rose (1986) has a young chimney-sweep – a thieving waif reminiscent of Smith in the early novel of that name – caught up in dubious affairs of state and high-level thuggery. Young Barnacle and his rescuer, Tom Gosling the Thames barge-man, are innocents protected by their innocence in a deeply devious world. This story has a finely ambiguous Garfield figure in Inspector Creaker, an upright man working in a bad cause and, at the end, with silent nobility, paying the ultimate price to settle all accounts. *The Empty Sleeve* (1988) shows Garfield still fiercely creative in a nightmarish Grand-Guignol mystery of deceit, villainy, dark comedy, tangled secrecy, murder, guilt, remorse and redemption – the whole tinged with what may be supernatural or may be fevered imagination and superstition. Besides these and other novels, Garfield has written splendid ghost stories set in the past – among them *Mister Corbett's Ghost* (1968) and *The Ghost Downstairs* (1972).

The children's-literature specialists have long since grown used to Leon Garfield; he is not the exciting phenomenon he once was; but in the wider worlds of film and television, and outside Britain, his reputation has continued to grow. His is undoubtedly one of the major talents working in children's books in the late twentieth century. But he is not a writer to be imitated. As a stylist, and also as a creator of plots and characters, he sails spectacularly close to the wind and heels his craft at a perilous angle; anyone trying to follow him would be likely to capsize into a sea of bad writing.

Geraldine McCaughrean has observed that 'rich imagery, full-blooded adventure and characters of interest and depth characterize my books . . .'[7] In spite of her Whitbread and Carnegie Medal awards, this description, coming from herself, may seem a shade immodest; but I am not going to challenge it. *A Little Lower than the Angels* (1987), set in medieval England, has a brilliant opening in which beautiful, angelic-looking Gabriel, reluctant apprentice to a brutal stonemason, finds himself cast in the role of angel as part of the presentation of Heaven and Hell by a troop of travelling players. The picaresque story that follows might well have had the title 'Pageant's Progress'. Gabriel, joining the troop, is credited with 'miraculous' cures, which he more than half believes to be genuine and which keep the show on the road. There is another brilliant scene towards the end in which the players are mobbed by the entire population of a plague-ridden village:

They heaved like a single body rising up out of the earth, still covered in clinging soil; their arms round one another's shoulders, their hair matted to a uniform colour by sweat and filth, their clothes the same moth-eaten, slept-in brown, dangling straw from their beds. Some were carrying children, as though the tiny shapes were molten lead running out of their grasp and heavy past holding. They squeezed across the narrow bridge ten abreast — one hideous, brown, pestilential beast with a hundred buckling legs. Others came behind on hands and knees. Two wicker stretchers tossed on the beast's back, half spilling their shroud-covered loads.

The villagers are begging to be cured. And Gabriel sees himself for what he is: 'a bogus angel standing between God the Creator and the people He had created, as they crumbled back into the clay they were made from.' There is no cure for the people; only terror for the players. The story is one of ups and downs; it cannot sustain throughout its course the power and intensity of the best passages, but it offers a colourful panorama of medieval England.

The action of K. M. Peyton's 'Flambards' books takes place just before and just after the First World War. Originally there were three novels – *Flambards* (1967), *The Edge of the Cloud* (1969) and *Flambards in Summer* (1969) – which for twelve years stood complete as a trilogy. In the first book Christina, who will be rich when she comes of age, is sent to live with her Uncle Russell and his two sons in a decrepit country house, financially undermined by Uncle's passion for horses and hunting. The handsome elder son, Mark, would like to marry her and keep what he calls 'all this' going; but Christina prefers Will, the gentle younger son who rejects the family obsession and longs to fly aeroplanes. The second book centres on Will's perilous life as an aviator; at the start of the third he is dead, and Christina returns to the old run-down house to bear his posthumous child, work the home farm, and marry the ex-groom Dick, who loves her. As well as a romantic story there is obviously a social theme – the death of an old way of life and its rebirth in a new form – and the connection between theme and period is organic. It was the First World War that broke up the old framework: the trilogy could not be transferred to any other time and retain its force.

In 1981, after the huge success of a television adaptation, Mrs Peyton added a fourth book, *Flambards Divided.* Inevitably, this changed the meaning of the other three: instead of completing the story they were leading up to a new conclusion. And the new conclusion was very different.

At the end of the third book, Christina had successfully carried Flambards into a new era; the omens, in her own phrase, were good. In *Flambards Divided,* these omens turn out to have been misleading. Christina's marriage to Dick doesn't work. Dick is reliable and hard-working but narrow, class-conscious and different from Christina in temperament and interests. Handsome Mark, home from the war, not knowing about anything but hunting and fighting, wins her affections after all. The squire, it could be said, is back in the saddle – even if it's now the driving seat of a motor car. If the author had written the fourth book straight after the other three, my guess is that she would have done it differently and poor Dick would have fared better. In twelve years illusions can be lost. The new ending may be truer to life, but I find it somewhat saddening.

18

After 'Johnny Tremain'

IN THE YEARS immediately after the Second World War, American historical fiction for young people stood in the shadow of Esther Forbes's *Johnny Tremain*, published in 1943 and discussed in an earlier section of the present study. *Johnny Tremain* was the novel that, above all others, was known and respected by everyone who had even the slightest acquaintance with the field. In 1976, however, it was damned by the historian Christopher Collier for allegedly embodying an old-fashioned interpretation of the American Revolution:

Johnny Tremain, with its message of ideologically motivated war, is so much the product of World War II that one who grew up in the 1940s must honor its clear one-sidedness . . . But, without denying its outstanding literary merit, Miss Forbes's presentation of the American Revolution does not pass muster as serious, professional history. Not so much because it is so sharply biased, but because it is so simplistic. Life is not like that — and we may be sure it was not like that two hundred years ago . . . To present history in simple, one-sided — almost moralistic — terms is to teach nothing worth learning and to falsify the past in a way that provides worse than no help in understanding the present or in meeting the future.[1]

As a British commentator, I have to observe that *Johnny Tremain*, though undoubtedly inspirational, does not seem to me to be one-sided. But a war so complex in its social, political and economic causes will obviously bear more than one interpretation and more than one fictional approach. After thirty years' change in attitudes, something like *My Brother Sam is Dead* (1974), which Christopher Collier wrote in collaboration with his brother James Lincoln Collier, was bound to come. *My Brother Sam* presents, to a generation of young people no longer expected to respond with simple patriotism to the inspirational, an unromantic picture of the war, and counts the cost of victory in terms of individual grief and suffering and the tearing apart of families.

While American historical fiction ranged over a good deal of foreign ground, it has continued to be at its most interesting in dealing with America's own past. It must be admitted that the liveliest fiction has not always had the rigour of 'serious, professional history'. Patricia Clapp's sprightly *Constance*

(1968) takes a familiar subject – the early years of Plymouth Colony, from 1620 to 1626 – and is built upon undoubted facts. By Jill Paton Walsh's definition it is a historical novel. But it is a costume novel, too; and perhaps rather more so. The sexy heroine who so disturbs the unattached young men of the colony, and enjoys herself vastly in doing so ('"Am I pretty?" I asked. "Pretty and sweet and ripe," he said, and leaned down to kiss me again') is a younger sister of the fetching creatures who frequently decorate romantic fiction. The book presents, so to speak, a twentieth-century seventeenth century; and the mayhaps and perchances of the dialogue don't reduce but if anything add to the sense of anachronism.

Elizabeth George Speare's *The Witch of Blackbird Pond* (1958) has hardly any archaisms in its dialogue, and sounds much more natural. And Kit Tyler, arriving in Connecticut from Barbados in 1687 with trunkloads of finery and an absence of Puritan conditioning, provides a convincing pair of eyes through which a stiff-and-stern community can be observed. The book is not entirely about witch-hunting; it is at least as much a discovery of old New England and New Englanders, an insight into a hard life in a hard-won land. The stiffness is also uprightness, the sternness is also strength; above all, there is a stolid endurance that sees things through. One never really believes that a court drawn from the sensible community portrayed here will commit Kit for witchcraft; but the dramatic last-minute evidence that brings her acquittal at least provides a strong climax to the story.

Near the beginning of this book, Kit remarks in passing that to pay for her passage from Barbados 'I had to sell my own Negro girl'. The other side of such a financial transaction is the starting point for Ann Petry's *Tituba of Salem Village* (1964). Tituba, an intelligent slave with 'good strong hands', finishes up in Salem; and, in a novel based on the first of the Salem witchcraft trials in 1692, comes under suspicion through the hysteria of several young girls. Along with two old women, she is convicted; alone of the three she survives. ('Remember, always remember, the slave must survive. No matter what happens to the master, the slave must survive.') The Salem witchcraft theme is well worn; the special merit of this book comes from the way in which superstition and hysteria are made credible in terms of character and background, and even more from a sense that real evil is here being engendered.

Escape from slavery has been a recurrent theme of American fiction from *Uncle Tom's Cabin* and *Huckleberry Finn* onward. Thomas Fall's *Canalboat to Freedom* (1966) is one of a number of novels published since 1945 that have featured the 'underground railroad', by means of which escaping slaves were smuggled from the South to Canada and the North. Ben, bound in service to a canalboat captain, joins a former slave called Lundius in working on the railroad, and learns why fugitives may be called the North Star People:

'Sometimes . . . when black folks run away, they don't have anything but the North Star to guide them through the swamps and the woods. If they follow the North Star, they'll get to freedom.'

This is an immensely strong theme, with obvious opportunities for combining an exciting escape story with social, moral and personal conflicts. But to my mind it has not yet inspired a modern children's novel of the highest class. Too often it has been unintentionally trivialized. It is all too easy to write with moral hindsight rather than insight, and consequently to produce stereotypes of villainy, bigotry or courage. In *Looking for Orlando*, by Frances Williams Browin (1961), it is hard to be convinced by the speed with which the hero and his friend are converted to anti-slavery, or by the Uncle Tommish innocence of the only black man who makes more than a fleeting appearance. In Jean Fritz's *Brady* (1960), slavery seems little more than an abstraction, and a runaway boy a pawn in a chess game. (But this is really the story of how Brady grows up under the responsibility of having people's life and liberty dependent on him.)

A more recent novel on this theme, *Underground to Canada* (1977) by the Canadian writer Barbara Schmucker, is based on first-hand accounts of experiences by runaway slaves, and tells its story from the point of view of two of them, Julilly and Liza. The incidents are such as might be expected – cruel treatment by overseer, escape, pursuit, hardship, and perilous passage from station to station on the railroad – but the story is one that grips, and the reader is bound to identify with the slaves themselves. There's a brief reminder at the end that arrival in Canada was not a simple happy-ever-after ending, and life for arriving blacks would still be hard.

The outstanding novel about slavery, and perhaps the most impressive American historical novel of its day, was Paula Fox's *The Slave Dancer* (1973). This is a first-person narration by Jessie Bollier, a New Orleans boy who is kidnapped and taken aboard a slave ship on its way to Africa to pick up black cargo. Jessie plays the fife, and he is wanted on the ship to 'dance' the slaves and thereby keep them in good enough condition for the market. It is a story of adventure at sea and eventual shipwreck; it is also an adventure into the depths of human nature, and a terrifying reminder of the inhumanity of which people who would regard themselves as decent can be capable. The crew of the slaver *Moonlight* are 'not especially cruel, save in their shared and unshakable conviction that the least of them was better than any black alive'. The slaves, crammed into the stinking hold, become sick and hopeless, most of them suffffering from 'the bloody flux', which makes the latrine buckets inadequate. Jessie finds that 'a dreadful thing' is happening in his mind:

> I hated the slaves! I hated their shuffling, their howling, their very suffering! I hated the way they spat out their food upon the deck, the overflowing buckets, the emptying of which tried all my strength. I hated the foul stench that came from the holds no matter which way the wind blew, as though the ship itself were soaked with human excrement. I would have snatched the rope from Spark's [the mate's] hand and beaten them myself! Oh, God! I wished them all dead! Not to hear them! Not to smell them! Not to know of their existence!

The *Moonlight* is wrecked (as was an actual slaver called *Moonlight* in the Gulf of Mexico in 1840). Jessie and a black boy named Ras are the only survivors. Ras is set on the road to freedom; Jessie returns home to live out an ordinary, modestly-successful life.

> I no longer spoke of my journey on a slave ship back in 1840. I did not often think of it myself. Time softened my memory as though it was kneading wax. But there was one thing that did not yield to time.
> I was unable to listen to music. I could not bear to hear a woman sing, and at the sound of any instrument, a fiddle, a flute, a drum, a comb with paper wrapped around it played by my own child, I would leave instantly and shut myself away. For at the first note of a tune or of a song I would see once again, as though they'd never ceased their dancing in my mind, black men and women and children lifting their tormented limbs in time to a reedy martial air, the dust rising from their joyless thumping, the sound of the fife finally drowned beneath the clanging of their chains.

Jessie Bollier fights in the civil war on the Unionist side, though this is not part of the substance of the novel. From slavery to the Civil War, in fact, is no great step. Irene Hunt's *Across Five Aprils* (1964) spans the wartime years, beginning with April 1861. But it is not a war story in the accepted sense of the phrase. It is about those left behind to struggle on with daily life and to suffer by proxy. The civil war prowls in the background; it is — as Matt Creighton, father of the hero Jethro, puts it — 'a beast with long claws'; and it is a beast that devours men and tears families apart.

Scott O'Dell (1898-1989) set most of his books in the American West — a West that was Spanish or Indian in flavour rather than White Anglo-Saxon Protestant. He came late to writing for children, and was not sure that he came to it at all; it was rather, he said, that he wrote 'in the emotional area that children share with adults'.[2] *Island of the Blue Dolphins* (1961) tells in the first person the true and moving story of an Indian girl who, in the middle third of the nineteenth century, lived alone for eighteen years on an island off the coast of California. *The King's Fifth* (1966) has as its hero a young cartographer in the days of the Conquistadors. Esteban, who yearns to map unknown lands, is caught up in a physically and morally perilous partnership with a band of unscrupulous treasure-hunters. The story of their quest unrolls side by side with that of its consequences; for Esteban writes it in prison, charged under Spanish law with depriving the King of his lawful fifth share.

O'Dell was in his late sixties when *The King's Fifth* appeared, but he went on to write more than twenty books for the children's list. He had a remarkable gift for assuming not only a feminine but an Indian identity. *Sing Down the Moon* (1970) is concerned with the sufferings of the Navajo Indians who were forced into the long dreadful march to Fort Sumner in 1864. It is told with a lovely grave simplicity by a young Navajo girl, Bright Morning. In 1986, at 88, O'Dell published one of his finest novels, *Streams to the River, River to the Sea*, in the same mode of first-person narration. This is the story, based on fact, of Sacagawea (Bird Woman), a girl of the nomadic Shoshone tribe in the Rockies, who accompanied the explorers Lewis and Clark on their epic journey to the Pacific at the start of the last century. It is, once more, an extraordinary feat of empathy; and it is an impressive achievement in late old age by a writer of major talent.

Elizabeth Borton de Trevino's *I, Juan de Pareja* (1965) is one of the best of American historical novels with non-American settings. This is the story, told in the first person, of the half-caste slave who became assistant, friend and fellow-artist to the Spanish painter Velazquez. Much of the book is built around actual Velazquez paintings; indeed, one suspects that the character and manner of the narrator are based on the Velazquez portrait of Pareja himself — grave, noble, immensely dignified, and looking to the untutored eye more like a grandee of Spain than a slave.

Historical fiction is one of two equally powerful strands in the work of Katherine Paterson (the other strand being formed by her novels of present-day or recent America, discussed in a later chapter.) The historical novels are set in the East: an East that is close to Katherine Paterson's roots, for she was born in China of missionary parents, learned Chinese as her first language, and was herself, as a young woman, a missionary in Japan for four years. Her first two books, *The Sign of the Chrysanthemum* (1973) and *Of Nightingales that Weep* (1974), are set in the feuding Japan of the twelfth century; their hero and heroine respectively are the children of Samurai but find their own ways to live — Muna (in *Chrysanthemum*) by becoming apprentice to a swordsmith, and Takiko (in *Nightingales)* by the eventual acceptance of the ugly potter who has become her stepfather.

Katherine Paterson has said that 'Setting for me is not a background against which a story is played out, but the very stuff with which the story will be woven. The characters will not determine the setting, but the setting to a great extent will determine both what they will be like and how they will act'.[3] The truth of this is evident, especially in her historical novels. The third, *The Master Puppeteer* (1975), is set in a world-within-a-world: the highly-ordered Bunraku, or Japanese puppet theatre, in disordered eighteenth-century Osaka. The hero is Jiro, the apprentice who, after many perils, makes good, but the most intriguing character is the bandit Saburo, an ambiguous Robin Hood figure.

Rebels of the Heavenly Kingdom (1983) followed a sequence of highly-acclaimed books with American settings, and was seen by some American observers as a disappointment. This must surely however have something to do with the dominance of contemporary realism as an American fictional mode, for *Rebels* is up to Katherine Paterson's highest standard. The setting and period are southern China in the mid-nineteenth century, when the Manchu empire, after being defeated by the 'long-nose barbarians' (the British), was under attack from within. Wang Lee, a peasant boy kidnapped by bandits and sold into slavery, is rescued by a girl called Mei Lin — who has herself been enslaved as a soldiers' whore — and recruited to the rebel cause of the Taiping Tienkuo, the Heavenly Kingdom of Great Peace. It seems a great cause: peace, freedom, and a kind of Christianity. But the leadership is corrupt, claiming divine descent and direct communication with God; and the 'heavenly peace' becomes ruthless slaughter, in which Wang Lee himself, all too credibly, takes part. At the end he and Mei Lin return to the soil to scratch an honourable peasant living. This novel, written by a committed Christian, faces with impressive honesty the distortions and excesses to which religion can be turned. It is also, to use Katherine Paterson's words in another context, 'a plea for justice and compassion'; and a plea which is all the more powerful because it is not made explicit but cries out from the heart of the story itself.

In the field of 'period' rather than 'historical' writing, the nearest American parallel to Leon Garfield is Sid Fleischman, who tells picaresque tales full of entertaining roguery. Like Garfield, Fleischman is fond of flamboyant, larger-than-life characters, and of mysteries of origin and identity; a recurrent theme is the discovery of a father or father-substitute. His principal literary influence appears to be Mark Twain, but there are other echoes, too; Mrs Daggatt's orphanage, for instance, in *Jingo Django* (1971), has a ring of Dickens about it. I have a special liking for *By the Great Horn Spoon!* (1963), in which the immaculate English butler Praiseworthy is found in the California Gold Rush, coping unflappably with all emergencies and respectfully claiming the hand of his young lady employer in the last chapter.

In *Humbug Mountain* (1978) Father is mostly around – he's an itinerant newspaper proprietor, who travels in a horse-drawn wagon with a hand-press and three cases of type, and can 'start up another newspaper quicker'n a hen lays an egg' – and the search is for Grandpa, Captain Tuggle, last heard of thrashing along the Missouri in his own riverboat. It's a quest that involves the steamboat *Prairie Buzzard,* the *Humbug Mountain Hoorah,* the founding of the city of Sunrise, the villainous Shagnasty John and the Fool Killer, the nickel-novel hero Quickshot Billy, and a supposedly petrified man – to name but a few. Fleischman is in fact a humorist and the modern master of the tall tale; and he has written a number of stories about McBroom and his wonderful one-acre farm, where the soil is 'so amazing rich we could plant and harvest two-three crops a day'.

In 1985, by coincidence, two books appeared in which the prairie, at a time in the past after the arrival of the railroad but before the motor-car, was both the setting and a crucial part of the emotional pattern of stories of basic yet profound human relationships. Patricia MacLachlan's *Sarah, Plain and Tall* has a classic brevity and simplicity. Papa farms; Mama died when small boy Caleb was born. Papa and Mama used to sing together; now Papa doesn't sing any more. Caleb and his older sister Anna, who narrates, need a mother as much as Papa and the farm need a working wife. Papa advertises for one. A reply comes from Sarah Wheaton in Maine; and, invited for a month's stay to see how it works, Sarah replies: 'I will come by train. I will wear a yellow bonnet. I am plain and tall.' In a postscript she adds, *'Tell them I sing.'*

Sarah, strong and capable, is just what this little family needs; but she misses her own people, and she misses the sea. She must detach herself from what what she has known and loved, and attach herself to the people and place she will love in future; no easy passage. The book has a mere fifty-eight pages, but it has the substance of a novel, and a fine one.

Prairie Songs, by Pam Conrad, brings to the Nebraska prairie, with its 'clear, pure nothing for miles and miles', a new doctor and his pretty, pregnant wife from New York. But Emmeline is no Sarah; she is afraid of Indians, coyotes and snakes; she longs for 'horses and carriages and angry drivers and cobblestone and shops with the wares displayed on the sidewalks, and people in finery, and huge ships docked with their masts reaching up into the sky.' She teaches the narrator Louisa from a neighbouring farm to read and enjoy poetry; but when she loses her baby it is all too much for her; she sinks into madness and despair, and dies in a tragic incident. A sad story, but two things remain of her: a picture by a pioneer photographer and a love of poetry born in Louisa.

The master of the difficult craft of making stories of the past attractive and comprehensible to the younger age group is Clyde Robert Bulla, who has written, for instance, about a boy's voyage to Vinland in *Viking Adventure* (1963), about the Pilgrim landings in *John Billington, Friend of Squanto* (1956), about life on the big river in *Down the Mississippi* (1954), about Coronado's quest for the city of gold in *Conquista!* (1978, with Michael Syson), and about an unwilling immigrant to early nineteenth-century America in *Charlie's House* (1983). Bulla's stories are clear, straightforward and without con-descension, and they are paced to the reading speed of a young child. Though short, they have sufficient action to satisfy; when you have read one you have read a whole, real book.

Very small children have little sense of the past; and although picture books and picture-story books quite often have period settings (and on principle ought to get them right) they remain basically picture books. An unusually pleasing and popular quartet was created by the American writer-artist Brinton Turkle with *Obadiah the Bold* (1965) and its successors, about a small Quaker boy in early nineteenth century Nantucket. The books convey a strong and colourful sense of the way of life of a community, in one of New England's historically and visually most interesting towns. Early nineteenth-century New England is the setting, too, of Donald Hall's *Ox-Cart Man* (1979), with affectionate, evocative pictures by Barbara Cooney that show a small farmer completing the year's work of the family by taking their produce and the things they have made on the ten-day trip 'over hills, through valleys, by streams, past farms and villages' to Portsmouth Market. Books like these open windows on the past but should not perhaps be burdened with the description 'historical'.

19

Re-expanding the far horizons

LIKE the historical novel, the 'good gripping yarn' of high adventure has had a hard time in the post-1945 years, though not for the same reasons. The wide, wide world has shrunk; trips to the other side of it are routine, and even those who sit at home can now see Tibet or Borneo, the Nile or the Andes, on the small screen. And probably the adventure story has suffered more than other fictional genres from the competition of films and television. Adventure is visual, and by definition is full of action and excitement – qualities that can more easily be exploited on the screen than on the printed page.

Yet adventure, however external and visible, must also involve thought and emotion; and where these are to be conveyed the printed page can do with ease what the screen can still only do clumsily. Moreover, books offer much more scope than films or television for identification: for projecting *yourself* into situations of excitement and peril. On the screen, the participants are clearly not *you*; you are watching them from the outside; but in reading a book you can be right in there yourself. The young eye at the centre of the story can be yours. Nina Bawden remarked some years ago that she aimed to put before children

what I hope are exciting adventure stories in a world that is real to them, and include situations and feelings they know. Adventure stories are important to children, not just the what-happens-next excitement, but because they can see themselves taking part in the action and test themselves: would they be brave in such a situation, or would they run away? Few children have a chance to do this in real life.[1]

The Second World War gave rise to a great deal of real-life adventure, most of it unsought. Yet although the war figured prominently in adult novels, in films and in comic books, it was not at first a source of inspiration to the most able children's writers. In early wartime Britain there were several novels about evacuee children which are now of only historical interest; and there was Mary Treadgold's *We Couldn't Leave Dinah* (1941), set in an imaginary Channel Island at the time of its Nazi occupation. But it was eleven years before a front-rank war book for children by a British author appeared. This was *The Silver Sword* (1956), in which Ian Serraillier described the trek of three Polish children across Europe in search of their parents, taken away by the Nazis. Though told in a matter-of-fact tone, this story holds enough incident and suspense for half a dozen books; it introduces a succession of people of different nationalities, and the children are seen growing up rapidly under the stress of experience.

Eleven years later still, Erik Haugaard, a Dane who writes in English, told a similar and equally touching story in *The Little Fishes* (1967). Guido, a waif on the streets of Naples in 1943, teams up with Anna and small brother Mario for a cross-country journey in search of a hoped-for benefactor. On their travels they encounter many people: the good, the bad, the indifferent, the ambivalent. There's a sadly-experienced but still childlike wisdom in Guido's narrative. These are the 'little fishes', the innocent and unimportant victims of war. At the end Mario has died but the other two are still wandering hopefully. We are not told what became of them; and in this case it is the right ending.

As the years passed, views on what could be put before young people became less and less restrictive. Writing on the same theme in *Tug of War* (1989), her most powerful novel so far, Joan Lingard dealt unflinchingly and often harrowingly with the ordeals, agonies and indignities suffered by two Latvian families fleeing from their homes in 1944.

By the time of *The Little Fishes,* World War II was coming into its own as a major fictional subject. A difficulty with war as a theme for children's fiction is that children can rarely be presented credibly as active combatants. But Jill Paton Walsh's *The Dolphin Crossing* (1967) has two boys in a small boat taking part in the famous rescue of British troops from Dunkirk in 1940, and the Dunkirk rescue also figures in Hester Burton's *In Spite of All Terror* (1968) and Philip Turner's *Dunkirk Summer* (1973).

Most war books of this period, however, featured the home front; and there were some very good ones. Jill Paton Walsh's *Fireweed* (1969) is set in London in 1940. An uprooted boy and girl, surviving dangerously through the blitz, set up house in the cellar of a bombed building, earn money, take in a lost child. And what develops between them is a true form of love, growing – like the fireweed, or willowherb, that gives the book its title – on the scars of ruin and flame. Their love is innocent, but is symbolically consummated on the cold night when the girl comes to sleep in the boy's arms. It cannot last;

Julie, rescued from rubble when the cellar collapses, is returned to her parents, who are much grander than Bill's, and the class barriers close around her. This is an exceptional novel for young people: poignant and haunting.

Carrie's War, by Nina Bawden (1973), shows a quieter corner of the home front, from the viewpoint of a child rather than an adolescent. Carrie and her younger brother Nick are evacuees from London, staying in a small Welsh town with narrow-minded, tight-fisted Councillor Evans ('Up and down the stairs, soon as my back's turned,' he complains, 'wearing out the stair carpet') and his downtrodden sister. Careful, conscientious Carrie and unregenerate Nick are themselves surviving the wartime hazards of uprooting, separation from parents, and being thrust into an uncongenial home in a strange community.

Michelle Magorian's hugely popular *Goodnight, Mister Tom* (1981) was another evacuee story, and one that struck a strong sentimental chord in readers of all ages. It is about Willie, a skinny, unloved, bed-wetting child from the East End of London, who not only thrives in the country but thaws out the frozen heart of the old man on whom he is billeted. But the home-front story that had the strongest and most authentic smell of danger and violence came from Robert Westall, with *The Machine-Gunners* (1975). This is about a gang of boys (and one girl) who smuggle a machine-gun out of a crashed German bomber, perilously determined to make their own contribution to the war effort. It is a powerful story with no punches pulled, crowded with character and incident.

Westall has returned more than once to World War II, which obviously exerts a powerful pull on his imagination. *Blitzcat* (1989) traverses the home front in the war's early years by following a female cat on its wanderings, through bombing raids and other dangers, in search of its owner. The story is episodic and violent, with death and mutilation, as well as a good deal of sexual reference and strong language; the acrid smell of war lies over everything. There is no young person as a main character, and the question arises which we hear from time to time: is this really a children's book? It depends, I think, on how you look at it. If the episodes were to be regarded as the substance of the novel, with the cat as a mere linking device, there would be a strong case for classing it as 'adult'. But if, as a young reader must, you identify with the cat, it becomes a children's book, for you are moving, vulnerable and uncomprehending, through a dangerous adult world which the author rightly portrays in the harsh colours of the time.

American homes were farther than British from the scenes of wartime action, and the stories referred to so far in this chapter could not have been written in American contexts. Several good books have been published in the United States however which have settings in occupied Europe. *The Upstairs Room,* by Johanna Reiss (1972), is based on its author's wartime experience as a child in Holland, and tells movingly how two young Jewish girls were confined for more than two years in the upstairs room of a Dutch farmhouse. The author explains in a note that she tried to write 'a simple, human book, in which my sister and I suffered and complained, and sometimes found fault with the Gentile family that took us in'; in which 'the members of that family were not heroes but people, with strengths and weaknesses.' Aranka Siegal's *Upon the Head of the Goat* (1981) is also a first-person autobiographical account — this time of a Hungarian Jewish family's life in the five years or so up to the time when what remains of it is sent in the trucks to Auschwitz. It is cumulative: first the straws in the wind, then the minor discriminations and inconveniences, and then the gradual buildup of oppression to the ultimate horror. The air of truthfulness and simplicity makes the appalling story all too credible.

Both of the books just mentioned were Newbery honour books. Lois Lowry's *Number the Stars* was the Newbery Medal winner for 1989. It is on a closely related theme, but the wartime experience on which it draws is at a remove from the author, being that of a Danish friend. The heroine, Annamarie, aged 10, helps a Jewish family escape from occupied Denmark to Sweden. This book does not seem to me to be as powerful as either of the other two. The telling is somewhat commonplace and the general attitude morally simplistic; the Danish characters are all brave and loyal, the German soldiers rude and aggressive. A fine first novel with a wartime setting in America however was Bette Greene's *Summer of my German Soldier* (1973), in which a Jewish girl living in a small town in Arkansas harbours an escaped German prisoner of war.

Among post-war but not war-based American adventure stories, one of the most distinguished, *My Side of the Mountain,* by Jean George (1959), is in essence a Robinsonnade. Sam Gribley, in the former book, runs away from his home in New York and lives for a year in a tree house in the Catskill

Mountains. Sam survives largely by hunting and fishing, but he also eats wild plants; he tames a falcon, which hunts for him, and he becomes friendly with several wild creatures. The details have an air of great authenticity; the author, with her husband John George, has written a number of books based on wildlife. The ending is not as might be expected. Sam does not go back to his family in New York; they come to him, and are going to build a house on the mountain.

Richard Armstrong, who sailed with the British Merchant Navy for many years, wrote a number of sea adventure stories that have had less attention in recent years than they deserved. His last two books, *The Mutineers* (1968) and *The Albatross* (1970), written when he was well into his sixties, were probably his best. *The Mutineers* can be compared, not absurdly, to William Golding's *Lord of the Flies*. It is about a gang of late-teenage boys who, after a successful mutiny, finish up on a desert island, where a power struggle throws up a dominant but brutal leader. But a positive ending contrasts with Golding's bitter cynicism. *The Albatross* (1970) is about four apprentice seamen who find a huge treasure and make off with it; but they have not really taken possession of it so much as it has taken possession of them. They are changed terribly, and it is clear that they are heading not for lifelong wealth but for disaster. Treasure in fact is sinister, and not only because it is often hidden, discovered and fought over in circumstances of violence and treachery. The truth is also that the hope of great unearned gain can be one of the most corrupting ever to get men in its grip.

Gillian Cross's *Born of the Sun* (1983) has the shape of the classic story of exotic adventure brought up to date. Paula is taken from school to accompany her father, Karel, a well known explorer and TV personality, with her mother and a young photographer, on a quest to find a lost city of the Inca. There are clashes and disasters, due to Karel's erratic behaviour; it emerges that an advanced cancer is affecting his brain. The city is found, but Karel doesn't see it, and anyway it is dead, lost in the dark. Karel, on the point of death, is apparently cured by an ancient tribal healer. That is a bald summary which cannot convey the resonances of this intriguing and stimulating, though by no means flawless, book. The exploration is not only what it is, but is of human nature; the discovery is that there are more things in heaven and earth than are dreamed of in our philosophy. At the end is a quotation from Richard Jefferies: 'In the heart of most of us there is always a desire for something beyond experience. Hardly any of us but have thought, some day I will go on a long voyage, but the years go by and still we have not sailed.' *On the Edge*, by the same author (1984), is a 'quality' thriller, written with great psychological insight: it is about the kidnapping of a boy by crazy terrorists and his struggle for his life and identity.

Leon Garfield's books in general are discussed elsewhere in the present study, but his first, *Jack Holborn* (1964), must be mentioned at this point as an adventure story in the best tradition, with murder, treachery, shipwreck and ultimate fortune. It has a finely ambiguous villain, Mister Solomon Trumpet, who can stand comparison with Long John Silver. Long John indeed continues to fascinate writers. Allan Campbell McLean, who has written several adventure stories set in the Isle of Skye, has a Stevensonian heroic villain in *Master of Morgana* (1960), where one-legged John MacGregor, 'with the face of an old pirate', stumps away with the story. And in Robert Leeson's *Silver's Revenge* (1978), an enigmatic Mr Argent, now a pioneer industrialist with a false leg that moves on ball-bearings, turns up in the later life of Jim Hawkins, and off they all go again to Treasure Island.

The obvious genre to which we may look for a re-expansion of the far horizons is science fiction. It enables writers to get around the limits of physical possibility, to invent new forms of life and marvellous gadgetry, and to explore rich and strange worlds of their own. True, a spaceship doesn't really have any more adventure built into it than a sailing ship. Yet on top of its other advantages, SF is a splendid vehicle for ideas, setting human nature and human problems in new contexts, and catching the attention of bright young minds at that point – the early years of high school, perhaps – at which they often lose interest in reading for pleasure.

SF writers for adults have made full use of the scope the genre gives them; their versatility and ingenuity are often startling. And 'adult' SF is of course widely read by young people. In England, though not so much in the United States, SF for children tended for many years to be looked down on by the children's literature pundits as an inferior genre, more suitable for pulp magazines than for respectable print.

In the first twenty years after the Second World War, the best known and most strongly established practitioners of SF for children in their native United States, and probably in Britain as well, were Robert Heinlein (1907-88) and André Norton. Both wrote mainly 'space opera', about journeyings among other worlds or galaxies. Heinlein began with *Rocket Ship Galileo* (1947), in which a group of youngsters build their own rocket and fly to the moon, where they uncover a Nazi plot. An unlikely story, to say the least; but Heinlein's characters are real people, he seems entirely at home with astronomy, mathematics and space technology, and he knows very well how to maintain suspense. Sometimes the opportunities he offers for wishful self-identification by the reader are rather obvious. In *Starman Jones* (1953) a boy who longs to be an 'astrogator' makes his way on to a spaceship, duly gets his chance, and finishes up as acting captain, no less. Space navigation will never actually be as Heinlein described it in 1953, but his account generates its own conviction and remains satisfying.

Heinlein was skilful at constructing future societies on foundations adapted from the past:

'Lot ninety-seven,' the auctioneer announced. 'A boy.' The boy was dizzy and half sick from the feel of ground underfoot. The slave ship had come more than forty light years; it carried in its holds the stink of all slave ships, a reek of crowded, unwashed bodies, of fear and vomit and ancient grief . . .

These are the opening words of *Citizen of the Galaxy* (1957); and they offer incidentally an object-lesson in how to seize the reader's interest. Heinlein did not claim any male monopoly of space; his *Have Space Suit – Will Travel* (1958) co-stars an extremely bright female child of ten; *Podkayne of Mars* (1963) – his last children's book, though he went on publishing fiction for adults until the year before his death – has a sixteen-year-old girl as its heroine.

André Norton has also put girls into space, but her SF is written in a hard, dry style which one might well take to be deliberately masculine. Her heroes are apt to be loners with little home background and few friends; her worlds of the future are bleak and perilous, and it is something even to stay alive. But the flow of action and invention is strong, and she holds her readers. Her best book among those known to me, and the one with most human warmth, is *Dark Piper* (1968), in which a group of young people take refuge underground when their civilization crumbles and bands of pirates infest the skies.

Probably the best known and most ambitious of American SF

stories for young people is Madeleine L'Engle's *A Wrinkle in Time* (1962). Heroine Meg Murry, who wears spectacles and has braces on her teeth, sets off with precocious small brother Charles and friend Calvin O'Keefe to rescue her scientist father from the grip of IT, a great brain that controls the lives of the zombie population of a planet called Camazotz. The power of love and the help of three witches, who appear also to be angels, enable Meg to triumph over evil (evil being the extermination of individuality). There is a luminous confusion about *A Wrinkle in Time;* it seems to be trying to do too many things at once. But it is an attractive book, splendidly unafraid of being clever or out-of-the-ordinary, and not concerned to reinforce the image of the regular guy or girl.

Laurence Yep began his career with a highly promising SF novel, *Sweetwater* (1973), though he then turned to writing on Chinese-American themes. *Sweetwater* has a pattern of interlocking conflicts: between a boy and his father, between colonists on a planet and an indigenous population, and among the colonists themselves. These transposed problems from our own world have also greatly concerned the Canadian writer Monica Hughes in *Crisis on Conshelf Ten* (1975) and other novels.

William Sleator has said that 'try as I might, I can't seem to keep outer space, time travel, and aliens out of my work.' He has also referred to science as 'the ultimate reality' − surely an unprovable proposition − and added that 'actual scientific facts are as peculiar as anything I could dream up',[2] which is undoubtedly true. He is clearly fascinated both by scientific concepts and by the stock-in-trade of science fiction. *Interstellar Pig* (1984) is an extremely clever book. Expectation rises as it becomes clear that the three handsome strangers who are so interested in the old house by the shore are something other than people, and that the galactic adventure-game into which they draw the teenage narrator Barney is much more than a game. Yet in the end the story goes over the top. When Barney becomes part of a creeping mass of voracious pink carnivorous lichen, while the other characters take shapes that are caricatures of SF monsters, it is hard not to feel that the whole thing has dissolved into a giggle, and that the author must know it. *The Green Fingers of Tycho* (1981) makes ingenious use of time travel and the paradoxes that surround it. *Singularity* (1985) is based on the supposition that an outhouse on a farm could be built over a singularity, or black hole − a dead star that has collapsed to a minute volume with enormous gravity — and would become a 'time contraction field'. A few hours spent in it could be years in the world outside. Harry, the narrator, uses it — unwisely, one might think — to age himself and become senior to brother Barry. A singularity like this might also be an opening to another universe, and for good measure a ferociously-jawed monster comes through, but fortunately eats itself up.

In Britain, little of value was achieved in SF for children until John Christopher, already well established as a writer of science and other fiction for adults, turned to books for the children's list with *The White Mountains* in 1967. This was the first book of a trilogy, of which the other two titles were *The City of Gold and Lead* (1967) and *The Pool of Fire* (1968). The world is ruled by Masters, from a distant planet, who have imposed upon it a stagnant, neo-medieval peace, reinforced by a process of mental castration known as capping. The theme of the trilogy is the apparently forlorn struggle of a few uncapped men to overthrow the Masters — who look on humans rather as we look on the beasts — before the Masters convert the earth's atmosphere to one which is fit for them but poisonous to the natural inhabitants. Some of the ideas are familiar; but the cool, clean style, the controlled intelligence with which the plot is unfolded, and the touches of true imagination on large or small scale, together with strong professional storytelling, made the trilogy an immediate success both with children and commentators.

John Christopher followed the *White Mountains* trilogy with *The Lotus Caves* (1969), in which two boys belonging to the frugally-administered colony on the Moon find their way into the strange, seductive realm of the Plant; and *The Guardians* (1970), which polarizes existing British class distinctions to the point where there are two separate nations — the crowded, horrible Conurb and the stately County. A second trilogy, consisting of *The Prince in Waiting* (1970), *Beyond the Burning Lands* (1971) and *The Sword of the Spirits* (1972), again postulates a post-cataclysmic neo-medieval England, now made up of small warring city-states. The hero, Luke, prince-to-be of Winchester, has a mission to unite his fragmented country against external peril, and there are strange echoes of Arthurian legend; but in the end Luke, loser in love to his best friend, turns the rediscovered forces of technology against his own people. The hero in short is fatally flawed, a greater

Illustration by David Smee from *The Blue Hawk*,
by Peter Dickinson

danger than any mere villain. Later books by John
Christopher, up to the time of writing, seem to me to have
been less impressive than those already mentioned.

Some of Peter Dickinson's books could be called, in his own
phrase, science fiction without the science. His first three
books on the children's list are about the 'Changes', which
have caused the people of contemporary England to turn
against machinery and withdraw into a dark age of ignorance
and malice. In the first to appear, *The Weathermonger* (1968),
Geoffrey, aged 16, and his sister Sally set off through hostile
countryside in a splendid antique Rolls-Royce to find out how
the Changes came about. This part of the book is a vivid
adventure story, and the passages in which Geoffrey practises
his mysterious art of conjuring up a different weather are fine
and poetic, but in my opinion the book goes badly wrong at
the end with its incongruous attribution of the Changes to a
revived but drug-sick Merlin.

In the second book, *Heartsease* (1969), two children, using
horses and an old tugboat, contrive the escape of a young man
who has been stoned as a witch and left for dead; in the third,
The Devil's Children (1970) the heroine, Nicola, attaches
herself to a band of Sikhs who themselves are unaffected by

the Changes but who are feared and hated by the people of the village near which they settle. The three books were reissued together in 1975 as *The Changes*.

Dickinson's early books were far excelled by *The Blue Hawk* (1976), a remarkable feat of the speculative imagination. It is set in a time that may be the distant past or the distant future, but is most likely a time-that-never-was, in a country that strongly suggests ancient Egypt. It is a priest-ridden country, ruled by ritual, in which nothing can ever change. Tron, a boy priest, breaks the pattern, opening up the closed land and closed minds. This is a fast-moving adventure story and at the same time a story about political intrigue and the conflict between personal relationships and hierarchical ones. It is also about the existence of the gods and — if they do exist — their nature.

Tulku (1979) is as exotic as *The Blue Hawk,* and as hard to classify. We are now in Tibet, where young Theodore, escaping from China at the time of the Boxer Rebellion, becomes the companion of rich ex-actress Mrs Jones. At a great monastery, Mrs Jones's unborn child by her guide, Lung, is declared to be the Tulku, a great reincarnated lama, and as with *The Blue Hawk* there follows a tale of interwoven religion and politics. And again there are questions of belief: it seems that belief and cynicism perhaps even belief and unbelief, can coexist in the same person.

In *Healer* (1983) sixteen-year-old Barry sets out to rescue Pinkie, a small girl with a gift of healing, from the charlatan Freeman who is exploiting her. His doing so is the main part of the plot. But there's another, internal, drama; for Barry feels that he has a divided personality; there is an animal inside him — he calls it Bear — which is violent and uncontrollable and almost causes him to kill Freeman. Pinkie's parting gift is to make him whole by integrating Bear into himself, and all ends well.

He turned towards home. The September noon was bright and pleasant. Somehow, despite the traffic fumes, it felt like a spring day. His skin crawled pleasantly in the warmth. He stretched and yawned, easing the muscles below the skin, feeling the wholeness of himself settle peacefully into place, as though he had just woken from winter sleep, sleep fretful with intrusive dreams, and now was prowling out into the sun, blinking at the last quick-melting snowdrifts, sniffling the air of a world made new.

Eva (1988) is about a girl whose mind has been transplanted into the body of a chimpanzee, after her own body has been wrecked in a car crash, some time in the future. She thinks as a human but feels as a chimp; she is exploited in an over-commercialized, over-populated world, and the story is concerned largely with an attempt to establish a chimp colony in a natural environment. The 'green' implications are obvious. With the death-wish growing among humans, Eva dies a chimp.

Peter Dickinson's books for young people − he has also written crime and other fiction for adults − are the products of an energetic, questing mind and a fine professional grasp of story-telling.

Jan Mark emerged in the mid-1970s as a major talent in children's writing. Much of her fiction, discussed elsewhere in this study, is set in the everyday world of childhood, but in the late seventies and early eighties she made three excursions into imagined worlds that reflected the harsher tendencies of our own. *The Ennead* (1978) is set on the dusty satellite-planet Erato; *Divide and Rule* (1979) in a corrupt, dilapidated theocracy, and in both books individuals are defeated by cynically-operated systems. But at least in *The Ennead* the human spirit goes down fighting, in the persons of the doomed lovers Moshe and Eleanor and of the unheroic hero Isaac, who has hitherto devoted his efforts to his own survival but in the end is willing to sacrifice himself. *Divide and Rule*, starker still, shows its hero still alive at the end but cast out by the system as a mere husk.

Aquarius (1982) is bleakest of all. The water-diviner 'hero', Viner, is a totally dislikeable figure who winds his way doggedly through ordeals and endurance tests to survival and success by the exploitation of others. At this point Jan Mark seemed to have journeyed to the farthest frontier of children's literature, and possibly beyond it, but she returned in the next few years to more familiar and less forbidding landscapes.

'Nicholas Fisk caters for children bred on television,' wrote Joy Whitby in an essay in *Twentieth Century Children's Writers*. 'Much of his work ends up on television . . .'[3] Fisk began a successful career as a writer mainly of SF with *Space Hostages* (1967), in which a group of children are kidnapped on to a spaceship by a dying airman and left alone in space. One of them can control the ship, but another is determined to be boss. The struggle for power is as gripping as the struggle for survival, and comes to the same thing in the end. Other notable books by Nicholas Fisk include *Trillions* (1971), *Grinny* (1973) and *A Rag, a Bone, and a Hank of Hair* (1982).

Science fiction of any quality for younger readers has not been plentiful. *Miss Pickerel Goes to Mars* (1951), by Ellen

MacGregor, has a spinster of uncertain age, accustomed to nothing more rapid than her 18-year-old, 20-m.p.h. car, coping resourcefully with the hazards and discomforts of a space trip. Then there were Ruthven Todd's *Space Cat* (1952), Eleanor Cameron's *Wonderful Flight to the Mushroom Planet* (1954) and its successors, and the Danny Dunn books of Jay Williams and Raymond Abrashkin. William Sleator contributed *Into the Dream* in 1979; and *The Green Book* (1981), by Jill Paton Walsh, was another welcome addition to this small sub-genre.

Books on the children's lists that have attempted to deal with a projected nuclear cataclysm have tended to be gruesome, heavily didactic, or both, and of limited literary merit. By far the best of those known to me is Robert C. O'Brien's *Z for Zachariah* (1975). This is in fact an after-the-cataclysm story; the actual horrors of nuclear war are not described, though sufficiently hinted at. The sixteen-year-old narrator, Ann Burden, in an American valley, is apparently the world's only survivor, managing to live by cultivating land and keeping a little farm stock, while also drawing on the village store (the equivalent of Crusoe's wreck). A second survivor arrives, a cold-blooded scientist named Loomis, who clearly intends to take over the establishment and Ann with it. One can't help seeing one of the book's themes as being the re-entry of evil into Eden. Ann gets away, and sets off on foot for a place that she has dreamed of that may exist: a schoolroom full of children waiting for someone to teach them. At the end there's just a slight indication of acceptance and reconciliation on Loomis's part, and the conclusion, though tentative, is positive: Ann's last words are 'I am hopeful'. And indeed a book for young readers without hope would be a terrible thing. This plain, spare but strong story was one of the most impressive of its decade.

20

Modern fantasy (i): Just like us

IN SPITE OF advancing technology, the materialism of the age, and the growing sophistication of children, fantasy has maintained its position in English-language children's literature. It has continued to some extent to be a British speciality, but much less so than in the nineteenth and early twentieth centuries. Distinguished fantasies have come from America and, in very recent years, Australia. Twenty years or more ago, I used to hear it suggested frequently in discussion that fantasy was an airy-fairy, flimsy-whimsy business, a form of 'escape from reality', which should be discouraged. But for some years now I have heard very little of this. Perhaps the quality of the books available has silenced the detractors; perhaps it is now being recognized that fantasy is as deeply rooted in human nature, and as relevant to the actual living of life, as any other literary mode.

The form is in fact an extremely varied one. It ranges from simple stories of magic to profound and complex imaginative constructions. For the purposes of this chapter and the two that follow, I have divided it into three categories: anthropomorphic fantasy, in which animals or inanimate objects are endowed with human qualities; fantasies that create imaginary worlds or countries; and fantasies that inhabit the world we know but require some disturbance of the natural order of things. This classification, like others in the book, is for convenience of discussion; I do not claim any special importance for it, and it would be easy (though unrewarding) to argue about borderline cases.

Animal fantasy is perhaps the most endearing category of children's fiction over the period under review. While there are animal villains — Manny Rat, for instance, in *The Mouse and his Child,* or General Woundwort in *Watership Down* — animal characters on the whole are presented sympathetically, and this sub-genre lends itself to cheerful and tolerant approaches. Perhaps this is because animals are essentially innocent — an animal only knows how to be the kind of animal it is — whereas innocence has taken rather a beating in recent years in fiction for older children.

In picture story books, easy readers and young children's fiction, anthropomorphism is often a kind of metaphor. For small or large animal, you read child or grown-up. Little Bear, in Elsa Minarik's *Little Bear* (1957) and its successors, is obviously a small child; Mother Bear is a loving, infinitely reliable parent to whose arms he returns from his adventures, and who will never forget his birthday or fail to make a cake. Similarly, Russell Hoban's Frances in *Bedtime for Frances* (1960) and other titles, although the illustrations show a badger, is really a little girl; and her ploys, such as wanting a drink of milk, asking for her doll, remembering that she didn't brush her teeth, and wondering whether she got her goodnight kiss, are the age-old techniques of small children for putting off the inevitable hour.

Arnold Lobel's *Frog and Toad are Friends* (1970) and its successors offer slightly different perspectives. Frog and Toad are childish grownups rather than children: active, relatively-sensible Frog the senior partner, and slow, well-meaning but not-very-bright Toad the junior. There's a likeable, happy humour in these stories; the animals have a curious dignity of their own and their mutual affection shines from the page — a celebration of friendship.

Paddington, in Michael Bond's *A Bear Called Paddington* (1958) and many later titles, lives with a human family and is treated as one of the children. Mortimer the raven in Joan Aiken's *Arabel's Raven* (1972) likewise lives with a family, the Joneses; he has a vocabulary consisting of the appropriate word 'Nevermore', likes diamonds and potato crisps and slot machines, and gets his family into the most extraordinary and hilarious predicaments. All these are only a few of the many fictional animals who in varying degrees are really people.

Dolls are people, too; and often they are people who have a hard life.

> It is an anxious, sometimes a dangerous thing to be a doll. Dolls cannot choose; they can only be chosen; they cannot 'do'; they can only be done by; children who do not understand this often do wrong things, and then the dolls are hurt and abused and lost; and when this happens dolls cannot speak, nor do anything except be hurt and abused and lost.

The quotation is from *The Dolls' House* (1947), by Rumer Godden, the most celebrated writer of doll stories. Her later books include *The Story of Holly and Ivy* (1958) and *Impunity Jane* (1955), which is my personal favourite. Impunity Jane has spent fifty years sitting on a bead cushion in a dolls' house, but at last gets out into the world, where she sails a model yacht, goes up in an aeroplane, and lives in igloos and wigwams. Miss Godden has also written neatly about human-ized mice in *The Mousewife* (1951) and *Mouse House* (1957). Discarded toys of long ago can induce adult nostalgia, and Jane Gardam's *Through the Dolls' House Door* (1987), which takes the dolls' house inhabitants through years of neglect and banishment before they are rescued for a new generation, has an undertone of wistfulness, and suggests a grown-up's rather than a child's-eye view. For that matter, dolls can be a vehicle for acid satire on human behaviour, as in 'Mr and Mrs Johnson', one of *Two Stories* by Jan Mark (1984).

Anthropomorphism can extend a long way: to railway engines (the Rev. W. Awdry and others), automobiles (Leila Berg's *Little Car*, Val Biro's *Gumdrop*), tugboats (Hardie Gramatky), steamshovels, cable-cars and houses (Virginia Lee Burton), and even computers (*The Little Red Computer*, by Ralph Steadman, 1969). Catherine Storr's *Clever Polly and the Stupid Wolf* (1967) is a different kind of fantasy for small children: a fantasy of competence, superiority and triumph over a big fierce creature.

The Iron Man (1968; American title *The Iron Giant*) is a 'story in five nights' by Ted Hughes, now Britain's Poet Laureate. The iron man, with his dustbin-shaped head as big as a bedroom, is clearly not a figure of the television-and-computer age, even if he does chew up old cars in the scrapyard. There is primitive power and magic in him; he falls off a cliff but reassembles himself; is buried and rises again; competes with a dragon from space in withstanding the heat at the sun's heart; restarts the music of the spheres. The mythological elements are obvious; the author himself has expounded their significance for children in psychoanalytical terms,[1] but leaves one feeling that a writer's interpretation of his book, though it must be looked on with respect, is still only one person's view, and is not necessarily 'correct' to the exclusion of all others.

E. B. White (1899-1985) was a major American literary figure – an influential writer and columnist for the *New Yorker* in its formative years, a witty and stylish essayist, collaborator with James Thurber, and winner of a Pulitzer Prize. But his lasting reputation is likely to be as the author of classic children's books, especially the splendid and perennially popular *Charlotte's Web* (1952). This story – in which Charlotte the spider saves little pig Wilbur from the usual fate of fat pigs by

Wilbur and the daughters of Charlotte: a drawing by Garth Williams
from *Charlotte's Web,* by E. B. White

weaving words of praise about him into her web — is far-stretched; but like the web, it is cleverly spun, and stronger than it looks. And it is more than merely playful. The point about loyal, intelligent Charlotte is that she is our kin, one of us. So is poor fat unheroic Wilbur, gulping and slurping in the warm slops or wallowing in the manure-heap; so are the gobble-obble-obbling geese and the greedy self-seeking rat Templeton. The death of Charlotte, which makes small girls weep, is the death of a person, made bearable by the continuance of life through her offspring. The barn and farmyard are a world. The passage of seasons, the round of nature, are unobtrusively indicated.

Outside the life of the farmyard there is another world, not perhaps more real but on a different plane, which is that of commonplace human life; and perhaps the most poignant thing in the book is the passage of small girl Fern from involvement with the animals as people to a perfectly normal, but imaginatively regressive, preoccupation with the glittering actualities of the fairground. Fern has begun the saving of Wilbur, but by the end she has forgotten him; that is life, too. Childhood passes. *Charlotte's Web,* though a short and apparently straightforward story, is astonishingly full and rich. White's *Stuart Little* (1945) takes the idea of animals-as-people to its logical conclusion. Stuart is not only a mouse; he is also the child of a human family. The book is a funny one with serious undertones. The comedy is partly Lilliputian, as when Stuart takes the helm of a model yacht in a race on the pond, and partly derived from a deadpan presentation of the absurd:

> The doctor was delighted with Stuart and said that it was very unusual for an American family to have a mouse . . . Everything seemed to be all right, and Mrs Little was pleased to get such a good report.
> 'Feed him up!' said the doctor cheerfully, as he left.

But the story ends in what appears to be midstream, with Stuart searching for the vanished bird Margalo whom he loves. Perhaps the ending is right; Stuart's is a quest for freedom and beauty, and such a quest is never completed.

The Trumpet of the Swan (1970) has much in common with *Stuart Little*. Once again the basic notion is simple and absurd: what if a trumpeter swan actually played the trumpet? And again much of the comedy is based on straightfaced acceptance. When Louis the swan goes to school, the first-graders 'liked the look of the new pupil and were eager to see what he could do'. And Louis grabs a piece of chalk in his bill and draws a perfect A. There is a memorable account of how Louis goes to stay the night at the Ritz Carlton Hotel in Boston – 'Has he any luggage?' asks the clerk suspiciously – and after ordering watercress sandwiches from room service goes luxuriously to sleep in the bathtub. Yet *The Trumpet of the Swan* is not 'flat' comedy; there is a third dimension in which fantasy blends with the real life of the wild and our kinship with the creatures is once again evident. It is a loving book as well as a funny one. George Selden's *The Cricket in Times Square* (1960) and its successors should be mentioned alongside the E. B. White books; they are very much in the same spirit. Here is another testament of friendship; and Chester the concert chirpist, Tucker the smart city mouse, and Harry the benignly unfeline cat are as odd and engaging a trio as Charlotte and Wilbur are a pair.

The hero of *Abel's Island*, by William Steig (1976), is a perfect gentleman – surely a Bostonian – as well as being a mouse. (Steig, being his own illustrator, has no difficulty in reconciling these characteristics.) It is the summer of 1907. Separated from his lovely wife Amanda and cast away on an island in the middle of a river, Abel sets to work, resourcefully and sagaciously, to get himself to the mainland; but a full year passes and he is a ragged mouse Crusoe before at last he is restored to Amanda's arms.

The humanized-animal fantasies of White, Selden and Steig, gentle and amiable as they are, may be seen as establishing a modern tradition which is sophisticated and distinctively American. Though they do not fall into either of the traps of avuncular condescension or of winking to the adults, there is a dryness in their wit. It appears at its dryest in *A Rat's Tale,* by Tor Seidler (1986), in which Montague Mad-Rat, member of a New York City rat family that is mocked for its artistic leanings, wins popular acclaim and the paw of the aristocratic Isabel Moberly-Rat when his sea-shell paintings fetch real dollars and buy off a human threat of mass rat-poisoning. One does not have to be unduly cynical to suspect a satirical sub-text. Art, it is clear, is not to be despised; it can be profitable, prestigious, and an aid to successful wooing.

Back in 1939 Robert Lawson (1891-1957) had written *Ben and Me,* a life of Benjamin Franklin as told by his mouse Amos, to whom Ben seems to have been indebted for some of his brightest ideas. In 1953 Lawson added *Mr Revere and I,* the story of Paul Revere's ride and other matters as told by his lady horse Scheherazade, the late pride of His Majesty's 14th Regiment of Foot. (I cannot bring myself to call this distin-guished quadruped a mare.) And in 1956 came *Captain Kidd's Cat,* narrated in the salty style of an old sea-cat by McDermot, whose drink is warm milk and Jamaica rum. According to McDermot, Kidd was a meek-and-mild man really; and McDermot should know, for 'didn't I sell the ruby ring out of my left ear to buy him a decent clean shirt for the hanging?' These are hearty, humorous stories, based on a splendid idea and a sufficiency of research, and they are accompanied by the author's own hearty, humorous drawings. To my mind, they show Robert Lawson at his best.

Russell Hoban's *The Mouse and his Child* (1967), about the quest of a pair of linked toys to find a home and be self-winding, is a multi-layered book, accessible at more than one level. It can be read by children quite simply as a story of the adventures of clockwork toys, and by adults as a haunting human progress. The pathos of a toy's life – the decline from freshness, beauty and efficiency towards the rubbish dump, the rusting of bright metal, the rotting of firm plush – is the pathos of human life transposed. The mouse and his child are loving *people*, totally interdependent. There are clear allegorical meanings — any child can understand the longing to be self-winding — and strong, often funny, sometimes savage satire, though some of this may be beyond the grasp of children. Manny Rat, who rules the rubbish dump and deals with recalcitrant toys by consigning their innards to the spare parts can, is a splendid villain.

The background to *The Mouse* is clearly North American, but the book has never been esteemed as highly in the United States as in Britain, where it is regarded by many, including myself, as a classic. In the 1969 revision of the *Critical History of Children's Literature* by Meigs and others, it is not mentioned; in the 1986 edition of *Children and Books,* by Zena Sutherland and May Hill Arbuthnot — the latest available to me at the time of writing — it gets only a brief paragraph under the heading 'Other Stories About Inanimate Objects'. I have never quite understood the book's lack of appeal to Americans, but at one level it may be a matter of hygiene, for I have to report the (separate) reactions of two graduate students to whom it was introduced: 'I guess Americans aren't into garbage' and 'Those old toys should have gone right back on that dump.'

The notion underlying Robert C. O'Brien's *Mrs Frisby and the Rats of NIMH* (1971) is that laboratory rats, raised to a high standard of intelligence and with the ageing process inhibited, might plan to escape and set up an unratlike community of their own. But the story that embodies this notion is told in retrospect by one of the rats involved, in the course of a rather ordinary 'outer' story about Mrs Frisby the fieldmouse and the rescue of her family from the ploughing-down of their home. The construction is awkward, and there is a lack of memorable characters, but there are some nice touches of detail. Look at the farmer's cat Dragon, as seen from a mouse's height:

He was enormous, with a huge broad head and a large mouth full of curving fangs, needle-sharp. He had seven claws on each foot and a thick, furry tail, which lashed angrily from side to side. In colour he was orange and white, with glaring yellow eyes; and when he leaped to kill he gave a high, strangled scream that froze his victims where they stood.

Richard Adams's *Watership Down* (1972), a first novel of formidable length, began its rise to fame by winning two major children's book awards, though its readership rapidly became a general one. The story is about a band of rabbits who leave their doomed warren to set up a new one, and are drawn into war with a totalitarian warren ruled by the fierce General Woundwort. The author has much to say by implication about the nature and relationships of people and the organization of society. Yet these animals are not just people in fancy dress; they truly are rabbits, and rabbits rather than bunnies; they perform their natural functions, they look for mates. Ingeniously, Richard Adams has provided them with a vocabulary and even a folklore of their own.

It is not surprising that *Watership Down*'s remarkable success was followed by the appearance of other books with similar story-lines. Some of these also did well, but they do not seem to me to be of impressive literary quality.

In Dodie Smith's *The Hundred and One Dalmatians* (1956), anthropomorphism runs riot. It's the story of Cruella de Vil and the ninety-odd Dalmatian puppies she has immured in Hell Hall, intending to make a fur coat out of their skins. Pongo and Missis are a married pair of dogs who lope bravely to the rescue, aided by the friends they meet along the way through the Twilight Barking. There's a good deal here that could be regarded as shamelessly corny; yet it is quite irresistible, a natural for the successful Disney film that it became. If dogs could read, they would be unable to put it down.

'Pigs of the Tamworth breed', according to an anonymous pig fancier quoted by way of introduction to Gene Kemp's *The Prime of Tamworth Pig* (1972), 'are creatures of enchantment'. When a small boy named Thomas has his face pushed into the stream by the inappropriately-named Christopher Robin Baggs and his henchman Lurcher Dench, it's Tamworth — 'a huge, golden pig, a giant of a pig, the colour of beech leaves in autumn, with upstanding furry ears and a long snout' — who comes to the rescue. Tamworth is a pig with a mission, and wants to launch a 'Grow More Grub' campaign — more of everything except, of course, meat. This cheerful fantasy freewheels to and fro across the borderline between the barely-possible and the gloriously-impossible.

Dick King-Smith has added notably to the modest supply of recommendable novels for under-twelves with his amiable stories of farmyard animals. In *The Fox-Busters* (1978), the chickens of Foxearth Farm, 'in their little island fortress surrounded by the armed might of all the foxes in the sandy dells and thick woods of that piece of country,' are in the position of beleaguered Britain in 1940. The rooster who leads them promises that they will fight in the milking-parlour, in the farrowing-house, in the silage-pit and on the dung-heap: 'We will never surrender!' And thanks to three intrepid young pullets the dreaded enemy is defeated.

In *Daggie Dogfoot* (1980) the eponymous piglet-hero is the runt of the litter, and moreover has unorthodox trotters; he finds that he can't, as he had hoped, fly, but he can swim, and he turns this ability to the common good. *The Mouse Butcher* (1981) has a plebeian cat hero winning the paw of a beautiful Persian, and in *The Sheep-Pig* (1983) the piglet brought home by Farmer Hoggett yearns to emulate the sheepdogs and, thanks to adoptive mother Fly, achieves the ambition. He succeeds brilliantly with the sheep by treating them as (so to speak) human beings. Like the best creators of humanized animals from Beatrix Potter onward, Dick King-Smith works from an affectionate understanding of the creatures he's adapting; he knows which qualities to point up and which are the telling parallels with human nature.

The greatest story of people and animals is that of Noah and the Ark, and Dick King-Smith embroidered it with *Noah's Brother* (1986). Noah, a huge, bearded, bossy old man, had, it seems, a small, bald, timid older brother, who was made to do all the work on the Ark and would then have been left behind if the animals hadn't got him on board and looked after him. As we all know, the old man doesn't appear in the official account – Noah succeeded in keeping him out of it – but King-Smith brings him and his equally-forgotten friends the white doves, Peace and Goodwill, to us in a fable with a rather obvious moral.

Most of us share our homes with other creatures: some, like dogs and cats, by choice; some, like mice and insects, because we can't get rid of them. Penelope Lively's *A House Inside Out* (1987) tells of the adventures of various residents, four-legged and more than four-legged, in the Dixon household. Among them are Willie, the dog, who adores Mrs Dixon and means well, but perpetually gets into mud and trouble and can be coaxed by a wily cat into digging up the rose-bed; Sam, the big-mouth mouse whose weakness for showing off is nearly the end of him; and Nat the woodlouse who in the story called 'Nat and the Great Bath Climb' reaches the summit of wood-louse ambition. Mrs Lively can add to her other literary distinctions that of being surely the only novelist to write a story with a woodlouse as hero.

21

Modern fantasy (ii): Imagined lands

CHILDREN's literature, I wrote in 1971, has wild blood in it; its ancestry lies partly in the long ages of storytelling. Myth, legend, fairy tale are alive in their own right, endlessly reprinted, endlessly fertile in their influence.[1] Epic and saga, I might have added, have their modern descendants, in which the features of the originals can still be discerned.

The twentieth-century figure who, above all, combined and reinvigorated these ancient influences was J. R. R. Tolkien (1892-1973). Tolkien wrote what he himself called fairy-story. By this he meant stories of 'Faerie, the Perilous Realm,' which 'contains many things besides elves and fays, and besides dwarfs, witches, trolls, giants or dragons: it holds the seas, the sun, the moon, the sky; and the earth and all things that are in it: tree and bird, water and stone, wine and bread, and ourselves, mortal men, when we are enchanted'.[2] *The Lord of the Rings,* discussed in an earlier part of this study, was intended by its author for adults; but Tolkien thought there should be fairy-story (in his sense of the phrase) within the measure of children. *The Hobbit* is undoubtedly a children's book, and the influence of Tolkien is recognizable (sometimes all too recognizable) over wide areas of children's and indeed of general literature.

The first writer in whom the influence was strong and evident was Tolkien's friend and colleague C. S. Lewis, whose Narnia sequence began to be published in 1950. Tolkien did not think much of the Narnia stories, and is said to have received the first of them with a snort of contempt. His biographer, Humphrey Carpenter, speculates that Tolkien 'was perhaps irritated by the fact that the friend and critic who had listened to the tales of Middle Earth had as it were got up from his armchair, gone to the desk, picked up a pen, and "had a go" himself'.[3]

Lewis's intentions were serious, however. He insisted that his only reason for writing a children's story would be that it was the best art form for something he had to say.[4] The Narnia books, which began with *The Lion, the Witch and the Wardrobe* in 1950 and ended with *The Last Battle* in 1956, soon became immensely popular. They are about four children, Peter, Susan, Edmund and Lucy, who enter the imaginary land of Narnia through the back of a wardrobe in the house of the old professor with whom they are staying, and are caught up in events of profound allegorical importance.

Lewis was learned in medieval allegory, in Norse myth and classical legend; and in addition to Tolkien he was influenced by George MacDonald and E. Nesbit. The allegory is the most important element, and it is Christian allegory. Narnia has its special lord, Aslan the lion; and in a passage in *The Lion, the Witch and the Wardrobe* Aslan gives himself up to save the life of the child who has betrayed him. He is 'neither angry nor afraid, but a little sad'; he dies and afterwards he rises from the dead. At the end of the last book, Aslan tells the children that so far as the ordinary world is concerned they are dead; that they have been killed in a railway accident. 'And as He spoke He no longer looked to them like a lion; but the things that began to happen after that were so great and beautiful that I cannot write them.'

For an adult, a return to Narnia after a lapse of years can be disconcerting: there is much in the books that now seems derivative, condescending, dated, even at times shoddy, and the Christian allegory can occasionally cause queasiness. And the four children are not equal to the parts they have to play in the story; as Marcus Crouch pointed out back in 1962 'it was always difficult to accept the translation of the schoolboy Peter into the High King Peter of Narnia'.[5] But the books have been greatly loved by large numbers of young readers, and have established a momentum which may well carry them on through years to come.

When Alan Garner's first book, *The Weirdstone of Brisinga-men*, appeared in 1960, there were many who thought that Garner was indebted to Tolkien. In fact he did not then know Tolkien's work, but undoubtedly he knew some of Tolkien's sources. *The Weirdstone* and its sequel, *The Moon of Gomrath* (1963), are fierce, wild fantasies that draw heavily on ancient legend. Their stories – of the loss and recovery of a stone of power, and of the capture of two children by evil forces – are full of non-stop action. Yet their use of magic is intricate and sophisticated, and the magical world is made credible by being firmly anchored to the solid ground of Alderley Edge, in Cheshire.

In his third book, *Elidor* (1965), Garner introduced a secon-dary world, a blighted land which four present-day children

– mysteriously transported to it from the back streets of Manchester – have the task of saving. *Elidor* has great richness of theme and connotation, and there is a splendid climax in which a unicorn is chased through slum streets to its glorious and life-renewing death. But the book does not entirely succeed: perhaps because, for all its richness, it has some big bare patches. The four children and their parents are uninteresting; the land of Elidor is a dead land where nothing really happens.

Garner's fourth novel, *The Owl Service* (1967), is set in a Welsh valley. It is based on the legend of the wife made of flowers, who betrayed her husband and brought death on her lover, and in punishment for her unfaithfulness was turned into an owl. The story, which comes from the great body of Welsh legend, the Mabinogion, is supposed to have been re-enacted in the same valley again and again through the centuries, often ending tragically. This time round, it involves two young English people and a bitter, passionate Welsh boy; and an almost unbearable tension is built up before disaster is narrowly, precariously averted. This book was a great advance on its predecessors; Garner added to his gift for absorbing old tales and retransmitting them with increased power a new grasp of the inward, emotional content of an incident or situation.

Red Shift (1973) was six years in the making. It had been eagerly awaited, and gave rise to a great deal of comment: some awed, some baffled. In my view it is not so much a difficult book as a daunting one. A reader who faces it head-on, determined not to be beaten by sudden leaps through time and changes of personnel, by staccato and elliptical dialogue, or by obscure echoes and allusions, will in the end be rewarded. The book does however ask a lot from any reader, especially a young one who has not yet developed concentration and persistence in the reading of fiction. Although first published on a children's list, it should, I think, be regarded not as children's or teenage reading but simply as a novel.

It is a novel with three distinct strands. A present-day story of separated young lovers is interwoven with others about ex-Roman legionaries in tribal Britain and about villagers who take refuge in a church during the English civil war. Tom, the brilliant but precariously balanced main character in the contemporary story, is paralleled by Macey in the earliest one and Thomas in the middle one; they are linked by a stone axe which Macey buries in the first story to be found by Thomas, and which Thomas will hide to be discovered by present-day Tom. All three suffer from psychotic disturbance, and all are catastrophic to those around them. Macey goes berserk and kills; Thomas helps to bring death to the villagers; Tom murders love.

Thomas and Macey are obviously alter egos of present-day Tom, and events in all three stories may be seen as being set in a single continuous present; in fact they all come together at the end. The phrase 'red shift' denotes a phenomenon, observed in the light from stars, that led to the theory that the universe is perpetually expanding. 'Things fall apart; the centre cannot hold'; and, looking inward rather than out, we can see in Tom the disintegration of a personality.

Like all Garner's fiction, *Red Shift* has power. Its weakness is that the foreground story, of Tom and his girl Jan, is a thin one, and its connection with the other two is not truly organic. The disastrous nature of present-day Tom is sufficiently accounted for by his narrow-minded, possessive parents, who turn innocent love into guilty sexuality. The stories from the past, it seems to me, are shadows within which the present one moves; and they are shadows that dwarf it. The Barthomley massacre, which actually happened, is so much bigger than the sorry little affair of Tom and Jan.

Susan Cooper began a large-scale fantasy sequence with *Over Sea, Under Stone* in 1965, and continued it, after an eight-year gap, with *The Dark is Rising* (1973), *Greenwitch* (1974), *The Grey King* (1975) and *Silver on the Tree* (1976). The second, and best, of the books, *The Dark is Rising*, gave its name to the quintet. The theme is the long-running war between the Light and the Dark, and the author draws heavily on myth and legend.

Except in the first, rather ordinary book, the writing is powerful. Yet the sequence does not quite cohere, and the clash of conflict seems sometimes to degenerate into noise. In the first two books the author launches different central child characters, whom she subsequently has difficulty in bringing together and keeping employed, and who, like the children in *Elidor* and the Narnia books, are unequal to the parts they have to play. In particular, it is hard to believe that ordinary-seeming Will Stanton is the last of the Old Ones and wields awesome power in a cosmic struggle. The Light and the Dark are obviously good and evil forces, but it is difficult to work out just what the Dark is, what it intends to do and what it actually *does*, other than create scenic and atmospheric effects.

But Susan Cooper has the rare gift of being able to send a sudden electric shudder through the reader; and there are loving, perhaps nostalgic evocations of English and Welsh landscape.

Major legend is dangerous stuff to handle. In comparison with the power, authority and durability of the original, a modern writer's efforts are likely to seem weak, presumptuous and ephemeral. If an author as able as Susan Cooper has difficulty in managing it, the less experienced should beware. In Jenny Nimmo's award-winning *The Snow Spider* (1986), nine-year-old Gwyn inherits the powers of the magicians Math and Gwydion from the *Mabinogion* and, armed with mysterious gifts from his mysterious grandmother, sets out to seek the sister who disappeared four years ago and to face evil supernatural forces. As an indication to readers of around Gwyn's age that Welsh legend is alive and active, this may be a valuable book, but as literature it will not stand up to scrutiny.

A second book, *Emlyn's Moon* (1987; American title *Orchard of the Crescent Moon)* features Nia, the under-appreciated child of a neighbouring family. Gwyn and his magic come into it, but it is at its best in dealing with personal and family problems and in conveying a sense of Welsh life and landscape.

In contrast to large allegorical and mythic themes is the small-scale, magnifying-glass fantasy of Mary Norton's *Borrowers* series which began with *The Borrowers* (1952). These books create, with perfect consistency and attention to detail, a tiny world within our own. Borrowers are little people who inhabit odd corners of houses: under the floorboards, for example, or anywhere else that provides a safe retreat. They live by 'borrowing' from the human occupants of the house. Over the years Borrowers have grown smaller and fewer, and now you only find them in 'houses which are old and quiet and deep in the country – and where the human beings live to a routine. Routine is their safeguard: it is important to them which rooms are to be used, and when. They do not stay long where there are careless people, unruly children, or certain household pets.'

'Our' particular family of Borrowers are Pod, the father, Homily, the mother, and little Arrietty (even their names are scraps of borrowed human names). They live below the wainscot under the grandfather clock, and Clock is their family name. Here is a glimpse of them at home:

The fire had been lighted and the room looked bright and cosy. Homily was proud of her sitting-room: the walls had been papered with scraps of old letters out of waste-paper baskets, and Homily had arranged the handwriting sideways in vertical strips which ran from floor to ceiling. On the walls, repeated in various colours, hung several portraits of Queen Victoria as a girl; these were postage-stamps, borrowed by Pod some years ago from the stamp-box on the desk in the morning-room. There was a lacquer trinket-box, padded inside and with the lid open, which they used as a settle; and that useful stand-by — a chest of drawers made from match-boxes . . . The knight [from a chess set] was standing on a column in the corner, where it looked very fine, and lent that air to the room which only statuary can give.

Homily is a houseproud, nervous little woman. Pod is a tough, resourceful little man, but he is beginning to feel his age, and a Borrower's life is not an easy one — it involves perilous mountaineering exploits over tables and up to kitchen shelves. And poor Arrietty, at nearly fourteen, is bored and lonely.

In *The Borrowers,* a human boy comes to stay in the house and meets Arrietty; he does some borrowing himself on the Borrowers' behalf, so that for a time they enjoy a life of undreamed-of affluence. But he borrows more than is wise; things are missed and the Borrowers' household is exposed; they are smoked out and have to take to the fields. *The Borrowers Afield* (1955) and *The Borrowers Afloat* (1959) trace their adventures after this forced emigration. In *The Borrowers Aloft* (1961) they find a home in the model village built by a retired railwayman, Mr Pott, but are kidnapped by his unpleasant rival Mr Platter. Ever-resourceful, they build themselves a balloon in order to escape from an upstairs window of Mr Platter's house.

The author then indicated that the series was complete, but in 1982 *The Borrowers Avenged* effortlessly jumped a gap of twenty-one years and followed straight on from its predecessor. After their escape from Mr Platter, the Borrowers are again looking for a home, and this time they find an ideal one in a rambling old rectory with only caretakers and the odd ghost in residence. Arrietty still has a dangerous longing to talk to Human Beans, and another for the fresh air and wider world; and there's a hint of romance when she meets Peregrine Overmantel, a Borrower of the vestigial upper class and also a poet and painter. The Platters get their come-uppance and the Borrowers are safe — or as safe as Borrowers can ever be.

Another small world was created by Pauline Clarke in *The Twelve and the Genii* (1962; American title *The Return of the Twelves*). A boy called Max finds, under the floorboards of an old house not far from Haworth, the toy soldiers of the Brontës, as described by Branwell in *The History of the Young Men*. It seems that the chief genius Brannii breathed life into them. Now they can revive. And when they do, their faces become bright and living, sharp and detailed instead of blurred and featureless with age. These tiny men are characterized not only as a group – they are *soldiers*, organized and resourceful in all they do – but as individuals: most strikingly their patriarch, the kindly and dignified Butter Crashey. And what more natural than that when in danger they should 'freeze' into mere wood?

Joan Aiken's sequence that began with *The Wolves of Willoughby Chase* (1963) is set in an England that never was: an England in which the Hanoverian succession did not happen and Good King James III came to the throne. It is an England where conspiracies are centred not on Bonnie Prince Charlie but on Bonnie Prince Georgie:

> My bonny lies over the North Sea,
> My bonny lies over in Hanover,
> My bonny lies over the North Sea,
> Oh why won't they bring that young man over?

There are wolves and wild boar in the remoter parts of Britain; they migrated through the recently-opened Channel Tunnel. *In The Wolves of Willoughby Chase,* Sir Willoughby and Lady Green go abroad, leaving their daughter Bonnie and niece Sylvia in the care of wicked governess Miss Slighcarp; and there follows a tale of double-dyed villainy, with right triumphant in the end.

Joan Aiken's writing has a high Dickensian colour and a tendency to burlesque and caricature. She is good at titles: the next two in the sequence were *Black Hearts in Battersea* (1964) and *Night Birds on Nantucket* (1966); and she went on to write *The Whispering Mountain* (1968) and *The Cuckoo Tree* (1971). In the last of these, King James III has gone to his rest and King Richard IV is to be crowned. Resourceful Cockney waif Dido Twite, who first appeared with her friend Simon in *Black Hearts* and has established herself as the central character of the series, arrives on the back of an elephant just in time to prevent a dastardly Hanoverian deed at the Coronation. Dido is in action again in *The Stolen Lake* (1981), when an expedition goes to Roman America to help Britain's oldest ally, New Cumbria, to recover the stolen Lake Arianrod from neighbouring Lyonnesse. How, you may wonder, do you steal a lake? No problem; not in Miss Aiken's world, anyway. You wait until it freezes, then carry it away in blocks.

In *Dido and Pa* (1986), action continues unabated; Dido's no-good father is involved in more plots against the newly-crowned Richard IV but comes to an uncomfortable end, eaten alive by wolves. Dido's friend Simon, who is now Duke of Battersea, invites her to become a duchess; she declines with thanks, but will no doubt be asked again.

Rosemary Harris created an Ancient Egypt that (it seems safe to say) never was, in her three books *The Moon in the Cloud* (1968), *The Shadow on the Sun* (1970) and *The Bright and Morning Star* (1972). Talking animals are the least of the improbabilities. With delicate irreverence, the first book mixes Miss Harris's Egypt with a story of the Biblical Flood. The second is concerned largely with the determination of King Merenkere to marry for love: a determination which is much needed, for he has a Great Royal Wife and ninety-three lesser wives already. The last book centres on a plot by No-Hotep, sinister Priest of Set, against this same Merenkere, a monarch who (as the chief royal crocodile remarks) is a wise man but has the fault of clemency. 'Clemency is no good. It doesn't feed crocodiles.'

Helen Cresswell, another writer with a strong comic gift, set *The Piemakers* (1967) and *The Signposters* (1968) in an England that may have been − or may not have been − at some time in the indefinite past. *The Piemakers* is about the enormous pie baked for the King by the Roller family of Danby Dale − the crust alone requires two hundred pinches of salt and eight hundred teaspoonfuls of water − and *The Signposters* about the efforts of Dyke Signposter, whose pleasant job it is to pace out afresh each year the distances between signs, to organize a great family reunion.

The Night Watchmen (1969) has a present-day setting. Josh and Caleb − two eccentric tramps whose ingenious practice is to pitch their shelter beside a hole in the road − are pursued by the jealous Greeneyes. Helen Cresswell is a great believer in spontaneity, the freedom of the creative spirit; and the implications of *The Night Watchmen* strike me as pessimistic. Josh and Caleb get away from the Greeneyes by whistling up a night train, but they cannot be said to have come out on top. They are still on the run, and it seems that they always will be.

Miss Cresswell, a prolific writer, has made many excursions away from the fictional path indicated by the three titles just mentioned: in particular with her comic Bagthorpe Saga, which has been hugely successful, though I have to confess that I do not find it enjoyable. She returned to what I think is her best vein with *The Secret World of Polly Flint* (1982), in which Polly meets the 'time gypsies' from Grimstone, a village that years ago 'slipped the net of time' and was lost beneath the waters of a lake.

Another prolific writer, Diana Wynne Jones, created one of the more successful post-Tolkien secondary worlds in *Cart and Cwidder* (1975) and *Drowned Ammet* (1977). Dalemark is a land ruled by feudal earls, divided between the liberal ones of the North and the tyrants of the South, where you 'dare not put a foot, or a word, out of place for fear of being clapped in jail.' Dalemark is well provided with myth and history; and a third book, *The Spellcoats* (1979) goes far back into its past to tell how a girl struggles against an evil magician in a conflict that will eventually become legend.

In the comic *Charmed Life* (1977) and its successors *The Magicians of Caprona* (1980), *Witch Week* (1982) and *The Lives of Christopher Chant* (1988), Diana Wynne Jones exploits the notion of a parallel England in which things have turned out differently. The principal difference is that magic is practised by all kinds of people from the humble Certified Witch with a notice in her parlour window, to the lofty eminence of the great enchanter Chrestomanci.

In *Charmed Life*, a boy called Cat Chant and his magically talented but obnoxious sister Gwendolen, are carried off from seedy Coven Street to Chrestomanci Castle, where Gwendolen gets her drastic deserts. It turns out to be Cat who has by far the greater gifts, is a Nine-Lifed Enchanter, and will be successor to Chrestomanci himself. *The Lives of Christopher Chant* tells of a great enchanter's apprenticeship, his travels among other worlds, the misuse of his powers under the influence of a wicked uncle, and the loss of several of his nine lives.

Another different and ingenious world is created in *Power of Three* (1976), which is set on the Moor, a sunken plain occupied by the People, or Lymen, and by the strange, water-dwelling, shape-shifting Dorig. There are also the noisy Giants, who trample over the place from time to time; and a brilliant revelation about the Giants, guaranteed to make the reader blink, changes the whole scale of the story. *Fire and Hemlock*

(1984) blends a great deal of traditional material with real-life relationships in a long and ambitious book for older readers.

In Lionel Davidson's *Under Plum Lake* (1980), the secondary world is under the sea. Barry Gordon finds the entrance to it while on holiday on the Cornish coast. It is a world supposed to be far in advance of ours: people live in beautiful surroundings, enjoy exquisite food and drink, and don't appear to do any work. In the mountains around glorious Plum Lake, they take their recreation: thrillingly dangerous power-skiing, tobogganing, and soaring on kites. Barry thinks it's marvellous. But a thoughtful reader is bound to wonder, Is this all? Is Utopia, or Xanadu, a place where there's nothing left to do but seek sensation?

American writers have also created fantasy worlds: some in unknown locations 'out there', some hidden, and some miniaturized. The most remarkable one of the early post-war years was portrayed in *The Twenty-one Balloons* (1947), by William Pène du Bois, a writer and draughtsman of elegant idiosyncrasy. This story is about the last days of Krakatoa, and the extraordinary discovery by the balloonist William Waterman Sherman of a civilization built upon solid diamond but otherwise remarkably shaky foundations. An audaciously devised Other World is the setting for the same author's reverently irreverent *Lion* (1956) which tells and shows how the celestial artists responsible for animal design created this masterpiece, and how the Chief Designer, giving His approval for the making of two lions and their dispatch to Planet Earth, suggests the final brilliant touch: that Lion should ROAR LIKE THUNDER.

James Thurber (1894-1961) slipped in a handful of stories for children among his extensive and famous output of writings and drawings. *Many Moons* (1943), *The White Deer* (1945) and *The 13 Clocks* (1950) are set in fairylands and are burlesques of fairy tales, with beautiful princesses, handsome princes, dim or villainous potentates, and hilarious twists given to familiar plots. *The Wonderful O* (1955) seems to me the most interesting of Thurber's books for children. It begins as a burlesque of pirate-and-treasure stories, but for most of its course it leaves that aim on the sidelines and pursues the notion of a regime that banishes the letter O from the language, so that floors and roofs become flrs and rfs, and s n. This may seem an absurd fancy, but there's a serious implied message about what happens when language is corrupted. Four O-words are celebrated by the rebels who finally throw the vandals out: hope, love, valour and freedom.

Delight in word-play is a feature of Thurber's stories, and is equally to be seen in *The Phantom Tollbooth*, by Norton Juster (1961). Milo finds in his room a package containing a self-assembly turnpike tollbooth; having put it together and driven through it in his little electric car he finds himself in the Lands Beyond. He visits the cities of Dictionopolis and Digitopolis, and eventually rescues the Princesses Rhyme and Reason from the Castle in the Air in the Mountains of Ignorance. The influence of that distinguished player-with-words Lewis Carroll seems evident throughout.

The Minnipins, or Small Ones, in Carol Kendall's *The Gammage Cup* (1959; British title *The Minnipins*) live in the green and pleasant Land Between the Mountains. They are secure, peace-loving, conventional and unadventurous; and it is just as well for the rest of them that a small band of non-conforming individuals led by Walter the Earl – a kind of village Churchill – is there to defeat an invasion by their ancient enemies the Mushrooms, or Hairless Ones.

The appeal of the book lies largely in the neatness and consistency of the portrayal of the Minnipins' country. The valley of the Watercress River, with its dozen villages – Great Dripping and Little Dripping, Slipper-on-the Water and Deep-as-a-Well – is exactly the place in which to find such a right little, tight little, smug little people. *The Whisper of Glocken* (1965) is a sequel.

Lloyd Alexander's five books of Prydain are worked on a broader canvas. They began with *The Book of Three* (1964) and continued with *The Black Cauldron* (1965), *The Castle of Llyr* (1966), *Taran Wanderer* (1967) and *The High King* (1968). The Prydain chronicles were inspired by Wales and its legends; but Prydain is not exactly Wales, and Lloyd Alexander dipped at will into that great general cauldron of story which, as he says, has been 'simmering away since time immemorial'.[6]

In these books the forces of evil, under Arawn, Lord of Annuvin, are eventually defeated by the good powers under the leadership of the Sons of Don. The hero Taran, from being Assistant Pig-Keeper to the old enchanter Dallben, at length becomes a companion in arms of Gwydion, war leader of the Sons of Don. The books tell of his advance to manhood and, between whiles, of his growing love for the Princess Eilonwy. At the end of the last book, when the Sons of Don must return to the Summer Country from which they came, and 'all enchantments shall pass away and men unaided guide their own destiny', Taran becomes High King of Prydain and Eilonwy his queen.

Lloyd Alexander earns the respect due to one who has conceived and carried out a large, complex design. I cannot feel however that he has caught the true spirit either of Wales or of Welsh legend; or that he has created a satisfying epic in its own right. Part of his trouble, I think, comes from an imperfect marriage of ancient and modern. He has rejected antique language, which is right; but the proper purpose of such a rejection is to secure greater naturalness. In making his dialogue obtrusively contemporary-colloquial; in giving his hero the title of Assistant Pig-Keeper; in causing (for instance) the King of the Fair Folk to sound like a harassed, self-important and not very competent business man, Lloyd Alexander has created an atmosphere of anachronism which works against credibility.

Taran is a good hero. He is brave, loyal, well-meaning, a leader – a fit figure for identification – and at the same time he sometimes fails, is sometimes wrong, does not always think clearly enough or far ahead. And the spirited Princess Eilonwy is an attractive heroine, although, to an adult reader at least, her tone of voice eventually grows tiresome. The lesser characters depend too much on one or two endlessly stressed features or phrases: the bard Fflewddur Flam, forever letting his tongue run away from the truth and causing strings of his magic harp to break; Taran's faithful follower, the hairy creature Gurgi, worrying about his poor tender head and the prospects of crunchings and munchings, slashings and gashings, or beatings and cheatings. And although admittedly in a five-volume romance you cannot build up tension steadily towards a single climax, there is too much to-ing and fro-ing, too frequent a feeling that one is not really getting anywhere. Only in the last fifty pages or so of *The High King*, I feel, does Lloyd Alexander rise close to the considerable heights at which he has aimed.

The outstanding 'secondary world' devised by an American writer is Ursula Le Guin's Earthsea, in *A Wizard of Earthsea* (1968), *The Tombs of Atuan* (1971) and *The Farthest Shore* (1972). Earthsea is much like the world we know, though made up of archipelagoes rather than continents. It is a world in which there are craftsmen, peasants and seafarers, but no machines. And it is a world suffused by magic: a world where every village has its small-time sorcerer who can manage simple stuff like weatherwork:

> In a land where sorcerers come thick, like Gont or the Enlades, you may see a raincloud blundering slowly from side to side and place to place as one spell shunts it on to the next, till at last it is buffeted out over the sea where it can rain in peace.

Higher levels of magic, more powerful, sophisticated and dangerous, are taught at a central university of wizardry, to which the hero Ged is sent. The first book tells of his growth in power and his arrogant loosing into the world of a great evil, a sinister Shadow, which he must pursue and confront. And in a climactic scene at the world's end Ged reaches out to the Shadow: 'Light and darkness met, and joined, and were one.' This is a striking contrast to simplistic presentations of Light and Dark as in effect goodies and baddies; and alert readers may well detect another shadow – that of Carl Gustav Jung.

In *The Tombs of Atuan*, a young girl is priestess, ruler and prisoner all at once in the dark ancient Place of the Tombs, where only women and eunuchs may live. And one day in the black sacred underground Labyrinth she finds an intruder, a full man, Ged. His life is in her hands, her freedom in his. She talks to him, comes to know him, and eventually escapes with him. Whereas the other two books of this trilogy are out in the open, and their action ranges over wide areas of land and sea, *The Tombs of Atuan* is dark, enclosed, claustrophobic. Yet it is a hopeful book. The escape of the girl, Tenar, is clearly a triumph of life, and indeed of sexual life, over darkness, isolation and repression.

In *The Farthest Shore* a great but corrupted mage has threatened the world's equilibrium by opening the door to immortality; and Ged must assert the ultimate claim on humankind, the claim of death, for 'death is the price we pay for our life, and for all life'. Wizardry and wisdom, it is clear, are hardly distinguishable; nor is one kind of power essentially different from another. So our world of science and technology is not so remote from the Earthsea world of magic as might be supposed. In either world, the greater the power the greater the responsibility, and the vital balance cannot lightly be disturbed.

There have been many more excursions into Tolkienish or Le Guinish countries. Among the more interesting of recent voyagers is the American writer Robin McKinley, who has said that Girls Who Do Things are the only subject she talks about, and who had noted Tolkien's 'unwillingness to deal with women at all, except as tersely and tangentially as possible, and with teeth visibly clenched'.[7] But she was inspired by one brief reference in Tolkien to a warrior maiden to create what she calls her 'lady heroes': Angharad, called Harry, in *The Blue Sword* (1982) and Aerin in the Newbery Medal-winning *The Hero and the Crown* (1984). Here are dragons, good and bad wizards, blue sword and hero's crown and other appropriate properties; and, above all, here are tall, formidable, totally-unlanguorous female protagonists.

Imaginary countries tend to be romanticized. The kingdom of Thyrne, in Betty Levin's *The Ice Bear* (1986) is one of gritty reality. The local lord is a brute and oppressor; the people's idea of a good time is to watch a bear-fight. The hero Wat, who makes a dangerous journey in the company of a strange girl to deliver a bear cub to the king, has no magic sword or flying horse and is not particularly brave or noble; in fact he's doing it in the hope of a reward. Yet it is in the end an achieved quest, and Wat is rewarded, though not in the way he had in mind.

22

Modern fantasy (iii): On the margin

NEWLY invented worlds and talking animals are obviously in the realms of fantasy; but there are other subjects that are barely inside its frontiers. Much fiction that is essentially naturalistic, concerned with what actual people do in the actual world, puts a foot across the border into fantasy in search of some degree of freedom that realism, strictly interpreted, would not allow. The border is in any case an elusive one. There is fantasy so minimal that the reader is left in doubt whether anything outside the bounds of possibility has happened at all. In K. M. Peyton's *A Pattern of Roses* (1972), for example, does present-day Tim Ingram 'really' brush against ghosts from the past, or does he merely have the impression of doing so? Tim himself doesn't know; possibly the author doesn't know; probably it doesn't matter. It is the haunting sense of the past that counts.

In *The Children of Green Knowe* (1954) and *The Chimneys of Green Knowe* (1958; American title *Treasure of Green Knowe*), by L.M.Boston (1892-1990), similar questions arise. A small boy named Tolly goes to stay with his wise old great-grandmother, Mrs Oldknow, in her ancient house. (The house is in all but name the manor house at Hemingford Grey, Cambridgeshire, where Lucy Boston lived for fifty years and in which she died at the age of 97; and Mrs Oldknow is Mrs Boston herself in equally slight disguise.) Mrs Oldknow tells Tolly stories of children who lived there in former days: Toby, Alexander and Linnet, who died in the Great Plague of 1665; blind Susan and little black boy Jacob, from the late eighteenth century. Tolly hears the children's voices and seems to meet them. But does he do so 'really', or has his imagination been quickened into extra activity by the influences of Mrs Oldknow and the house? We do not know, and are not obliged to choose; our minds are capable of holding both possibilities at once.

There are four more Green Knowe books, of which the best is *A Stranger at Green Knowe* (1961). The stranger is Hanno, a gorilla escaped from the zoo, befriended in the grounds of the old house by Ping, a small Chinese boy who is visiting Mrs

Drawing by Susan Einzig from *Tom's Midnight Garden*,
by Philippa Pearce

Oldknow. In the end Hanno is shot, and Ping says, 'He's dead.
It's all right. That's how much he didn't want to go back. I saw
him choose.' The sixth and last of the books, *The Stones of
Green Knowe*, appeared in 1976, twelve years after its predecessor. It goes back to the beginning, in 1120, with a boy
called Roger watching the fine new manor-house being built.

'All my water is drawn from one well,' Mrs Boston once said
– the well being the house itself.[1] She used words with great
beauty and precision, and never more so than when describing
house or garden: as when Tolly returns to Green Knowe at the
beginning of *Chimneys*, at a time when 'the wide and wandering garden was silky with daffodils'. Her style, clear rather than
coloured, has the endlessly varied flow and sparkle of spring
water; it is unsurpassed by that of any other British children's
writer, and rivalled by very few.

One of the few is Philippa Pearce, whose qualities as a stylist
are combined with the novelist's power to create memorable

people and with the almost architectural ability to complete a perfectly constructed and proportioned work. *Tom's Midnight Garden* (1958) is a haunting, evocative fantasy, yet is firmly rooted in the actual world.

Tom goes to stay with his dimly-intellectual Uncle Alan and yearning childless Aunt Gwen in their flat in a converted house whose owner, old Mrs Bartholomew, lives spiderlike at the top. One night when the grandfather clock strikes thirteen, Tom finds his way into the large beautiful garden that belongs to the house — but belongs to it only in the past. He plays with a late-Victorian little girl named Hatty; she, alone of the family who live in the house at the time in which Tom is visiting it, can see him, for to most people he is invisible.

Tom visits his garden and Hatty night by night; but in the world of the past, time is passing much more quickly than in that of the present. In that world his visits are at long intervals, and Hatty is growing up before his eyes; at length he realizes that she is now a young woman. And on the last day of his stay with his aunt and uncle, Tom meets old Mrs Bartholomew at the top of the house and discovers that she is Hatty; night after night she has been dreaming him into her own past life. The book has a profound, mysterious sense of time; it has the beauty of a theorem but it is not abstract; it is sensuously as well as intellectually satisfying. The garden is so real that you have the scent of it in your nostrils. 'Masterpiece' is not a word to be lightly used, but in my view *Tom's Midnight Garden* is one of the tiny handful of masterpieces of English children's literature.

Clive King's *Stig of the Dump* has been perennially popular in Britain since its first publication in 1963. A small boy named Barney explores the dump at the bottom of the chalk-pit near where he is staying, and finds there a cave-boy, from ages long past, who has made himself a house out of junk, with bottle-glass windows and a tin-can chimney, and has done all the marvellous things that small boys are sure *they* could do with what you find on rubbish dumps, if only their mean old parents would let them. Once again there is an open question: does the cave-boy, Stig, 'really' exist or is he a figment of a lonely child's imagination? And once again, it is not essential to answer the question.

Penelope Lively made her name as a children's writer with the splendidly comic fantasy *The Ghost of Thomas Kempe* (1973), in which a bad-tempered apothecary whose spirit has been bottled up in a wall for three and a half centuries emerges to make a nuisance of himself in the present day. It was followed by an even better book, *The House in Norham Gardens* (1974). This memorable novel involves, in part, a dream-fantasy about a strangely-painted shield from New Guinea; but its true centre, as the title implies, is a big Victorian house in North Oxford, where fourteen-year-old Clare lives with her aged academic aunts. Past and present, far and near are brought together; and perhaps the most appealing feature is the unsentimental yet touching affection between young and old. The book contains one of the most inspired birthday presents in fiction: Clare's gift to her Aunt Susan, aged eighty-one, of a young copper-beech tree that will outlive her by two or three hundred years.

Time-slips are a standard fictional device but, handled with perception and delicacy, can be marvellously effective. In Penelope Lively's *A Stitch in Time* (1976), Maria is a solitary, imaginative child who doesn't talk to other people much, but has conversations with animals, plants and petrol pumps. She is just the person to hear sounds that seem to come from the past, and to speculate on Harriet, who lived a century ago in the house where Maria is now on holiday, and who never finished the sampler she was making. This is a quietly distinctive story, itself as carefully stitched and patterned as a Victorian sampler.

A novel that rises above the commonplace in a similar way is *Charlotte Sometimes,* by Penelope Farmer (1969). Charlotte, on her first night at boarding-school, finds herself changing places with a girl called Clare who slept in the same bed in 1918, the last year of the First World War. For a while they change places daily; then it seems they may become fixed in each other's role. In the end Charlotte returns to be safe in the present, yet she will never in her life escape entirely from being Clare. There are subtle webs here, both of thought and feeling about identity, about reality and illusion, and about time itself.

In the same author's *A Castle of Bone* (1972), Hugh, his sister Jean, and their friends Penn and Anna, find that the cupboard bought in a junk-shop can time-change what is put into it. A pigskin wallet becomes a sow; Penn becomes a baby. Three planes of fantasy intersect: simple through-the-cupboard fantasy that recalls E. Nesbit and C. S. Lewis; complex fantasy with mythological origins; and a personal fantasy that relates especially to Hugh and is a metaphorical quest for self-knowledge. Finally emerging from the fantasy world into daylight,

Hugh finds that 'the void had gone. Walls had closed around Hugh, confining him, imprisoning him in the narrowest of castles; a castle of bone, he thought. But the castle of bone was himself.'

This could be described as psycho-fantasy, a type of fiction in which the real problems of young people are worked out in fantasy form. An outstanding example, a few years earlier, was *Marianne Dreams,* by Catherine Storr (1958). Marianne, aged ten and ill in bed, draws a house and dreams herself into it; dreams an actual sick boy, Mark, into it, too; then, in anger, scribbles over his face, draws prison bars and walls around the house, and changes boulders around it into malignant one-eyed creatures. The real-life Mark's illness gets worse. But Marianne helps dream Mark in a brave escape, and real-life Mark gets better.

The atmosphere in the dream sequence is one of real fear; and, although everything is resolved, the awareness comes across with great force that one person can do terrible things to another person. *Marianne Dreams* is strong stuff for children of the fairly low age-group (about nine to twelve) for which I have seen it suggested. But I would not say it is unsuitable. The realization that we all have power for evil must come some time, and could take far more disturbing forms than this.

William Mayne's ambitious and harrowing *A Game of Dark* (1971) clearly looks to an older readership than *Marianne Dreams,* and indeed may be thought to slip off the top of the children's list. Donald Jackson, nearly fifteen, suffers the pain and guilt of not loving his dying, Methodist lay-preacher father; has adopted as father-figure the Church of England clergyman who is indirectly responsible for his sister's death and his father's maiming; and, under unbearable pressure, retreats into a medieval chivalric world in which he has to kill the huge, preying Worm. This he achieves at length by unfair play, stabbing its under-belly from the protection of a hole in the ground; there is no honour in it; yet at last he can love his father, who now dies, and can accept reality.

Fantasy here is the dramatization in a boy's mind of an external situation. The Worm is hugely symbolic; in the context I take it to be a compound of Donald's monstrous guilt, his father's ugly pain, and − Freudianly speaking − Father himself. The psychoanalytical implications could be discussed at length. Artistically I cannot feel that the book succeeds. The fantasy action and setting are too flimsy, too unreal to make an impact;

there is no involvement. For Donald the charade may be a necessary one, but for the reader it is still a charade.

A Game of Dark came five years after *Earthfasts*, Mayne's first venture into fantasy in what was already a distinguished career. *Earthfasts*, in which a drummer boy who marched into a hillside in 1742 in search of the burial place of King Arthur, marches out of it into the 1960s carrying a candle with a cold white everlasting flame, is a weirdly credible story, and was probably Mayne's best up to that time. It was followed by *Over the Hills and Far Away* (1968; American title *Hill Road)* in which he reversed the process and had modern children pony-trekking into the distant past.

Mayne has worked in many forms – several of his books will be discussed in a later chapter – and has always been able to surprise. *Antar and the Eagles* (1989) made one of his most extraordinary and perilous imaginative flights. Antar is a small boy carried away to be reared with eagles and entrusted by them with a quest that only a small human being can achieve. Antar learns to talk to the eagles, and makes wings with which he can fly; the eagles become familiar to him, but at the same time are utterly strange, a different species. The relationship is made wholly credible in a distinctive Mayne *tour de force*.

Mayne's finest achievement in fantasy may however have been a book for younger readers, *A Year and a Day* (1976) – if in fact this is fantasy, for the border between fantasy and naturalistic writing is particularly elusive at this point. Two little girls in Cornwall, more than a century ago, find a small naked boy who is said by the local wise woman to be a fairy child, here for a year and a day only. The children's parents, poor cottage folk, take the boy in and call him Adam; he doesn't speak, but imitates the sounds he hears. The little girls love him, but when the year expires they find him 'sleeping cold'. Yet soon there's a new Adam, a fine lusty natural ordinary boy, to console them. This is a brief, beautiful story, with a still, sad music of its own.

A Year and a Day is an affectionate book; Robert Westall's powerful *The Scarecrows* (1981) seems full of anger. Simon Brown loathes his stepfather and resents his mother's marital happiness; and it is obviously his own fury and malice that bring to life the Scarecrows, grown from clothes left in the nearby ruined water-mill by the participants in a long-past, murderous triangle of passion.

The outstanding modern American fantasy of the kind where everything follows naturally from a single displacement of the natural order of things is Natalie Babbitt's *Tuck Everlasting* (1975). Winnie, a small girl of the 1880s, meets the Tuck family, who are 'as plain as salt' but are immortal, because eighty-seven years ago they drank from the little spring near Winnie's house. They have been unchanged ever since. The theme here – the implications of immortality – is the same as that of Ursula Le Guin's *The Farthest Shore,* though the treatment is very different, and well within children's reach. Would one *want* to live for ever? Mr Tuck gives Winnie the answer:

> 'Everything's a wheel, turning and turning, never stopping . . . Being part of the whole thing, that's the blessing. But it's passing us by, us Tucks . . . If I knowed how to climb back on the wheel I'd do it in a minute. You can't have living without dying. So you can't call it living, what we got. We just *are*, we just *be*, like rocks beside the road.'

An epilogue tells us that Winnie has not drunk from the spring and has died at a ripe age. 'Good girl,' says Mr Tuck, seeing her grave. This is a quiet, thoughtful book, and beautifully written: Natalie Babbitt is a stylist with an eye for the precise and telling detail and an ear for the sound of a sentence; one notes such small felicities as (with my italics) 'a *capable* iron fence' and a tree's thick roots '*rumpling* the ground'.

Jane Langton's fantasies are powered transcendentally by the historic town of Concord, Massachusetts, and the ghosts of Henry Thoreau and Ralph Waldo Emerson, to whom she happily acknowledges her indebtedness on every possible occasion. Her main work for children is the brief series of books, appearing at longish intervals, about the Hall family who live in a wildly gabled and turreted house in Concord: Edward and Eleanor and small cousin Georgie and eccentric Uncle Freddy who opens the Concord Academy of Transcendental Knowledge, and others. A memorable cast also includes dreadful Mr Preek the bank president and his secretary Miss Prawn who boasts that 'my own dear grandfather put Henry Thoreau in jail'. The first book, *The Diamond in the Window* (1962), features a quest for 'transcendental treasures' which turn out to be jewels of human wisdom and experience. This, and the next two books in the sequence, make somewhat Nesbit-like use of magical objects to open doors out of everyday reality; in the fourth, *The Fledgling* (1980), Georgie learns from a goose 'mighty in wing spread' to fly over Concord; and in the fifth, *The Fragile Flag* (1984) Georgie marches – almost – out of fantasy to lead a cumulative peace crusade of children behind an ancient flag that sometimes fades and sometimes blazes bravely.

Jane Louise Curry, an American who has lived in England from time to time, has set books in both countries. Most of them are concerned with interaction between past and present – the involvement of present-day people in past events or the living influence of the past on the present. Time slips are a recurrent feature. In *Poor Tom's Ghost* (1977), the best of those known to me, thirteen-year-old Roger's actor father Tony inherits an ugly Victorian house which turns out, on a bit of probing, to be concealing an Elizabethan one. The exposure of the old house, which was built by Tom Garland, a player in Shakespeare's theatre, opens a gap in the time fabric; Tony becomes in part possessed by the ghost of Tom, in agony over supposed deception by his wife during a plague year; and Roger must intervene in the past to put right a wrong and lay Tom's ghost. By changing the past he also changes the present: a recurrent problem in time-travel stories. In this book it is solved by cancelling the events of the past five days.

Exploration of the past is readily contrived in England, with its long recorded history. It is more problematic in America, but Jane Curry has ambitiously attempted it in a series of novels beginning with *Beneath the Hill* (1967) and continuing at intervals through her career. The sequence centres on Apple Lock (formerly Abaloc), West Virginia, and builds up, with the aid of myth and magic, a 'mystical history' (and prehistory) of the land.

The Shrinking of Treehorn, by Florence Parry Heide (1971), is about as different from this as any fantasy could be; yet fantasy it undoubtedly is. It is also a sharp satire on some adult attitudes to children. Treehorn is a small boy who's getting rapidly smaller, and no one will take his predicament seriously. 'Nobody shrinks,' says his father at first; then, 'I wonder if he's doing it on purpose. Just to be different.' 'I'll let it go for today,' says his teacher. 'But see that it's taken care of before tomorrow. We don't shrink in this class.' And so on.

Does Treehorn 'really' shrink? Perhaps my query reflects the kind of reaction that the book is satirizing. Certainly he shrinks on the page. The stoicism of Treehorn himself and the imperviousness of adults are perfectly rendered in the deadpan drawings of Edward Gorey – an inspired choice of illustrator. Treehorn stops himself shrinking, but at the end he's turning green. 'I don't think I'll tell anyone,' he thinks. 'If I don't say anything they won't notice.'

There are deep divisions among adults over the children's books of Roald Dahl, a writer of peculiar talent and strong individual flavour. While popularity is not the ultimate test of worth — if it were, the maps both of 'adult' and children's literature would look very strange — it is a quality that naturally appeals to parents and teachers who wish to get children reading.

The Dahl books are fantasies unlike any others. That they go down well with children is unquestionable; that Dahl is a gifted writer on a different plane from the mass purveyors of junk is also undeniable. I am however among those who would leave children to find his books for themselves, rather than take pains to introduce them. They appeal, I think, to the cruder end of childish taste: to a delight in rumbustious rudery and in giving people one-in-the-eye. *Charlie and the Chocolate Factory* (1964), about the wonders of Mr Willy Wonka's vast sweet-making establishment and the sticky fate therein of four spoiled children, seems to me to be a thick, rich, glutinous candy-bar of a book, which children are all too likely to enjoy but which we need not urge them to consume. *The Twits* (1980) is sufficiently characterized by the author's remark in passing that 'we can't go on forever watching these two disgusting people doing disgusting things to each other'.

I like *The BFG* (1982) more than most of the Dahl books: the Big Friendly Giant is harmless and well-intentioned and has a vocabulary of his own:

'All of them' (the other giants) 'is guzzling human beans every night . . . That is why you will be coming to an ucky-mucky end if any of them should ever be getting his gogglers on you. You would be swallowed up like a piece of frumpkin pie, all in one dollop.'

The nine bad giants are going to raid England and gorge themselves on girls and boys, but heroine Sophie and the BFG thwart them by means of a night approach to the Queen, in whose presence the BFG releases one of the resounding rectal blast-offs that are his speciality.

Dogs' droppings and spikes in bottoms are among the less savoury items to be found in *The Witches* (1983), in which witches plan to turn all the children in England into mice. The Whitbread Award judges, honouring this book, found it 'deliciously disgusting'. It's a matter of taste.

Traditional stories — legend and folktale — have continued to be reissued in various forms and formats throughout the years under review. As they are not original work of the period, I have in general not included them, but a few exceptions must be made where imaginative retelling and outstanding artwork have combined to form a distinguished new book. The world-famous novelist Isaac Bashevis Singer turned to writing for children when he was over sixty with *Zlateh the Goat and other stories* (1966), and has told or retold a great many stories on folk themes, mainly from Eastern Europe. The most impressive of them is *The Golem* (1982), about the enormous figure of a man, fashioned by a rabbi with divine authority out of clay, brought to life for a good purpose but afterwards misused. The Golem has huge strength and no intelligence, yet it can feel; it is a pathetic as well as a dangerous figure. Uri Shulevitz's illustrations − in my view the best work of this talented artist − are sombre, menacing, yet at times grotesquely humorous.

In *The God Beneath the Sea* (1970), Leon Garfield and Edward Blishen reshaped Greek myth to form a continuous narrative, and − rightly, in my view − sought to match the magnificence of their material with a highflown style which predictably brought condemnation by some who saw the result as floridity rather than splendour. The same partnership produced *The Golden Shadow* (1973), a further selection of myth and legend linked by the figure of a travelling storyteller. Both books are powerfully illustrated by Charles Keeping.

Virginia Hamilton's extraordinary *Magical Adventures of Pretty Pearl* (1983), brings its heroine, a god child, down from the African equivalent of Olympus, on Mount Kenya:

What good is it bein' a god child, she thought, if I got to hang around up here all de time? What there for me to do when I beat all de god chil'en at de games, and I learns everythin' so fast?

In the shape of albatrosses, she and her older brother John de Conquer, the greatest god, cross the ocean to America, where Pretty joins a post-Civil-War community of freed slaves, surviving with Amerindian cooperation in the forests of upland Georgia. The book mixes elements of myth, legend, folklore, national and racial history, and makes superb use of Black English as the language both of gods and mortals.

Kevin Crossley-Holland, a distinguished poet and editor, is particularly noted in the field of children's literature as a teller and reteller of stories set in distant times. A trio of medieval stories written primarily for young children were made into exceptional picture books by Margaret Gordon. The most appealing perhaps is *The Green Children* (1966), about a boy and girl who arrive unaccountably in East Anglia from a mysterious land where all is green. Kevin Crossley-Holland retells this in the manner of a modern short story. Margaret Gordon's drawings are equally modern, with their boldly stylized children, peasants and sheep. Interestingly, the result has less of an air of anachronism than a pseudo-medieval approach would have had.

In *The Kingdom Under the Sea* (1971), Joan Aiken re-created eleven East European folk tales with a fierce vitality that was matched by Jan Pienkowski's spectacular silhouette-style

A Jan Pienkowski silhouette from *The Kingdom Under the Sea*, by Joan Aiken

illustrations. Another Aiken-Pienkowski partnership was *A Necklace of Raindrops,* in which Joan Aiken triumphed in the difficult genre of the modern fairy-tale. The properties in these tales include a train, an aeroplane and a motor-bus, which Jan Pienkowski portrays as endearingly antiquated and perfectly at home in a world of magic. Good original fairy tales in the traditional manner are rare; among the few who can catch the authentic note is the prolific American writer Jane Yolen. While using time-honoured magical ingredients, Yolen often relates her stories to present-day themes. An instance is *The Seventh Mandarin* (1970), whose young hero, having fulfilled a quest to retrieve the king's soul — lost in the form of a kite — comes back through the poorest part of the city and, shocked by what he sees, has hard truths to tell the king.

Susan Price's *The Ghost Drum* (1987) is not folk-tale — it is a full-length book — but uses traditional folk-tale motifs and breathes the air of folktale. The setting must be Russia; the great and good witch Chingis, whose house runs — as it should — on chicken legs, magically rescues the young son of the dead Czar from being killed on the orders of his wicked aunt; but a villainous shaman in league with the aunt causes Chingis to be killed and the young Czarevich handed over. Chingis returns from the spirit world to save the day once more, before returning there and taking the Czarevich with her. The tale is told by the memorable, compelling, almost hypnotic figure of a learned cat on a golden chain, walking round and round a tree; and it is an assured, crystal-clear telling.

There are strong elements of Russian folk-tale, too, in *The Dream Stealer* (1983), by the American writer Gregory Maguire. The people of a remote village live by selling what they can to passengers on the Imperial Express train that halts there. Rumours that a legendary demon wolf is on the prowl terrify the villagers and deprive them of their livelihood. Two children venture out to seek the advice of the famous witch Baba Yaga, and when the train comes — empty — into the village their salvation is at hand. The story makes rich and resonant use of magic, and is equally rich in robust humour.

23

Realism, British-style

REALISM, like all such holdall words, can be defined and redefined indefinitely. It tends to connote the seamy side and the 'let's face-it' approach; but for present purposes I take it simply to indicate fiction in which the events described are such as might actually happen in real life, and in which the setting is the present rather than the historical past. Even such simple definitions as this raise problems of drawing the line; and I shall arbitrarily include a sub-genre of stories whose settings are in the past, but a past that is within living memory or not far beyond it. The Moffat books of Eleanor Estes, referred to in an earlier chapter, are an example; their pre-1914 setting was not contemporary when the books were written, but clearly they are neither 'historical' nor 'costume' stories.

British writers have contributed interestingly to this sub-genre. Gillian Avery's books are set in the late Victorian period, but they are not explorations of the past. Miss Avery has simply moved the present back a little; the action of her stories is undoubtedly happening 'now', but 'now' is not quite in its usual place. In *The Warden's Niece* (1957) Maria runs away from school and takes refuge with her uncle, the head of an Oxford college. He puts her under the same tutor as the sons of his colleague Professor Smith. The three boys are the capable, somewhat awe-inspiring Thomas, apprehensive Joshua and outrageous eight-year-old James; and their tutor is long, thin Mr Copplestone, who in any emergency heads straight for disaster. Maria, who is timid but determined, has the ambition to become Professor of Greek, and gatecrashes the Bodleian Library for the sake of a piece of original research.

A Likely Lad (1971) is an endearing piece of social comedy. This is the story of William Cobbett Overs, whose father, a small shopkeeper in Manchester around the year 1900, is determined to push him onward and upward to success, beginning with an office stool in an insurance company headquarters. Bookish Willy, a likely lad in his own way, is horrified by the prospect, and has a nervous doggedness which enables him to escape it. And happily, though Mr Overs sees

Drawing by Faith Jaques, from Gillian Avery's *A Likely Lad*

little point in book-learning, his faith in Willy and capacity for being right whatever happens are enough to encompass a total change of direction.

There were other books that similarly looked backward to time recalled – even if at a remove – rather than to 'historical' time. Noel Streatfeild (1895-1986) showed her best form for the last time in *Thursday's Child* (1970), about a decisive young person who although a foundling is undoubtedly a lady, for she was discovered on a Thursday somewhere around the turn of the century 'in a basket on the church step with three of everything of the very best quality'.

A Sound of Chariots, by Mollie Hunter (1973), tells of Bridie McShane, a spirited, sensitive child in a hard-up family just after the First World War. Bridie stands up for herself against various foes; grieves for her handsome, admired father who dies of war wounds; realizes her own mortality; delights in language and is determined to be a writer. The book is made compelling by a profound sense of involvement, a feeling that the author is right in there with the main character, a passionate participant. Yet for the same reason I find it not entirely likeable; there is a disturbing sense of the author's absorbed admiration for her protagonist.

The Children of the House, by Brian Fairfax-Lucy and

Philippa Pearce, first published in 1968, was placed in its actual setting when reissued in 1989 as *The Children of Charlecote*. This is the lightly-fictionalized family story of four neglected children: neglected not by foster-parents in some squalid slum but by their own grand, chilly father and mother in a great house in England just before the First World War. It is a strange, touching story with some terrible moments, as when the children literally dance for joy at their parents' temporary absence; but there is reassurance, for they find comfort and affection in one another and in the pitying servants.

The Children of Charlecote apart, Philippa Pearce has written a small number of highly-acclaimed novels and many short stories. The novels have appeared at longish intervals over the years, as and when their time came. Her first book, *Minnow on the Say* (1955; American title *The Minnow Leads to Treasure)* was an intricately plotted treasure-hunt: a clear, bright book with the sparkle and also some of the depth of the river that flows through it. *Tom's Midnight Garden*, discussed in the preceding chapter, came between this and *A Dog So Small* (1962), which explores the depths of a child's longing. Ben, the middle child of five, is promised a dog by his grandfather, but the promise cannot be properly kept, and all he gets is a picture of a dog worked in wool. In his disappointment Ben imagines a dog of his own, which he can only see with closed eyes; and while crossing the street, lost to the world, he is run over and goes to hospital. At last all comes right, for Ben's grandparents are able to give him a pup after all; his parents move to a place near the Heath where a dog can be kept; all that is needed is that Ben should learn to live with the dog he has, an ordinary animal, rather than an exotic creature of daydream.

The Battle of Bubble and Squeak (1978), a short novel with strong appeal for readers down to the age of eight or even less, is an unpretentious and easy-to-read but quietly perceptive story on the perennial theme of children's fight against parental opposition to keep a pet. Bubble and Squeak are gerbils, and although they belong to Sid, his sisters Peggy and Amy are just as fond of them. It's Mum who can't stand animals, particularly small, messy ones. But the outcome of the battle is predictable. 'She may never *enjoy* gerbils,' says Sid when he can see that he's winning, 'but at least she's facing up to them.'

The Way to Sattin Shore (1983) was Philippa Pearce's first full-scale fictional work for more than twenty years. It was greatly praised; it has some splendid characters and finely evoked settings, but as a warm admirer of Philippa Pearce I have to say that I don't think it quite succeeds. The plot is complex, almost melodramatic. Kate Tranter tries to find out what happened to her father, who appears to have died on the day of her birth, and as the threads are unravelled they lead back to Sattin Shore, a desolate fringe of estuary. Here, ten years ago, the tide welled up to cover the face of a man lying unconscious on the sand. The shadow of tragedy, of past hatreds and jealousies, falls heavily on the present, particularly in the person of Kate's watchful, sinister Granny; and although there's a happy ending much of the story is sombre.

Kate is a wholly believable child in a wholly believable family. Not least of the characters is beautiful, golden Syrup, the cat, who weaves in and out of the story in cool pursuit of his own interests, and who is entertained in other houses under the names of Ginger, Sunshine, and Sunny Jim. Philippa Pearce's sense of place is acute, and she has a vivid gift for catching the heightened moments of life: there is a chapter on tobogganing in which you can feel the bite of snow and the heady perils of downhill speed. The trouble with *Sattin Shore,* I think, is that its best features are independent of the storyline and do not coalesce with it to form a satisfying whole. It does not gain from the dark intricacies of its plot.

Philippa Pearce's short stories are of equal excellence with her novels. *Lion at School* (1985) is a splendid collection of tales suitable for reading aloud to young children, or for those who can read for themselves. *What the Neighbours Did* (1972) contains eight short stories for an older age group. Mainly they are about ordinary happenings to ordinary children and grown-ups in ordinary places. But little is ordinary when looked at freshly with clear eyes, and Philippa Pearce is particularly good at conveying the strangeness that lies behind the everyday. This gift enables her to step outside the borders of realism without any loss of conviction in *The Shadow-Cage and Other Tales of the Supernatural* (1977) and *Who's Afraid and Other Strange Stories* (1986).

Treasure-hunts not unlike the one in *Minnow on the Say* were characteristic also of the early work of William Mayne in the 1950s, though the treasures were never ordinary ones, and they were most often discovered by the solution of complicated mysteries from the past. Mayne's first major book, *A Swarm in May* (1955) was one of the most brilliant of its decade. John Owen, a Singing Boy at a cathedral choir school, becomes the Beekeeper, whose task is not to keep bees but to sing a solo before the Bishop. The action, too intricate to summarize here, involves a real swarm of bees and a long-hidden secret, as well as the daily life of the school; and the cathedral itself, alive and enduring and dominating everything, is like a great three-dimensional frame to the story.

A Grass Rope (1957) is set in the Yorkshire Dales, Mayne's own country. The present-day participants are Nan and Mary from the farm, Adam the head boy at Nan's school, and Peter who lives at the inn; but there is an older story, now half legend, which involves these children's remote ancestors together with a pack of hounds, a unicorn and (maybe) a treasure. Mary is a small girl who believes in fairies; Adam is a mature schoolboy who believes in science; and though the answer to the puzzle is scientific it is Mary, setting off to fairyland with a grass rope for catching the unicorn, who leads the way to the treasure.

There were several more of these elaborate treasure-hunts, ingenious in conception and elegant in execution, but they lacked a vital element – a sense of emotional involvement. Eventually this deficiency was remedied. *Ravensgill* (1970) had superficial resemblances to *A Grass Rope* – both are set in the Dales, and in each of them a problem from the past is solved by present-day young people – but in *Ravensgill* at last there is depth of feeling. The mystery is one of crime and punishment; the process of solving it revives old bitterness in a new generation; and when, with the final solution, a feud dies, it is too late; the damage is done.

There is depth of feeling, too, in *The Jersey Shore* (1973), a book that differs startlingly in its American and British editions. Arthur, an American boy staying on the coast of New Jersey in the 1930s, meets his grandfather, who came from England and was married three times, though never to the girl he really loved. Grandfather tells Arthur of old unhappy far-off things: of rural poverty and hardship, illness and child-death, in the fenlands of eastern England. In an epilogue Arthur, now grown-up Art, flies to England with the wartime US Air Force and visits Grandfather's country.

Here the editions diverge. In the British version, it becomes clear at the very end that Art's grandmother was black, a former slave; and she was 'next thing in looks' to Grandfather's true love, back in England, who was dark-skinned and slave-descended too. The story ends with Art's love-at-first-sight meeting with a beautiful girl of the same clan who has 'the same skin as himself, the same skin as his grandmother'. This can only mean that they are both black. The link will be completed at last, and 'between them they had enough years of freedom to be truly free'. In the American version all this is dropped; the book ends tamely with an act of natural piety on Art's part towards his vanished family. I will not speculate on the reasons for the change, but it is hard not to see it as crucial and damaging, for in the British edition one notes how many arrows have been pointing the same way, and how the ending makes sense of what has gone before.

While Mayne is best known for his complex and sophisticated novels for older children, he has in fact written well for younger readers. *No More School* (1965) is a gem of a book for the eights to tens or thereabouts. Two small girls decide to keep the village school open when its one teacher is away ill; and problems of the curriculum, of discipline and of catering are resourcefully dealt with.

In later years Mayne has continued to be active and prolific; by the end of the 1980s he had more than seventy titles to his name. With such an output, he had left most of the commentators panting far behind; and possibly he had produced more than his audience could absorb, for he has never been a popular writer in the sense of having easy appeal and achieving large sales. Yet all through his long career he has pushed out frontiers and set standards for other writers. *Drift* (1985), set in the frozen north of North America, where a dangerous journey is experienced first as it seems to the limited vision of a white boy and then with the alert senses and instincts of an Indian girl, was one of his finest pieces of work, and showed him still well able to break new ground.

Writing of the late 1940s, Geoffrey Trease has told how teachers used to ask him, 'Why are there no modern stories with working-class settings? Nannies and ponies mean nothing to the children we teach'.[1] There was in fact Eve Garnett's *Family from One-End Street*, surviving from the 1930s and still popular; but this book, though warm-hearted, was written from outside. In Britain at least, there was little else, the most obvious reason being that authors themselves came from a restricted social group. Children's writers were more likely to have gone to private than to local authority schools, and more likely to be acquainted with nannies and gardeners than with dwellers in back streets.

Times were changing, however; the base was beginning to broaden. In 1958 E. W. Hildick published *Jim Starling*, the first of a series of books set, as the author said, in the industrial working-class north of England, where he was brought up, worked and taught until the mid-1950s. Jim Starling goes to Cement Street Secondary Modern School, Smogbury, and is taught not by formidable gowned pedagogues but by ordinary teachers doing their best in grim surroundings. The books however are of no great merit.

In 1960, Frederick Grice (1910-83), who grew up in a Durham pit village, published his episodic *The Bonnie Pit Laddie*, which introduced such features as strike, hardship and disastrous accident, and had the unmistakable ring of authenticity. Bill Naughton's tales of the adventures and vicissitudes of working-class lads in *The Goalkeeper's Revenge and Other Stories* (1961) were told humorously, sometimes touchingly, and with a firm base of personal experience. In *Gumble's Yard* (1961; American title *Trouble in the Jungle*) John Rowe Townsend – forced many years ago into the use of his middle name to distinguish him from another John Townsend – wrote about city streets similar to those he knew as a child. Kevin and Sandra, the eldest of four children abandoned by their elders, fight to keep the family together, even though this means a moonlight flit to a derelict warehouse on a canal bank. *Goodbye to Gumble's Yard* (1965), originally known as *Widdershins Crescent* and in America as *Goodbye to the Jungle*, takes the same family to a new housing estate, where Kevin and Sandra now have to cope with financial entanglements and problems of social adjustment and how to keep the dishonest, dimwitted head of the household out of trouble. Townsend's later books have ranged widely in subject and setting; they include *The Intruder* (1969), *Noah's Castle* (1975) and *The Islanders* (1981).

Sylvia Sherry, in *A Pair of Jesus-Boots* (1969; American title *The Liverpool Cats)* took the tougher kind of contemporary realism as far as it had then gone. Her hero Rocky O'Rourke, who lives in the back streets of Liverpool, is rough, reckless, destructive, without any respect for the law or any sense of right and wrong; his main ambition is to 'do a job' like elder brother Joey. Rocky in fact has attractive human impulses, but there is no accepted social and moral order to which he owes his loyalty. At the end of the book he looks as if he'll come good in his own way; but, reappearing years later, after the success of a TV adaptation, in *A Pair of Desert Wellies* (1985) and *Rocky and the Ratman* (1988), he seems unregenerate and still pretty lawless.

Nina Bawden, already an established novelist, wrote her first books for children in the 1960s. *A Handful of Thieves* (1967) was one of several that showed contemporary children having sometimes-improbable adventures in settings that were mostly those of daily life. If the adventures were improbable, the children were not; they were portrayed with shrewd insight and with a sympathy that never became sentimental. *Squib* (1971) is about children who come across a grossly-neglected small boy, living in a decrepit bus on a caravan site. The younger ones think he is held captive by a witch who might eat him; the older ones know that something is terribly wrong but cannot quite comprehend it. The difficulty, for children, of knowing what's going on, and doing anything about it if they do know, is a recurrent Bawden theme.

In *The Peppermint Pig* (1975), Nina Bawden is at her best. Poll is the youngest of the four Greengrass children. It's the turn of the century; Father has gone to America to seek the family's fortune, and Mother has taken the children to live in a small Norfolk town. This is the quiet, episodic story of a year in Poll's life; and that year encloses the whole life of Johnnie, the peppermint pig (runt of a litter), who arrives in the milkman's pocket, becomes a family pet, and grows towards his inevitable end. Poll comes to accept his death; she has him 'fixed and safe in her mind for ever'. This is an apparently simple but actually subtle book, written in the admirable Bawden style of unobtrusive precision. *Rebel on a Rock* (1978) brings an unusual kind of realism into a children's novel. When children become involved in a plot to remove a dictator, in a country very like the Greece of the colonels' regime a few years ago, they do not merely fail to forward the plan; they unwittingly give it away and cause it to collapse. This runs counter to the fictional tradition by which children triumph over villains, but is a far more likely result of children's intervention in such matters.

Among British writers of the 1970s who set out to deal realistically with problems of contemporary life were Bernard Ashley, with *The Trouble with Donovan Croft* (1974), *A Kind of Wild Justice* (1978) and other titles, and Jan Needle, with

Albeson and the Germans (1977) and *My Mate Shofiq* (1978). Ashley's understanding of young people is based on long teaching experience. Donovan Croft is a black boy, fostered out with a well-meaning white family, who feels himself to have been betrayed and switches off from the world. Occasionally there's an air of the case-history, but there's also shrewdness and penetration. Ashley's novels have grown tougher over the years; increasingly his young protagonists face a harsh, sometimes merciless world. In *A Kind of Wild Justice,* which has pace and tension, Ronnie Webster struggles to survive amidst adult crime and turpitude. Kevin, in *High Pavement Blues* (1983), has to look after the family market-stall, and defend it against the unscrupulous enmity of the next-door stallholders, when his father, the Big Fellow, an ex-Army trumpeter, walks out. Jan Needle's Albeson, a dockland child, is drawn into a horribly convincing bout of vandalism at his school, and runs away into further trouble; Bernard, in *My Mate Shofiq,* gets into a variety of complications through his friendship with a Pakistani boy; and with a particularly interesting form of realism Jan Needle manages to take the reader into his heroes' well-meaning but naive and muddled minds.

A great deal was written and said in the 1960s and 1970s about the need for books for children living in multi-racial communities. This need was and is a real one. Several good writers − notably Andrew Salkey, James Berry and C. Everard Palmer, all discussed in Chapter 26 − have written for children in Britain about West Indian life, culture and tradition; but there has been a dearth of black writers of the first or second rank to contribute fiction about black children growing up in this country. White writers have been reluctant to write as if out of black experience, and I would not care to say they are wrong: it is a perilous undertaking. A scatter of black faces in illustrations, and of token black characters in fiction as (for instance) members of gangs of children is not really good enough, though better than nothing.

Probably however the most vivid and vigorous realism of the 1970s − and an indication of the rich potential of mixed communities as a fictional setting and source of inspiration − is to be found in work of an Indian living in Britain, Farrukh Dhondy. In his story collections *East End at Your Feet* (1976) and *Come to Mecca* (1978), Dhondy writes with tolerance, sympathy and wry humour about black, white and (especially) Asian youngsters in London; his stories revolve around the culture-differences, generation gaps and misunderstandings that surround them. The stories in *Poona Company* (1980), which draw on Dhondy's own childhood experience, are even more spicy and colourful. A further but slightly disappointing collection, *Trip Trap*, appeared in 1982, since when Dhondy seems to have been largely occupied with the theatre and television and to have stopped writing for the children's lists.

The old sex stereotypes died a slow death over the post-war years. It was hardly even a gesture when Jean Ure wrote, in *A Proper Little Nooryeff* (1982) about a boy who – not without misgivings – dances in ballet and has the courage to face 'the jeers, the ribaldry, the jokes chalked up on the blackboard'. Jean Ure, who had a stage training herself, has written well about theatre and ballet. Among her books for children – she has also written adult novels – I particularly like *Hi There, Supermouse!* (1983), in which tall, gangly Nicola is played, or rather pushed, off the stage by her younger, pink-and-pretty sister Rose. Nicola is endearingly human, not above jealousy or spite. Perceptive professionals around her can see that actually she's more promising than Rose, though lacking in kittenish child-star quality. She *might* be a dancer, if she doesn't decide to be a doctor instead.

Jill Paton Walsh, demonstrating that there is a realism of the emotions as well as of the social situation, wrote two of the best novels of the decade to be published on a children's list in *Goldengrove* (1972) and *Unleaving* (1976). The two titles together form a quotation from a poem by Gerard Manley Hopkins:

> Margaret, are you grieving
> Over Goldengrove unleaving?

Goldengrove is the name of Madge's Gran's house on the Cornish coast, where the action of both books takes place. Madge and Paul, who think they are cousins, have stayed there summer after summer; but in the year of *Goldengrove* everything is changed; their relationship is not what they thought it was; Madge is growing into new emotions and new kinds of awareness; and, meeting a blind professor, eager to help him, she learns with horror that a person can retreat behind the locked doors of self, refusing love and trust. In some ways this is a sad book, sad with the loss of childhood and the burden of knowledge; and we are reminded that 'some wounds cannot be healed, some things are beyond helping and cannot be put right'. But this is also a book full of light, of the sense of landscape, of sea and sky. In *Unleaving*, Madge has inherited Gran's house and has let it to a university reading party; the professor's son Patrick — like Madge a creature of feeling — makes, or seems to make, a fearful decision over his small mongol sister Molly. Tragedy follows; Patrick suffers for it and Madge saves him. Interwoven with this story of storm and stress is a portrayal of a serene Cornish summer with grandchildren at play; and the two strands finally meet in a surprising but, once grasped, inevitable revelation.

Gaffer Samson's Luck (1985) is a simple but not shallow story about a boy who meets and survives the challenge of village life — the gulf between natives and incomers — and who makes a friend of a dying old man. The Gaffer's 'luck' is a small black stone which he believes preserves his life, and which he has hidden. This is an old folktale motif which Jill Paton Walsh has ingeniously adapted: the Gaffer asks James to find his luck for him so that he can give it away and die. He passes the luck to James, and James passes it to a village boy who's in hospital and needs it. The story is about these things and more; and it's also about the strange but fascinating Fen country. Fenland is short of hills, it's true; but hills, as the Gaffer sagely observes, cost a lot of sky.

Jane Gardam, like several other novelists, has written both for adults and children. *The Summer After the Funeral* (1973) was published on a children's list but is a witty and distinctive novel that can be enjoyed by adults as much as by young readers. Athene Price, rising seventeen, is beautiful, intelligent and innocent. Her father, who has just died at the outset of the story, was an aged clergyman, and she identifies herself with Emily Brontë. In a series of encounters with a reality which is sometimes as bizarre as her fantasies, Athene wins through to self and sense. There are some very funny touches: for instance, when schoolmistress Miss Bowles tells Athene about her friend Primrose Clarke.

> 'I've always had holidays with Prim. She's English.'
> 'English?'
> 'Yes.'
> 'But, aren't you —?'
> 'No, I'm Geography.'

Anne Fine's first book, *The Summer-House Loon* (1978), was light and frothy and deliciously absurd. It's about Ione and her blind, unsentimentally-treated professor father and his secretary

Caroline and one of his students, Ned, who is in love with Caroline; and after disagreements and misunderstandings, and a hilarious but far from erotic bedroom scene, it all ends with strawberries on the lawn and imminent wedding bells. Ned's proposal to Caroline is a classic: 'Marry me, you stubborn old bat, and be my only sweet love for everandevermore.'

Anne Fine's subsequent books have ranged between the comic and the serious, being generally more successful at the comic end of the spectrum. *Goggle-Eyes* (1989) is probably her best. Kitty's parents are divorced; Mum has a new man, Gerald, in her life, and Kitty detests him. He's conventional, conservative, and everything Mum isn't. But as Kitty's narrative goes on it becomes clear that he's shrewd, sensible, not without dry humour, and just what Mum and Kitty need. There's a brilliantly funny account of a wire-cutting expedition to a nuclear site, with Mum and Gerald on opposite sides, so to speak, of the fence. I would guess that the author's sympathies are with Mum, but one of the joys of this book is that it's engagingly tolerant.

Vivien Alcock has written largely fantasy, but *The Cuckoo Sister* (1985) is a realistic story and is, like *Goggle-Eyes*, about a resented newcomer. (The word 'cuckoo' refers to nests, not to craziness.) Kate's sister Emma was snatched from her pram many years ago; now an appallingly-dressed, spiky-haired, hard-eyed teenager called Rosie turns up with a letter saying she's the lost baby. But is she? It's an intriguing situation, and the way it develops is the matter of the book. In the end Kate and Rosie/Emma become sisters, so all is well; but one sees clearly enough that it could have been disastrously otherwise.

The traditional boarding-school story has not revived and does not look likely to do so, though Antonia Forest bravely kept it alive by adding *The Cricket Term* (1974) and *The Attic Term* (1976) to her earlier books about the Marlowes at Kingscote, *Autumn Term* (1948) and *End of Term* (1959). There are other books about the young Marlowes, set away from school in holiday times. School naturally makes an appearance in many stories that are not primarily school stories; and the hugely successful television series set in a day school called Grange Hill produced a spin-off in book form with *Grange Hill Rules, OK?* (1980) and other Grange Hill titles by Robert Leeson.

The Turbulent Term of Tyke Tiler, by Gene Kemp (1977) is

about a trouble-prone but likeable child's last term in primary school. It is mainly episodic, though a serious thread running through it is provided by Tyke's efforts to look after not-very-bright Danny Price. At the end Tyke climbs to the school roof to ring the old bell, and causes the collapse of the building. 'That child', says Chief Sir (the head teacher), 'has always appeared to me to be on the brink of wrecking this school, and as far as I can see has at last succeeded.' A good line; and there's a marvellous, although once-for-all, surprise at the end which I had better not reveal.

Jan Mark's *Thunder and Lightnings* (1976) cannot be called a school story, but some of its most entertaining events take place in school. It is about the friendship of two boys, middle-class Andrew and less-privileged Victor. The viewpoint is Andrew's, but the book is more about Victor, who is supposed to be backward but who has carefully hidden depths. Victor has a passion for aircraft, especially the Lightnings that rend the Norfolk air with sonic booms; but he doesn't condescend to write about them for his yearly school project, which is always about fish. 'Fish are easy,' he tells Andrew. 'They're all the same shape.' And he shows Andrew his book:

His fish were not only all the same shape, they were all the same shape as slugs. Underneath each drawing was a printed heading: BRAEM, TENSH, CARP, STIKLBAK, SHARK. It was the only way of telling them apart.

Victor, who suffers from living in a spotlessly uncomfortable home, enjoys the easygoing atmosphere of Andrew's, but is cheerfully resigned to his own situation, and doesn't expect too much from this world.

Jan Mark is prolific and has written a variety of books, including the speculative fiction referred to in an earlier chapter. *Hairs in the Palm of the Hand* (1981) is a pair of hilarious long-short stories about goings-on in school. In *Handles* (1983) Erica, who wants to be a motor-cycle mechanic, works her way into the tatty repair shop run by Elsie (a man), who has a nickname for everybody. Erica longs to earn a handle for herself, and gets one in the end – a rather grand one. Erica is struggling against what is expected of her; so is Elsie, a married schoolmaster turned mechanic. The story, in fact, though light and cheerful, is shot through with tensions between what people are and what they are supposed to be.

Alan Garner's *Stone Book Quartet*, appearing in the late 1970s, may well be its author's finest achievement. In four brief books, each of which covers the events of only one day,

Garner traces five generations of village families, their crafts and their relationships. Each story has a boy or girl at its centre; each is concerned with the transmission of skills, the wisdom that resides in work, and continuity of life in an intimately known landscape.

In the order of the events they describe, not of publication, the four are *The Stone Book* (1976), *Granny Reardun* (1977), *The Aimer Gate* (1978) and *Tom Fobble's Day* (1977). The most masterly, I think, is *Tom Fobble's Day*, the ending of which sums everything up. The time is World War II. Grandad, a smith, just before his death, has made a new sledge for William. That night, with anti-aircraft guns firing and search-lights swivelling around the sky, William sledges perilously down the snowy hillside, again and again; and 'he was not alone on a sledge. There was a line, and he could feel it. It was a line through hand and eye, block, forge and loom to the hill. He owned them all; and they owned him.'

Before this quartet it was possible to feel that Garner, though undoubtedly brilliant, lacked a humanity which would have given greater depth to his work. In the *Stone Book* quartet, that humanity is abundantly present. Granny Reardun, by the way, is not somebody's name. A granny reardun is a person brought up by his grandmother.

The outstanding new writer to appear in Britain in the early 1980s was Janni Howker. Though young and emphatically regional — living in and writing about the North of England — she is a sophisticated writer, and her first two books, *Badger on the Barge* (1984) and *The Nature of the Beast* (1985), are far from being prentice work. *Badger* is a group of five longish short stories. In each story there is an old person with whom a young one becomes involved, but no story is concerned only with such a relationship; all have other themes and show the young protagonist in some other significant relation. All are touching, carefully shaped, delicate in feeling; the most poignant is *Jakey*, in which an old boatman is going to die, and young Steven dreams of a dark shape following the old man's boat: 'a great grey shape, like a shark, swimming behind, slowly, secretly'. It is Jakey's death.

In *The Nature of the Beast*, the urban setting, as often happens in the North, is on the edge of open country. The story is about the weeks following the closure of the mill on which the community depends. A rumoured Beast is prowling around, savaging farmers' stock and frightening people; and the Beast, whether or not it exists, has obvious symbolic aspects.

Unemployment also prowls around and destroys; the Beast embodies it. And in the end the Beast, in the shape of fury, anger, hatred, frustration, is inside the boy as well: 'I'm going to take over where the Beast left off. They've not seen nothing yet.'

Isaac Campion (1986) takes the form of an account supposedly given to the author by the aged Isaac just before his death in 1984 at the age of 96; it tells of events when he was 'twelve, rising thirteen,' so goes back in time to the farthest reach of living memory. At the centre of the story is Isaac's father, a horse dealer and a harsh, violent man. Isaac's older brother is killed as a result of a reckless dare by the son of Father's enemy; Father, swollen with hatred, plans a dreadful revenge, and Isaac, on impulse, thwarts him. The story is one of ferocious passions, intense and sometimes suffocating family relationships, in a world from which Isaac knows he must escape; but all is not darkness, for in Isaac himself the human spirit shines through, and even in Father's relentless drive there is something heroic. These last two novels are arguably general rather than specifically young people's fiction; they are grim yet rich and complex, the work of a high and promising talent.

Badger on the Barge was widely acclaimed and won several awards, but not the Carnegie Medal. Two years later — almost as if in compensation — the Carnegie was awarded to another book with a strongly northern flavour which was in effect a group of short stories, although in this case linked together by family ties and framed by a celebration. The episodes in *Granny was a Buffer Girl*, by Berlie Doherty (1986) are mainly love stories of three generations of a Sheffield family. A buffer girl's nasty job was to put the shine on the products of a cutlery works; the best episode, and the one that gives the book its title, is a Cinderella tale in which the prince, who is the boss's son, doesn't recognize his Cinders in her working clothes, and she falls back on the available local lad. This is a respectable piece of work, but not of the quality of *Badger on the Barge*. Regional writing in the realistic mode can be of high excellence, but it can also be mediocre, and one has to wonder whether the award committee could tell the difference.

24

Realism, American-style

ONE OF THE MOST striking features of post-1945 American realistic writing for children has been a determined and continuing attempt to widen the scope of fiction to include the experience of minority groups: especially (so far) blacks. The position of the black American in a white-dominated society is of course no new theme; it goes back to *Uncle Tom's Cabin* and *Huckleberry Finn*. Among stories of the 1940s which were 'contemporary' at the time of their publication but which have now dated were John R. Tunis's *All-American* (1942) and Jesse Jackson's *Call Me Charley* (1945). The Tunis book was concerned with the admission of black (and Jewish) boys to sport teams; *Call Me Charley* with the acceptance of a black boy in a suburban community generally.

In these books the black characters bear injustice with a patience that now seems excessive. Ned LeRoy in *All-American*, told he will be left out of a football team in Miami because 'they don't permit colored boys to play down there', accepts the situation and merely says 'I sure hope they broadcast that game'; Charley Moss's mother in *Call Me Charley* advises him on the last page, 'As long as you work hard and try to do right, you will always find good [white] people like Doc Cunningham or Tom and his folks marching along with you in the right path.' Actually Charley is not without spirit; when someone addresses him as Sambo he says, 'My name is Charles. Sometimes I'm called Charley. Nobody calls me Sambo and gets away with it.' Hence the book's title. Nevertheless, in the attitudes of the time there is some resemblance to the treatment of the poor by well-meaning Victorians. Just as the poor were expected to rely on and be grateful for the beneficence of the rich, so the black must rely on and be grateful for the beneficence of the white.

In the later 1950s and early 1960s, 'integrationist' novels began to be numerous. A fair example, and better than most, is Dorothy Sterling's *Mary Jane* (1959). Mary Jane is one of the first tiny group of blacks to be integrated in a rather superior junior high school. She has to walk behind policemen through hostile crowds to the school door — there is a frighteningly vivid account of this — and faces isolation in class and in the cafeteria. But she becomes friendly with a white girl who is also a misfit, and by the end of term she is integrated sufficiently for the Junior Science Club to decide that it will not visit any place that does not admit coloured students.

Mary Jane's father is a lawyer and her grandfather an eminent biologist; so the class aspect of racism is somewhat obscured. Educated black people have a very different problem from that of uneducated ones. There were many innocuous stories on similar themes to that of *Mary Jane,* written by well-intentioned white writers and, unconsciously, still white-orientated. The idea that there were true and valuable differences between the races did not occur. The authors were unlucky; they lacked foresight, as we all do on many occasions, and their approach became discredited. The black writer Julius Lester, in a published exchange of letters with George Woods, children's book editor of the *New York Times,* said:

When I review a book about blacks (no matter the race of the author) I ask two questions: 'Does it accurately present the black perspective?' 'Will it be relevant to black children?' The possibility of a book by a white answering these questions affirmatively is almost nil.[1]

A problem in the earlier post-war years was that there were not yet enough good black writers for children. This lack has largely been remedied, and excellent black writers have emerged. Probably the most distinguished is Virginia Hamilton, who made an impressive debut with *Zeely* (1967). Zeely Tayber is immensely tall, black and beautiful, and helps her father to keep hogs. An imaginative younger girl, Elizabeth Perry, from whose viewpoint the story is told, is spending her summer on the adjoining farm. She sees Zeely first as a ghostly night traveller, then as a Watutsi queen, finally and not least impressively as herself. This is a book without bitterness or paranoia, but it is deeply concerned with black dignity: the splendour of Zeely in contrast with her humble occupation, the association of night travelling with escape from slavery. It is easy to read a message into the book — walk tall — but this does not detract from its merit.

Virginia Hamilton's second book, *The House of Dies Drear* (1968) is a complicated mystery-story and treasure-hunt set in the big old house of an abolitionist who had made it into an underground railroad station and had been murdered there. The story itself has a curious, almost-architectural resemblance to the house it describes: large, dark, rambling, and leading off in strange directions. *The Planet of Junior Brown* (1971) is of a different and higher order. It is, if I interpret it correctly, a story of the creation in love and pain of refuges from loneliness and non-communication. It is not fantasy, but it is not wholly realistic either; for such conceptions as the 'planets' of homeless boys dotted around the big city, each with its 'Tomorrow Billy' as leader, are acceptable symbolically rather than literally.

After *Junior Brown* came the remarkable *M. C. Higgins the Great* (1974). M.C. is a barefoot black youth who spends much of his time sitting atop a forty-foot pole on the side of a mountain to which his great-grandmother Sarah came long ago, a slave with a child in her arms. The book doesn't have much of a storyline, but has powerful emotional cohesion, and it has a theme, which as I understand it is the bond between M.C.'s family and the place they have made their own. The most important event happens in M.C.'s mind: the acceptance of his rootedness in Sarah's Mountain and his resolve to build a wall which may, perhaps, hold back the spoilheap that threatens his home. And though the title 'the Great' is self-awarded, a joke, it is deserved, for this poor, rough boy will always take risks to ride high. *M. C. Higgins* was followed by the equally distinctive and mysterious *Arilla Sun Down* (1976), in which a girl of part black, part American Indian ancestry discovers her identity and comes into her inheritance.

Several of Virginia Hamilton's books have crossed or hovered around the uncertain line that divides realism from fantasy. *Sweet Whispers, Brother Rush* (1982) is a ghost story, in which the beautiful and beautifully-dressed Brother (actually her dead uncle) appears to the heroine Tree as a ghost; but the ghost element is not there for its own sake, and the concerns of the story are entirely with human relationships. The intervention of Brother Rush enables Tree to learn crucial facts of the family past, and to cope with a desperate-looking present.

Virginia Hamilton won the 1975 Newbery Medal for *M. C. Higgins,* and observed in her acceptance speech that she was 'the first black woman and black writer to have received this award'.[2] The 1977 Newbery winner was a book by another black writer, Mildred D. Taylor: *Roll of Thunder, Hear My Cry.* Mildred Taylor said in her Newbery speech that she had been dissatisfied with books about black families by white writers, 'not because a white person had attempted to write about a black family, but because the writer had not, in my opinion, captured the warmth or love of the black world and had failed to understand the principles upon which black parents brought up their children and taught them survival.' She herself wanted 'to show a black family united in love and pride, of which the reader would like to be a part'.[3]

Roll of Thunder is about the Logans, living in Mississippi in the 1930s, and better off than most black families, for they have land and are determined to hold on to it in spite of hardships, injustices, and all the troubles you make for yourself by fighting for fair treatment. It is a substantial novel, with a strong feeling for land and landscape as well as for people; and in spite of the tragic episode with which it ends, its spirit is positive and heartening. The chronicles of the Logan family had begun with the brief *Song of the Trees* (1975) and continued with *Let the Circle be Unbroken* (1981) and *The Friendship* (1987), all of which showed the Logans still grappling with oppression and sustained by family loyalty and pride.

The white writer to whose book the 'black experience' is the basic material is on perilous ground. William H. Armstrong's Newbery-winning *Sounder* (1969) – about the poor black sharecropper, arrested for stealing food for his hungry children in a hard winter, and about the great coon dog, shot and terribly injured but holding on to life until his return – is attributed by the author to the grey-haired black man who taught him to read fifty years ago; but this has not saved it from being comprehensively trounced for lack of authenticity, white supremacism, and emasculation of the black.[4]

Some of the charges made against *Sounder* seem obviously misguided. The fact that the sharecropper's family are referred to as the father, the mother, the boy, rather than by name is surely not because 'within the white world, deep-seated prejudice has long denied human individualization to the black person'. It must have been the author's intention that his characters should appear universal, not tied down to a local habitation and a name. *Sounder* seems to me to have the ring of authenticity that comes from truth to human nature; and human nature does not have a skin colour. It is not necessary or desirable that a writer be restricted to what he knows from direct experience; otherwise no man could write about women or woman about men, no middle-aged person could write about old age, no one at all could write about the past. It is the task of the creative imagination to leap across such frontiers. *Sounder* is a brief, bleak book that tells an elemental story of hardship and endurance; tells it memorably and well.

Paula Fox's *The Slave Dancer,* discussed in Chapter 18, has come in for much the same kind of criticism as *Sounder,* and to my mind with equal lack of justification. Paula Fox had already shown, in her admirable *How Many Miles to Babylon?* (1967), that true authenticity in portraying character and experience comes from the heart and mind of the author. The story is of the journey through city streets and through strange imagined vistas of a small black boy from Brooklyn. James is black, and has to be black for the story to work; but the mystery of *How Many Miles to Babylon?* is one of the profound and complex mysteries of life from which no one element can be abstracted on its own.

Other books published by Paula Fox in the sixties illustrate the change that was taking place in the relationship between the generations. Old certainties were dissolving; everything was much more fluid. In Paula Fox's books of that time the implication was that children would be all right if only grown-ups would let them develop in their own way. Maurice's parents in *Maurice's Room* (1966) are baffled by their son's devotion to junk, and attempt uncomprehendingly to interest him in the kind of things they think a boy ought to be interested in. Lewis, in *A Likely Place* (1967), is oppressed by his elders until mercifully left in the erratic care of unpredictable Miss Fitchlow; Ivan, in *Portrait of Ivan* (1969), realizes that 'in nearly every moment of his day he was holding onto a rope held at the other end by a grown-up person . . . It was frightening to let go of that rope, but it made him feel quick and light instead of heavy and slow.'

In later work, Paula Fox has broadened her scope. An outstanding novel is *One-Eyed Cat* (1984). Given an airgun for his eleventh birthday, Ned fires it from an attic window at something moving in the moonlight; and when a scrawny one-eyed cat turns up in the woodshed of elderly neighbour Mr Scully, Ned is sure that he shot it. He and Mr Scully struggle to keep the cat alive through the winter; the cat lives, though Mr Scully dies. Ned lives for long months with his guilt; enmeshed, too, in a web of concealment, until eventually all must be brought into the open, expiated, forgiven. As with *How Many Miles?,* it is the mystery of life, of relationships between people, and between people and the world in which they move, that in the end is expressed in a book of cool beauty and understanding.

Cool beauty and understanding, and some sadness, are also at the heart of Paula Fox's *The Lost Boy* (1987). Almost-adolescent Lily, her brother Paul and her parents are getting near the end of a long summer stay on a Greek island when Jack appears: tall, arrogant, anti-social, and hugely attractive to Paul, who turns away from his own family. Jack is the lost boy, but lost only metaphorically; he is the son of a remittance man who doesn't bother with him. Much of the book is an evocation of the island as discovered by Lily: the sea, the landscape, the antiquities, the friendly villagers; yet there's something ominous in the air, and because of Jack's recklessness a child dies. Lily, sorry for Jack, makes brief contact with him afterwards; she and Paul will go home, older, to resume American life, but having glimpsed 'a world of feeling and of loss.'

One pleasant result of the disappearance of old assumptions about the infallibility of parents and the duty of children to toe the line has been the arrival of a number of highly-individual child characters – usually girls – whose personalities have been allowed by their authors to develop without too much regard for what constitutes a proper example. Harriet, in *Harriet the Spy* (1964) by Louise Fitzhugh (1928-74), lives in Manhattan, is eleven, and intends to be Harriet M. Welsch the famous writer when she grows up. After school each day she goes round her 'spy route', observing people and writing down her comments in a notebook. She also puts down what she thinks about her classmates:

> MY MOTHER IS ALWAYS SAYING PINKY WHITEHEAD'S WHOLE PROBLEM IS HIS MOTHER. I BETTER ASK HER WHAT THAT MEANS OR I'LL NEVER FIND OUT. DOES HIS MOTHER HATE HIM? IF I HAD HIM I'D HATE HIM.

Understandably, when Harriet's notebook falls into the hands of her classmates she becomes highly unpopular. Yet she is without malice; the truth is that she actually has the dedication, devastating honesty and ruthlessness of the artist. *Harriet the Spy* is one of the funniest and most original children's books of its day.

Claudia, in E. L. Konigsburg's *From the Mixed-up Files of Mrs Basil E. Frankweiler* (1967), is another heroine who is her own child and nobody else's. Claudia has decided, coolly, to run away from home, returning only when everyone has learned a lesson in Claudia-appreciation. Since she believes in beauty, education and comfort, and lives within commuting distance of New York City, where better to run away to than the Metropolitan Museum of Art? And since there are money problems, whom better to take with her than her financial wizard of a younger brother, Jamie?

Harriet and Claudia; big tough Veronica who beats up the boys in Marilyn Sachs's *Veronica Ganz* (1968); rock-throwing Queenie in Robert Burch's *Queenie Peavy* (1966); lanky, self-deprecating Sara in Betsy Byars's *Summer of the Swans* (1970), who remarks drily that 'the peak of my whole life so far was in third grade when I got to be milk monitor'; suspicious Carlie in the same author's *The Pinballs* (1977); bright, sharp, outrageous Gilly in Katherine Paterson's *The Great Gilly Hopkins* (1978): they all form part of a gallery of real, live, idiosyncratic heroines.

Vera and Bill Cleaver (William J. Cleaver 1920-81), have contributed more to this gallery than most writers. The heroine of their first book, *Ellen Grae* (1967), is the child of divorced parents and a famous teller of tall stories – so much so that when she is burdened with a terrible secret and then made to disclose it to Authority, Authority simply will not believe her. Fourteen-year-old Mary Call Luther, in *Where the Lilies Bloom* (1969), struggles to hold together a poor, parentless family of four, bosses everyone around, and is rewarded by being called mean and ugly; yet this resourceful, awful, splendid child is as much a heroine as any in fiction. Annie Jelks, in *I Would Rather be a Turnip* (1971), resents her illegitimate nephew Calvin; and when, bad-temperedly, she saves his life, she cannot bear his thanks: 'Oh, be quiet, Calvin. You get on my nerves. Did I ever tell you that? Well, you do. You get on my nerves.' There is not much that is outwardly appealing about Annie Jelks, yet by the end of the book one likes and even admires her, and knows that her loyalty to Calvin, her family, or an accepted friend would be grudging but unbounded.

The Cleaver band of doughty heroines continued to grow, with (among others) Littabelle in *The Whys and Wherefores of Littabelle Lee* (1973) and Wilma in *Queen of Hearts* (1978), who look after aged grandparents in very different but equally desperate circumstances, and Evelyn in *The Kissimee Kid* (1981), whose dogged integrity comes into conflict with family loyalty and affection.

After her husband's death, Vera Cleaver went on writing books of much the same kind as before. Amy Blue, in *Sugar Blue* (1984), gets little attention from her busy parents and has withdrawn into a protective shell, from which she is coaxed out by the four-year-old niece who comes to stay and (surprisingly) loves her.

Dicey Tillerman, in Cynthia Voigt's *Homecoming* (1981) and *Dicey's Song* (1982), seems to me to go over the top. She is too good to be true in a late twentieth century sense of the word 'good', with resourcefulness substituted for piety. *Homecoming* follows the trek of the four Tillerman children in search of a home after their mother has abandoned them; *Dicey's Song* is concerned with their settling in to a new way of life with their crusty, eccentric grandmother. Dicey is sturdily independent, open-hearted and right-minded, and endlessly protective of her siblings (who are beset, in the second book, with a well-chosen assortment of problems). Cynthia Voigt has added further books about the Tillerman family and their friends; at the time of writing there are six. They have their admirers.

Boys as well as girls have been freed by some writers from the traditional stereotype. Grover, in the Cleavers' Ellen Grae books and in *Grover* (1970), and Ussy Mock, in *The Mock Revolt* (1971), would never have done as heroes of the old clean-limbed adventure story. And the narrator of Betsy Byars's *The Midnight Fox* (1968), though he bears that most masculine of names, Tom, is a splendidly un-hearty hero. Tom is sent to Aunt Millie's farm for the summer while his parents are in Europe. He goes under protest; he says that 'animals hate him', and he is sure he will never leave his bedroom by the tree outside the window, as Aunt Millie's boys always did. But Tom is ready for the experience he has in the story: the perception of beauty in, and feeling for, a wild creature. It begins when he sees the black fox:

Her steps as she crossed the field were lighter and quicker than a cat's. As she came closer I could see that her black fur was tipped with white. It was as if it were midnight and the moon were shining on her fur, frosting it. The wind parted her fur as it changed directions. Suddenly she stopped. She was ten feet away now, and with the changing of the wind she had got my scent. She looked right at me . . .

Suddenly her nose quivered. It was such a slight movement I almost didn't see it, and then her mouth opened and I could see the pink tip of her tongue. She turned. She still was not afraid, but with a bound that was lighter than the wind — it was as if she was being blown away over the field — she was gone.

And Tom knows that this will change his life.

The Midnight Fox is a fine book — beautiful in glimpses, and between the glimpses often truly funny. Betsy Byars, a prolific writer, belongs unmistakably to the TV and advertising age. Her prose style is quick and witty, accomplishing a great deal in a few strokes. Her protagonists are smart, up-to-date children or teenagers, but at the same time they are inexperienced, naive, often out of their depth. Next to *The Midnight Fox*, my favourite among her earlier books is *The Eighteenth Emergency* (1973), whose unheroic hero Benjie Fawley is called Mouse because he acts like one. The eighteenth emergency is that of being pursued by the school bully. The book is very funny, in a dry, contemporary urban-American way, and at the same time has a didactic element: Mouse comes to feel some sympathy and understanding for the bully, and copes with the eighteenth emergency in neo-Victorian style by taking his punishment like a man.

Several of the now-numerous Byars novels touch on difficult and sensitive subjects – a retarded younger brother in *The Summer of the Swans* (1970), abused or abandoned children in *The Pinballs* (1977), a battered mother and baby in *Cracker Jackson* (1985), a teacher suspected of a suicide attempt in *The Burning Questions of Bingo Brown* (1988) – and are sharply realistic in the perception that comedy and even farce can accompany harrowing drama. It is also a truth sometimes overlooked in fiction that children coping gamely with adult-sized problems are still children and can at times be childishly silly rather than consistently and prematurely adult. In spite of this, one is sometimes left with an uneasy feeling that a light, slight Byars treatment has not measured up to the seriousness of the subject.

Slake, in *Slake's Limbo*, by Felice Holman (1974), is another unorthodox hero – unwanted, short-sighted and bullied – who takes refuge from his pursuers in the New York subway and stays there for 121 days. Slake makes some human contacts, culminating in a 'moment of mutuality' (the author's phrase) with the motorman who stops on the line and picks him up when he's ill and in danger. At the end he feels that his 'general direction is up'. But essentially the story is a Robin-sonnade; its fascination, like that of *Robinson Crusoe*, lies in the detail of how the hero survives.

The tackling of tough subjects has been increasingly charac-teristic of American fiction, not only for teenagers but for children. Katherine Paterson's moving *Bridge to Terabithia* (1977) has death as a theme. Jesse Aarons is introduced to the world of the imagination by his new friend Leslie (a girl); together they set up a secret kingdom in the woods beyond the creek. One day Leslie falls into the creek and is drowned; Jesse must survive his grief, and does so to the extent of building a (surely symbolic) bridge across which he can bring his small sister. Leslie's death is sudden and not witnessed by Jesse, so to some extent the reader is spared; in Lois Lowry's *A Summer to Die* (1977) thirteen-year-old Meg must live through her sister Molly's terminal illness, and sees Molly in hospital close to death.

In *Jacob Have I Loved* (1981) Katherine Paterson portrays an isolated, Methodist community, living in 'the fear and mercy of the Lord' on a small island in Chesapeake Bay. Louise is the elder of twins; her younger sister Caroline is a talented singer, praised, admired, and (by Louise) resented. Poisonous Bible-quoting Grandma doesn't hesitate to supply Louise with the text, from Romans 9.13: 'Jacob have I loved, but Esau have I hated.' The story's many Biblical allusions are a reminder of the richness of that now neglected literary source, and it may be noted that there is something of Martha/Mary as well as of Esau/Jacob in Louise's relationship with her sister. Louise has to work her way out of the resentment that imprisons her; the book has to cover a sizeable time-span and is somewhat lacking in narrative drive; but as a portrait of a place, a way of life and a family situation it is impressive.

In *Park's Quest* (1988), Katherine Paterson seems to me to fail — as other writers have done — by unwisely seeking to embody ancient and powerful legend in a contemporary story that cannot sustain it. Parkington Waddell Broughton the Fifth's relationship with his stricken grandfather is touchingly portrayed, but to identify Park with Parsifal, the Grail Knight, and the old man with the Grail King, is to cast them in roles for which they have not the stature; and the equating of the closing events of the book with fulfilment of the quest for the Holy Grail seems rashly audacious rather than awe-inspiring.

The death of Sylvia Cassedy (1930-89) came, regrettably, when after many years of silence she had begun to publish fiction of unusual distinction. In *M.E. and Morton* (1987), the snobbish and rather repulsive narrator Mary Ella (who would like to be known by her initials) is understandably friendless and has an older, backward brother, Morton, of whom she's ashamed. A poor child, Polly, arrives one summer, willing to be M.E.'s friend for part of the time and Morton's for another part. Polly is casual, says she never misses people when they're not there, and by negligence allows Morton to have an almost-fatal accident.

But Polly is imaginative, and wonderfully good for both of them. She revolutionizes M.E.'s relationship with Morton — not by being virtuous but by being, as she herself claims, magical.

The magic, I will guess with some confidence, is compounded of imagination and spontaneity.

Lucie Babbage's House (1989) is Sylvia Cassedy's outstanding novel. Its opening chapters gently mislead the reader; Lucie seems to go to a private school, to have a well-off, rather old-fashioned family with a living-in servant, and to set up a correspondence with a pen friend in England. But it emerges that the school, the house, the pen friend are not what they seem. Lucie, inattentive in class and the butt of her schoolmates, is a refugee in her own imagination; and the story, unfolding, gradually reveals the cause. At the end there is a sign — no more than a sign, from just a few spoken words — that she will come back into the world when she is ready. A second reading is needed to appreciate the subtleties of the story; it certainly is not for every child, but for some it holds rare rewards.

To write enjoyably and well for the sevens-to-tens or thereabouts requires an unusual gift — a gift possessed most notably by Beverly Cleary, whose books about Henry Huggins, his dog Ribsy, his friend Beezus, and Beezus' little sister Ramona, appeared over a period of some 35 years. It all began with *Henry Huggins* (1950):

Henry Huggins was in the third grade. His hair looked like a scrubbing-brush and most of his grown-up front teeth were in.

In the first story, Henry finds a mongrel dog which he calls Ribsy and which he tries to bring home on the bus, with disruptive results. The formula for many of the remaining stories is the same: a probable incident developed into hilarious improbability. In *Henry and Ribsy* (1954), Henry has to keep Ribsy out of trouble for nearly two months if he is to go on a fishing trip with his father; and this is difficult when Ribsy tries to protect the garbage from the garbage man (thus earning the name of garbage-hound) and has a dispute over a bone with Ramona. But Henry does go salmon-fishing — and catches a 29-pounder with his bare hands. *Ramona the Pest* (1968) is a misnomer; Ramona is not really much of a pest, she's just a lively little girl beginning kindergarten. In later years, Ramona has rather taken over the series; she reached her seventh book, a little older and maybe wiser, in *Ramona Forever* (1984).

25

How young is an adult?

THE TEENAGE NOVEL is an American speciality. The need for it was succinctly put by S. E. Hinton in *The New York Times Book Review:* 'Teenagers today want to read about teenagers today'.[1] Many British writers have tried their hands at so-called young-adult fiction, and some British publishers and comment-ators have encouraged them; but I am now inclined to think that the more successful of British books that I formerly regarded as falling into this genre did not need to be so classified. They were fiction of general interest, accessible to older children and young people, and acceptable also to adults who happened to come across them. The subject-matter of the teenage novel in its purest form is 'being a teenager'. I have the impression that most British adolescents are less interested in teenage as a mode of being than they are in doing the things they want to do. This is not to deny that novels about the specific problems of teenagers may be very good novels.

In the late 1940s and in the 1950s, the nothing-barred American young-adult novel did not exist. Teenage fiction mostly took the form of the romantic novel for girls, as written by Betty Cavanna, Mary Stolz and others. Beverly Cleary's *Fifteen* (1956) has stayed the course better than most, and illustrates both the qualities and the limitations of this kind of story. It is not so much about first love as about first boyfriend and first dating. Jane is an ordinary girl, Stan an ordinary boy. She meets him when she is baby-sitting and he is delivering horsemeat from the Doggie Diner. Jane suffers the agonizing hesitations of adolescence − is she saying or doing the right thing? − and the even more agonizing fears: is Stan taking another girl to the high-school dance? The first boyfriend emerges not simply as a person but also as a status symbol: '"Hi, everybody," said Stan, while Jane smiled happily beside him. Not many sophomores had dates for the junior-class steak bake.'

The change began in the early 1960s, and clearly was connected with the change, already noted, in relationships between the generations. Adults felt less sure that they knew best and were entitled to tell the younger generation what to do. And young people themselves were not automatically inclined to listen. They were in reaction against received values, not much impressed by their elders or in any hurry to achieve acceptance as adults. They might well have entered fields of experience that their parents did not know at their age and perhaps never knew at all. The developing young-adult novel reflected these trends and was also a product of literary influences: above all, that of J. D. Salinger's *Catcher in the Rye.* The number of lesser Holden Caulfields, narrating in the first person and in the same tone of voice, defies computation.

Emily Neville's *It's Like This, Cat* (1964) is a story of contemporary life which at the time of publication seemed refreshingly different from some of the staider books that were around, but now appears, like *Fifteen,* innocuous in the extreme. True, it is 'children's' rather than young-adult; but it offers indications of what is to follow. Dave Mitchell, who is fourteen and lives in New York City, fights with Father; adopts a stray cat called Cat; meets Tom, a college dropout who is trying to pick up the pieces of himself; gets acquainted with a nice girl called Mary, and in the end realizes by the sensible way his father helps Tom and copes with one or two practical problems that basically Pop is all right. Things have moved on; fathers do not have to be perfect or even nearly perfect; but the parental position, although no longer deeply entrenched, is holding out.

It is still holding out – though rather desperately – in *The World of Ellen March,* by Jeanette Eyerly (1964). Here a teenage girl, knocked off balance by her parents' impending divorce, concocts a childish plan to reunite them by kidnapping her little sister. The plan misfires, of course; Ellen is reprimanded by Father for foolish, irresponsible behaviour and realizes that she must 'grow wiser, or wise enough to order her own life properly rather than try to make over the lives of her parents'. In other words, the burden of adjustment is on her, and she is at fault for not having the maturity and stability to deal with the situation her parents have placed her in.

That was in 1964. By the end of the decade there was little left of the assumption that parents are always right. More and more fictional parents were useless to their children or even positively vicious. In John Donovan's *I'll Get There, It Better be Worth the Trip* (1969), the hero's mother is a heavy drinker; his father has remarried, and 'when we see each other everything has to be arranged'. Davy's love goes to his dog and the male friend he's made at school. In *The Dream Watcher,* by Barbara Wersba (1968), the hero's parents are living together, but the father is a pathetic death-of-a-salesman figure and the mother is a dissatisfied, self-indulgent woman who has destroyed her husband and could easily destroy her son.

In Paul Zindel's *The Pigman* (1968), there are two narrators, boy and girl, John and Lorraine, and they have no constructive relationship with their parents at all. John's father is always referred to by John as 'Bore'. Lorraine's mother has an obsession with the awfulness of men, and all she has to say to Lorraine is on the lines of 'Don't get into cars' and 'Don't let a man into the apartment.' In the same author's *My Darling, My Hamburger* (1969), parents are no less than the villains of the piece. Liz's stepfather is so brutally abusive when she is out late for an innocent reason that she feels she may as well give him something to be abusive about. She lets her boyfriend have his way. Then she becomes pregnant. And the reason why she has an abortion instead of marrying the boy, whom she loves and who is willing to marry her, is the odious cynicism of the boy's father, who tells him it is cheaper to pay a few dollars and get rid of the embarrassment.

The mother of Dinky Hocker, in *Dinky Hocker Shoots Smack!*, by M. E. Kerr (1972), is an interesting variation on the unsatisfactory parent; she is too busy do-gooding to have time for her daughter's problems until Dinky − whose actual addiction is to food, not drugs − plasters the town with the shocking graffito that gives the book its title. But by the early 1970s parents had probably touched bottom. True, Paul Zindel created some obnoxious specimens in the parents of 'Marsh' Mellow in *Pardon Me, You're Stepping on my Eyeball!* (1976) and of Sibella in *The Girl Who Wanted a Boy (1981)*; but the assault was easing. By the early eighties, parental iniquity was no longer a major theme. None the less, parents had been toppled from their former pedestal, and there was no way of putting them back.

The great communicator with adolescents, and children approaching adolescence, is undeniably Judy Blume. *Are You There, God? It's Me, Margaret* (1970) belongs perhaps in a special category: the pre-teenage novel. The heroine, not yet twelve, chats frequently with her Maker and has anxious appeals to make: 'I just told my mother I wanted a bra. Please help me grow, God. You know where.' The physical signs of growing up dominate the minds of Margaret and her friends.

This story, highly popular among girls of eleven and twelve, is a sad one, really. Growing up is difficult enough without becoming a competitive jostle.

The title of *Forever* (1975) is ironical. The narrator Katherine, sleeping with Michael, sheds her romantic illusions; forever is a long time. At the end there's a new boyfriend in the offing, and one assumes that there will be other affairs. This debunking seems to me to devalue love and indeed sex; the inference is that they aren't all that important after all. *It's Not the End of the World* (1972) deals with parental divorce and offers a similar arid reassurance; it's as if profound human issues can be resolved by means of trivializing them.

But Judy Blume's ability to reach young people should not be undervalued. She has been accused of 'an astonishing incapacity to show that people are different from one another in the way they think and feel and talk';[2] but this observation, differently phrased, could be seen as indicating her strongest point. Obviously people differ; but the areas of life in which they think and feel and talk in very similar ways are extensive and basic. Surely it is because she has located these areas, and found the common factors among so many young people, that Judy Blume receives literally thousands of letters from readers who say in effect 'You are writing about me.'

Judy Blume has in fact matured as a writer, and with the passage of time has come to seem less shocking than she did at first to many adults. *Tales of a Fourth-Grade Nothing* (1972) and its sequel *Superfudge* (1980) deal humorously with the little-brother problem. *Tiger-Eyes* (1981) is a thoughtful story of a teenage girl's first year after the violent death of her father, and gives a credible account of the girl's and her mother's changing emotions and the difficulties of living with kind, well-meaning but somewhat tiresome relatives. The fact that Davey is an ordinary teenager, without any striking idiosyncrasy that would make reader-identification more difficult, is probably not a disadvantage in a 'situation story'. None the less, Ursula Le Guin's *Very Far Away from Anywhere Else* (1976), though decidedly value-laden, came as a refreshing contrast to many teenage novels of its day; it shows a friendship between an intelligent boy and girl who aren't going to be pushed into sex or anything else by pressure to do what everyone does.

Few if any areas of life, however harrowing, unsavoury or frightening, are closed to the modern young-adult novel. As long ago as 1970, Jeanette Eyerly, a vigorous realistic writer already mentioned, was described as 'a pioneer in exploring such subjects as unwed motherhood, school dropouts, mental illness, and the problems confronting children of divorced or alcoholic parents'.[3] Premarital sex, drug abuse, homosexuality, running away from home are hardly remarkable any more. Squalid surroundings do not have to be avoided, and degrees of violence that were once unacceptable are now commonplace. S.E.Hinton was herself a teenager when she published, in 1967, *The Outsiders,* a novel of gang warfare which then seemed startlingly tough. While I believe it is deplorable sensationalism to pile on the squalor or violence for the sake of doing so, there is no denying that some writers have used the freedom now available to them to good effect.

Rosa Guy's Harlem trilogy, which began with *The Friends* (1973) and continued with *Ruby* (1976) and *Edith Jackson* (1978), has an unmistakable air of harsh authenticity. The books are about the interacting lives of three black teenagers, and each story hinges on a betrayal. Phyllisia, in *The Friends,* is ashamed of the shabby poverty of her friend Edith, and then even more ashamed of her failure to stand by Edith when she is in need. In *Ruby,* Phyllisia's sister forms a homosexual relationship with her classmate Daphne, only to be discarded when Daphne goes to college; in *Edith Jackson,* Edith is seduced and left pregnant by worthless James. Rosa Guy's young people come through; but it is a bitter struggle against deprivation and adversity.

The central character of *The Disappearance* (1979), and of *New Guys Around the Block* (1983) is Imamu Jones, a black Harlem teenager living in a world of decay and desperation. Both these books are fast-moving mysteries, but are memorable less for their plots than for their pictures of crumbling Harlem streets and rotting people: surroundings where a car crash is followed not by help but by looting, and the injured are stripped of their clothes. A third book, *And I Heard a Bird Sing* (1987) completes a powerful trilogy; Imamu battles through dangers and dramas, including a murder for which he is scapegoat, towards a hard-won maturity. Crime and violence usually belong to a different fictional genre from the portrayal of daily life and personal relationships, but in these books the two come together all too convincingly, for crime and violence are part of daily life.

Virginia Hamilton has (as Betsy Hearne puts it) 'crossed boundaries of time, space, style and genre'.[4] *A Little Love* (1984) is a teenage romance; it is also a considerable novel, displaying some of its author's best qualities. Sheema, at 17, is large and slow, as well as black, but doing well enough at vocational college. Her mother is dead; her father went away long ago; she lives with her grandparents, and she and her boyfriend Forrest make love when they can, 'letting loose all their wanting and needing. . . Simply loving, they knew one another.' The day comes when Sheema, impelled from within, must find her father, and she and Forrest set off on the quest in his old Dodge. Father, when found, is ashamed of himself; he is willing to support Sheema, but he doesn't want her; he has a new wife and family. And Sheema, after grief and rage, comes through to acceptance of those who do love her, and to womanhood.

This is a simple story, and in summary sounds trite; but simplicity is no bar to excellence. It is brilliantly characterized. Sheema may be inarticulate, but her profound depth of feeling wells out of the story. We move constantly into and out of her mind, and when we are in it we hear her thoughts in the same black English as the dialogue. Granmom and Granpop are old and poor and afraid of death, especially of dying first; Granmom is losing her grip and Granpop is a bit shifty, but love still binds and supports them. And as so often with Virginia Hamilton, the book has echoes and resonances that go far beyond the printed page.

Nat Hentoff made an impact with his first novel, *Jazz Country* (1965). Tom Curtis, who wants nothing but to be a jazz trumpeter, is an outsider in the world he wants to enter because he is white: whether he will make it is uncertain, and in the last chapter, appropriately titled 'Open End', he is 'trying college for a while', and keeping his options open. Other Hentoff novels known to me have been about 'issues' – arising from Vietnam in *I'm Really Dragged but Nothing Gets Me Down* (1968) and student unrest in *In the Country of Ourselves* (1971). Such subject-matter of course risks losing its interest when the issue ceases to be topical. *The Day They Came to Arrest the Book* (1982) examines the question of censorship, as raised by the charges of racism levelled at *Huckleberry Finn*. It has only slight characterization, and virtually no action outside the progress of the campaign to have Huck banned in the George Mason High School. The arguments are presented very fairly, but the effect is curious: the book becomes a kind of extended seminar in which the author is speaking in turn for all the participants. There's a villain of the piece – the school principal, 'Mighty Mike'

Moore, who is solely concerned with protecting and promoting his own interests, and at the end is satisfied that he has done very nicely in this inglorious endeavour.

In Robert Cormier's novels, violence takes complex and alarming shapes. The protagonists of his first three books for young people are all defeated by corruption. At the end of *The Chocolate War* (1974), Jerry Renault is brutally beaten up by a vicious school gang, called in by the appalling acting-headmaster Brother Leon to support a fund-raising effort. In *I Am the Cheese* (1977) Adam Farmer and his father are victims of secret agencies of government; Ben, in *After the First Death* (1979), commits suicide after being betrayed by his high-ranking military father as a ploy in the defeat of terrorists. Barney, in *The Bumblebee Flies Anyway* (1983), is one of a group of terminally-ill youngsters who are being used as subjects in a clinic for experimental medicine; the aims of the clinic may not be malign, but there is an ambience of malignity about it. The most chilling aspect of the Cormier books is the sense one gets that the Mafia is not outside the pale but is here, inside, part of the system.

There is a time in adolescence when, for many young people, cynicism is almost a necessity. And, of course, in real life the good guys don't always win. Cormier has said that he is 'frightened by today's world, terrified by it. I think that comes out in the books. I'm afraid of big things . . . Big government frightens me, so does big defence'.[5] In the light of this, his claim to be an optimist seems somewhat frail, and his remark that what he is saying to the reader is that 'choice is always possible . . . Terrible things happen because we allow them to happen' is hardly reassuring.

It can be strongly argued that fiction for young people should not present an unduly rosy view of the world, but Cormier's novels seem to me to err the other way — to suggest that decency is a loser, that evil is great and will prevail. Strangely, in *Beyond the Chocolate War* (1985), while numbers of lesser characters weave in and out of the action, it is hard to avoid seeing the gang boss — cool, subtle, unscrupulous Archie Costello — as the hero.

Aidan Chambers's novels for adolescents are the nearest British approach to American-style teenage fiction. Chambers has expressed admiration for work by Zindel and Cormier; he has also praised, at the expense of the British, the 'breezy uninhibitedness' of American writing and the absence of stultifying class and cultural assumptions.[6] The central characters of his novels *Breaktime* (1978) and *Dance on my Grave* (1982) are English, but their flip articulacy doesn't sound like the speech of imaginable British teenagers. Ditto, in *Breaktime,* gets involved in a drunken escapade and (separately) loses his virginity; Hal, in *Dance on my Grave,* has a homosexual affair with an older boy, Barry, and becomes deeply disturbed when, after a quarrel, Barry rides off and is killed in a motor-cycle crash. Sexual matters are dealt with, not perhaps with breezy uninhibitedness, but at any rate with dogged attention to detail.

Chambers has ranged widely in arriving at his convictions as a writer, claiming that 'story' must now take account of recent explorations of both outer space and inner (psychological) space, of 'gender within the personality', nuclear fission and television techniques.[7] It seems clear that he has been influenced by Kurt Vonnegut in the United States and B. S. Johnson in England. It would not be grossly unfair to say that the nature and technique of fiction are largely what the two books are about. Traditional narrative sequence is discarded in favour of fragmentation and the use of various devices. The sub-title of *Dance on my Grave* is 'A Life and a Death/in Four Parts/One Hundred and Seventeen Bits/Six Running Reports/ and Two Press Clippings/with a few jokes/a puzzle or three/some footnotes/and a fiasco now and then/to help the story along.' It is too facetious, too self-conscious, too much. Aidan Chambers is an interesting and energetic writer, but these books appear to demonstrate his convictions rather than inner creative power. It is hard to see them as heralding a new age in British fiction for young people.

26

Around the world

OUTSIDE the United States and Britain, the most impressive contribution to English-language children's literature in the decades after 1945 was made by Australian writers. Indeed, proportionately to population, the Australian achievement has probably been more notable than the American or British. Interestingly, the transition from innocence to experience, which can be traced through the whole field of writing for children during the period, can be seen in conspectus within the work of individual Australian writers. The leaders — Ivan Southall, Joan Phipson, Patricia Wrightson — have been writing since the early fifties and have shown this progression in their own books: Southall from old-fashioned 'boys' stories' about a super-hero airman, Phipson and Wrightson from harmless family adventures, and all in the direction of deeper and more demanding subjects.

Southall has long been the best known and most controversial of the Australians. He had a distinguished war record, and for years after the end of the Second World War he wrote adventure stories about stiff-upper-lipped Squadron Leader Simon Black of the Royal Australian Air Force. But after nine books he tired of Simon, and of that kind of children's writing:

For the first time, I found myself looking at my own children and their friends growing up round about me. In their lives interacting one upon the other at an unknown depth, I began to suspect with genuine astonishment that here lay an unlimited source of raw material far more exciting than the theme itself [for a novel that had occurred to him]. Thus there came a positive moment of decision for me.[1]

The result was *Hills End* (1962), the story of a group of ordinary children cut off by storm and flood in a remote small town, forced to fend for themselves in the absence of adults, and somehow muddling through. Four novels which followed — *Ash Road* (1966), *To the Wild Sky* (1967), *Finn's Folly* (1969) and *Chinaman's Reef is Ours* (1970) — had strong similarities to *Hills End*. In each book, children were faced with a situation too large and menacing for them to handle; their courage and endurance taxed to the limit, their innermost characters emerging under almost intolerable stress, their relationships with each other brought out into searching light. *To the Wild Sky* and *Finn's Folly* in particular are harrowing books which appear to force a confrontation; to demand of the reader how much punishment he can take.

To the Wild Sky was the most baffling and to many readers the most frustrating of all. Six children in a private plane whose pilot has suddenly died of a heart attack crash-land on a remote island off Australia's north coast; at the end they have little food and no water and there is no sign of current human life. We are not told what happens to them. For many years the author resisted pressure to add to the story; but in 1985, after eighteen years, he published a sequel, *A City Out of Sight*. The outcome is reassuring: in spite of various perils and the tensions and cross-purposes among themselves, the children find means of survival and it's a happy ending. Yet there is something not quite satisfying about it; one has, surprisingly and perhaps perversely, a sense that doors have been closed, possibilities diminished. It could be (though I have said otherwise in my time) that there is occasionally a case for a story that leaves the final decision to the reader.

In the year after *To the Wild Sky,* a shorter book, *Let the Balloon Go* (1968) indicated the way Southall would move next. This story about a spastic boy who climbs to the top of an eighty-foot tree is tense enough, yet its real action takes place within the mind of one boy, and so does the real action of *Bread and Honey* (1970) and the Carnegie Medal-winning *Josh* (1971). Against a background of war commemoration, Michael in *Bread and Honey* faces the private implications of resistance to violence; experiences the clash of literal and imaginative, of conventional and spontaneous; comes through an ordeal into the beginnings of manhood. Fourteen-year-old, town-bred, poetry-writing Josh survives an ordeal, too; he falls foul of the earthy local youngsters in Ryan Creek, where his family used to be leading citizens. Josh's stream of consciousness is effectively, painfully presented; and although he comes through he still has no real communication with the locals. He leaves to walk a hundred miles home to Melbourne, alone. The taste remaining in the mouth is of bitterness and alienation.

What About Tomorrow (1977), which seems to me to be one of Southall's best books, tells of the journeyings in 1931 of a boy called Sam, who runs away from home after the disaster of crashing his bike and losing eight shillings' worth of newspapers. Through a series of encounters Sam is growing up; but the question is, what is he growing up towards? A series of forward flashes shows him as captain of a wartime seaplane, flying to meet his fate. Once again, the sense of personal involvement is profound.

In *The Long Night Watch* (1984), members of a fringe religious cult, SWORD (the Society for World Order under Divine Rule) are shipped during the Second World War to a Pacific island to await the coming of their saviours, the Heroes of Light. Those who actually arrive are the attacking Japanese. It's the end of SWORD; but are the elect wiped out or is it just conceivable that something else happened? Southall showed in this book that he could still surprise and disconcert.

There are moments of joy, even of exultation, in the Southall novels, yet when one looks back on the long line of them it is hard not to feel that for him life is earnest and often painful, and that his work expresses his pain. In a note written in 1981, he referred to 'a life-long fear and repugnance of physical, mental and emotional violence', and went on:

To this day I am distressed when my work confronts me with the understanding that major components of life throughout the universe are very violent indeed and that it is my eventual responsibility to explore and express them.[2]

Often in fact Ivan Southall's books have been more challenging than enjoyable; but they have been widely read in many countries, and young readers thrive on challenge as well as on enjoyment.

Joan Phipson began her writing career with stories of ponies and holiday adventures, and her numerous books include several family stories. Of those I have read, *The Family Conspiracy* (1962), in which the Barker children go into action to raise money for Mother's operation, is the most successful. Gradually Joan Phipson widened her range through a series of more ambitious books in which she explored on the one hand the relationships among groups of young people and the nature of leadership; on the other hand the wide, varied and often mysterious landscapes of Australia.

Eventually everything came together in an admirable novel, *The Cats* (1976). Jim and younger brother Willy are kidnapped by tough Socker and his hanger-on Kevin after their parents have won a huge lottery prize. They are driven to a derelict farmhouse, deep in the bush, where, under pressure of hardship and difficulty, the relationships between captors and captives subtly change. It is Willy, who has often gone off on long lone trips and whose eyes sometimes 'seemed to be looking at something that wasn't there', who has the knowledge and the inner strength to cope. The cats of the title are large, feral cats that live in the wild, around the farmhouse; and when, in a startling passage, Socker dashes out the brains of a kitten, only Willy can save him from the vengeance of the cats. And he does so more to protect the cats from human investigation than to save the life of Socker.

In a writing career extending over more than thirty years, Patricia Wrightson has built up a well-deserved international reputation. Her work is varied and does not fit into neat descriptive pigeon-holes. *The Rocks of Honey* (1960) is in the main a realistic story, yet one of its chief points is that reality is not enough; that there is more to life than common sense can take account of. Farmer's son Barney and aboriginal boy Eustace take part together in a search for an ancient stone axe; and when it is found, a strangeness comes between them. They have caught a fringe of the past; there is something here that Eustace and his uncle, as aborigines, know how to deal with, but that is baffling to practical Barney.

I Own the Racecourse (1968; American title *A Racecourse for Andy*) was Mrs Wrightson's best book up to that time. Andy is the boy who isn't quite like the rest, who doesn't always understand, who goes to a separate school. The other boys play the game of buying and swapping property in imaginary deals. And innocent Andy does a deal to beat them all, because he thinks he has really bought the racecourse; he paid a tramp three dollars for it. Naturally Andy wants to help in running his property, and the men who work there indulge him and call him 'the boss'. But he becomes a nuisance. Somehow it has to end. And the author ends it perfectly.

With *An Older Kind of Magic* (1972), Patricia Wrightson introduced figures from aboriginal folklore, contrasting this ancient, rooted magic with the cheap, shoddy modern kind exemplified in big-business wizardry and the TV commercial. Since then her fictional explorations have taken her more and more deeply into the land of Australia itself and those who have lived in it from the most distant times: the People, the indigenous spirits, the creatures. *The Nargun and the Stars* (1973) has at its centre the huge, patient thing that resembles a great rock but is, in its slow way, alive: 'Sometimes it remembered the world's making and cried for that long agony . . . It had a sort of love: a response to the deep, slow rhythms of the earth; and when it felt the earth's crust swell to the pull of the moon it sometimes called in ecstasy.' In comparison with this, the incomers of a couple of centuries are johnnies-come-lately, with only a precarious hold: the land and the old things will be there when they are gone. The defeat of sturdy old Mrs Tucker in *A Little Fear* (1983), driven from her lonely cottage by the small, cunning Njimbin, which rallies the rats, the ants, even an ocean of midges against her, must be seen as symbolic. In this book and in *Moon-Dark* (1987) the sense of place and atmosphere, the command of natural history, are formidable; these books are also notable for two splendid dog characters – Hector in *A Little Fear,* Blue in *Moon-Dark* – and for the ingenious use of language to convey the communications of spirits and of animals.

The Book of Wirrun is Patricia Wrightson's most ambitious venture: an epic trilogy. In an author's note to *The Ice is Coming* (1977), the first part, she observes that she knows a country 'as powerful and as magical as Earthsea or Middle Earth. It is the only one I know, and the one I want to write about.' It is of course Australia, the 'old south land' that 'lies across the world like an open hand'. Wirrun, a young aboriginal, defeats the Ninya, frosty creatures who would clench the country in a fist of ice, and becomes a hero of the People.

In the second book of the trilogy, *The Dark Bright Water* (1979), Wirrun defeats a threat to the People and falls in love with a water-spirit; in *Behind the Wind* (1982) he must descend among the dead in order to save the People once more. Wirrun in fact dies, but this is a happy ending, for his spirit can be reunited with the water-nymph while his memory remains in the People's stories.

One needs staying-power to read this trilogy; it is often slow-paced, occasionally confusing, sometimes sombre. Walter McVitty, writing of *The Dark Bright Water*, found 'something almost Wagnerian about its ominous, shadowy landscapes, noble purpose and high ideals, its mortals engaged in terrifying enterprises with terrifying supernatural figures . . .'[3] It is not, to my mind, fully successful, but it is a work of weight and substance, a major imaginative endeavour.

Nan Chauncy (1900-1970) was senior to the three writers just named, and did much to establish the reputation of Australian writing for children. Her setting was Tasmania. There is still a sense of pioneering in her books about the Lorenny family, surviving stoutly in a remote area, in *Tiger in the Bush* (1957) and *Devil's Hill* (1958). In *Tangara* (1960), a sad and searching book, a present-day girl makes mysterious contact with an aboriginal child of more than a century before, and, seeming through her to relive long-past experiences, becomes aware of a dreadful slaughter of aborigines. The fate of the Tasmanian aborigines is also the concern of *Mathinna's People* (1967).

In the 1960s, Eleanor Spence wrote historical novels with Australian backgrounds: notably *Lillypilly Hill* (1960) and *The Switherby Pilgrims* (1967), which tells how a determined English spinster emigrates in the 1820s with a party of orphans to New South Wales, and how they set out to take possession of their land grant – a few acres of bush. In the 1970s Mrs Spence turned more to contemporary subjects, with *The Nothing-Place* (1972), featuring a deaf boy, and *The October Child* (1976), an autistic one.

H. F. Brinsmead has written mainly for and about teenagers. Her first and best book, *Pastures of the Blue Crane* (1964) is about toffee-nosed, mean-spirited Ryl, who finds herself joint owner of a farm with her proletarian grandfather Dusty. The story is of her reconciliation to the neglected farm, to the New South Wales/Queensland border country, the ordinary but kindly neighbours, old Dusty himself, and at last the truth about her own parentage. Ryl becomes more likeable as her shut-in personality expands in the open air; she changes, but she is recognizably the same person.

Beat of the City (1966) follows a mixed foursome of young people in Melbourne as they pursue happiness in their various ways and discover that some of the ways are dead ends. *Long-time Passing* (1972) is about the life and hard times of a settler's family, growing up through the Depression in the Blue Mountains. According to the author it is 'at least half true', though told as fiction.

In Ruth Park's *Playing Beatie Bow* (1980), Abigail, aged fourteen, follows a mysterious child into the Sydney of 1873, becomes involved in the lives of the Bow family, and finds she has a role to play in the perpetuation of a supernatural 'gift'. This is a cross-genre novel, since much of it is really period fiction about life in nineteenth-century Sydney slums, with the fantasy element providing an outside eye. (Abigail notices what we would notice but a person of the time would not.) The fantasy also ties together present and past and allows a neat romantic conclusion. The children's game of Beatie Bow is an ingenious conception: it commemorates a formidable head teacher, who was in fact the child whom Abigail first met.

Judith O'Neill, an Australian living in Britain, set her first three novels for young readers in Australia in different, but not distant, times. *Deepwater* (1987), the best of them, tells in the voice of 14-year-old Charlotte of the lives of farming families in a remote valley in Victoria in the early months of the First World War. The immediate enemy is drought; at last the rain comes and everyone rushes joyfully out to be drenched; but in the background is the darker, longer-lasting menace of war, brought home by news of the casualties at Gallipoli.

Robin Klein, in a few highly productive years, has become a well known and popular writer. In a comedy series that began with *Penny Pollard's Diary* (1983), she launched an ingenious, articulate and not too dangerously subversive small girl who has counterparts in existing children's literature but is distinctively Australian. *People Might Hear You* (also 1983) is a serious, admirably crafted novel about a girl called Frances who is removed from ordinary life into the appalling household ruled over by her aunt's new husband, 'Uncle' Finley, member of a self-isolating religious sect. Frances in fact is in a prison, from which she must and finally does escape.

The same author's *Halfway Across the Galaxy and Turn Left* (1985) could hardly be more different. It uses a few science-fictional props but is best described as comic fantasy with a dash of satire. The alien family who land on Earth from a second-hand spacecraft after getting into a spot of bother on Zyrgon are people much like us — though five-year-old Qwrk is by Earth standards a genius, while beautiful Dovis can literally tread on air. Father is an amiable crook and financial wizard, Mother a dress-designer, so they are well equipped to make a living here. Life on Earth strikes them as odd, to say the least, but has its compensations, and long before the end we can guess that they're going to stay.

The partnership of Jenny Wagner and the artist Ron Brooks produced Australia's most distinguished picture books. In *The Bunyip of Berkeley's Creek* (1973) a large, baffled creature emerges from the mud, finds that he is a bunyip, and wants to know what a bunyip looks like. Nobody can tell him; as a man points out, 'bunyips simply don't exist'. But happily he meets a lady bunyip, and they find out what they look like: each other. *Aranea* (1975) is the story, illustrated in fine-spun black-and-white, of a spider's indefatigable determination to spin the perfect web. Best of all is *John Brown, Rose and the Midnight Cat* (1977). Widowed Rose lives with her four-footed, doggily-devoted friend John Brown, and they're quite content until Rose sees the strange, beautiful, midnight-black cat out in the garden. John Brown doesn't share Rose's fascination with the

Illustration by Ron Brooks from *John Brown, Rose and the Midnight Cat,* by Jenny Wagner

cat; cats are something he just doesn't want to know about; but when Rose pines and takes to her bed he thinks better of it and opens the door to the midnight cat. Possessiveness, the nature of love, the needs of the spirit: this simple but profound picture-story raises questions about them all.

In Canada, though library work with children has long been excellent, the actual writing of books lagged behind for many years. This situation is changing, helped by support from public funds, and at the time of writing there is something of an upsurge of creativity. Much Canadian writing is limited in its impact by not being published in New York or London. The tradition of Ernest Thompson Seton and Charles G. D. Roberts has however been continued by Farley Mowat and James Houston, whose books, like theirs, have straddled the border between children's and general literature.

Houston has written much about Inuit (Eskimo) and West Coast Indian life. His best-known books on the children's list, illustrated by himself, are *Frozen Fire* (1977), in which

American Matthew and his Inuit friend Kayak set out by snowmobile on a rescue expedition and have to survive in the Arctic wilderness, and its sequel *Black Diamonds* (1982), a search for a 'river of gold' that ends in the discovery not of gold but of oil. Farley Mowat's stories of the wild have mostly been published for adults. Most appealing of his work for children is *Owls in the Family* (1961), a cheerful and relatively domesticated children-and-animals story. Narrator Billy has thirty gophers and a garage-full of white rats, besides his garter-snakes and pigeons and rabbits and a dog called Mutt; so it's not surprising that Dad says 'Oh NO! not owls too.' Here are recollections of a boyhood in Saskatchewan, as well as an account of the adoption and adventures of the bold Wol (spelled as in *Winnie-the-Pooh)* and the timid Weeps.

The Incredible Journey (1960), by Sheila Burnford (1918-84), is about a long homeward trek through the perils of the wilderness made by a retriever, a Siamese cat and a bull terrier. In an admittedly compelling piece of anthropo-morphism that has been immensely popular and has become a successful film, human loyalties, emotions and ways of thought are projected on to the animals; and it is hard to avoid Sheila Egoff's conclusion that 'the journey remains incredible'.[4]

Barbara Schmucker's underground-railroad novel *Underground to Canada* and the science fiction of Monica Hughes have been mentioned earlier, in the context of non-Canadian books to which they can be related. Probably Canada's best known writer of realistic fiction for children on contemporary themes is Jean Little. Her early books, *Mine for Keeps* (1962) and *Home from Far* (1965) were described by Sheila Egoff as 'a conventional attempt at bibliotherapy' and 'contrived'.[5] But authors develop, and after several books in which children either triumph over or come to terms with problems or handicaps, Jean Little wrote *Mama's Going to Buy you a Mockingbird* (1984), which is one of the best of such 'situation stories'. Here the situation faced by Jeremy and small sister Sarah is that Father is dying, and in the course of the book does die, of cancer. Jeremy has his share of common failings and is hard-pressed to rise above them; but friendship with tall odd-girl-out Tess, who has also lost a parent, helps him on the way to a warmhearted if somewhat sentimental conclusion. *Lost and Found* (1985) is an engaging story for younger children about a small girl, without friends in the town to which she's moved, who 'finds' a dog that isn't actually lost; but all ends happily, for she finishes up with two friends and a dog as well.

Janet Lunn's novel *The Root Cellar* (1981) begins and ends as a time-slip fantasy, about lonely orphan Rose, who is sent to live with relatives on an island off the Canadian shore of Lake Ontario, and finds a door into the past through the root cellar of an old house. But the heart of the story is an account which is realistic, though set into the fantasy frame, of a difficult journey to Washington which Rose makes in 1865, in search of a boy who lived at the house long before her and enlisted on the Union side in the American civil war. It's an unusual but effective blend of forms. The same author's *Shadow in Hawthorn Bay* (1986) is set wholly in the past, but is also a blend of fictional forms. Mary Urquhart, a Scottish highland girl, has the second sight, and sails for Canada because she hears her cousin Duncan calling to her. When she arrives, Duncan is dead, but only at the end of the book can she free herself from his disastrous shadow. In between, the story is of her adjustment to a Canadian rural community, but it is tinged throughout with the supernatural.

Robert Munsch is a word-of-mouth storyteller, and his books cannot capture his brilliance in that capacity; but they have been highly successful all the same. *The Paper Bag Princess* (1980), made into a picture book by Michael Mortchenko, is about a princess called Elizabeth who is going to marry Prince Ronald. Elizabeth reverses the traditional order of things by rescuing her prince from a dragon. Her reward is to be told after her exertions that she looks a mess. Then:

'Ronald,' said Elizabeth, 'your clothes are really pretty and your hair is very neat. You look like a real prince, but you are a bum.'
They didn't get married after all.

Andrew Salkey's Jamaican stories of natural disaster – *Hurricane* (1964), *Earthquake* (1965) and *Drought* (1966) – can hardly escape comparison with Ivan Southall's early books. They are descriptively vivid, but they are far less harrowing and they do not convey anything like the same tension. The author seems to have gone out of his way, and perhaps too far out of his way, to avoid making his narrative too fearsome for children. To my mind, the best West Indian stories written for children in the 1960s and early 1970s were those of C. Everard Palmer. Big Doc, the showman-charlatan in *Big Doc Bitteroot* (1968), hoodwinks nearly everyone in the Jamaican village of Kendal, but goes too far when he takes money to cure somebody who is really ill. The undeserving but engaging rogue comes out of it all right, though. *My Father, Sun-Sun Johnson* (1974) tells of the local 'big man' who loses wife, home, money and most of his family to his great rival, but picks himself up, bounces back undaunted, and in the end dies a hero's death. Palmer moved to Canada some years ago, and after 1974 the West Indies played a dwindling role in his fiction.

James Berry's Jamaican short stories in *A Thief in the Village* (1987) are the stories of a poet, vividly graphic in their use of language, rich and racy in their Caribbean English dialogue. They are stories of poverty: the treats and joys, the problems and the desperately humble longings are those of poor children. When Gustus is injured in a foolhardy attempt to protect his banana tree in a hurricane, his father asks him why he did it. 'I did wahn buy mi shoes, Pappy', says Gustus. 'I cahn go anywhere 'cause I have no shoes.' And his father weeps.

The outstanding children's novel of recent years with an Indian setting has been Anita Desai's *The Village by the Sea* (1982). Lila and Hari are the eldest of a family of four children living in a fishing village little changed by 'progress'. Their father is a drunkard, their mother ill; the burdens all fall on the young people. Hari seeks work in Bombay, where he is a naive country boy in the big city; Lila struggles to keep the home going. Meanwhile there are plans to set up a fertilizer factory in the village: good for jobs, or bad for the environment? Hari sees at the end that 'the wheel turns' and the need is to adapt. Anita Desai's book is slow-moving but rich in detail and description, humane and perceptive.

Ruskin Bond, who had a British father but grew up Indian and lives in India, has written several books for quite young children which combine attractive storytelling with an ability to convey the feeling of being a child in present-day India. *Cricket for the Crocodile* (1986) describes entertainingly the hazards of a boys' cricket match in which some of the fathers insist on playing – and in which Nakoo the croc intervenes. *Tigers Forever* (1983) is more serious. Because of the encroachment of man on the forests, a fine old tiger starts killing the villagers' buffalo. The villagers cannot let this go on, and mount a tiger hunt. Happily the tiger is not killed but swept away down-river, where he finds a new habitat. The day is saved, but the encroachment continues. The main human character is a village boy, Chottu, who has encountered the tiger and misses him: 'Let there be tigers forever,' he whispers.

New Zealand's most distinguished writer for children is Margaret Mahy. In twenty prolific years, beginning in 1969, she published something like 45 books, not counting school readers. They span the whole age-range of the children's list, from picture books to teenage novels. *A Lion in the Meadow*, illustrated by Jenny Williams (1969), and *The Man Whose Mother was a Pirate*, illustrated by Brian Froud (1972), are brief, brilliant fantasies that celebrate the power of the imagination; this indeed is a motif that runs through her work.

Her first full-length novel, *The Haunting*, appeared in 1982, and *The Changeover* two years later. Barney, in *The Haunting*, is haunted by supposedly-dead Great-Uncle Cole, whose prime need is for his company; Laura, in *The Changeover*, must actually become a witch in order to defeat a malign ancient spirit that is drawing the life out of her small brother. In both books, supernatural phenomena are set in the context of complex family relationships, and are possibly metaphors for developments in real life; Laura's changeover is evidently a passage not only to witchhood but to womanhood.

The Catalogue of the Universe (1985) is a teenage novel of which the most attractive element is the friendship between tall, beautiful Angela and short, odd-looking Tycho, an aspiring astronomer. Tycho and Angela are enjoyably *clever,* and take pleasure in the play of minds, though bodies have their moments too. *The Catalogue of the Universe,* by the way, is the title of the book that Angela gives Tycho for his birthday. And it doesn't only indicate the range of his interests; it forms a step for him to stand on to reach Angela's height at a crucial juncture.

Lynley Dodd created as author-artist the series that began with *Hairy Maclary from Donaldson's Dairy* (1983.) The first book tells in lolloping rhyme of Hairy Maclary, a black dishmop of a dog, and his friends, including the mastiff Hercules Morse, as big as a horse, the Dalmatian Bottomley Potts, covered in spots, and others, all of whom are put to flight by the appearance of the arch-cat Scarface Claw, the toughest tom in town. In *Hairy Maclary, Scattercat* (1985), the canine hero, feeling 'bumptious and bustly, bossy and bouncy and frisky and hustly', chases cat after cat, until Scarface Claw chases *him.* There's energy in every line of Hairy Maclary's ridiculous body, and the pictures are dog's-eye views from just about his height.

27

Virtuosity in verse

VERSE anthologies for children fall thick and fast from the presses. Some are excellent; some merely reflect the fact that an anthology of a kind can be compiled by anybody. It is easier to choose from among other people's poems than to write poetry oneself. The present study is not concerned with anthologies but with original verse published for children since 1945, of which there has been a substantial amount.

Several good poets, including the present British Poet Laureate, Ted Hughes, have contributed to the children's lists, as well as many lesser lights and some who would not claim to be more than versifiers. Two major American poets, while they did not write for children in particular, made selections for young readers from the body of their work: Robert Frost (1874-1963) with *You Come Too* (1959) and Carl Sandburg (1878-1967) with *Wind Song* (1960). The general trend over recent years has been from the 'poetic' to the demotic and from the garden to the street, and poets have tried to speak to children at their own level rather than as adults addressing their juniors.

The most characteristic American qualities have been a light, dry humour and a good deal of technical virtuosity, frequently combined in the work of the same writer. David McCord has been a lifelong versifier, and his first book for children, *Far and Few* (1952) was actually his fifteenth book of verse. Under the headings 'Write me a Verse' in *Take Sky* (1962) and 'Write me Another Verse' in *For Me to Say* (1970), he explains various verse-forms in the forms themselves. Here for instance are three of a group of haiku:

> Syllable writing,
> Counting out your seventeen,
> Doesn't produce poem.

> Good haiku need thought:
> One simple statement followed
> By poet's comment.

> The town dump is white
> With seagulls, like butterflies
> Over a garden.

McCord's collected poems for children were issued in 1977 under the title *One at a Time*.

Haiku are particularly associated with the name of another American poet: Harry Behn (1898-1973) who translated *Cricket Songs* (1964) and *More Cricket Songs* (1971) from the Japanese. Behn has written verse for young children of perhaps five or six upwards in *The Little Hill* (1949), *Windy Morning* (1953) and other volumes. Many verses show the child at play, and recall − not always happily − Robert Louis Stevenson's *Child's Garden*. A selection of his verse, made by Lee Bennett Hopkins and called *Crickets and Bullfrogs and Whispers of Thunder*, was published in 1984.

The verse of Ogden Nash (1902-71), with its *ad hoc* scansion and its tendency to wander off in search of a rhyme and come back with something monstrously ingenious, is often childlike in a good sense of the word. Among the 'elderly poems for youngerly readers' in *Parents Keep Out* (1951), the 'Adventures of Isabel' are particularly appealing:

> Isabel met an enormous bear,
> Isabel, Isabel didn't care.
> The bear was hungry, the bear was ravenous,
> The bear's big mouth was cruel and cavernous.
> The bear said, Isabel, glad to meet you,
> How do, Isabel, now I'll eat you!
> Isabel, Isabel didn't worry,
> Isabel didn't scream or scurry.
> She washed her hands and she straightened her hair up,
> Then Isabel quietly ate the bear up.

Ingenuity with words is a mark also of the work for children of John Ciardi (1916-86); other marks are a wry wit and a tendency to set up a playful war-of-the-generations. Russell Hoban, who published The *Pedalling Man* in 1968, has a sad awareness of the lapse of time and a remarkable empathy with people, animals, and even inanimate objects. The pedalling man of the title-poem is a weather-vane with legs propelled by wind-pressure. Spring, summer and fall he rides the winds, but a winter blizzard brings him down. Perhaps there is more man in him than metal.

The change in expression, most obvious in the sixties, can be neatly illustrated with two brief quotations from Myra Cohn Livingston, a talented and long-established poet and anthologist. 'Whispers', from *Whispers and Other Poems* (1958) begins:

> Whispers
> tickle through your ear
> telling things you like to hear.

By 1969, the same poet was writing (in 'The Sun is Stuck', from *A Crazy Flight and Other Poems*):

> The sun is stuck.
> I mean, it won't move.
> I mean it's hot, man, and we need a red-hot poker to pry it loose.

But not every poet has found it necessary to keep up with the times. *Father Fox's Pennyrhymes,* by Clyde Watson (1971), have been described as 'a lovely freak' and as having the 'daft battered quality of old nursery verse'[1]:

> Knickerbocker Knockabout
> Sausages & Sauerkraut
> Run! Run! Run! The hogs are out!
> Knickerbocker Knockabout.

Perhaps the most distinctive American contribution during the period was made by black poets. Langston Hughes (1902-67) did not intend his poetry for children, but a selection from his work which was made by Lee Bennett Hopkins *(Don't You Turn Back,* 1969) made a deep impression. Pride of race can be a proper subject for poetry, though often an intrusion into fiction:

> The night is beautiful,
> So the faces of my people.
>
> The stars are beautiful,
> So the eyes of my people.
>
> Beautiful, also, is the sun.
> Beautiful, also, are the souls of my people.

And there is the reminder:

> I am the darker brother.
> They send me to eat in the kitchen . . .
>
> Tomorrow,
> I'll be at the table
> When company comes.

The Pulitzer prize-winning poet Gwendolyn Brooks has written mainly for adults, but published for children in 1956 the well-known *Bronzeville Boys and Girls.* And in 1970 came

Lucille Clifton's *Some of the Days of Everett Anderson,* the first of six picture-books of verse about a small black boy, the first two illustrated by Evaline Ness and the other four by Ann Grifalconi.

> Afraid of the dark
> is afraid of Mom
> and Daddy
> and Papa
> and Cousin Tom.
>
> 'I'd be as silly
> as I could be,
> afraid of the dark
> is afraid of Me!'
>
> says ebony
> Everett
> Anderson.

June Jordan's *Who Look at Me?* (1969) is a long, uneven poem, at the heart of which is a line that follows on from the title:

> I am black alive and looking back at you.

Here again the 'black experience', sought so painfully, and often unsuccessfully, in prose, comes out clearly and simply in verse:

> In part we grew
> as we were meant to grow
> ourselves
> with kings and queens no white man knew.

Two highly popular versifiers, Shel Silverstein and Jack Prelutsky, are somewhat similar in appeal. Silverstein's *Where the Sidewalk Ends* (1974) and *A Light in the Attic* (1981) are illustrated with his own drawings. *Where the Sidewalk Ends* has some decidedly ruthless rhymes in it: 'Someone ate the baby', for instance, is about as far from edifying as one can get. Jack Prelutsky has an equally strong line in the gruesome: the 'poems to trouble your sleep' in *Nightmares* (1976) feature the Haunted House, the Vampire, the Troll, the Ogre, the Werewolf and so on, culminating in the Dance of the Thirteen Skeletons. *The Headless Horseman Rides Tonight* (1980) contains a further selection of equally dire creatures. *It's Hallowe'en* (1977) offers gentler chillings for smaller spines: it shows children pretending or trick-or-treating and is not in fact scary.

At the other extreme from Silverstein and Prelutsky is Paul Fleischman, whose *I am Phoenix* (1985) and *Joyful Noise* (1988) surely call for adult mediation. These are 'poems for two voices' − about birds in *Phoenix* and insects in *Joyful Noise* − and are printed in parallel narrow columns, to be spoken sometimes by one or the other voice, sometimes in unison. 'Mayflies' is a fair example:

Your moment

                  Mayfly month

Your hour

                  Mayfly year

Your trifling day

                  Our life

We're mayflies   We're mayflies
just emerging   just emerging
rising from the river,
born this day in May

                  birthday

and dying day,

                  this particle of time

this single sip of living

                  all that we're
                  allowed . . .

This is poetry as a performance art, and likely to work well in classroom or drama group; but it is difficult for one person to read, either aloud or silently, and few children are likely to organize themselves spontaneously for choral reading. There is patient, sympathetic observation of the creatures in both books, and sometimes pathos, as in 'The Digger Wasp' ('I will never/see my children') or humour, as in the happy marriage of two book lice ('We honeymooned in an old guide book on Greece.') But these are teachers' books more than children's books.

A few years after the Second World War the British poet James Reeves wrote two books of verse for children: *The Wandering Moon* (1950) and *The Blackbird in the Lilac* (1952). It is more usual for a book of poems to be collected than written all in a piece like a novel, but in fact Reeves wrote each of these books during a spell of concentrated effort, cutting himself off from the distractions of the moment, and sometimes composing three or four poems in a day.[2] The books thus have exceptional unity as the products of one writing personality at one time, and in my view they contain some of the best poems written for children in the present century. A surprising number are humorous in various ways: wryly, affectionately, inventively, or even mysteriously. And a rich rural tone of voice combines with comedy and with a verse-form unlike any other in 'Cows':

> Half the time they munched the grass, and all the time they lay
> Down in the water-meadows, the lazy month of May,
>   A-chewing,
>   A-mooing,
> To pass the hours away.
>
>   'Nice weather,' said the brown cow.
>   'Ah,' said the white.
>   'Grass is very tasty.'
>   'Grass is all right . . .'

Here and there is a hint of poignancy, no more than a suggestion of an autumn nip in the air; and a simple descriptive poem can have its undertones and implications:

> Slowly the hands move round the clock,
> Slowly the dew dries on the dock.
> Slow is the snail — but slowest of all
> The green moss spreads on the old brick wall.

The distinguished British poets who have written most successfully for children in the more recent post-war decades have been Ted Hughes and Charles Causley. Hughes began in comic vein with *Meet My Folks!* (1961), which reflects the tendency of its time to break old moulds. Discarding the charming harmlessness long associated with children's verse, it describes a family you might not particularly want to meet, still less to acknowledge for your own. Sister Jane is 'a bird, a bird, a bird, a bird.'

> Oh it never would do to let folks know
> My sister's nothing but a great big crow.

Father is the Chief Inspector of Holes ('A hole's an unpredictable thing — Nobody knows what a hole might bring') and Mother is a cook who concocts some disconcerting dishes:

> I took her a rattlesnake that had attacked us:
> She served it up curried with Crème de la Cactus.

Hughes's poems have frequently been carried forward to new collections and revised editions, and this can be confusing. In *The Earth-Owl and Other Moon-People* (1963), Hughes looks at the strange creatures inhabiting what have been called 'the worlds within us . . . the thought-planets drifting somewhere beyond the rim of the mind'.[3] There were more moon poems — together with some of the poems about birds and beasts which Hughes does so admirably — in *Moon-Bells and Other Poems* (1978); and the moon poems were then drawn together in *Moon-Whales* (1988). Many of these poems, such as the title poem and 'The Moon-Lily', are strangely beautiful. We learn about moon-whales that

> They plough through the moon-stuff
> Just under the surface
> Lifting the moon's skin
> Like a muscle
> But so slowly it seems like a lasting mountain . . .
>
> The music is immense
> Each note hundreds of years long
> Each complete tune a moon-age . . .

Other poems are funny or grotesque or grotesquely funny; and the last two of this last collection are, in different ways, quite terrifying; dream has become nightmare.

Season Songs (1976; revised with additions in 1985) follows the turning year and contains some of Hughes's finest nature poems: sometimes tough, sometimes beautifully tender, as in the description of the newly-born calf, 'half of him legs,/Shining-eyed, requiring nothing more/But that mother's milk come back often.' *What is the Truth? A Farmyard Fable* (1984) brings together many fine Hughes poems about animals and birds, told in the persons of the farmer, his wife, their son and daughter, the poacher and others. They are linked by a quest for 'the truth', which God knows but people don't: namely, that God is in all these creatures.

Charles Causley's contribution to poetry for children is no less splendid than Hughes's. Like Hughes, Causley does not condescend to his audience or draw too much distinction between his work for children and that for adults. 'If there is a "best" way to set about writing poems for children,' he has said, 'I think it may be by concentrating first on trying to produce a *poem*, and by deciding afterwards on its most appropriate audience. The test of an authentic "children's" poem, surely, is that it should work equally successfully with both the child and the adult'.[4]

Causley, a Cornishman, is storyteller as well as poet; his work is imbued with the spirit of the old ballads, and with folklore and legend. The swiftly-moving narrative poems of

Food fit for a king: drawing by Pat Marriott for the title poem
of Charles Causley's *Figgie Hobbin*

Figure of 8 (1969) range from Balaam and his famous donkey
to the modern tall tale of Stoker Rock and the baby he
incautiously adopted while in foreign parts. The short poems
of *Figgie Hobbin* (1970) are set firmly into Cornish contexts.
They are tough, vigorous and concrete (surely no poet could
use fewer abstract nouns than Causley does); they sound out
loud and clear; and as the sound dies away sometimes the
echo steals back:

> Mother I hear the water
>   Beneath the headland pinned,
> And I can see the sea-gull
>   Sliding down the wind.
> I taste the salt upon my tongue
>   As sweet as sweet can be.
>
> *Tell me, my dear, whose voice you hear?*
>
> It is the sea, the sea.

In the years after *Figgie Hobbin*, Causley did a great deal of
work for children, as writer and anthologist; and in 1986 and

1987 came a blaze of poetic creativity with *Early in the Morning* and *Jack the Treacle Eater*. The first of these, a collection of new poems and modern nursery rhymes, was made into a lovely book — a work of art in its own right — with illustrations by Michael Foreman and music by Anthony Castro. And *Jack the Treacle Eater* shows Causley, at the age of 70, as capable as ever of producing, without apparent effort, poems that are in turn (and sometimes all together) humorous, touching, simple yet profound or evocative. He is not ashamed to use strong, full rhyme and bounding rhythm. And he is still an ancient mariner of a storyteller.

Cara Lockhart Smith's work is not widely known and not for every reader, but seems to me — in *Riding to Canonbie* (1972) and still more in *Old Merlaine* (1975) — to have distinctive, wry humour and a thin sharp vein of true poetry. Old Merlaine is an imaginary country. Its inhabitants include Miss Jessamine, thin as a pin; Colonel Silver Shankskin, of the Regiment of Flowers; the grocer who once took tea with three mermaids and has never been the same since; and the sinister King and Queen in cobwebbed Whirligig Castle. The realm is under some kind of spell, but through it all the children go their ways unharmed, running as free as air.

A wave of 'urchin verse' had struck Britain in the 1970s. In this country, the move from the poetic to the demotic was headed by Michael Rosen, whose *Mind Your Own Business* (1974) was the exemplar. Here was family life in the raw, with its backchat, fury and muddle, and instead of woods and meadows were disused railway lines, building sites and junkheaps. Other collections followed, whose tendency to cock a snook at social or literary pretension is summed up in the opening of a four-liner from *Wouldn't You Like to Know* (1977): 'Down behind the dustbin/I met a dog called Sid.' The perky, unregenerate narrators of Rosen's verses were hit off perfectly by the illustrator Quentin Blake in several successive books. With *When Did You Last Wash Your Feet?* (1986), Rosen moved up the age-range to take an equally unromantic view of adolescence.

Among other poets whose most obvious characteristics are energy and down-to-earth humour are Roger McGough, who put his verses together with Rosen's in *You Tell Me* (1983) and followed on with *Sky in the Pie* (1983), and Kit Wright, with *Rabbiting On* (1978), *Hot Dog* (1981) and *Cat Among the*

Pigeons (1987). Kit Wright has a pleasing way of slipping in a few 'straight' poems to lie like benevolent traps among the comic verse. Gareth Owen's poems, in *Salford Road* (1976) and *Song of the City* (1985) are likewise mainly comic but sound an occasional note of sadness, usually over the passage of time.

Black poetry for children has been late to make an impact in Britain, where it has aroused not so much hostility as incomprehension − or perhaps the fear of incomprehension. In a brief, helpful introduction to his collection *When I Dance* (1988), James Berry, referring to a teacherly attitude summed up in the words 'Nobody'd expect me to read *that*,' points out that it isn't tremendously difficult; when honestly sought and accepted a poem will yield itself up. Berry, born in Jamaica and living in Britain, moves easily between Jamaican and British scenes and ways of life, and just as easily between standard English and Caribbean Nation language. His work is designed to bring together rather than separate, for, as he says, 'surely everybody needs a bit of everybody.' Another black poet, Grace Nichols, in *Come on into my Tropical Garden* (1988), offers readers and hearers some intriguing glimpses of the Caribbean from which she came to Britain in 1977. Here are poems full of colour and flavour, offering brief intense experiences of sea and sun, vivid animals and plants, and people of different voice and appearance but a familiar human nature. As with Berry, the telling voice is interestingly varied: some poems are in accepted English English, others depart from it an enjoyably long way:

> Me mudder pound plantain mek fufu
> Me mudder catch crab mek calaloo stew...
>
> Ain't have nothing
> dat me mudder can't do.

Maybe you've never encountered fufu or calaloo stew, but what does that matter? You can still like the sound of them.

28

Picture books in bloom: USA

PICTURE BOOKS have blossomed since 1945. Technological advances, already in train before the war, have continued; in particular, developments in offset-lithography have made it possible to obtain visual effects that the old picture-book artists could hardly have dreamed of. Many respectable and some outstanding talents have found creative satisfaction in picture-book work. And among enlightened parents and teachers there has been growing recognition of the importance of a child's first books.

A distinction should be drawn between picture-book art and illustration. Although many contemporary illustrators are also picture-book artists, the two functions are not the same. Illustration explains or illuminates a text, helps (or, sometimes, hinders) the working of the reader's imagination, but is subordinate; it is the text that counts. In a picture book the artwork has at least an equal role to that of the text, very probably has the major part, and occasionally is unaccompanied by any text at all. This chapter and the next will be concerned, respectively, with some leading modern American and British picture-book artists. Unfortunately it is not possible in the small space available to discuss artists who are known primarily as illustrators in an auxiliary role. Work by some of them however is included among the illustrations to this book.

The picture book is a genre on its own, an impure art form. It tells a story or (occasionally) conveys information; in either case it is doing a job of work that is not required these days of 'pure' painting. Donnarae MacCann and Olga Richard, in their generally valuable study *The Child's First Books,* seem to me to go astray when they carefully separate for discussion the literary and graphic elements of the picture book and consider the latter on the same basis as the work of the pure painter. 'The meaning of his picture,' they say of the picture-book artist, 'comes from the way he arranges colours, lines, shapes, and textures into a special synthesis, one that will please the senses and provide an aesthetic experience for the reader'.[1] This is true and needs saying, but it is not the whole truth about picture-book art, which operates in the time dimension as well as the spatial ones, and which shares with the text in the complicated achievement of the told-and-pictured story. A picture book is not like a painting, or even, as a rule, like a sheaf of paintings; it forms a whole, from its beginning to its end, and the picture-book artist is involved in the shaping of action, the creation of character and place, the evocation of atmosphere, as functions of storytelling.

An opposite view to that of MacCann and Richard – and to my mind equally mistaken – is taken by Brian Alderson in *Sing a Song for 6d*. Alderson complains of the intrusion of 'artistic bravura' into the picture book, dismisses 'modish graphic styles' and 'fanciful central European theories', and insists with determined insularity that the 'English' style (as exemplified by Randolph Caldecott) is 'a touchstone for the judging of all picture-book art'.[2]

There is nothing wrong with the English style, which is a perfectly good style; Edward Ardizzone's work remained firmly grounded in it throughout his working lifetime. It is still giving good service. But it is not the only style. I am thankful that picture-book art as a whole has not in fact cut itself off from the wider world of the visual arts. It is easy to detect (say) classical, medieval, African or Oriental elements in the work of individual artists. Impressionism, expressionism and abstract painting have made some impact; so have advertising, poster design and typography, cartoons and comic strips, and much else. Some of these influences interact with one another; and direct influences may be filters for more distant ones. Picture-book artists have taken their inspiration where they could find it. It is all gloriously complicated.

Maurice Sendak is an eclectic artist whose work has been based on traditional models. (MacCann and Richard do not include Sendak among their 'outstanding contemporary illustrators', though they include him as an 'outstanding narrative writer'.) His dominance in the picture-book field today is indisputable. I agree with the general verdict on Sendak; indeed, I am prepared to say that he is the greatest creator of picture books in the hundred-odd years' history of the form. And, notwithstanding MacCann and Richard, I have no doubt that he is also a fine illustrator of other people's books – and one who never seeks to bludgeon his text into submission.

Much of Sendak's early work (in the 1950s) was black-and-white illustration. He began, in effect, by illustrating Ruth Krauss's book of children's definitions, *A Hole is to Dig*

(1952); and the small, squat, jaunty children he drew soon became associated with his name. As an admirer of the great Victorian illustrators he has also frequently used a gentle, fine, carefully archaic monochrome style which can be seen, subtly varied, in his illustrations to books by George MacDonald, Randall Jarrell and others. He made two almost-forgotten short stories by the American writer Frank R. Stockton (1834-1902), *The Griffin and the Minor Canon* and *The Bee-Man of Orn*, into splendid picture story books in 1963 and 1964 respectively.

Best of all the work of his early and middle years (leaving *Wild Things* apart) may well be *Hector Protector,* the first half of *Hector Protector and As I Went Over the Water* (1965). Here Sendak had a brief, inconsequent text that implied a story but didn't tell it and allowed the artist to make of it what he would. Sendak approached it in the manner of the Caldecott picture books, improvising from line to line and from page to page; and the resulting pictures, with their wiry bounding-lines and dynamic composition but delicate tinting, are both a tribute to Randolph Caldecott and a triumph of visual story-telling.

Sendak has said that 'if I have an unusual gift, it's not that I draw particularly better or write particularly better than other people – I've never fooled myself about that. Rather, it's that I remember things other people don't recall: the sounds and feelings and images – the emotional quality – of particular moments in childhood'.[3] And he has said of his famous trilogy that began with *Where the Wild Things Are* (1963) and continued with *In the Night Kitchen* (1970) and *Outside Over There* (1981), that the three books 'are all variations on the same theme: how children master various feelings – anger, boredom, fear, frustration, jealousy – and manage to come to grips with the realities of their lives'.[4]

Surely everybody knows the story of *Wild Things*. Max, sent supperless to bed for being naughty, sails off 'through night and day in and out of weeks and almost over a year' to the land of the wild things, who 'roared their terrible roars and gnashed their terrible teeth and rolled their terrible eyes and showed their terrible claws'. He tames them by staring unblinkingly into their yellow eyes, becomes their king, and then leads these huge, ugly, but not really very fearsome creatures through pages of wild rumpus. Then Max the king of all wild things is lonely and sails back to his own room, where his supper is waiting for him; 'and it was still hot'.

That very night in Max's room a forest grew: a page from
Maurice Sendak's *Where the Wild Things Are*

As the story opens out from the confines of Max's home to
the fantasy world he is creating for himself, the pictures
expand. From postcard-size with broad white surround, they
grow to near-page, full-page, page-and-a-bit; then the 'wild
rumpus' fills three great wordless double-page spreads, and on
the return journey everything gradually closes in again. The
text is strong and sounding, the story sails swiftly along, and
the ending has the right comforting and comfortable note.

In the Night Kitchen shows Mickey falling from his bed
down and down into the basement, where the bakers are all
ready with the Mickey Oven to make a delicious Mickey cake.
He emerges to make a floppy flight by dough-plane and find
milk for the batter; and, triumphant in full-frontal nude, cries
'Cock-a-Doodle-Doo!' He finishes safely back in bed, 'cakefree
and dried'; it looks very much as if he has gone through a
symbolic process of conception, gestation and birth. The book
owes a lot to strip cartoons, movies and popular American art
of the thirties, and the three identical bakers all look just like
Oliver Hardy of the Laurel-and-Hardy films.

Outside Over There begins with the curiously haunting lines,

> When Papa was away at sea
> and Mama in the arbor,
> Ida played her wonder-horn
> to rock the baby still —
> but never watched.

Goblins snatch Ida's baby sister and substitute a baby of ice, but by an inspired use of that same wonder-horn Ida is able to win the baby back. This deeply allusive work was several years in gestation. It seems to have arisen in part from Sendak's own illustrations to *The Juniper Tree and other tales from Grimm,* translated by Lore Segal and Randall Jarrell and published in 1973. While working on this, he listened only to the music of his hero Mozart; and 'I made my own make-believe connections: this is Grimm country; this is the eighteenth century; Mozart died in 1791; it's proper the music should be only Mozart'.[5] And Sendak had for some time been meditating the 'changeling' and 'lost child' themes.

Outside Over There is more painterly than the other two books, mysterious and dreamlike in atmosphere; mysterious, too, in content. What are we to make of the storm at sea that we see through the window in the second and third openings? Why is Mama sitting useless in the arbour, leaving Ida to bear the responsibility (a burden symbolized by the weight of the baby in Ida's arms)? What is the significance of the magnificent dog that is so prominent in the arbour scenes but doesn't actually *do* anything? The book can be endlessly discussed, and has perhaps already been over-discussed, in literary, artistic and psychological terms. (The height of absurdity is surely reached in the solemn observation that '*Outside Over There* deserves attention every bit as serious and detailed as *Remembrance of Things Past*'.[6]) After an initially lukewarm response, I myself have found it more and more impressive; there is so much that lingers unforgettably in the mind.

Sendak has acknowledged many sources of inspiration, including King Kong for *Wild Things* and Mickey Mouse for *Night Kitchen.*[7] Many artistic influences on *Outside Over There* can be traced, but the debt that Sendak himself has emphasized is to Mozart, to whom he pays visual homage — the figure in the cottage — towards the end of the book. He has absorbed these influences and made them part of his identity as a creator; he is not merely a master but the one and only grandmaster of the picture book.

Sendak is not by any means the only modern picture-book artist to have produced his own texts; indeed, it has become more the rule than the exception. The results have not always been happy. The temptation to the artist must obviously be strong, since the text required is so brief, and if you do it yourself you can keep it under your own control and make it serve your purposes. You also get the whole of the royalty. But just as most authors are at best indifferent illustrators, so are most artists indifferent writers.

Robert McCloskey is exceptional in being a recognized author. (He wrote *Homer Price* and *Centerburg Tales*.) The broad humour and short but strong story-lines of his *Make Way for Ducklings* (1941) and *Blueberries for Sal* (1948) have kept these two cheerful books popular through the succeeding decades. The text of *Time of Wonder* (1957), a description in words and pictures of a vacation in Maine, is possibly a shade overwritten, but this is a lovely picture book, full of light and air and water, and with a sense of wonder that justifies the title. At the time of writing, unfortunately, McCloskey has published nothing for more than a quarter of a century.

Roger Duvoisin (1904-80), if not exactly an accredited author, had the gift of creating memorable characters, among them the silly goose in *Petunia* (1950) and the hippopotamus who gives her name to *Veronica* (1961). This engaging creature, feeling herself to be inconspicuous and wanting to make her mark in the world, goes to the city, where she is gloriously conspicuous. Then there's Jasmine, the independent-minded cow in *Jasmine* (1973), who won't give up wearing her fancy hat. And Roger Duvoisin collaborated with his wife Louise Fatio, who wrote the text, in *The Happy Lion* (1954), by now a picture-book classic. The lion whose human friends greet him warmly while he is safe in the French small-town zoo finds it is quite another matter when he walks through the streets.

Ezra Jack Keats (1916-83) did not have remarkable gifts as a writer, but succeeded where many artists have failed in creating effective picture books without the collaboration of an author. In his most successful books, his concepts were such as could be expressed and developed pictorially, without requiring too much help from the printed word. As an artist he demonstrated incidentally that although economy of means is a sound principle there is nothing *wrong* with using vivid colour and all the technical panoply of the day. Keats made extensive use of collage, sometimes employing such materials as patterned paper, dried leaves, strips of fabric and old

Valentines. His subjects were drawn largely from the lives of black city children.

The Snowy Day (1962), about a small black boy's excursion into a winter-white world, still seems as pleasing as any of his books. In one sense there is not much story; what is offered is an atmosphere, a discovery of the strange in the familiar; but in another sense this discovery *is* the story. And to look at *The Snowy Day* is to perceive and grant at once that pictures are indeed arrangements of colours, lines, shapes and textures, and that a picture-book page can provide an aesthetic experience for the reader. Peter, the small hero of *The Snowy Day,* appeared in several other Keats books, among which *Peter's Chair* (1967), with its clear bright dynamic shapes, effective use of white, and simple visual story, is notably successful.

Some of the best picture-book artists, denying themselves the benefits of an instantly-recognizable style, have varied their methods continually to meet the different needs of their material. Marcia Brown, in her best books, used old tales and devised appropriate styles for them. There is an earthy robustness about her rendering of *Stone Soup* (1947), the story of how three soldiers returning from the wars persuade a simple peasantry to help them make soup from stones (with a few added ingredients). *Dick Whittington and his Cat* (1950) has a busy medieval air. In contrast, Marcia Brown's *Cinderella* (1954) has the frilly elegance appropriate to a Perrault fairy-story, and in contrast yet again is the scrawny northern vigour of her *Three Billy-Goats Gruff* (1957). For *Once a Mouse* (1966), a fable from ancient India, she used woodcut, now back in favour, to get flat, stylized, almost primitive shapes.

Barbara Cooney is another artist who adapts her style to her subject-matter. Her *Chanticleer and the Fox* (1958), adapted from Chaucer's *Nun's Priest's Tale,* uses deceptively simple-looking shapes and clear bright medieval colours. Among many other books, *A Garland of Games* (1969) is an alphabet with a couplet to each letter, based on mid-eighteenth-century colonial America, and has a plain but sturdy elegance. Barbara Cooney was still in good form in 1982 with her salty *Miss Rumphius,* about the dauntless maiden lady who retires to the coast of Maine and there fulfils her lifelong aim of doing something to make the world more beautiful. And *Island Boy* (1988), another book with a lovely Maine coastal setting, covers a full human life-span in the 32 pages of a picture book.

Leo Lionni had already had a distinguished career in art and graphic design when he produced his first children's book at the age of nearly 50. This was the highly-original *Little Blue and Little Yellow* (1959). The 'characters' are mere blobs of colour, but the book tells what is clearly a story of human relationships. Lionni has said indeed that his characters are humans in disguise and that he deals with large themes: 'my books are fables and parables.' The books do have readily-discernible morals, but what is most striking about them is their offbeat ingenuity. In *Inch by Inch* (1960) an inchworm is asked by a nightingale to 'measure my song'; in *Frederick* (1967) an artist fieldmouse stores up sun-rays and colours against the winter; a chameleon wants to stick to one colour in *A Colour of His Own* (1975). For Leo Lionni, humans can come in strange disguises.

The best-known picture book of Evaline Ness (1911-86) is *Sam, Bangs and Moonshine* (1966). It is a beautiful book to look at; its line-and-wash pictures are strongly composed, and the grey-greens are exactly right for the sea-coast and fishing-harbour setting; but it is let down by a weak and heavily-didactic story. But Evaline Ness was a fine and versatile illustrator, and among many successes was the splendid picture book she made in 1966 out of the Joseph Jacobs telling of *Tom Tit Tot:* a satisfying integration of story, type and pictures into a designed whole that has a crusty, home-baked look about it.

Crockett Johnson (1906-75) made his name with a comic strip called *Barnaby*. Bright ideas rather than dedication to fine art are the stock-in-trade of the cartoonist and the comic-strip creator, and Johnson's reputation in the children's-book field rests on one brilliant notion: that of *Harold and the Purple Crayon* (1955). Beginning on the wall of his own bedroom, Harold draws a marvellous moonlight adventure, and finishes by drawing his way back to his own room and bed. There were more books about Harold, but none of them ever matched the first.

Among American picture-book artists, Eric Carle has made the most ingenious use of physical devices. In his ever-popular *The Very Hungry Caterpillar* (1969), the caterpillar eats his way through holes in the pages, to emerge triumphant and colourful as a butterfly in a final double-page spread. In *The Very Busy Spider* (1985), there are raised surfaces, so that you could 'read' the story with your fingers; in *Papa, Please Get the Moon for Me* (1986), Papa obligingly climbs up a ladder on a page that folds upwards.

Tomi Ungerer, award-winning illustrator, commercial artist

and cartoonist, was born in France but lived in the United States and afterwards Canada during the years in which his picture books were published. He has a comic, fertile and often gruesome imagination. *Zeralda's Ogre* (1967) shows a round-faced, round-eyed farmer's daughter winning an ogre away from his child-eating habits by her superb cuisine. Good. But there is something not altogether reassuring about the outcome, with Zeralda surrounded by the ogre's unprepossessing friends and (later) married to the reformed, clean-shaven

Benito, with wheel and topper, from Tomi Ungerer's *The Hat*

ogre and having a lot of children. 'And, *so it would seem,* (my italics) they lived happily ever after.' *The Hat* (1970) is less ambiguous: an inventive and truly visual creation with an air of comic opera about it. The curly-brimmed, magenta-ribboned topper, blown from a rich man's head onto the bald pate of old soldier Benito, has magic powers; and soon Benito's peg-leg is fitted with a silver wheel, he looks a perfect gentleman, and he goes on to riches and romance. The physical possibilities of a top hat (for holding things, catching things, putting a stopper on things) are exploited with great ingenuity.

The Beast of Monsieur Racine (1971) is Ungerer's most appealing picture book: absurd, funny, and even in its way tender. Monsieur Racine, a retired tax collector, makes a friend of the strange beast that has been stealing his pears; it looks from a distance like a heap of mouldy blankets and it loves cookies, chocolate and ice-cream. But when he goes to display it to the Academy of Sciences, it splits apart with laughter and resolves itself into two children. Uproar all round; but Monsieur Racine, 'who had a sense of humour', congratulates the children and takes them on a tour of the capital.

Cartoonists have contributed substantially to the modern American picture book. William Steig is essentially amiable. *Sylvester and the Magic Pebble* (1969) is the story of a young donkey – obviously in reality a child – who is turned into a rock but eventually rescued by his loving and yearning parents. The theme is one with meaning for every parent and child; the drawings are without artistic pretensions but affectionately in keeping with the text. Steig's later picture books include *Amos and Boris* (1971), about the friendship between a mouse and a whale, and *Doctor De Soto* (1982), in which a mouse dentist, having extracted a bad tooth for a fox, ingeniously forestalls his patient's ungrateful intentions. In *Solomon the Rusty Nail* (1985), Solomon the rabbit turns himself into (of all things) a rusty nail, and gets himself banged into the wall by a villainous cat. Only a fire – which causes him, while still in his nail form, to feel alive, inspired and bright – can return him to rabbithood. William Steig tells tall stories in a straight, deadpan style; he is never facetious and never winks to the adult reader over the child's head.

James Stevenson is another well-known cartoonist; his casual-looking line lends itself to a dry, affectionate but unsentimental humour which is the most attractive characteristic of his books. Friendship is the theme of *Monty* (1979), about the amiable alligator who gives himself a vacation from being taken for granted but is there when he's needed, all the same; of *Howard* (1980), about the migrating duck who only gets as far as New York City, but survives a winter there with the help of the new friends he's made, and of *The Night After Christmas* (1981), in which Chauncey the brown dog devises an unexpected but wholly believable way of finding homes for a couple of discarded toys.

Arnold Lobel (1933-87) was truly a writer-artist, equally able in either role, though he himself said that drawing gave him more pleasure than writing.[8] His original *Fables* (1980) are remarkably true to the spirit of Aesop, though my favourite is one of the least Aesopian. A camel wants to be a ballet-dancer, but after she's practised for months, her invited audience merely sneers at her. Never mind; she decides she'll dance for herself alone, and 'it gave her many years of pleasure'. Moral: satisfaction will come to those who please themselves. And the ungainly creature that cavorts in the accompanying picture is both ludicrous and lovable. Lobel's *Book of Pigericks* (1983) begins with a rhyme about 'an old pig with a pen' – unmistakably Lobel himself – and is thoroughly Learian, even to the extent of using the form of limerick in which the final line is a repeat. A particular joy is the light pig of Montclair who floats on air and is seen sailing along like an airborne dowager with a retinue of birds.

Margot Zemach, who died in 1989, was a prolific artist who adapted her style to her material. She made picture books out of a world-wide variety of folk-tales, many of them retold by her husband Harve Zemach; I particularly like the robust and different comedies of *Too Much Nose* (1967) and *Duffy and the Devil* (1973). But the best of the Zemach books must surely be *The Judge* (1969), which is 'an untrue tale' by Harve Zemach himself. The Judge, a marvellous figure of purblind judicial arrogance, gives short shrift to the succession of seedy characters who tell him that 'a horrible thing is coming this way, Creeping closer day by day'; but at the end we see with delight that even judges should sometimes believe what even seedy characters say.

John Steptoe (1950-89), using heavy Rouault-like outlines, brought black ghetto life into picture books with *Stevie* (1969) and *Uptown* (1970). In later work he extended his territory and developed his style, the culmination of his work being *Mufaru's Beautiful Daughter* (1987). The story here is a retold folk-tale from southern Africa, and its shape is universally familiar: of two sisters, one is proud and selfish, the other kind and gentle. In the end virtue is rewarded – in this case by marriage to the King. It is nothing special in itself, but the pictures are glorious. Wiry drawing and rich colouring combine to achieve a heightened naturalism, glowing and textured; and to this is added an air of enchantment when the heroine Nyasha gazes from on high at a distant city – inspired, we are told, by an ancient city discovered in Zimbabwe.

In 1983 Molly Bang featured a warm, happy black family with its pets, toys and possessions in a counting-down book for bedtime, *Ten, Nine, Eight*. Three years later she showed her virtuosity in the clear, bright collage-style outlines of *The Paper Crane*. Snapshots, a map, and glimpses through doors, windows and a hatch help to tell a story with an oriental flavour of a restaurant owner whose kindness to an old man brings him a paper crane that can come to life, dance, and bring in the customers.

The picture book as art was taken to its farthest point in one direction by Gerald McDermott in *The Magic Tree* (1973) and *Arrow to the Sun* (1974). Arising from McDermott's work in making animated films, these highly stylized and blazingly vivid adaptations of folk-tales were the artist's response to the challenge to 'discover visual evocations of the compelling myths of mankind'.[9]

In *The Garden of Abdul Gasazi* (1979) and *Jumanji* (1981) Chris Van Allsburg created, in black-and-white tone drawings with unorthodox perspective, an atmosphere of eeriness to match his disconcerting, surreal stories. With *The Wreck of the Zephyr* (1983) he went into full colour to tell the story of the boy, determined to excel as the greatest sailor of all, who sails his boat through the sky. But the boy pays the price of overweening pride, and as he flies over his own village the wind fails; the Zephyr crashes, and here, years afterwards, she still is. The boy, it seems, is still here, too: now an old man who has 'never amounted to much' but is still trying. With the use of colour, Van Allsburg achieves luminous, mysterious effects; but he is far from dependent on colour, and *The Mysteries of Harris Burdick* (1985) is back in black-and-white. This is a sheaf of fourteen drawings – weird, ominous, uncanny – belonging to the same number of supposedly-vanished stories about which we can only speculate. This was the enigmatic Van Allsburg's most enigmatic book so far. In *The Polar Express* (1985), a great train comes by to pick up a boy on Christmas

Eve, and carries him and other children northward through wintry landscapes to the North Pole, where a city of toy factories turns out the goods for Santa Claus. Evocative soft-focus double-page spreads convey an appropriate sense of mystery and dream. Santa gives the boy a bell from a reindeer's harness; 'it made the most beautiful sound my sister and I had ever heard', but their parents can't hear a thing. The narrator concludes, 'Though I've grown old, the bell still rings for me as it does for all who truly believe.' Or – a cynical commentator might add – for all who are truly sentimental.

Rosemary Wells has a witty eye and pen for small children's relationships with their siblings and peers. (The children may be shown as small animals, but they're 'ourselves in fur', so it doesn't make much difference.) Sometimes, as in *Morris's Disappearing Bag* (1975) or *A Lion for Lewis* (1982), it's the youngest child who is kept out of the older ones' games but finds a way to turn the tables; other times, as in *Stanley and Rhoda* (1978), it's the older ones who have their trials in coping with tiresome tinies. Nicest and most wickedly perceptive of those known to me is *Timothy Goes to School* (1981). Timothy is firmly put down by established and talented Claude, but finds a friend in Violet, similarly outshone by Grace; and on the last page 'Timothy and Violet laughed so much about Claude and Grace that they both got the hiccups'. Rosemary Wells has also brought quality to the board book for babies – traditionally a mass-market product – with a series of ten books about Max, a rabbit child: *Max's Toys, Max's Birthday* and so on.

I am ruefully aware that many more good artists could have been mentioned in this chapter. The modern American picture book is a rich and productive field.

29

Picture books in bloom: Britain

THE BRITISH picture book, after many disappointing years, came to vigorous life in the 1960s. The leading names of the decade were those of Charles Keeping and Brian Wildsmith, but many other artists also came to prominence. Keeping (1924-88) remained throughout his working life the most powerful and the most controversial of them all. He did not make concessions to supposed childish tastes, and his work raises in acute form the question whether picture-book artists sometimes demand too much of their audiences and waste their endeavours on those who cannot yet appreciate what they are doing.

I do not know of any study that has been made of the graphic preferences of small children. Certainly their tastes can be very different from those of visually educated adults. Grown-ups should not, I think, deprive children of what they find for themselves and enjoy; but in actually introducing them to books I believe it wise to stick to the principle that only the best is good enough. Picture books are a first introduction to art and literature, no less. To give a child crude, stereotyped picture books is to open the way for everything else that is crude and stereotyped. And even if children do not always appreciate the best when they see it, they will have no chance of appreciating it if they don't see it.

Judged as graphic art, I have no doubt that Charles Keeping's work is very fine. His first major success, *Charley, Charlotte and the Golden Canary* (1967) is an urban fairy tale: two children, parted when the old houses in Paradise Street are pulled down, are reunited when a canary flies from one to the other. As a story it's slight and unconvincing, but as a book to look at it's stunning; the colours are so wild, glowing and vibrant, and used with such lordly freedom. *Through the Window* (1970), considered as a whole, is a better book. Jacob's world consists of what he can see through the gap in the curtains. Excitement is followed by disaster when runaway horses from the brewery come galloping down the street, and the poor old woman picks up and cradles the limp body of her dog. But the conclusion, if not exactly happy, is positive, for Jacob, breathing on the window and drawing, has the old woman upright and smiling, her dog alive and alert in her arms.

In *Railway Passage* (1974), Keeping's colour has cooled a long way from the vivid blaze of *Charley, Charlotte and the Golden Canary,* and there is more emphasis on draughtsmanship and pictorial character-creation. The six tenants who live in Railway Passage are old and rather poor; the children call them uncles and aunties. They always fill in a joint football-pool coupon, and one day it comes up and they are rich. Not a child-centred subject, admittedly; but children, like the rest of us, are intrigued by the idea of sudden wealth, and we can all consider which of the uncles and aunties spend the money wisely.

In *Cockney Ding-Dong* (1975), Keeping, a Londoner in blood and bone, built a rowdy, energetic, eye-filling and massively nostalgic book on the foundations of the songs that were sung at the old London singsongs and in the music-halls. His presentation of the Alfred Noyes poem *The Highwayman* (1981) is stark, almost brutal, and exemplifies a sombre streak that ran increasingly through his work in later years. His last book, *Adam and Paradise Island* (1989), was set, appropriately, in his most-loved part of London: an old, almost-forgotten down-river urban area in the East End. Paradise Island is linked to the outer world by a couple of narrow bridges; the Council — a fine lot of rogues and nitwits, by the look of them — decide to build a fast road across it. The old shopkeepers are rehoused and go to work for the Neata supermarket. But the children save something from the wreckage by building for themselves, with help from old inhabitants, a playground on a patch of marshy ground unfit for development. The pictures of the children and the local people and places are cool, in fawns, greens, greys and browns; the splashes of gaudy colour are mostly for the new and nasty. The atmosphere of the book is one of wry realism lightened by hope; and it is the children who represent hope.

Brian Wildsmith is more painter than draughtsman. The richness of his *ABC* was astonishing when it first appeared in 1962; there was nothing else quite like his kettle aglow with heat or his lion on the next page aglow with sun. He has a gift for putting the pulse of life into representations of natural creatures; if ever there was an artist whose tigers burned bright it was Brian Wildsmith; and he produced, among others, books of *Birds* and *Wild Animals* (1967), *Fishes* (1968) and *The*

Circus (1970). Wildsmith has illustrated various folktales and fables, but gives the impression of turning constantly aside to pick flowers. This happens almost literally in *The Miller, the Boy and the Donkey* (1969), which at one point shows man and boy riding across a rich, deep flowerscape that is irrelevant to the story but is the principal interest of the double-page spread on which it appears. In *The Hare and the Tortoise* (1969), when the hare stops to eat carrots, we see a cross-section of growing, glowing carrots in the juicy black jewelled earth. Nothing could be farther from the idea of a race, and we may well wonder whether (endearingly) the artist shares the hare's tendency to be sidetracked. As a storyteller, Wildsmith has never seemed impressive, but he surpassed himself with *Professor Noah's Spaceship* (1980). This is a space-age revamping of the Biblical story, and at the same time a fable with an ingenious twist in the end. The animals, endangered by pollution, are taken by Professor Noah on a forty-day journey through space to find an unspoiled world, but a failure of the time guidance system brings them back to Earth — not now but as it was in the beginning, with a chance to start again. A splendid book; and full of Wildsmith's splendid animals.

John Burningham's early books were obviously the work of a gifted comic artist. In *Borka* (1963) and *Trubloff* (1964), the flat, slabby, idiosyncratic pictures show people and animals

Mr Gumpy and friends: a drawing by John Burningham from *Mr Gumpy's Outing*

self-possessed, even smug, however unlikely their situations. The composedly-deadpan manner extends to the (extremely tall) stories of these books, told without a twitch of the lips. Never let it be thought odd that a mouse should play the balalaika or travel a vast distance on skis. True, 'the innkeeper was amazed to see a mouse with a balalaika,' but 'he had to admit, after hearing him, that Trubloff played well.'

Burningham's *Mr Gumpy's Outing* (1970) is a perfect picture-book story. Mr Gumpy takes his children and a growing number of animals on a boat trip, and they all do just what they're told not to do (which always seems particularly funny to the very young). Disaster follows, but is quickly surmounted, for it all takes place in a world in which disaster doesn't stand a chance. *Come Away from the Water, Shirley* and *Time to Get Out of the Bath, Shirley* (1977 and 1978) have a satiric element, for the dailiness and 'don'tness' of parents is contrasted on facing pages with the vivid imaginings of Shirley herself.

Among Burningham's later books, *Granpa* (1984) and *Oi! Get Off Our Train!* (1989) have struck subtler and more serious notes. In *Granpa,* the conversations between grandparent and grandchild are beset by failures of communication across a long generation gap: the tangling of elderly memory of the past with juvenile fixation on the passing moment, the unawareness on a child's part of the limitations of time and of age — 'Tomorrow shall we go to Africa, and you can be the captain?' Towards the end we have 'Grandpa can't come out to play today'; finally there's an empty chair, but there's also a baby to push in the pram.

Oi! Get Off Our Train! combines a child's dream — a toy train becomes full size and can be driven off on a journey — with a conservation fable as animal after animal begs for a ride on the train because its habitat is being destroyed. There are other aspects of the story, too; some children, and adults, may find it a little confusing. Visually however this is surely the best thing Burningham has ever done; the full-page paintings of the train steaming through varied landscapes and weathers are splendid.

Quentin Blake's pictures are a cartoonist's pictures, but he uses his casual, sketchy-looking style with great versatility. *Patrick* (1968) is visual fantasy. Patrick, playing his violin, brings singing fish out of the sea, changes the leaves on the trees to all kinds of bright colours, and makes the trees grow 'pears and bananas and cakes and cream and slices of hot

Mr Magnolia, drawn by Quentin Blake

buttered toast'. A woeful tinker and his wife become bright and
happy behind a multi-coloured horse and cart . . . Does all this
epitomize the gifts conferred by art on humanity? Maybe; or
maybe it's just delicious nonsense. In *Jack and Nancy* (1969),
two children are blown away, clinging to an umbrella, to a
tropical island. The basic idea is by no means unique. It's the
scenes that are such fun: Jack and Nancy descending parachute-
fashion among foliage and parrots, swimming with many-
coloured fish, or living below deck with the sailors on the ship
that brings them home. 'Mr Magnolia has only one boot' is the
opening line of *Mister Magnolia* (1980); and the book itself is
based on a poem with only one rhyme. There's a line to a
page, approximately, and the lines may seem as zany as the
accompanying drawings, but at least they all rhyme with 'boot'.
At the end Mr Magnolia is sent a second boot as a present; it's
a different shape and colour, but it's a boot, and Mr M stands
on his hands and waves both boots in the air with delight.

Blake has joined with writers in several successful collaborations. Among the most notable is *How Tom Beat Captain Najork and his Hired Sportsmen* (1974), of which Russell Hoban wrote the text. Tom won't stop fooling around with sticks and stones and mud and shaky high-up things; so his fierce Aunt Fidget Wonkham-Strong, who wears an iron hat and makes the flowers droop, sends for Captain Najork and his men to play rough, muddy games against Tom and teach him a lesson. But it's Tom, the consummate fooler-around, who comes out on top. Blake's drawings here match the wit of the author and the aplomb of the hero. Tom and Aunt Fidget are around again in another amazing Hoban/Blake concoction, *A Near Thing for Captain Najork* (1975).

The world of Raymond Briggs, as seen in his *Mother Goose Treasury* (1966) and *Fairy Tale Treasury* (chosen by Virginia Haviland, 1972) is full-blooded and boisterous. Briggs's people are notably lacking in any hint of delicacy or sensitivity. They tend to have jutting chins and prominent, if scattered, teeth. In any situation where only the fittest could survive, they would be among the eaters rather than the eaten. Giants — a rough lot on the whole — seem particularly congenial to Raymond

Shirley Hughes's Chips and Jessie, with Barkis the dog
and Albert the cat

Briggs; he has created two separate and equally rumbustious ones to illustrate the old rhyme 'Fee Fi Fo Fum', and a rather pathetic one, to be happily transformed and made a hundred years younger with the aid of enormous teeth, wig and spectacles, in the hilarious *Jim and the Beanstalk* (1970).

Since then, Briggs has continued on his eccentric way. *Father Christmas* (1973) is in comic-strip form and portrays a grumpy old codger who complains about blooming snow, blooming cold, blooming chimneys and blooming soot; but at least, when his annual night's work is over, he enjoys a hot bath, dry clothes, his own Christmas dinner and a paper hat. And 'happy blooming Christmas to you, too!' *Fungus the Bogeyman* (1977), with pictures in muck-brown and slime-green, is really more suitable for grimy-minded over-tens and adults than for small children. I am told it sells well to students. Fungus is large, dank, dim, thick-green-skinned, small-eyed and big-eared, with six webbed fingers on each hand. He lives in a nice filthy underground home with his wife Mildew and has flaked corns for breakfast. But there's no malice in him, and he and Mildew are a devoted couple. 'Oh, Fungus, darkling!' she exclaims, 'I love your smell. You stink to high heaven!' *The Snowman* (1979) is wordless, beautiful, moving and sad, for the snowman who comes alive to be a child's playmate has only a snowman's expectation of life. *When the Wind Blows* (1982), using the comic-strip style to demonstrate the horror of nuclear war, is a picture book for adults, not children.

Shirley Hughes, an established illustrator with a special gift for drawing small sturdy flesh-and-blood children, had created a successful picture book as long ago as 1960 in the appealing *Lucy and Tom's Day*. In the 1970s and early 1980s she greatly increased her reputation in this field. Among the picture books written and drawn by herself were *Helpers* (1975), in which teenager George has an exhausting day looking after three tinies, and *Dogger* (1977), in which Dave's dearly-loved toy dog is sold by mistake at a summer fair but recovered through an act of remarkable generosity by bigger sister Bella. *Up and Up* (1979), a small girl's flying fantasy, is in comic-strip style and is wordless — the pictures on their own being quite enough to tell the story. *Alfie Gets In First* (1981) and other Alfie books are deceptively simple-looking explorations of the dramas and adventures that lurk in the (to adults) ordinary activities of ordinary days. *Chips and Jessie* (1985) is a clutch of five stories about two small friends and various relatives, schoolmates and pets, all combined together in a lively but by no means artless jumble of pictures, strip cartoons and narrative text.

Two picture books without text – Raymond Briggs's *The Snowman* and Shirley Hughes's *Up and Up* – have been mentioned in this chapter. A third that is wholly successful is *Changes, Changes* (1971), by Pat Hutchins, in which a resourceful round wooden man and woman make their home out of building blocks, then transform it to a fire engine when it catches fire, a boat to sail away on the resulting water, a truck, a train, and finally a house again. Any text would be superfluous. But such successes are rare, for in general the picture-book genre seems to be one that by nature walks on two legs and is crippled if one of them is removed.

In Pat Hutchins's classic *Rosie's Walk* (1970), the point of the text lies in what it doesn't say. We are told (in just thirty-two words, spread over twenty-seven pages), that Rosie the hen went for a walk across the yard, around the pond, over the haycock, past the mill, through the fence, under the beehives, and got back in time for dinner. That's it, verbatim. What we are not told in words is that Rosie is pursued all the way by a fox, who has a series of cartoon-film-style misadventures each time he tries to pounce on her. The book goes beyond cartoon-film, however, for the joke is that bird-brained Rosie remains happily unaware of her peril. The child reader or hearer can feel gloriously superior not only to Rosie and the fox but also to the silly old grown-up writer who failed to notice what was going on.

Janet and Allan Ahlberg, a prolific husband-and-wife, writer-and-artist team, have probably achieved the most rapidly-growing reputation as British picture-book creators in recent years. Among their already-numerous books, *Burglar Bill* (1977) is one of those that straddle the frontiers of story and picture book. Its text is no mere appendage to the pictures:

Burglar Bill lives by himself in a tall house full of stolen property. Every night he has stolen fish and chips and a cup of stolen tea for supper. Then he swings a big stolen sack over his shoulder and goes off to work, stealing things.

How's that for a beginning? Going about his business one night, Bill brings home a box and finds that there's a baby in it; and after some sniggery business of wetting and smelling and nappy-changing the baby turns out to belong to Burglar Betty, a poor widowed lady burglar. Fraternizing over cocoa,

Rosie, from *Rosie's Walk* by Pat Hutchins

Bill and Betty decide to get married, mend their ways and restore their ill-gotten loot; so it's a highly moral story. The pictures, appropriately, are cheerful, mildly grotesque and just a shade vulgar.

The Ahlbergs' *Each Peach Pear Plum* (1978) and *Peepo!* (in America *Peek-a-Boo!*) (1981) are for the really small. Both are based on nursery games. In *Each Peach*, each successive picture of a Mother Goose or fairy tale character is accompanied by an 'I Spy' couplet; and the 'I Spy' refers ahead to the next page's main character, who can be spotted by an alert young eye concealed in the picture on *this* page. *Peepo!* uses a hole in the page to show only part of a picture, which is seen in full, together with descriptive rhyme, when the page is turned. *Bye Bye Baby* (1989) is described on the title page as 'a sad story with a happy ending'. It begins with a baby who has no mummy. 'This baby lived in a little house all by himself. He fed himself and bathed himself. He even changed his own nappy.' But the baby goes out into the world and finds, in succession, various helpful creatures, an old uncle, a mummy who is pushing a pram but has no baby, and a daddy. In all these three books the pictures are sunny and reassuring, with plenty of detail to be explored, and totally without pretension. The hugely best-selling *The Jolly Postman* (1986) is a little way up the age range. It's a package of letters to fairy tale characters, notable among them a lawyer's letter to the wolf on behalf of his clients the Three Little Pigs: 'All this huffing and puffing will get you nowhere.'

Postmen obviously sell; John Cunliffe's series of *Postman Pat* books, with the innocently amiable Pat, and his van and his cat and the people of quiet Greendale, and the advantage of being televised, were one of the big successes of the eighties, and at the end of the decade looked well set to continue. Another success of the decade was that of Eric Hill's series about Spot, the puppy, which began with *Where's Spot?* in 1980. This makes use of flaps in a game of hide and seek: Spot's mother Sally looks for him in the grandfather clock, under the stairs and so on, until (hooray!) he is found in the shopping-basket. I have heard squeals of delight from the very small at this disclosure, which they had seen a hundred times and never tired of.

Mary Rayner is both writer and artist, and the story is the strength of *Mr and Mrs Pig's Evening Out* (1976). The Pig parents get a babysitter from an agency to look after their ten piglets. Mrs Pig asks the sitter her name. 'It's Mrs Wolf,' she says, crossing a pair of dark hairy legs; and she settles down with her knitting and Mrs Pig's copy of *Sow and Sty*. The piglets are in peril, but there's no need to worry; they are more than a match for Mrs Wolf. The presentation of suburban life in porcine terms, and the multiplication of numbers, with no fewer than ten youngsters fooling around in the bathtub and being shooed upstairs to bed, are all part of the fun. A demand for further Pig books was inevitable, and others followed in 1977 and 1981.

Fiona French has created picture books which are exotic both in subject-matter and pictorial treatment. Her first, *Jack of Hearts* (1970), is based on the playing-card dynasties – Spades, Hearts, Diamonds and Clubs – and designed from actual cards. *Huni* (1971) has an ancient Egyptian setting and introduces Egyptian gods; *City of Gold* (1974) has a medieval theme and the richness of stained glass. Perhaps the most extraordinary of all is *Snow White in New York* (1986), which transposes the well known tale into a glitzy, Scott Fitzgeraldy setting, with Snow White as a club singer, the seven dwarfs as seven jazzmen, and the prince a handsome reporter. Snow White's wicked stepmother, 'the classiest dame in New York', pops a poisoned cherry in her cocktail; but Snow White survives to marry the reporter in a big society wedding and cruise off on a glorious honeymoon. And presumably they live happily together ever after, or for a few months anyway. To the adult eye, this book is delicious fun, though I am not sure that it escapes the charge of being a children's book for grown-ups.

Mairi Hedderwick lived for ten years on the island of Coll in the Inner Hebrides. As long ago as 1972 she made a memorable picture book out of a retelling by Rumer Godden of a folk tale, *The Old Woman Who Lived in a Vinegar Bottle* (a round house with a pointed thatched roof); but it was not until 1984 that she produced a book written by herself. This was *Katie Morag delivers the Mail*, the first of − so far − four books featuring bright-eyed, red-haired small girl Katie Morag, and set on the 'Isle of Struay'. The books are in part celebrations of the Hebridean landscapes, seascapes and people. The outdoor scenes are full of light and air; you want to walk out into them; and the people are outdoor people, a community whose members know each other well. *Katie Morag and the Two Grandmothers* (1985) brings smartly-dressed Grannie Mainland to the island for the Struay Show, but the heroine of the occasion is Grannie Island, who helms a boat, drives a tractor, and needs all her resourcefulness to cope with a crisis.

Anthony Browne's was another rapidly rising reputation of the eighties. He had published in 1977 *A Walk in the Park,* a neat and witty picture story in which children and dogs fraternize happily but the class-divided adults who have taken them to the park have nothing to say to each other. The bonus of the book is to be found in its incidental, surrealist details: the topiary figure that exactly resembles the lady passing it; the gentleman walking his pig; the hippo in the fountain which itself is an extravaganza put together from impossible components.

The book that made Browne's name was *Gorilla* (1983). Its story is simple. Hannah longs to see a gorilla, but Father hasn't time to take her to the zoo or anywhere else. She asks for a gorilla for her birthday, but only gets a toy one, which she doesn't think much of. In the night a 'real', full-sized gorilla appears, puts on Father's hat and coat, and takes her on a glorious adventure. In the morning there's only a toy one again; but she tells Father, and Father's going to take her to the zoo after all. The book's attraction is the visiting gorilla himself: large, kind, reassuring, a person − indeed, a father − but with just a hint of pathos.

In *Willy the Wimp* (1984) the weedy little chimp who apologizes to everybody, even when it isn't his fault, takes a course of body-building, becomes muscular and walks tall − but at the end collides with a lamp-post, and apologizes to it.

Willy, of course, is endearingly human. *Piggybook* (1986) is a feminist picture book. As a man I wish I could say its message had become redundant; I hope it is becoming so. Mr Piggott and his sons expect to be waited on; call for their meals when they come in, then flop down in front of the TV. One day Mrs Piggott disappears, leaving a terse note to say 'You are pigs.' They have to make their own (horrible) meals, the house becomes a pig-sty, and the pictures show them with pigs' heads. And of course they learn their lesson: when Mrs Piggott comes back they do their share of the chores and 'Mum was happy too . . .' (turn over the page) . . . 'She mended the car.' Trenchant stuff, yet acceptable because it's funny; it would take a very piggy man or boy not to see the joke.

The Tunnel (1989) is also somewhat feminist. A brother (who is not named) doesn't want the company of his little sister (also unnamed); but when he crawls through a tunnel and doesn't come back she conquers her fears and follows him. She arrives in a frightening country, where she finds him turned to stone, and thaws him into life by putting her arms round him. They run home together, friends; and now at last they are named. The pictures in this book come close to being photographic; the girl's figure is even slightly blurred when she's running; but they are very cleverly devised, composed and scaled. In general Anthony Browne makes effective use of clear, bright outlines, often against blank white backgrounds that give a cut-out effect. He is an able, witty artist and − just as importantly − he has picture-book-shaped ideas.

In recent years there has been a revival and extension of the Victorian fashion for toy books − pop-ups, cut-outs manipulated by tabs, and other such devices − and a new profession has been established: that of paper engineer. Such productions are outside the scope of the present study, but they are of economic importance to the trade. 'If it bangs, rattles, squeaks, smells, pops up or has holes in it, we can sell it', a bookseller told me ruefully; and booksellers, like publishers, have to stay in business.

Besides the toy books, there have been lavish new editions of the classics, endless refurbishments of Grimm or Perrault fairy tales, novelizations of TV series, treasure-hunts, choose-your-own-adventure books: anything, one might think, to attract the unbookish buyer and keep the book trade going in whatever holes and corners are left unoccupied by the electronic media. At times it seems that those who still want to get 'real' books to children are whistling in the dark.

And yet, while fads and fashions come and go, the picture or story book that absorbs the child's attention and stimulates the imagination holds sturdily on to life. Not everything is against it, after all. Films and TV, with their millions of viewers, inevitably offer less variety than books; they, and new media arising out of them, are always likely to have much greater initial production costs and must be dependent on a high degree of general acceptability. They cannot afford to use much material which, though excellent, has limited appeal. A large part of the case for the book is that it is not really a mass medium; it can pay its way on a sale of a few thousand copies and an initial outlay which is still fairly modest. There can still be books for the exceptional reader. And, unlike a film or a TV programme, a book is 'open', unfinished: the child completes it in his or her own mind. The read book is a collaboration between writer and reader.

I still have faith in the ability of the book to keep going. It is a tough old bird, after all. People thought that the cinema and radio and television would kill it, but they have not done so yet. Perhaps it is not too wildly optimistic to hope that in the twenty-first century, when all the modern miracles, and some we have not yet dreamed of, have come to pass, a child will still be found here and there, lying face down on the hearthrug or whatever may have replaced the hearthrug, light years away from his or her surroundings, lost in the pages of a book.

Notes

Full bibliographical details are given only where the work quoted does not also appear in the bibliography that follows.

1. The beginnings

1. Modernized from the version printed, among many other such texts, by F. J. Furnivall in *The Babees' Book*, pp. 399-402.
2. Sir Philip Sidney, 'An Apology for Poetry', included in *English Critical Essays: XVI-XVIII Centuries*, edited by E. D. Jones, London, Oxford University Press, 1922 (World's Classics), p. 22.
3. See Sloane, *English Children's Books in England and America in the Seventeenth Century*, p. 68.
4. Heartman, *The New England Primer*, p. xxii.
5. Quoted by A. S. W. Rosenbach in his introduction to *Early American Children's Books*, p. xl.

2. Mr Locke and Mr Newbery

1. Penelope Mortimer, 'Thoughts Concerning Children's Books', New Statesman, 11 November 1966. Reprinted in *Only Connect*, edited by Egoff and others.
2. Locke, *Thoughts Concerning Education*, § 149, 156.
3. Boswell, *Life of Johnson*, vol. 1, p. 427.
4. Darton, *Children's Books in England*, 3rd edition, p. 7.
5. Quoted by Welsh in *A Bookseller of the Last Century*, p. 23.
6. Goldsmith, *The Vicar of Wakefield* (Everyman, 1908), p. 101.
7. Welsh, op. cit., p. 105.
8. Sir John Hawkins, *The Life of Samuel Johnson, Ll.D.* (1787), new edition, Jonathan Cape, 1961, p. 152.
9. Rosenbach, op. cit., p. xli.

3. Rousseau and the lady writers

1. Rosenbach, op. cit., p. lvii.
2. Darton, op. cit., p. 74.
3. Barry, *A Century of Children's Books*, p. 90.

3. Barry, *A Century of Children's Books*, p. 90.
4. *Letters of Charles and Mary Lamb*, edited by E. V. Lucas (Dent and Methuen, 1935), p. 326.
5. Darton, op. cit., p. 160.

4. Fact and fancy

1. Darton, op. cit., p. 96.
2. Goodrich, *Recollections of a Lifetime*, vol. 2, p. 320.
3. ibid., vol. 1, p. 172.
4. Darton, op. cit., pp. 221-8.
5. Targ, *Bibliophile in the Nursery*, pp. 436-7.
6. Alice M. Jordan, 'From Rollo to Tom Sawyer', included in *The Hewins Lectures 1947-62*, edited by Siri Andrews, pp. 8-9.
7. Meigs and others, *A Critical History of Children's Literature*, pp.124-5.
8. Catherine Sinclair, *Holiday House*, new edition, Hamish Hamilton, 1972, p. xiv.
9. Darton, op. cit., p. 214.

5. Nineteenth-century adventures

1. Darton, op. cit., p. 246.
2. Stevenson, prefatory verses to *Treasure Island*.
3. Quoted by Percy Muir, *English Children's Books 1600 – 1900*, p. 109.
4. Fenn, *George Alfred Henty*, p. 320.
5. Darton, op. cit., p. 295.
6. Letter to W. E. Henley, included in *Letters of Robert Louis Stevenson*, edited by Sidney Colvin, Methuen, 1911, vol. 1, p. 49.
7. Quoted by Darton, op. cit., p. 295.
8. Jacob Blank, *Harry Castlemon: Boy's Own Author*, New York, R. R. Bowker, 1941. Quoted by Meigs, op. cit., p. 221.
9. Louisa M. Alcott, *Eight Cousins*, Boston, Roberts Bros, 1875, p. 198. Quoted by Selma Lanes, *Down the Rabbit-Hole*, p. 137.
10. Arbuthnot, *Children and Books*, 3rd edition, p. 435.
11. Gardner, *Horatio Alger*, p. 199.

6. Domestic dramas

1. Salmon, *Juvenile Literature As It Is*, pp. 221-2.

2. Charlotte M. Yonge, article in *Macmillan's Magazine,* vol. xx, 1869, p. 309.
3. Battiscombe, *Charlotte Mary Yonge,* p. 61.
4. Quoted by Helen L. Jones, 'The Part Played by Boston Publishers of 1860-1900 in the Field of Children's Books', *Horn Book Magazine,* June 1969, p. 331.
5. Arbuthnot, op. cit., p. 43.
6. Jane Manthorne, 'The Lachrymose Ladies', *Horn Book Magazine,* 1967, pp. 375-84, 501-13, 622-31.
7. G. B. Stern, 'Elsie Reread', *New Yorker,* 14 March 1936.
8. Alice Payne Hackett, *Seventy Years of Best Sellers,* New York, Bowker, 1967. Quoted in Elizabeth Johnson, 'Margaret Sidney vs Harriet Lothrop', *Horn Book Magazine,* June 1971, pp. 313-9.
9. Egoff, *The Republic of Childhood,* p. 252.
10. Darton, op. cit., pp. 232-3.

7. *Imagination rehabilitated*

1. See discussion in Cook, *The Ordinary and the Fabulous,* p. 1.
2. Letter from Nathaniel Hawthorne to J. T. Fields, quoted by Fields in *Yesterday's Authors,* Sampson Low, 1852, p. 59.
3. Charles Dickens, 'Frauds on the Fairies', *Household Words,* October 1, 1853. Quoted in *Nineteenth Century Children,* by Gillian Avery with Angela Bull, p. 43.
4. Margery Fisher, introduction to *Memoirs of a London Doll,* by Richard Hengist Horne, new edition, Deutsch, 1967, p. xxi.

8. *The never-lands*

1. Edward Wagenknecht, *Utopia Americana,* p. 17.

9. *The world of school*

1. Mack and Armytage, *Thomas Hughes,* p. 86.
2. ibid., p. 100.
3. Brian Alderson, postscript to *The Fifth Form at St Dominic's,* new edition, Hamish Hamilton, 1971, p. 310.
4. Eyre, *British Children's Books in the Twentieth Century,* p. 82.

10. *Articulate animals*

1. Egoff, op. cit., p. 113.

2. Arbuthnot, op. cit., p. 398.

11. Writers in rhyme

1. Isaac Watts, preface to *Divine Songs*, new edition, Oxford University Press, 1971, pp. 145-6.
2. This vast subject is comprehensively covered in the classic works of Iona and Peter Opie, listed in the bibliography.
3. James Sutherland, *Early Eighteenth-Century Poetry*, publ. 1965, p. 25. Quoted by J. H. P. Pafford in introduction to new edition of *Divine Songs*, Oxford University Press, 1971.
4. Darton, op. cit., p. 180.
5. Augustus de Morgan, quoted by Darton, op. cit, p. 183.
6. Darton, op. cit., p. 193.
7. Noakes, *Edward Lear*, p. 227.
8. Arbuthnot, op. cit., p. 132.

12. Pictures that tell a story

1. Leigh Hunt, *The Town*, Oxford University Press, 1907, pp. 62-3.
2. Pitz, *Illustrating Children's Books*, p. 38.
3. See Robert Lawson, 'Howard Pyle and His Times', in *Illustrators of Children's Books 1744-1945*, edited by Mahony and others, pp. 105-22.
4. See Spielmann and Layard, *Kate Greenaway*.
5. Margaret Lane, *The Tale of Beatrix Potter*, p. 122.
6. ibid., p. 185.
7. ibid., p. 133.
8. ibid., p. 130.
9. Graham Greene, 'Beatrix Potter'. Reprinted from his *Collected Essays* in *Only Connect*, edited by Egoff and others, pp. 291-8.

13. Fantasy between the wars

1. Cecil Day Lewis, 'I've heard them lilting at loom and belting', from *Collected Poems*, Cape and Hogarth Press, 1954, p. 139.
2. See fuller account in Meigs, op. cit., pp. 384-97.
3. Eleanor Farjeon, introduction to *The Little Bookroom*, Oxford U.P., 1955.
4. Quoted by Edward Blishen in *Hugh Lofting*, p. 12.
5. ibid., p. 19.
6. Isabelle Suhl, 'The "real" Doctor Dolittle', *Interracial Books for*

Children, vol. II, 1969, nos. 1 and 2. Reprinted in MacCann and Woodard, *The Black American in Books for Children,* pp.78-88.

7. Blishen, op. cit., p. 16.
8. Milne, *It's Too Late Now,* p. 217.
9. Milne, introduction to *Winnie-the-Pooh,* 1926.
10. Tolkien, *Tree and Leaf,* p. 43.
11. Tolkien, foreword to *The Fellowship of the Ring,* 2nd ed., Allen and Unwin, 1966, p. 6.

14. History and brass tacks

1. Geoffrey Trease, author's note to new edition of *Bows Against the Barons,* Brockhampton Press, 1966, p. 152.

15. Craftsmen in two media

1. Milne, *It's Too Late Now,* p. 218.
2. ibid., p. 221.
3. Wanda Gág, quoted in Mahony and others, *Illustrators of Children's Books* 1744-1945, p. 309.
4. Milne, op. cit., p. 223.
5. Siné, *Je ne pense qu'à chat,* Paris, Le Livre de Poche, 1968.

16. The turbulent years

1. Ann Durell, 'If There is no Happy Ending: Children's Book Publishing — Past, Present and Future', *Horn Book Magazine,* February 1982, pp. 23-30 and April 1982, pp. 145-50.
2. Arbuthnot, op. cit., p. 5.
3. Nancy Larrick, 'The All-White World of Children's Books', *Saturday Review,* 11 September 1965, pp. 63-5 and 84-5.
4. A Feminist Look at Children's Books', *School Library Journal,* January 1971, pp. 19-24.
5. *Public Libraries and their book funds:* report from the National Book Committee, Book Trust, 1989.

17. Britons and their past

1. *The Times Literary Supplement,* 28 April 1972, p. 476.
2. These three books were reissued in Britain in one volume in 1980, under the title *Three Legions.*

3. Reviewer quoted by Margaret Meek in her Bodley Head monograph, *Rosemary Sutcliff*, p. 55.
4. Geoffrey Trease, 'The Revolution in Children's Literature', in *The Thorny Paradise*, edited by Edward Blishen, pp. 13-24.
5. Jill Paton Walsh, 'History is Fiction', *Horn Book Magazine*, February 1972, pp. 17-23.
6. John Rowe Townsend, article on Leon Garfield, *Guardian*, May 5, 1976.
7. Note by Geraldine McCaughrean in *Twentieth Century Children's Writers* (3rd edn, 1989), p. 654.

18. After 'Johnny Tremain'

1. Christopher Collier, 'Johnny and Sam: Old and New Approaches to the American Revolution', *Horn Book Magazine*, April 1976, pp. 132-8.
2. Scott O'Dell, article in *Psychology Today*, January 1968, quoted in John Rowe Townsend, *A Sense of Story*, p. 160.
3. Katherine Paterson, 'In search of a story: the setting as source', from *Gates of Excellence*, p. 85.

19. Re-expanding the far horizons

1. Nina Bawden, address to National Book League conference, Birmingham, November 1972, reported in *Signal* 11, May 1973, p. 106.
2. William Sleator, note in *Twentieth Century Children's Writers* (1989 edn), pp. 889-90.
3. Joy Whitby, essay on Nicholas Fisk, *Twentieth Century Children's Writers* (1989 edn), p. 345.

20. Modern fantasy (i): Just like us

1. Ted Hughes, 'Myth and Education', *Children's Literature in Education*, no. 1, March 1970, pp. 55-70.

21. Modern fantasy (ii): Imagined lands

1. John Rowe Townsend, introduction to *A Sense of Story*, p. 12, repeated in *A Sounding of Storytellers*, p. 12.
2. J.R.R. Tolkien, *Tree and Leaf*, Unwin pprback edn (1975), p.16.
3. Humphrey Carpenter, *J. R. R. Tolkien: A Biography*, Allen & Unwin, 1977, p. 201.

4. C .S. Lewis, 'On Three Ways of Writing for Children', reprinted from *Proceedings of the Library Association Conference, Bournemouth 1952*, in *Only Connect*, edited by Egoff and others, pp. 207-20.
5. Marcus Crouch, *Treasure Seekers and Borrowers*, 1962, p. 115.
6. Lloyd Alexander, 'High Fantasy and Heroic Romance'. Talk given at the Fifteenth Annual Storytelling Festival, Roxborough branch of the Free Library of Philadelphia, 10 June 1971.
7. Robin McKinley, Newbery Medal acceptance speech, *Horn Book Magazine*, July/August 1985, pp. 395-405.

22. Modern fantasy (iii): On the margin

1. Lucy Boston, in talk to the Children's Book Circle, November 1968. Extract published in John Rowe Townsend, *A Sense of Story*, pp. 36-7.

23. Realism, British-style

1. Geoffrey Trease, 'The Revolution in Children's Literature', in *The Thorny Paradise*, edited by Edward Blishen, pp. 13-24.

24. Realism, American-style

1. Julius Lester and George Woods, 'Black and White: an exchange', *The New York Times Book Review*, 24 May 1970.
2. Virginia Hamilton, Newbery Award acceptance speech, *Horn Book Magazine*, August 1975, pp. 337-43, reprinted in *Newbery and Caldecott Medal Books 1966-1975*, Boston, The Horn Book Inc., 1975.
3. Mildred D. Taylor, Newbery Award acceptance speech, *Horn Book Magazine*, August 1977, pp. 401-9.
4. Albert V. Schwartz, '*Sounder*: a Black or a White Tale?', *Interracial Books for Children*, Vol. III, no. 1, 1970. Reprinted by MacCann and Woodward, *The Black American in Books for Children*, pp. 89-93.

25. How young is an adult?

1. Susan Hinton, 'Teen-agers are for real', *New York Times Book Review*, 27 August 1967.
2. David Rees, *The Marble in the Water*, p. 177.

3. Jacket copy for *Radigan Cares*, New York, Lippincott, 1970.
4. *Twentieth Century Children's Writers* (1989 edn) pp. 423-4.
5. Interview with Robert Cormier by Anita Silvey, *Horn Book Magazine*, March/April and May/June 1985, pp. 145-55, 289-95.
6. Aidan Chambers, article, *Horn Book Magazine*, October 1976, pp. 532-8.
7. Aidan Chambers, article, *Signal* 40, January 1983, pp. 36-52.

26. Around the world

1. Ivan Southall, 'Depth and Direction', *Horn Book Magazine*, June 1968, pp. 343-6.
2. Ivan Southall, note in McVitty, *Innocence and Experience*, pp. 266-7.
3. Walter McVitty, *Innocence and Experience*, pp. 125-6.
4. Sheila Egoff, *The Republic of Childhood*, p. 126.
5. ibid., p. 203.

27. Virtuosity in verse

1. Edward Blishen, review in *Guardian*, 8 November 1972, p. 10.
2. See note by Eleanor Graham in *A Puffin Quartet of Poets*, Penguin Books, 1958, p. 53.
3. Charles Causley, article on Ted Hughes, *Twentieth Century Children's Writers* (1989 edn), p. 480.
4. Note by Charles Causley, *Twentieth Century Children's Writers* (1989 edn), pp. 181-2.

28. Picture books in bloom: USA

1. MacCann and Richard, *The Child's First Books*, p. 24.
2. Alderson, *Sing a Song for 6d*, pp. 91 and 8.
3. Selma G. Lanes, *The Art of Maurice Sendak*, p. 7.
4. ibid., p. 227.
5. ibid., p. 229.
6. Margaret Meek, 'Symbolic Outlining: the Academic Study of Children's Literature', *Signal* 53, May 1987, pp. 97-115.
7. Maurice Sendak, introduction to a portfolio of *Pictures by Maurice Sendak*, New York, Harper, 1971.
8. Arnold Lobel, Caldecott Medal acceptance speech, *Horn Book Magazine*, August 1981, pp. 400-404.
9. Gerald McDermott, 'On the Rainbow Trail', *Horn Book Magazine*, April 1975, pp. 123-31.

Bibliography

This list includes only books which were consulted and found helpful for the purposes of the present study. The literature on children's books is now very extensive, and there are many other works of merit or interest.

Alderson, Brian, *Sing a Song for 6d: the English picture book tradition and Randolph Caldecott*, Cambridge University Press, 1986.

Aldington, Richard, *Portrait of a Rebel: the life and work of Robert Louis Stevenson*, London, Evans, 1957.

Andrews, Siri (editor), *The Hewins Lectures 1947-1962*, Boston, The Horn Book, 1963.

Arbuthnot, May Hill, *Children and Books*, 3rd ed., Chicago, Scott, Foresman, 1964.

Arbuthnot, May Hill and Sutherland, Zena, *Children and Books*, 4th ed., Chicago, Scott, Foresman, 1972.

Aries, Philippe, *Centuries of Childhood*, London, Jonathan Cape, 1962.

Avery, Gillian, *Childhood's Pattern: a study of the heroes and heroines of children's fiction 1770-1950*, London, Hodder & Stoughton, 1975.

Avery, Gillian, *Mrs Ewing*, London, Bodley Head, 1961. (The Bodley Head Monographs series.)

Avery, Gillian, with Bull, Angela, *Nineteenth Century Children: heroes and heroines in English children's stories 1780-1900*, London, Hodder & Stoughton, 1965.

Bader, Barbara, *American Picturebooks, from* Noah's Ark *to* The Beast Within, New York, Macmillan, 1976.

Ballantyne, R. M., *Personal Reminiscences in Book-Making*, London, J. Nisbet, 1893.

Barry, Florence, *A Century of Children's Books*, London, Methuen, 1922.

Battiscombe, Georgina, *Charlotte Mary Yonge: the story of an uneventful life*, London, Constable, 1943.

Bell, Anthea, *E. Nesbit*, London, Bodley Head, 1960. (The Bodley Head Monographs series.)

Blades, William, *The Biography and Typography of William Caxton*, London, Trubner, 1882.

Bland, David, *A History of Book Illustration*, London, Faber & Faber, 1969.

Blishen, Edward, *Hugh Lofting*, London, Bodley Head, 1968. (The Bodley Head Monographs series.)

Blishen, Edward (editor), *The Thorny Paradise: writers on writing for children*, Harmondsworth, Kestrel Books, 1975.

Blount, Margaret, *Animal Land: The Creatures of Children's Fiction*, London, Hutchinson, 1974.

Boswell, James, *Life of Johnson*, London, Dent, 1906. (Everyman's Library.)

Briggs, Julia, *A Woman of Passion: the Life of E.Nesbit 1858-1924*, London, Hutchinson, 1987.

Briggs, Katharine, *A Dictionary of Fairies*, London, Allen Lane, 1976.

Brogan, Hugh, *The Life of Arthur Ransome*, London, Cape, 1984.

Bull, Angela, *Noel Streatfeild: a biography*, London, Collins, 1984.

Burnett, Vivian, *The Romantick Lady: the life story of an imagination* (Frances Hodgson Burnett), New York, Scribner, 1927.

Cameron, Eleanor, *The Green and Burning Tree: on the writing and enjoyment of children's books*, Boston, Atlantic-Little, Brown, 1969.

Campbell, Joseph, *The Hero with a Thousand Faces*, Princeton University Press, 1949.

Carpenter, Humphrey and Prichard, Mari (editors), *The Oxford Companion to Children's Literature*, Oxford, Oxford University Press, 1984.

Carpenter, Humphrey, *J. R. R. Tolkien: a biography*, London, Allen & Unwin, 1977.

Carpenter, Humphrey, *Secret Gardens: a study of the golden age of children's literature*, London, Allen & Unwin, 1985.

Carrington, Charles, *Rudyard Kipling: his life and work*, London, Macmillan, 1955.

Chambers, Aidan, *The Reluctant Reader*, Oxford, Pergamon Press, 1969.

Chambers, Nancy (editor), *The Signal Approach to Children's Literature*, Harmondsworth, Kestrel Books, 1980.

Chevalier, Tracy (editor), *Twentieth Century Children's Writers*, 3rd edition, London, St James Press, 1989.

Chitty, Susan, *The Beast and the Monk: a life of Charles Kingsley*, London, Hodder & Stoughton, 1974.

Chitty, Susan, *The Woman Who Wrote* Black Beauty, London, Hodder & Stoughton, 1971.

Chukovsky, Kornei, *From Two to Five,* Berkeley, University of California Press, 1963.

Clark, Leonard, *Walter de la Mare,* London, Bodley Head, 1960. (The Bodley Head Monographs series.)

Cohen, Morton, *Rider Haggard: his life and work,* London, Hutchinson, 1960.

Colwell, Eileen, *Eleanor Farjeon,* London, Bodley Head, 1961. (The Bodley Head Monographs series.)

Cook, Elizabeth, *The Ordinary and the Fabulous: an introduction to myths, legends and fairy tales,* Cambridge University Press, 2nd ed., 1976.

Coveney, Peter, *The Image of Childhood,* revised ed., Harmondsworth, Peregrine Books, 1967.

Crews, Frederick C., *The Pooh Perplex: a freshman casebook,* New York, Dutton, 1963.

Crouch, Marcus, *Chosen for Children: an account of the books which have been awarded the Library Association Carnegie Medal 1936-65,* London, The Library Association, 1967.

Crouch, Marcus, *Treasure Seekers and Borrowers,* London, The Library Association, 1962.

Cunliffe, Marcus, *The Literature of the United States,* London, Penguin Books, 1954.

Cutt, M. Nancy, *Mrs Sherwood and her Books for Children,* London, Oxford University Press, 1974.

Darton, F.J.Harvey, *Children's Books in England: five centuries of social life,* 3rd ed., revised by Brian Alderson, Cambridge University Press, 1982.

De Voto, Bernard A., *Mark Twain at Work,* Cambridge, Mass., Harvard University Press, 1942.

De Vries, Leonard, *Flowers of Delight,* London, Dennis Dobson, 1965.

De Vries, Leonard, *Little Wide-Awake: an anthology from Victorian children's books and periodicals in the collection of Anne and Fernand G. Renier,* London, Arthur Barker, 1967.

Donelson, Kenneth L. and Nilsen, Alleen Pace, *Literature for today's young adults,* 3rd ed., Glenview, Ill., Scott Foresman & Co., 1989.

Duff, Annis, *Bequest of Wings: a family's pleasures with books,* New York, The Viking Press, 1944.

Duff, Annis, *Longer Flight: a family grows up with books,* New York, The Viking Press, 1955.

Edgeworth, R. L., and Edgeworth, Maria, *Practical Education,* London, Joseph Johnson, 1798.

Egoff, Sheila, and others (editors), *Only Connect: readings on children's literature,* second ed., Toronto, Oxford University Press, 1980.

Egoff, Sheila, *The Republic of Childhood: a critical guide to Canadian children's literature in English,* Toronto, Oxford University Press, 1967.

Egoff, Sheila, *Thursday's Child: trends and patterns in contemporary children's literature,* Chicago, American Library Association, 1981.

Elledge, Scott, *E. B. White: a biography,* New York, Norton, 1984.

Eyre, Frank, *British Children's Books in the Twentieth Century,* London, Longman, 1971.

Fenn, G. M., *George Alfred Henty: the story of an active life,* London, Blackie, 1907.

Fenwick, S. I. (editor), *A Critical Approach to Children's Literature,* Chicago University Press, 1967.

Field, Mrs E. M., *The Child and His Book,* Redhill, Wells Gardner, Darton, 1892.

Fisher, Margery, *The Bright Face of Danger: an exploration of the adventure story,* London, Hodder & Stoughton, 1986.

Fisher, Margery, *Henry Treece,* London, Bodley Head, 1969. (The Bodley Head Monographs series.)

Fisher, Margery, *Intent Upon Reading: a critical appraisal of modern fiction for children,* new ed., London, Brockhampton Press, 1964.

Fisher, Margery, *John Masefield,* London, Bodley Head, 1963. (The Bodley Head Monographs series.)

Fisher, Margery, *Who's Who in Children's Books: a treasury of the familiar characters of childhood,* London, Weidenfeld, 1975.

Frye, Northrop, *Fearful Symmetry: a study of William Blake,* Princeton University Press, 1947.

Furnivall, F. J., *The Babees' Book,* London, Trubner, 1868.

Gardner, Martin (editor), *The Annotated Alice,* New York, C. N. Potter, 1960.

Gardner, Martin and Nye, Russel B. *The Wizard of Oz and Who He Was,* Michigan State University Press, 1957.

Garland, Madge, *The Changing Face of Childhood,* London, Hutchinson, 1963.

Goodrich, Samuel G., *Recollections of a Lifetime,* New York, Miller, Orton, 1857.

Graham, Eleanor, *Kenneth Grahame,* London, Bodley Head, 1963. (The Bodley Head Monographs series.)

Green, Peter, *Beyond the Wild Wood: the world of Kenneth Grahame, author of* The Wind in the Willows, (adaptation of *Kenneth Grahame: a biography),* Exeter, Webb & Bower, 1982.

Green, Peter, *Kenneth Grahame, 1859-1932: a study of his life, work and times,* London, John Murray, 1959.

Green, Roger Lancelyn, *J. M. Barrie,* London, Bodley Head, 1960. (The Bodley Head Monographs series.)

Green, Roger Lancelyn, *Lewis Carroll,* London, Bodley Head, 1960. (The Bodley Head Monographs series.)

Green, Roger Lancelyn, *C. S. Lewis,* London, Bodley Head, 1963. (The Bodley Head Monographs series.)

Green, Roger Lancelyn, *Mrs Molesworth,* London, Bodley Head, 1961. (The Bodley Head Monographs series.)

Green, Roger Lancelyn, *Tellers of Tales,* new ed., London, Edmund Ward, 1953.

Halsey, Rosalie V., *Forgotten Books of the American Nursery: a history of the development of the American story-book,* Boston, Charles E. Godspeed, 1911.

Hamilton, Charles, *The Autobiography of Frank Richards,* London, Charles Skilton, 1962.

Hardyment, Christina, *Arthur Ransome and Captain Flint's Trunk,* London, Cape, 1984.

Harrison, Barbara and Maguire, Gregory, *Innocence and Experience: Essays and Conversations on Children's Literature,* New York, Lothrop, Lee & Shepard, 1987.

Harrison, Barbara and others (editors), *Travellers in Time — Past, Present and to Come,* proceedings of the summer institute held at Newnham College, Cambridge, 1989, by Children's Literature New England; Cambridge, Green Bay Publications, 1990.

Haviland, Virginia (editor), *Children's Literature: a guide to reference sources,* Washington, Library of Congress, 1966.

Haviland, Virginia (editor), *Children's Literature: Views and Reviews,* Chicago, Scott Foresman, 1973.

Haviland, Virginia (editor), *The Openhearted Audience: ten authors talk about writing for children,* Washington, Library of Congress, 1980.

Hazard, Paul, *Books, Children and Men,* Boston, The Horn Book, 1947.

Hearn, Betsy, and Kaye, Marilyn (editors), *Celebrating Children's Books: essays on children's literature in honor of Zena Sutherland,* New York, Lothrop, 1981.

Heartman, Charles F., *The New England Primer Issued Prior to 1830: a bibliographical check-list for the more easy attaining the true knowledge of this book*, 3rd ed., New York, R. R. Bowker, 1934.

Heins, Paul (editor), *Crosscurrents of Criticism: Horn Book essays, 1968-1977*, Boston, Horn Book Inc., 1977.

Hewins, Caroline M., *A Mid-Century Child and Her Books*, New York, Macmillan, 1926.

Hudson, Derek, *Arthur Rackham: his life and work*, London, Heinemann, 1960.

Hudson, Derek, *Lewis Carroll*, London, Constable, 1954.

Hurlimann, Bettina, *Three Centuries of Children's Books in Europe*, London, Oxford University Press, 1967.

Judd, Denis, *Alison Uttley: the Life of a Country Child*, London, Michael Joseph, 1986.

Kiefer, Monica M., *American Children Through Their Books 1700-1835*, Philadelphia, University of Pennsylvania Press, 1948.

Kingman, Lee (editor), *Newbery and Caldecott Medal Books 1956-1965*, Boston, Horn Book Inc., 1965.

Kingman, Lee (editor), *Newbery and Caldecott Medal Books 1966-1975*, Boston, Horn Book Inc, 1975.

Kingman, Lee (editor), *Newbery and Caldecott Medal Books 1976-1985*, Boston, Horn Book Inc., 1986.

Kingman, Lee, and others (editors), *Illustrators of Children's Books 1957-66*, Boston, The Horn Book, 1968.

Kingsmill, Hugh, *After Puritanism*, London, Duckworth, 1929.

Kipling, Rudyard, *Something of Myself*, London, Macmillan, 1937.

Knox, Rawle (editor), *The Work of E. H. Shepard*, London, Methuen, 1979

Kresh, Paul, *Isaac Bashevis Singer: the magician of West 86th Street*, New York, Dial Press, 1979.

Lane, Margaret, *The Magic Years of Beatrix Potter*, London, Warne, 1978.

Lane, Margaret, *The Tale of Beatrix Potter*, revised ed., Harmondsworth, Warne, 1985.

Lanes, Selma G., *Down the Rabbit-Hole: adventures and misadventures in the realm of children's literature*, New York, Atheneum, 1971.

Lanes, Selma G., *The Art of Maurice Sendak*, New York, Abrams, 1980.

Landsberg, Michele, *The World of Children's Books: a Guide to*

Choosing the Best, London, Simon & Schuster, 1988.

Laski, Marghanita, *Mrs Ewing, Mrs Molesworth and Mrs Hodgson Burnett,* London, Arthur Barker, 1950.

Leeson, Robert, *Reading and Righting: the past, present and future of fiction for the young,* London, Collins, 1985.

Lennon, Florence Becker, *Lewis Carroll: a biography,* London, Cassell, 1947.

Linder, Leslie, and Herring, W. A. (selectors), *The Art of Beatrix Potter,* London, Warne, 1972.

Locke, John, *Educational Writings,* Cambridge University Press, 1922.

Lurie, Alison, *Don't Tell the Grown-Ups: subversive children's literature,* London, Bloomsbury, 1990.

MacCann, Donnarae, and Richard, Olga, *The Child's First Books,* New York, H. W. Wilson, 1973.

MacCann, Donnarae, and Woodard, Gloria, *The Black American in Books for Children,* New York, Scarecrow Press, 1972.

Mack, Edward C. and Armytage, W. H. G., *Thomas Hughes: the life of the author of* Tom Brown's Schooldays, London, Benn, 1952.

Mackail, Denis, *The Story of J. M. B.: a biography,* London, Peter Davies, 1951.

Mahony, Bertha E., and others (editors), *Illustrators of Children's Books 1744-1945,* Boston, The Horn Book, 1947.

Martin, R. B., *The Dust of Combat: the life and work of Charles Kingsley,* London, Faber, 1959.

McVitty, Walter, *Innocence and Experience: essays on contemporary Australian children's writers,* Melbourne, Nelson Australia, 1981.

Meek, Margaret, *Geoffrey Trease,* London, Bodley Head, 1962. (The Bodley Head Monographs series.)

Meek, Margaret, *Rosemary Sutcliff,* London, Bodley Head, 1962. (The Bodley Head Monographs series.)

Meek, Margaret and others (editors), *The Cool Web: the pattern of children's reading,* London, Bodley Head, 1977.

Meigs, Cornelia, *Louisa M. Alcott and the American Family Story,* London, Bodley Head, 1970. (The Bodley Head Monographs.)

Meigs, Cornelia, and others, *A Critical History of Children's Literature,* new ed., New York, Macmillan, 1969.

Miller, Bertha Mahony, and Field, Elinor Whitney, *Caldecott Medal Books, 1938-1957,* Boston, Horn Book Inc., 1957.

Miller, Bertha Mahony, and Field, Elinor Whitney, *Newbery Medal Books, 1922-1955,* Boston, Horn Book Inc., 1955.

Milne, A. A. *It's Too Late Now: the autobiography of a writer,* London, Methuen, 1939.

Milne, Christopher, *The Enchanted Places*, Eyre Methuen, 1974.

Moore, Doris Langley, *E. Nesbit: a biography*, new ed., London, Benn, 1967.

Morison, Stanley, *Talbot Baines Reed: author, bibliographer, typefounder*, Cambridge, privately printed, 1960.

Moss, Elaine, *Part of the Pattern: a personal journey through the world of children's books, 1960-85*, Bodley Head, 1986.

Muir, Percy H., *English Children's Books 1600-1900*, London, Batsford, 1954.

Nesbitt, Elizabeth, *Howard Pyle*, London, Bodley Head, 1966. (The Bodley Head Monographs series.)

Niall, Brenda, *Australia Through the Looking-Glass: children's fiction 1830-1980*, Melbourne University Press, 1984.

Noakes, Vivien, *Edward Lear: the life of a wanderer*, London, Collins, 1968.

Opie, Iona and Peter, *The Lore and Language of Schoolchildren*, Oxford University Press, 1959.

Opie, Iona and Peter (editors), *The Oxford Dictionary of Nursery Rhymes*, Oxford University Press, 1951.

Opie, Iona and Peter, *The Singing Game*, Oxford University Press, 1985.

Paterson, Katherine, *Gates of Excellence: on reading and writing books for children*, New York, Elsevier/Nelson, 1981.

Paterson, Katherine, *The Spying Heart: more thoughts on reading and writing books for children*, New York, Dutton, 1989.

Patterson, Sylvia, *Rousseau's Émile and Early Children's Literature*, New York, Scarecrow Press, 1971.

Philip, Neil, *A Fine Anger: a critical introduction to the work of Alan Garner*, London, Collins, 1981.

Pickering, Samuel F., Jr., *John Locke and Children's Books in Eighteenth-Century England*, Knoxville, University of Tennessee Press, 1981.

Pitz, Henry C., *Howard Pyle: writer, illustrator, founder of the Brandywine School*, New York, Bramhall House, 1965.

Pitz, Henry C., *Illustrating Children's Books: history, technique, production*, New York, Watson-Guptil, 1963.

Potter, Beatrix, *Journal, 1881-1897*, transcribed by Leslie Linder (new ed.), London, Warne, 1989.

Potter, Beatrix, *Letters: a selection by Judy Taylor*, London, Warne, 1989.

Quigly, Isabel, *The Heirs of Tom Brown: the English school story*, London, Chatto & Windus, 1982.

Rees, David, *The Marble in the Water: essays on contemporary writers of fiction for children and young adults*, Boston, The Horn Book, Inc., 1980.

Rickert, Edith, *The Babees' Book: medieval manners for the young, done into modern English from Dr Furnivall's texts*, London, Chatto and Windus, 1908.

Rose, Jacqueline, *The Case of Peter Pan, or The Impossibility of Children's Fiction*, London, Macmillan, 1984.

Rose, Jasper, *Lucy Boston*, London, Bodley Head, 1965. (The Bodley Head Monographs series.)

Rosenbach, Abraham S. W., *Early American Children's Books: with bibliographical descriptions of the books in his private collection*, Portland, Maine, Southworth Press, 1933.

Rousseau, J.-J., *Émile, ou de l'éducation*, London, Dent, 1911 (Everyman's Library.)

Salmon, Edward, *Juvenile Literature As It Is*, London, H. J. Drane, 1888.

Saltman, Judith, *Modern Canadian Children's Books*, Toronto, Oxford University Press, 1987.

Salway, Lance, *A Peculiar Gift: nineteenth century writings on books for children*, Harmondsworth, Kestrel Books, 1976.

Sawyer, Ruth, *The Way of the Storyteller*, new ed., New York, The Viking Press, 1962.

Saxby, H. M., *A History of Australian Children's Literature 1841-1941*, Sydney, Wentworth Books, 1969.

Saxby, H. M., *A History of Australian Children's Literature 1941-1970*, Sydney, Wentworth Books, 1971.

Scott, Sir S. H., *The Exemplary Mr Day*, London, Faber, 1935.

Shelley, Hugh, *Arthur Ransome*, London, Bodley Head, 1960. (The Bodley Head Monographs series.)

Sloane, William, *Children's Books in England and America in the Seventeenth Century: a history and checklist*, New York, King's Crown Press, Columbia University, 1955.

Smith, Lillian H., *The Unreluctant Years*, Chicago, American Library Association, 1953.

Smith, Naomi Royde, *The State of Mind of Mrs Sherwood*, London, Macmillan, 1940.

Spielman, Marion H., and Layard, G. S., *Kate Greenaway*, London, Black, 1905.

Streatfeild, Noel, *Magic and the Magician: E. Nesbit and her children's books,* London, Benn, 1958.

Strong, L. A. G., *John Masefield,* London, Longman, 1952.

Sutcliff, Rosemary, *Blue Remembered Hills: a recollection,* London, Bodley Head, 1983.

Sutcliff, Rosemary, *Rudyard Kipling,* London, Bodley Head, 1960. (The Bodley Head Monographs series.)

Sutherland, Zena, and Arbuthnot, May Hill, *Children and Books,* 6th ed., Chicago, Scott Foresman, 1986.

Targ, William (editor), *Bibliophile in the Nursery: a bookman's treasury of collector's lore on old and rare children's books,* Cleveland, World, 1957.

Taylor, A. L., *The White Knight* (Lewis Carroll), Edinburgh, Oliver and Boyd, 1952.

Taylor, Judy, *Beatrix Potter: artist, storyteller and countrywoman,* Harmondsworth, Warne, 1986.

Tebbel, John W., *From Rags to Riches: Horatio Alger, Jr., and the American Dream,* New York, Macmillan, 1963.

Thompson, Lawrence, *The Printing and Publishing Activities of the American Tract Society from 1825 to 1850,* Papers of the Bibliographical Society of America, Vol. 35, 1941.

Thompson, Stith, *The Folktale,* New York, Dryden Press, 1946.

Thwaite, Ann, *A. A. Milne, his life,* London, Faber, 1990.

Thwaite, Ann, *Waiting for the Party: the life of Frances Hodgson Burnett,* London, Secker and Warburg, 1974.

Thwaite, M. F., *From Primer to Pleasure in Reading,* new ed., London, The Library Association, 1972.

Tolkien, J. R. R., *Tree and Leaf,* London, Allen and Unwin, 1964.

Townsend, John Rowe, *A Sense of Story: essays on contemporary writers for children,* London, Longman, 1971.

Townsend, John Rowe, *A Sounding of Storytellers: new and revised essays on contemporary writers for children,* Harmondsworth, Kestrel Books, 1979.

Trease, Geoffrey, *Tales Out of School,* new ed., London, Heinemann, 1964.

Viguers, Ruth Hill, and others (editors), *Illustrators of Children's Books, 1946-56,* Boston, The Horn Book, 1958.

Viguers, Ruth Hill, *Margin for Surprise: about books, children and librarians,* Boston, Little, Brown, 1964.

Wagenknecht, Edward, *Utopia Americana* (Oz), University of Washington Chapbooks, 1929.

Warner, Oliver, *Captain Marryat: a rediscovery,* London, Constable, 1953.

Watts, Isaac, *Divine Songs Attempted in Easy Language for the Use of Children,* new edition with introduction by J. H. P. Pafford, London, Oxford University Press, 1971.

Welsh, Charles, *A Bookseller of the Last Century, being some account of the life of John Newbery,* Griffith, Farran, 1885.

Whalley, Joyce Irene and Chester, Tessa Rose, *A History of Children's Book Illustration,* London, Murray, 1988.

White, Gabriel, *Edward Ardizzone: artist and illustrator,* London, Bodley Head, 1979.

Wighton, Rosemary, *Early Australian Children's Literature,* Melbourne, Lansdowne Press, 1963.

Willey, Basil, *The Seventeenth Century Background,* London, Chatto and Windus, 1934.

Willey, Basil, *The Eighteenth Century Background,* London, Chatto and Windus, 1940.

Wintle, Justin, and Fisher, Emma, *The Pied Pipers,* New York, Paddington Press, 1974.

Wolff, R. L., *The Golden Key: a study of the fiction of George MacDonald,* New Haven, Yale University Press, 1961.

Index